Y0-BCT-867

Robert Henley Woody
and Associates

✿✿✿✿✿✿✿✿✿✿✿✿✿✿✿✿✿✿✿✿✿✿✿✿✿✿✿✿✿✿

The Law
and the Practice
of Human Services

 Jossey-Bass Publishers

San Francisco • Washington • London • 1984

THE LAW AND THE PRACTICE OF HUMAN SERVICES
by Robert Henley Woody and Associates

Copyright © 1984 by: Jossey-Bass Inc., Publishers
433 California Street
San Francisco, California 94104

&

Jossey-Bass Limited
28 Banner Street
London EC1Y 8QE

Library of Congress Cataloging in Publication Data
Main entry under title:

The Law and the practice of human services.

Includes bibliographical references and index.
1. Law—United States.   2. Public welfare—Law and
legislation—United States.   3. Social workers—Legal
status, law, etc.—United States.   4. Social workers—
United States—Handbooks, manuals, etc.   I. Woody,
Robert Henley.
KF390.S6L38   1984   349.73'02436   83-49269
ISBN 0-87589-602-2   347.3002436

Manufactured in the United States of America

JACKET DESIGN BY WILLI BAUM

FIRST EDITION

Code 8406

The Jossey-Bass
Social and Behavioral Science Series

Preface

Human services exist in large part to translate public policies into actions that will change and improve human behavior and living conditions. These actions are undertaken because society expects its members to conform to certain social and behavioral standards and wishes to promote optimum quality of life. In our society, human services professionals are expected to bear allegiance to these objectives and to carry them out.

Human services professionals are thus inextricably involved with public policies and, consequently, with the legal system. Practitioners in any human service necessarily operate within a socio-legal framework and need to have a certain level of expertise in legal matters. Regrettably, training programs rarely include courses on how the law and human services mesh. Most typically, the practitioner must seek legal knowledge and skills alone, a trial-and-error effort that is likely to meet many obstacles, misinformation chief among them. It is hoped that *The Law and the Practice of Human Services* will fill this void.

This book is designed to provide human services professionals in all fields—including psychology, social work, counseling, medicine, rehabilitation, nursing, education, and health services—with the fundamental legal information they need to fulfill their obligations to their clients, their disciplines, and society. Each chapter is an original contribution by an author who has obtained eminence in the area about which he or she writes. The contents are structured to inform the reader of *legal theory* essential to the analysis of human services problems and of the *legal principles* that must be applied in providing services to clients. Special emphasis has been placed on practicality, so that the legal information in this volume will help a practitioner formulate a strategy for dealing with a particular case. In addition, the contents encompass the breadth and depth of legal information that should be part of every human services training program. This single-volume compilation provides the reader with an extensive treatment of the topic area and lends itself to graduate studies on the law in relation to the entire spectrum of human services disciplines.

Contents and Organization

Simply because, in Pope's words, "a little learning is a dangerous thing," it is risky to try to "specialize" in or limit one's understanding to a single legal niche. To obtain a solid, functional sociolegal foundation, it is necessary to progress through an array of legal topics. Consequently, one goal of this volume has been to distill the complex field of law into a series of carefully delineated, comprehensible chapters that combine to provide a broad view of the law for human services professionals.

Chapter One, "Understanding the Legal System and Legal Research," lays the cornerstone for effective practice by explaining what human services data can and cannot be used as evidence in legal cases, and by showing the reader how to blend the law, be it from statutory or case sources, with behavioral science. It also demonstrates how human services professionals can draw upon legal sources, that is, conduct legal research, to enhance behavioral science practices.

Chapter Two, "Criminal Law," details the array of crimes that has been established by law, recognizing the influence of public policies. The reader is guided through the facets that must be proved by criminal legal procedure in order to obtain convictions. Defenses used to contradict guilt beyond a reasonable doubt and other legal principles and strategies are presented in a manner that will allow the human services professional to comprehend and knowledgeably enter into criminal proceedings. Special attention is given to the psychological aspects of crime and to critical cases, especially from the United States Supreme Court, that influence the use of social science information.

Chapter Three, "Juvenile Law," describes the various functions of the legal system as it is applied to youths. Distinctions between criminal offenses and juvenile offenses are made clear, with descriptions of the special programs and facilities that have been established to aid in attaining society's objectives for youthful offenders.

Chapter Four, "Family Law," discusses how family relations are influenced by the law, describes the types of cases human services professionals work with, and suggests techniques that have proved useful.

Chapter Five, "Personal Injury Law," provides instruction on the list of civil offenses that deprive an individual of a protected right; most commonly, such an offense takes the form of an injury to a person or to his or her property. By inspecting each civil or tort offense, the reader will be able to identify the legal principles that require behavioral science information that might be provided through expert testimony. Special consideration is given to cases that did, in fact, turn on psychologically related testimony.

Chapter Six, "Employment Discrimination Law," focuses on legislative sources that establish an employee's rights in the workplace. The emphasis is on the proscriptions against discrimination, as might be related to race, sex, and age. Numerous case examples are used to clarify how the legal system evaluates what are often nebulous and contradictory data, such as whether or not psychological testing is used for a legitimate purpose by an employer and whether or not it obtains the requisite standards for equal rights protection.

Chapter Seven, "Capacity to Make Contracts and Wills," opens up a legal area in which only a limited number of mental health professionals have trod, yet has historically relied upon psychological concepts (with the latter being defined and implemented by legalists and general medical personnel). Now there is a clear-cut expectation that specialized professional knowledge about a person's mental abilities for understanding the nature of testamentary actions be relied upon by the courts. This chapter explains the legal tests, as would have to be met by professional testimony, and presents numerous cases that reveal how the courts process mental health data.

Chapter Eight, "Rights of Institutionalized Patients," describes and analyzes numerous cases that are critical to professionals in the mental health disciplines. It has become a major legal concern, for example, that mental patients' legal rights not be denigrated, and the mental health professional is typically the front-line worker safeguarding these rights.

Chapter Nine, "Rights of Handicapped Children to an Education," explains the constitutional bases for the right to education and detailedly analyzes federal legislation that declares the extent and quality of education that must be afforded to all would-be students in our contemporary American society. Political postures are discussed, and court decisions are presented. The chapter is aimed at helping the practitioner both provide appropriate educationally related clinical services and adopt an advocacy stance for promoting changes within the educational system with which he or she must deal professionally.

Chapter Ten, "Professional Responsibilities and Liabilities," focuses on the unique nature of the relationship between the human services professional and his or her client, with special emphasis on informed consent, privileged communication, the duty to warn, and professional malpractice.

With clear memories of my first experiences giving expert psychological testimony in a court of law—with its imposing atmosphere of formality and bewildering rules and language—I offer this book with the hope that it will alleviate unnecessary reservations about and discomfort with the legal arena. In the subsequent years, I have come to believe that the quality of my psychological services is influenced by whether I am able to work effectively with legal issues. This conclusion holds true for virtually every human services professional: Our inauguration into human services professionalism by society compels us to become involved with and contribute to the legal system.

Omaha, Nebraska   Robert Henley Woody
January 1984

This volume is dedicated to my wife, Jane Divita Woody, to our children, Jennifer, Robert, and Matthew, and to the families of each of the contributors. Love and support are invaluable assets.

Contents

The Authors

Robert Henley Woody is professor of psychology at the University of Nebraska at Omaha and he maintains private practices in law and in clinical and forensic psychology. He received the Ph.D. degree in counseling psychology from Michigan State University (1964), the Sc.D. degree in health services research from the University of Pittsburgh (1975), and the J.D. degree from Creighton University School of Law (1981). During 1966–67, he was a postdoctoral fellow in clinical psychology at the University of London's Institute of Psychiatry (Maudsley Hospital), and in 1969, he received the two-year Postdoctoral Certificate in Group Psychotherapy from the Washington School of Psychiatry.

Prior to his appointment at the University of Nebraska at Omaha, Woody was assistant professor of rehabilitation counseling at the State University of New York at Buffalo, associate professor and director of psychological services in the schools training program at the University of Maryland, dean for student development and director of counseling and mental health services at Grand Valley State College, and professor of education and psychology at Ohio University. Woody has been a visiting professor at Ohio State University and the University of Reading in England. Before his current professorship, he was dean of graduate studies and research at the University of Nebraska at Omaha.

Woody is a fellow of the American Psychological Association, the American Association for Marriage and Family Therapy, the Society for Personality Assessment, and the American Society of Clinical Hypnosis. He has been accorded the status of Diplomate in Clinical Psychology by the American Board of Professional Psychology, Diplomate in Forensic Psychology by the American Board of Forensic Psychology, Diplomate in Professional Neuropsychology by the American Board of Professional Neuropsychology, and Diplomate in (Experimental) Psychological Hypnosis by the American Board of Psychological Hypnosis. He is licensed as a psychologist in Nebraska, Michigan, and Florida, and as a marriage counselor in Michigan and Florida. He has been admitted to the Nebraska and Florida state bars for the practice of law.

Woody has authored or edited thirteen books and approximately two hundred articles for professional journals. His books include *Behavioral Problem Children in the Schools* (1969), *Clinical Assessment in Counseling and Psychotherapy* (with J . D. Woody, 1972), *Psychobehavioral Counseling and Therapy* (1971), *Getting Custody* (1978), and the *Encyclopedia of Clinical Assessment* (1980).

Deborah Ann Karras, Ph.D., is a postdoctoral fellow in neuropsychology, Nebraska Psychiatric Institute, University of Nebraska Medical Center, Omaha.

Robert E. Mitchell, Ph.D., is associate professor and director of the Division of Behavioral Science, School of Medicine, Creighton University, Omaha, Nebraska.

Ronald J. Palagi, J.D., is a practicing attorney, Omaha, Nebraska.

Janet B. Porter, J.D., Ph.D., is associate professor of criminal justice, University of Nebraska at Omaha.

Roger A. Rapaport, J.D., is a practicing attorney, Lansing, Michigan.

Thomas J. Reed, J.D., is associate professor of law, Delaware Law School of Widener University, Wilmington, Delaware.

R. Barry Ruback, J.D., Ph.D., is assistant professor of psychology, Georgia State University, Atlanta.

Jeffrey C. Savitsky, Ph.D., J.D., is associate professor of psychology, Purdue University, West Lafayette, Indiana.

James R. Springer, Ed.D., is associate professor of psychiatry, Michigan State University at Grand Rapids.

Robert S. Stick, J.D., is a practicing attorney with Legal Services of Southeast Nebraska, Lincoln.

The Law
and the Practice
of Human Services

Robert Henley Woody
Robert E. Mitchell

1

Understanding
the Legal System
and Legal Research

❀❁❂❃❄❅❆❇❈❉❊❋

For a number of reasons, the law's involvement with (some would say intrusion into) human services has increased dramatically over the past several decades.

- The number of elderly has increased, with a concomitant increase in questions concerning competency (although the majority of elderly, of course, are not demented or otherwise incompetent).
- Mentally ill and mentally retarded citizens living in the community instead of in long-term institutions (thanks to the increased effectiveness of intervention techniques—biochemical, behavioral, and social management—as well as the community mental health movement and changes in commitment laws), have caused increased attention to be focused on such issues as the insanity defense, rules for civil commitment, and the right to receive treatment and to refuse treatment.
- The court has become increasingly involved in education, at first in regard to integration but now in a much broader context.
- There has been a great increase in the number of divorces and concomitant child custody decisions.
- There has been an increase in civil litigation, giving more notice to psychological factors and occasionally resulting in large

1

judgments. For example, legal remedies for personal injury commonly ask for psychological predictions about long-range effects.

- Human services professionals are being looked to by the legal profession for help and being held accountable for promises.
- Finally, one can only speculate on the effect of a large increase per capita of the number of attorneys and the number of human services professionals.

Because of this increased involvement, there is an increased need for human services professionals (herein referred to as "professionals) to know the law. More and more professionals are being called as expert witnesses; effective testimony implies familiarity with the legal issues in question and the process by which they will be decided. The principles upon which judgments of professional liability and malpractice are based are changing rapidly, and professionals must keep up with these changes in order to protect themselves and their clients. For instance, familiarity with the law will help them make more sophisticated judgments about when confidentiality applies and when they have a duty to warn third parties of possible danger from clients. In short, professionals need to understand the legal process and to learn how to research the law if they are to keep up with changes in an intelligent fashion. Also, there is a recent burgeoning of literature on subjects involving both the law and human services; to reap the benefits of or actually participate in this research, professionals must know how to find and make legal citations.

Becoming involved in the legal system is not a mere matter of introduction. It is necessary to make adaptations. In point of fact, human services professionals, as contrasted to professionals from other disciplines, may find movement into the legal system difficult—because of their philosophy and their methods.

Philosophically, many, if not most, human services professionals strive to individualize their helping. To be sure, there is an awareness of helping the client fit into and contribute to society, but society often remains "somewhere out there," to be dealt with indirectly at best. In the courtroom there is a reversal. While the individual's constitutional rights and human dignity are honored, there is an overriding reverence for societal development and welfare. The philosophical discrepancy between the individual and societal helping frameworks can produce a quandary for the professional. All too often the professional's training has been heavily influenced by "ivory tower" notions of *what should be;* as a result, academics are unprepared for *what actually happens* when they are ushered into the courtroom, where the emphasis is not on helping an individual client progress and become better but on reaching a fair decision that solves a practical problem in the here and now and that can be applied to similar cases in the same way. The philosophy of the courtroom seems to contradict the philosophy of the therapy room.

Methodologically, human services professionals may find that their commitment to advancing knowledge conflicts with the legal preferences for the established "truisms" of everyday life. The professional is well grounded in research methodology and finds "truth" in the .05 level of significance. Evidence for the professional is objective data that can be experimented on in replicable fashion. "Truth" for the court is a standard of proof that may range from "beyond a reasonable doubt" to "burden of evidence." Evidence for the court is defined by very strict rules, to be elaborated on below. For example, a professional may be prepared to cite laboratory research to document his or her testimony about a given party in a legal case—and then find that such documentation is unacceptable in the courtroom because the findings did not come from a real-life situation. Nevertheless, courts do seek expert testimony to facilitate the legal process by transforming such expertise into opinions that can enlighten the judge and the jury. Ironically, however, courts may give more weight to the expert's opinion than to the scientific merit of that opinion. Courts may accept opinion as a "fact."

Further difficulties can arise over a confusion of roles. In therapy the professional's role is to help an individual become better. In the courtroom the professional's role is to tell the truth. The attorney's role is to promote a client's interests within the boundaries of the law and the rules of the courtroom. The attorney is not there to discover the truth; the court itself seeks truth by weighing all the evidence presented to it in the context of an adversarial struggle.

The adversarial process may create a personal and ethical dilemma for professionals. Personally, they may sense that, in order to be a part of the legal proceedings, they will be pressured to relinquish integrity. Ethically, the adversary system itself creates a tendency to present data in a light most favorable to the side presenting it. The opportunity not only for personal bias, conscious or unconscious, but also for actual abuse of behavioral science data is great. An understanding of the law relating to human services as well as the legal system itself can relieve such pressures. Combined with an ethical professional stance, such an understanding will allow an appropriate and effective integration of behavioral science information into legal decision making.

The Legal System: Laws and Courts

The legal system can be roughly categorized into theoretical processes (statutory and case laws) and institutional implementation (courts).

The law, whether from statutory or case sources, can be broken into criminal and civil categories. Criminal law involves offenses against the state or society, such as treason, felonies, or misdemeanors. Civil law involves disputes by private individuals, with one individual alleging that the other has breached an agreement or a duty imposed by law.

Statutory Law. Statutory laws are created by various lawmaking bodies, such as Congress, the state legislatures, and city councils. Preeminent in statutory law is the federal Constitution. Constitutional rights will proscribe (forbid) and prescribe (mandate) certain types of actions for or against the individual. For example, the Constitution proscribes the use of cruel and unusual punishment and prescribes the right to legal counsel. A court's findings in individual cases, whether heard before a jury or just a judge, may demonstrate the relevance of specific constitutional rights to the human services. For example, note the many judicial decisions on the rights of mental patients, such as the right to quality-controlled treatment, cited in Chapter Eight.

State statutory law makes a similar proscriptive/prescriptive contribution to human services. In some ways it reaches more directly into day-to-day human services operations, since many state statutes and regulations spell out how an agency (for example, an agency that provides rehabilitation programs) or an institution (for example, a mental health facility) will operate; similarly, state licensure laws spell out how a professional will practice (for example, by specifying what services the professional may offer or by proscribing certain unethical practices).

An interesting blend of constitutional rights and state regulation can be found in statutory definitions of the rights of patients in mental health facilities. Exemplifying how the legal process evolves in general, a new generation of state laws may well reflect the preceding generation of court interpretations of constitutional law in regard to mental health procedures. Section 394.459 of the *Florida Statutes*, for example, specifies that, among other rights, mental health patients have the right to individual dignity, to treatment (and inability to pay will not lead to denial of services), to the least restrictive treatment alternative, and to informed consent to procedures. The *Florida Statutes* recognize only one right of mental health professionals: "No mental health professional shall be required to accept patients for treatment of mental, emotional, or behavioral disorders" (sec. 394.460).

Case Law. Case law, often referred to as "common law," is a body of legal decisions that, when taken collectively, creates legal rules for decision making. Typically, the statutes will prescribe a certain legal principle—for example, that a substantial change of circumstances is required before a child custody placement can be changed; a series of case decisions will then define that principle—indicating, for instance, what constitutes a "substantial change of circumstances" in the custody context. Case decisions also determine what exactly a statute means. The court looks at a law and its "legislative history" and decides what the lawmakers actually intended by the law. Court opinions take into account any bearing that "higher" laws (such as the state or federal constitution) may have on the interpretation of the statute in question. There are many legal nuances that determine whether federal or state law will apply in a given case. In general, however, suits must consider state law first; if a federal issue, such as a constitutional right or a conflict between states or between parties from different states, is involved, the federal laws will come into play. Depending on the nature of the case, a federal court may apply a state law, even when considering a federal issue. This is not a simple matter, and it would be ill-advised to open it up beyond this nominal mention.

Types of Courts. As for the types of courts, the basic distinction is federal and state.

The federal judicial system starts with one of the ninety-four U.S. District Courts. Among the kinds of cases heard at this level are those in which one party is the federal government, when one state sues another, and when a Constitutional issue or federal legislation is involved. If a decision of one of those courts is appealed, the case may move to one of the eleven circuits of the U.S. Court of Appeals. On rare occasions a case may reach the ultimate: the U.S. Supreme Court. There are also a number of specialty courts, such as the U.S. Tax Court, the Court of Customs and Patent Appeals, and the Court of Claims.

In some instances the judicial process requires that an administrative agency process a case before it can move into the federal courts. For example, labor relations cases (depending on their nature) might have to start with litigation before the National Labor Relations Board.

The state judicial system is unique to every state. Contrary to the commonly held belief, the highest state court is not always the "supreme court." In New York, for instance, the supreme court is an appellate court (called "Supreme Court, Appellate Division") below the New York Court of Appeals. In other words, the name for a court of a particular level is different from state to state.

Another feature unique to the state is the number of courts in the legal chain. For example, in Nebraska, cases can start in a state district court and, on appeal, move to the state supreme court; there is no intermediate court. In Florida, however, a case starting in a circuit court or county court must move to a district court of appeal before it can potentially reach the state's supreme court.

Jurisdiction is a critical concept. It involves two questions: (1) Which court, federal or state, should receive the case? (2) Once that determination has been made, which court (such as a specialty versus a general court) should hear the case? In other words, which court has the power or authority to act on the merits of the case—to resolve the dispute and to grant relief (or a remedy)? A court must have jurisdiction over both the subject matter (the type of case) and the person. For example, a state does not have jurisdiction over a citizen of another state unless that person has done a substantial amount of business in the state or has some other adequate connection to it.

Within a geographical jurisdiction, there may be alternative jurisdictions with which to reckon. For example, a teenager accused of a criminal act could be bound over to a general court or assigned to juvenile court (which would commonly allow for a more therapeutically oriented processing of the case). Another good example is the divorce case. Many jurisdictions have special facilities, sometimes labeled conciliation courts (or something similar), that are intended to promote family life (that is, contradict divorce), if at all possible. Two other examples of specialty courts are the small claims court, authorized to settle disputes (frequently without lawyers being involved) involving small amounts of money (for example, Nebraska limits claims to $1,000); and the workers' compensation court, established to administer and enforce provisions of the state's workers' compensation statute (for example, the determination of benefits resulting from industrial accidents or occupational diseases). Finally, the size of a population center may result in the presence of municipal courts or county courts.

With the caution that every state is unique, the state of Florida will be used to exemplify jurisdiction. Since there are differences between types of cases, two separate descriptions of criminal and civil courts are necessary.

In Florida a criminal case alleging a misdemeanor or a violation of an ordinance (except a misdemeanor connected to a felony) must have its first appearance in a *county court.* All felonies, misdemeanors joined with felonies, and juvenile cases come before the *circuit court.* If a criminal case heard initially in a county court is to be appealed, it must go to a circuit court—although certain cases, such as those involving a constitutional issue, may bypass the circuit court and move directly to the state *supreme court.* Following a decision on a criminal case in a circuit court, the appeal is to a *district court of appeal,* wherein final orders are entered for cases that are not directly reviewable by any other court, such as the supreme court.

It is far more difficult to reach the supreme court, either in a state or in the federal system, than the average person realizes. In most instances, a distinct error in a lower court's decision has to be documented. There are some exceptions, however. In Florida, for example, the state supreme court reviews all final orders for cases that involve the imposition of a death sentence; and in many states cases involving alleged unethical conduct by attorneys fall under the original jurisdiction of the supreme court (usually preceded by a series of grievance proceedings in the state bar association).

Turning to civil cases, the sixty-seven Florida county courts deal with matters not exceeding $5,000; and the twenty circuit courts have general trial jurisdiction for all cases not directly aligned with county courts and for actions on probate and estate cases, actions of ejectment, and a number of other exclusive areas. The five district courts of appeals hear appeals of all final orders (unless they can go directly to the state supreme court) and nonfinal orders that deal with technicalities such as venue, injunctions, and jurisdiction. Again, there are innumerable legal nuances that influence whether a given court will or will not accept a case, but that is beyond the scope of this discussion. Finally, the state supreme court has both mandatory appellate review (such as in death penalty cases) and discretionary appellate review (for instance, when a decision in one district court of appeal conflicts with a decision of another district court of appeal).

A court decision in one state may be different from a decision on a seemingly comparable case in another state. Even within the same state, there may be contradictions. Judges are human; and, by role definition, each is accorded great judicial discretion for the decision making. Consequently, one judge may rule one way and another judge may rule another way, and an appeal will be possible only if reversible error can be alleged. Generally, appellate courts strain to uphold the decisions made at the lower level.

Since judicial discretion has sometimes produced deleterious legal results, legislatures tend to specify by statutory language what criteria a judge must apply in a given type of case. Also, the judicial system has promulgated "model acts," which represent the collective thinking of foremost legal authorities on a particular subject, and these acts are adopted by (or serve as a framework for) state legislation that shapes legal decisions.

Rules of Evidence

Earlier mention was made of the adaptations the human services professional must make to function effectively in the legal system. One of the most fundamental adaptations involves an understanding of the rules of evidence. These rules have evolved to promote the goals of the law and specifically to facilitate a fair trial. Scientific investigation can always await further experimentation or the development of new methods to arrive at its conclusions. The psychotherapist can tailor a therapeutic regimen to the needs of the individual patient; and, if one technique does not produce the desired results, the therapist may shift to another. The court can afford neither of these luxuries. It must solve a pressing problem in a timely fashion, and its solution must be applicable to persons with similar problems. The court reaches its solution to the problem on the basis of evidence that has been presented to it. The rules of evidence are, therefore, of utmost importance because they determine what will be allowed to come before the court. No professional function in the legal system can occur without an allegiance to the rules of evidence.

Human services professionals are frequently disheartened by their initial exposure to the rules of evidence. In his treatise on psychiatry and the law, Slovenko (1973, pp. 5–7) captures the discomforting nature of the proceedings:

> The judicial process was initially a contest and has always been subject to restrictive rules which set the lawsuit squarely in the domain of orderly, antithetical play. . . . Traditionally, a trial has been regarded as a type of drama and is preeminently a theatrical form. . . . Much "truth" is accepted through faith . . . . The relationship of judge or jury and litigant is institutionalized in an attempt to exclude the many irrelevancies which spring from human frailty. . . . A trial . . . . evaluates only the evidence brought forth by the parties. . . . It is not expected that a trial, however fair, will produce all the evidence that exists. . . . Results in law are primarily practical, and only secondarily theoretical.

Noting that one famous attorney won seven hundred cases, while losing only one, Slovenko adds, "It was clearly not the rightness of the client's case that won all these decisions in his favor" (p. 6). He notes also that the rules of evidence are the legal system's method of screening data and that "much evidence may be rejected in a court of law, even though in other disciplines it is considered substantial enough from which to draw inferences" (p. 8). In short, "The law's method of arriving at a result is often purposely nonscientific or dependent upon a nonprofessional assessment" (p. 9).

Slovenko's descriptions of the law are likely to produce a shudder in some human services professionals. They are accurate nonetheless, however antithetical they may be to the "ivory tower" leanings of many professionals. A closer examination of the rules of evidence may help the professional understand how the adversarial struggle between two parties can produce the kinds of data that will allow the court to arrive at a fair decision.

Expert Testimony. Subject to the rules of evidence, which vary by jurisdiction, almost anyone who is "professionally acquainted with, skilled, or trained in some science, art, or trade, and thereby has knowledge or experience in matters not generally familiar to the public" can serve as an expert witness (Schwitzgebel and Schwitzgebel, 1980, p. 238). Expert testimony is predicated on the requirement of firsthand knowledge; that is, knowledge from observation. Relatedly, the party who is calling on the expert testimony must first satisfy the court that the expert has had adequate opportunity to observe whatever is receiving attestation. (More will be said on this topic in the later discussion of the *Florida Evidence Code.*)

The expert witness may offer opinions or inferences and may respond to hypothetical questions. The lay witness may not offer opinions or inferences, and the observation criterion is applied differently to lay persons. While the lay person must have had direct contact with the action or expression (otherwise the testimony would be hearsay), the professional may be allowed to offer testimony based on indirect observation. For example, many jurisdictions will allow a professional to testify about data collected by another professional who is part of a team effort; in child custody cases, for example, a psychologist may be allowed to cite a home visitation report made by a social worker. Usually, however, any source of information, such as the social worker in the preceding example, is expected to be available personally for testimony to accommodate cross-examination by the attorney for the party being testified against (known as the "party-opponent").

Opinion testimony must be aligned with the ultimate issue, and there must be a concrete description of facts: "The purpose of the testimony has had an effect on the degree of concreteness required. In the outer circle of collateral facts, near the rim of relevancy, evidence in general terms will be received with relative freedom, but as we come closer to the hub of the issue, the courts have been more careful to call for details instead of inferences" (Cleary, 1972, p. 26). The court prefers facts to inferences because it does not want the testimony to "usurp the function" of the jury. That is, the jury should make an independent analysis of facts, rather than let the expert's statements preordain their decision.

Since expert opinions must be qualified, expert witnesses usually are asked to cite their qualifications relevant to professional knowledge on the subject being considered and to enter a copy of their professional credentials into the record.

Expert testimony cannot be accorded elevated importance unless it is on a subject that is "so distinctively related to some science, profession, business, or occupation as to be beyond the ken of the average layman" (Cleary, 1972, p. 9). Moreover, "Opinion evidence is not admissible if the court believes that the state of the pertinent art or scientific knowledge does not permit a reasonable opinion to be asserted even by an expert" (p. 31). Therefore, the examining attorney may ask the expert, "Have you derived or formed an opinion based on your professional knowledge and with a reasonable degree of professional certainty?" All this procedure is part of the qualification phase for expert testimony.

Hypothetical questions comprise an area where experts may be allowed to testify without firsthand observation-based knowledge of the parties. The trial judge is free to decide whether to allow testimony on hypothetical facts (which closely parallel the characteristics of the parties or the circumstances of the case); if such testimony is erroneously admitted, it might be the basis for an appeal. For example, a judge might believe that certain data were obtained through normal data-collection methods of a profession and thus qualified as an exception to the hearsay rule, when in fact the methods were not commonly used and the information was therefore hearsay—and the case was determined by that evidence.

Some jurisdictions allow the testimony of other witnesses to be the basis for the expert's later testimony on hypothetical questions. For example, again from a child custody case, a series of professionals who had actually assessed, firsthand, the parents and children could testify about their findings; then (with the court's approval) another professional, who had not conducted a firsthand assessment, could be called to the stand to testify about what, if the preceding testimony were true, the diagnoses for the parents and children might be. In this instance the expert must be established as a person with special skills for this sort of secondhand diagnosis—for instance, through teaching university courses or conducting research on psychodiagnostics or supervising the case data presented by other professionals.

Some jurisdictions will allow reports to be submitted as evidence, whereas other jurisdictions will not allow reports unless the author is available for in-court cross-examination (or else is available, for cross-examination under oath via a deposition). Cleary (1972, pp. 43–44) emphasizes the importance of cross-examination:

> For two centuries, common law judges and lawyers have regarded the opportunity of cross-examination as an essential safeguard of the accuracy and completeness of testimony, and they have insisted that the opportunity is a right, and not a mere privilege. . . . And the premise that the opportunity of cross-examination is an essential safeguard has been the principal justification for the exclusion generally of hearsay statements, and for the admission as an exception to the hearsay rule of reported testimony taken at a former hearing when the present adversary was afforded the opportunity to cross-examine. Finally, state constitutional provisions guaranteeing to the accused the right of confrontation have been interpreted as codifying this right of cross-examination.

The availability for cross-examination may create barriers to using certain types of behavioral and health science information. For example, if a psychologist calls a colleague in another state to seek a "second opinion" on a diagnosis, that colleague's opinion may be inadmissible because he or she is unavailable for cross-examination.

There are some exceptions to being available for cross-examination. These include illness, incapacitation, and death. Written reports are admitted, if qualified for authority, in only some states, and often other rules are attached, such as the report writer must be available for cross-examination by deposition. In any event, the concept of "fair play," which is so critical to our justice system, would support that cross-examination is essential in all but the most rare circumstances.

Federal Rules of Evidence. Relevance is the password for all evidence. The rules of evidence are structured to increase the chance that the decision maker will reach a correct verdict. The primordial safeguard, therefore, is to restrict admissible evidence to that which aids understanding of valid factors. The *Federal Rules of Evidence* (1979), which is the precursor for state rules of evidence, indicates: "All relevant evidence is admissible, except as otherwise provided by the Constitution of the United States, by act of Congress, by these rules, or by other rules prescribed by the Supreme Court pursuant to statutory authority. Evidence which is not relevant is not admissible" (Rule 402). The exceptions are intended to ensure constitutional rights (for example, against self-incrimination) and judicial fair play: "Although relevant, evidence may be excluded if its probative value is substantially outweighed by the danger of unfair prejudice, confusion of the issues, or misleading the jury, or by considerations of undue delay, waste of time, or needless presentation of cumulative evidence" (Rule 403).

As for a definition of relevant evidence: " 'Relevant evidence' means evidence having any tendency to make the existence of any fact that is of consequence to the determination of the action more probable or less probable than it would be without the evidence" (Rule 401).

Even relevant evidence, however, may be excluded for policy reasons. Most notable is hearsay: " 'Hearsay' is a statement, other than one made by the declarant while testifying at the trial or hearing, offered in evidence to prove the truth of the matter asserted" (Rule 801). Clearly, the hearsay rule could undermine the expert testimony of human services professionals, since that testimony is based largely on out-of-court assertions by others. Before the alarm is sounded, however, it should be underscored that Rule 803 provides a long list of hearsay exceptions—conditions that will admit testimony even though the declarant is unavailable. (The declarant is the person who originally made the statement and is now being quoted.) While the hearsay exceptions vary greatly among the states, several allow the professional to testify about information that would likely be excluded as hearsay if uttered by a nonprofessional witness. Subsection (3) allows statements about existing mental, emotional, or physical conditions. Subsection (4) admits statements for purposes of medical diagnosis or treatment (the word "medical" is usually defined generically and would extend to any health-related diagnosis or treatment). Also admissible are recorded recollections (subsection 5), records of regularly conducted activity (subsection 6), learned treatises (subsection 18), reputation concerning personal or family history (subsection 19), reputation as to character (subsection 21), and the "catch-all" exception that allows the court to admit hearsay evidence if it has "equivalent circumstantial guarantees of trustworthiness" and if "the general purposes of these rules and interests of justice will best be served by admission of the statement into evidence" (subsection 24).

If there is any doubt about the admissibility of a bit of evidence, the opposing attorney can be expected to object to it as "immaterial," "inadequate foundation," "hearsay," or whatever. Of course, similar objections may be raised about the form or substance of questions being posed to the expert giving testimony.

As mentioned several times, the rules of evidence are unique to every state. While the *Federal Rules of Evidence* cast the mold for state rules, not all rules may be included. For example, the "catch-all" hearsay exception does not win universal favor.

Florida Evidence Code. One state's rules—the *Florida Evidence Code* (Title VII, Chap. 90, 1981)—will be used here to show how such rules apply to one area of human services, psychology. For brevity, the *Florida Evidence Code* will be referred to simply as "the rules," and subsection citations will be omitted.

Before a witness is allowed to testify, the Florida rules indicate that the "court shall determine preliminary questions concerning the qualification of a person to be a witness, the existence of a privilege, or the admissibility of evidence." "A witness may not testify to a matter unless evidence is introduced which is sufficient to support a finding that he has personal knowledge of the matter." To avoid an unfair emphasis on the testimony, "A judge may not sum up the evidence or comment to the jury upon the weight of the evidence, the credibility of the witnesses, or the guilt of the accused." If a psychologist were to make use of a writing or a recorded statement, "an adverse party may require him at that time to introduce any other part of any other writing or recorded statement that in fairness ought to be considered contemporaneously." If adequately documented by psychological research, an idea testified to may receive "judicial notice," meaning that the court recognizes that the "facts are not subject to dispute because they are capable of accurate and ready determination by resort to sources whose accuracy cannot be questioned."

The expert witness is accorded special significance because of academic preparation. The rules indicate:

> If scientific, technical, or other specialized knowledge will assist the trier of fact in understanding the evidence or in determining a fact in issue, a witness qualified as an expert by knowledge, skill, experience, training, or education may testify about it in the form of an opinion; however, the opinion is admissible only if it can be applied to evidence at trial.

> The facts or data upon which an expert bases an opinion or inference may be those perceived by, or made known to, him at or before the trial.

> If the facts or data are of a type reasonably relied upon by experts in the subject to support the opinion expressed, the facts or data need not be admissible in evidence.

Relevant evidence—evidence tending to prove or disprove a material fact—may be excluded on grounds of prejudice or confusion. Thus, psychological testimony that is especially complex, theoretical, or abstract may not be admitted because "its probative value is substantially outweighed by the danger of unfair prejudice, confusion of issues, misleading the jury, or needless presentation of cumulative evidence."

Character evidence is a subject of much debate. In general, "Evidence of a person's character or a trait of his character is inadmissible to prove that he acted in conformity with it on a particular occasion," but, as is so often the case, there are exceptions. For example, "Similar fact evidence of other crimes, wrongs, or acts is admissible when relevant to prove a material fact in issue, such as proof of motive, opportunity, intent, preparation, plan, knowledge, identity, or absence of mistake or accident, but it is inadmissible when the evidence is relevant solely to prove bad character or propensity."

The rules also declare: "Evidence of measures taken after an event, which measures if taken before it occurred would have made the event less likely to occur, is not admissible to prove negligence or culpable conduct in connection with the event." Thus, the evidence that a defendant accused of child abuse sought psychotherapy after the alleged abuse *might* be inadmissible as a means of proving the allegation.

Privileged communication (discussed further in Chapter Ten) is carefully restricted. In general, the rules specify: "No person in a legal proceeding has a privilege to (1) refuse to be a witness, (2) refuse to disclose any matter, (3) refuse to produce any object or writing." Statutory privileged communication is, of course, endorsed for certain professional relationships, such as attorney-client, psychotherapist-patient, and husband-wife.

In the Florida statutes, "psychotherapist" is defined as "a person licensed or certified as a psychologist under the laws of any state or nation, who is engaged primarily in the diagnosis or treatment of a mental or emotional condition, including alcoholism and other drug addiction." Under the present rules (although they may be changed to coincide with a revised licensing statute that encompasses psychologists, school psychologists, clinical social workers, mental health counselors, and marriage counselors under one statutory umbrella), only psychologists have privileged communication. Physicians also have it—but only when they are treating a mental or emotional condition.

Another point of special interest is the privilege granted to husbands and wives: "A spouse has a privilege during and after the marital relationship to refuse to disclose, and to prevent another from disclosing, communications which were intended to be made in confidence between the spouses while they were husband and wife." What of the statements made during marriage counseling? If the counselor is not eligible for psychotherapist-patient privilege, reliance would have to be on the husband-wife privilege. And what if a divorce action follows, and one of the spouses wants the marriage counselor to give testimony about what was said (threats, admission of abuse, plans to conceal assets, and the like). At first glance the Florida rules seem to allow the dissenting spouse to "prevent another" (such as a marriage counselor) "from disclosing communications." However, since the rule applies only to communications "intended to be made in confidence," the spouse who wants to bring in the testimony may claim that the counseling sessions were not intended to be confidential. In fact, most states would probably view a discussion with a marriage counselor, if not specifically deemed eligible for privileged communication by statute, as creating a circumstance where a third party's (the counselor's) presence negated the confidentiality attributed to any marital privacy right. There is also a trend away from any kind of privileged communication. Finally, there can be no marital privilege between husbands and wives when they are party-opponents.

Being a behavioral or health scientist, the human services professional wants to remain objective, but seldom will the "other side" (the attorney for the party who did not call the professional to testify) give unreserved acceptance to testimony. The outcome will be an attempt to "impeach": "Any party, except the party calling the witness, may attack the credibility of a witness by introducing statements of the witness which are inconsistent with his present testimony . . . , [by] showing that the witness is biased . . . , [and by] presenting] proof by other witnesses that material facts are not as testified to by the witness being impeached."

It is often disturbing for the professional who agrees to testify, thereby fulfilling a societal duty, to encounter a "hostile" attorney from the other side, who laces into the professional's testimony in a manner that creates a sense of personal attack and professional denigration. In point of fact, the party-opponent's attorney is making sure that justice is at work. The right to cross-examination, as discussed previously, necessitates attempts to "shake the story" in an effort to get at the truth.

The impeachment process is a sound reason for never entering a courtroom without having done one's "homework." For example, the testimony of one psychologist was clearly impeached when a second psychologist, brought in by the other side, told the court that the first psychologist did not meet the standards of care required of psychologists because he had failed to score the Rorschach, to administer all eleven subtests of the Wechsler Adult Intelligence Scale (he had administered only six subtests), and to adhere to the standardized administration of the Thematic Apperception Test (instead of using the established sequence of cards, he had randomly selected only a few cards that would "give me what I was looking for"). Likewise, any terminology used should be studied beforehand. One psychologist referred to a type of psychopathology and on cross-examination could not define it. His credibility dropped sharply.

In giving testimony, then, professionals should not attempt to speak on subjects outside the area of their expertise. The rules state: "Cross-examination of a witness is limited to the subject matter of the direct examination and matters affecting the credibility of the witness." Thus, the examining attorney should avoid questions on a topic that might "open the door" to the cross-examining attorney. Of course, most skilled attorneys can "open the door" themselves by making a tangential connection between what was brought out in the direct examination and what they want to cover in the cross-examination; or they can bring up a new area as a pretext for establishing credibility—for example, to determine how knowledgeable a professed expert is about the broad scope of the discipline.

Some professionals erroneously believe that their case notes or test protocols have sanctity. As the rules state: "When a witness uses a writing or other item to refresh his memory while testifying, an adverse party is entitled to have such writing or other item produced at the hearing, to inspect it, to cross-examine the witness thereon, and to introduce it, or, in the case of a writing, to introduce those portions which relate to the testimony of the witness, in evidence." The cautious professional will study carefully any folder of documents beforehand and will not bring a document to the courtroom if he or she does not want it to be introduced as evidence.

Even if the materials are not taken to the witness stand, they can be ordered to be produced. For example, if there are materials in a briefcase or even elsewhere, the court can require that they be brought into the record, and used for cross-examination. One psychologist was asked whether he had any materials not previously submitted to the court, and he responded that there was a folder in his office. He was ordered to obtain it during the luncheon recess. When his testimony resumed in the afternoon, a single sheet of hand-scribbled notes became the focus of cross-examination for several hours, since the party-opponent's attorney wanted to use those penned ruminations to show that the professional was not testifying with scientific objectivity but, rather, was an advocate (as witnessed by his notes about how to present his ideas most convincingly on behalf of the party calling him to testify).

Some jurisdictions exclude professional treatises from court proceedings, but the Florida rules permit them under certain conditions: "Statements of facts or opinions on a subject of science, art, or specialized knowledge contained in a published treatise, periodical, book, dissertation, pamphlet, or other writing may be used in cross-examination of an expert witness if the expert witness recognizes the author or the treatise, periodical, book, dissertation, pamphlet, or other writing to be authoritative, or, notwithstanding nonrecognition by the expert witness, if the trial court finds the author or the treatise, periodical, book, dissertation, pamphlet, or other writing to be authoritative and relevant to the subject matter." This rule clearly mandates that, before accepting a role as an expert witness, the professional must definitely be well read, or else be prepared to have his testimony impeached.

In one case the attorneys for both parties entered the courtroom with the third edition of the American Psychiatric Association's *Diagnostic and Statistical Manual of Mental Disorders (DSM-III)* to use as a point of reference in cross-examination of each other's expert witnesses only a few days after the *DSM-III* had been shipped from the publishers. It is not beyond the astute attorney to seek one or more treatises that only the most diligent of professionals would have studied, yet all professionals theoretically should have studied.

As mentioned earlier, statements made by other than the person testifying, offered to prove the truth of the matter asserted, are potentially hearsay and excludable from the legal proceedings, but "Statements made for purposes of medical diagnosis or treatment by a person seeking the diagnosis or treatment, or made by an individual who has knowledge of the facts and is legally responsible for the person who is unable to communicate the facts, which statements describe medical history, past or present symptoms, pain, or sensations, or the inceptions or general character of the cause or external source thereof, insofar as reasonably pertinent to diagnosis or treatment" constitute an exception to the hearsay exclusionary rule.

Another exception to the hearsay rule, under certain conditions, is "Testimony given as a witness at another hearing of the same or a different proceeding, or in a deposition taken in compliance with law in the course of the same or another proceeding." Although the conditions permitting this testimony are spelled out in a complex fashion ("[Such testimony is allowed] if the party against whom the testimony is now offered—or, in a civil action or proceeding, a predecessor in interest—had an opportunity and similar motive to develop the testimony by direct, cross-, or redirect examination") the rule does allow the professional's testimony in another hearing to be introduced in the instant hearing as potential evidence. At worst, this rule could enable an opposing attorney to impeach the professional's testimony by pointing out that in a comparable case the professional had maintained a different opinion. For example, child custody cases often require an answer, based on research findings, to the question "Is there a particular age when a boy needs his father [or mother] more than his mother [or father]?" No matter which parent has called the professional to testify, his or her answer had better be the same in all child custody cases.

In one fairly small jurisdiction, a psychologist is consistently impeached because of self-contradictions from one case to the next. He has gained the reputation of "saying whatever you pay him to say." Similarly, one judge regularly asks psychologists their views about splitting up siblings (allowing one child to live with the father and one child to live with the mother) in custody cases. The judge does so, seemingly, to check on whether the psychologist is being consistent with previous testimony the judge has heard from the person, as well as to evaluate the psychologist's general knowledge of factors related to child development.

This somewhat cursory overview of the *Florida Evidence Code*, as it applies particularly to psychological testimony, should create at least a sense of the legalese that is used to spell out the rules for testimony. Any human services professional who anticipates giving expert testimony would be well advised to read through the rules of evidence for his or her state and discuss them with an attorney. Relatedly, there are differences among jurisdictions (from one county to the next and even between judges) relevant to procedures and protocol. These matters, too, should be a subject of discussion with a local attorney before entering the courtroom to give testimony.

Evidence Based on New Techniques. New methods on which testimonial ideas are based typically receive limited acceptance from the courts. It has been stated: "When faced with a novel method of proof, [the California courts] have required a preliminary showing of general acceptance of the new technique in the relevant scientific community" (*People* v. *Kelly,* 17 Cal. 3d 24, 30 (1976)). This judicial caution reflects an awareness that lay jurors place a high value on scientific evidence from experts and that there may be, as a result, a "misleading aura of certainty which often envelops a new scientific process, obscuring its currently experimental nature" (at 32). Professional ethics require that such testimony be acknowledged as new and evolving, even though such an admission might reduce a witness's credibility.

A distinct example of legal skepticism directed at a behavioral science method is hypnosis. Like any behavioral science method that can claim to reveal human behavior, hypnosis has received progressive endorsement by law enforcement personnel. Many police departments even have an officer especially trained to conduct hypnotic interviews. This endorsement, however, is far from universal. Margolin (1981, p. 43) asserts: "The professional consensus is that hypnosis should not be used in courts and should be used more carefully, if at all, in investigations." The concern about using hypnosis seems to be twofold. First, there is doubt that a hypnotist other than a psychiatrist or psychologist—for example, a police officer who has learned the rudiments of hypnotic induction and interrogation—can properly elicit valid and reliable evidence. Second, there is doubt that hypnosis will yield untainted testimony. A Minnesota court clarifies:

In addition to its historical unreliability, a
"memory" produced under hypnosis becomes hard-
ened in the subject's mind. A witness who was unclear
about his "story" before the hypnotic session becomes
convinced of the absolute truth of the account he made
while under hypnosis. This conviction is so firm that
the ordinary "indicia of reliability" are completely
erased, and hypnotic subjects have been able to pass lie
detector tests while attesting to the truth of statements
they made under hypnosis which researchers know to
be utterly false. It would be impossible to cross-
examine such a witness in a meaningful way [*People
v. Mack*, 292 N.W.2d 764, 769 (Minn. 1980)].

This legal opinion reveals why the testimony by human services
professionals on matters that they believe to be derived from legitimate methodology may still fail to reach the level of probative value
required by the legal system.

Special Guidelines for Expert Witnesses

Expert testimony is a professional function, not a personal
mission. It should be treated accordingly. Some professionals become committed to a particular area of service, such as the rights of a
special interest group. As expert witnesses they should avoid an
apostolic zeal—promoting the area to the point that personal preference dilutes professionalism. The legal system does not accommodate zealots of any cloth, even if robed by academia. Similarly,
professionals should not let their roles become confused. In criminal
cases, for example, the expert witness's role is not to save a defendant's life or to protect society from wanton criminals. The expert's
place is to serve the court in the interest of justice and to do so within
the legal system and not the human services system. To do otherwise
is to ensure impeachment of testimony.

Professionals also should avoid taking the opposing attorney's activities as a personal attack. Seldom does an attorney, at least
if he or she is a properly developed legalist, attempt a personal
vendetta against a professional giving testimony. Consequently, the
expert witness should view impeachment efforts by an attorney dis-
passionately, answering the attorney's questions in a straightfor-

ward, academically based manner. To slip into personal defensiveness—for instance, when one's credentials are questioned—is to succumb to the goal of impeachment.

No single set of rules will, in every case, prevent problems for the expert witness; some general guidelines, however, may be of help. Before agreeing to become an expert witness, the professional should have clarified exactly what his or her role is to be. Frequently, the first step is to determine who the patient or client is. If, for instance, a prosecuting attorney asks a psychologist to determine a criminal defendant's sanity or competence to stand trial, then the prosecutor is the client. In such a case, the psychologist should inform the defendant prior to examination that he or she has been retained by the prosecution and that what the defendant reveals may well be used against him or her at the trial. In general, before they assume the expert role, professionals must learn what use will be made of their reports or their opinions.

Professionals also must be able to work closely with the attorney and to understand the attorney's role as well. In particular, they will need to understand the precise legal questions that the attorney wants answered. Many, if not most, legal questions are unanswerable on a purely scientific basis. In a sanity evaluation, for instance, who (except possibly the defendant) knows what a psychotic defendant thought about a criminal act at some given moment in the past? Understanding the legal issues in question and the legal process in general, however, will help the professional decide how to examine the defendant in such a way that the best possible expert testimony will be provided. At the same time, professionals should not become so enamored of the legal issues (which ultimately are for the judge and/or jury to decide) that they are distracted from doing a thorough evaluation. In the above example, the psychologist should have done a complete assessment of the defendant, so that he or she can testify to the individual's current mental status, diagnosis, life history, and the results of appropriate psychological testing. This type of material, of course, represents the core of the psychologist's expertise. He should communicate to the attorney the complete results of the evaluation and their significance, so that the attorney is able to frame the appropriate questions. Additionally, the psychologist should have become familiar with the case in general, so as to provide a framework for his or her contribution. In sanity cases it is sometimes extremely helpful to have available police reports or other eyewitness accounts of the defendant's behavior at the time of the alleged criminal act. Such accounts might well shed light on the question of whether the patient was acting in a mentally disordered fashion at that time. Indeed, it may be helpful to interview close family members or other people who observed the defendant at or about the time of the crime.

Prior to taking the stand, professionals should have a good understanding of what will be asked during direct examination; they will not be of service to justice if they become confused by the attorneys who have retained them and consequently are misunderstood by the jury. When they have taken the stand, they should listen very carefully to the questions asked and make sure that they understand a question before they attempt an answer. If a "yes" or a "no" response is not possible to a specific question, they should say so; at the same time, they should confine their responses to the actual question asked.

Throughout their testimony, professionals should be meticulously honest, remembering that, although one or the other side has retained them, their role is to serve the interests of justice. Professionals should not be afraid of admitting weaknesses in their opinions or in the methods used; they should, at the same time, be prepared to outline specifically what facts they relied on. Finally, professionals should be able to give their testimony in relatively plain language, so that the jury and/or the judge can understand it.

Legal Research

The human services professional is typically well equipped to understand legal research, at least from the content point of view—since behavioral scientists are trained to analyze data, and data analysis is the foundation of legal research. There are, however, fundamental differences between behavioral science data and those of law. Seldom will the legal reference rely on numerical data or even experimental conditions. Rather, the legal data are commonly contained in descriptions of cases or statutes, and the legalist's results will be a subjective analysis of the quality of the descriptive material.

The legal scholar must be able to analyze and evaluate the significance of a case or statute and to make comparative analyses of various sources; but any subjective analysis is vulnerable to differences of opinion. This is the very essence of what happens in the courtroom. The two sides have different legal analyses, based on the same set of facts, legal theories, or rules; and the advocacy is directed at establishing which of the parties is advancing the correct interpretation. Of course, the court may conclude that neither party is totally correct and that the correct way of interpreting the significance of the legal data is in the manner issued by the court.

Briefing an Opinion. As a student the human services professional likely spent hours in the university library, laboriously taking notes on articles from professional journals. The similar practice in legal research is termed "briefing an opinion." When reading a legal case, one must glean certain kinds of information—information that subsequently will be provided to the court. That information appears in the brief. There is no fixed outline or form for a brief of an opinion. The important thing is to follow a plan that is meaningful and consistent, that allows reliable retrieval of "data," and that achieves needed goals: "The ultimate reason for analyzing opinions is to be able to predict, on the basis of what courts have done in past cases, what a court will do in a current or future case. In analyzing for reasons of prediction, [one must relate] the contents of a particular opinion to a current problem" (Rombauer, 1978, pp. 10–11). This type of analysis requires comparing the facts and legal questions of the present case with those of the previous case or cases.

More specifically, Rombauer (p. 11) notes that briefing an opinion enables the legal scholar to develop "instinctive analytical and evaluative reactions" and "the ability to pinpoint legal questions"; to learn what matters are considered relevant and what types of reasoning are persuasive to courts; to identify past legal questions and the courts' answers to them; to become familiar with "existing" law (currently recognized rules and principles, the reasons for their development, and the factual situations where they have been applied); and to identify "unsettled areas of law."

In general, a brief of an opinion should include the following sections: the reference citation; the nature of the case or what kind of action was taken; a summary of the facts, detailed enough to allow for the derivation of distinctions from other cases; the legal issue; the legal holding or decision, including the rule(s) of law established, and the legal reasoning that justified the ruling; and possibly a summary of the writer's own analysis of the case. A sample case brief (intended only as a guide and not as a prototype that would negate personalized analysis) appears at the end of this chapter (Exhibit 1). It is a commercially prepared brief, often referred to by law students as a "canned brief" (with a negative connotation sometimes attached because it minimizes individual scholarship; yet law students quickly learn that the rigors of law school press toward any form of "study aid," including "canned briefs").

Briefing a Statute. Briefing a statute, at the state or the federal level, is somewhat different from briefing a case and will likely tax efforts to follow a set outline or plug information into uniform sections. The true meaning of a statute often rests with the legislative intent. Therefore, to determine what the lawmakers intended when they passed the law, one must study not only the actual wording of that law but also the "legislative history" (committee reports, debates, executive messages, records of hearings).

The briefing of a statute mandates that every word be weighed, since every word is significant. Finding a consistent interpretation in the midst of sometimes inconsistent language can be a challenge; but, again, the legislative intent will usually be the connecting rod between words and rule.

Legal Briefs. Briefing an opinion or a statute should not be confused with the widely heralded "legal brief." The legal brief represents an attorney's analysis of the law for the benefit of the court. That is, the court relies on the legal brief for the research background from which the decision or verdict will be fashioned. Needless to say, the legal brief must be impeccably accurate, and the party-opponent's attorney must be diligent to ascertain that the other attorney's brief tells the story correctly. Of course, there will be points in the brief that will give rise to legitimate debate. Indeed, one of the values of the brief is that it provokes healthy legal debate.

Many human services professionals may actually have a hand in the writing of the legal brief—for instance, by providing a review of behavioral or health science research, which the attorney then incorporates into the brief. Since *Muller* v. *Oregon*, 208 U.S. 412

(1908), courts have been receptive to the "Brandeis Brief" (named after Supreme Court Justice Louis D. Brandeis, who endorsed its usage), which incorporates research, including behavioral and health science data, into the legal persuasion. An understanding of the nature of the legal brief, therefore, may be of help to professionals in working with attorneys.

The legal brief is more than a summary of legal principles and citations; it is a comprehensive treatise on the facts and law pertaining to the case at hand. Pittoni (1967, p. 4) specifies the following contents:

1. A résumé of the facts in narrative form and, where possible, in chronological order.
2. Quotations, abstracts, or digests of the Constitution, statutes, regulations, orders, etc., involved.
3. Abstract or digest of the pleadings, with reference to the paragraph numbers of the original pleadings.
4. Information for probable and possible questions in examining the jurymen.
5. List of witnesses, both in the order in which you expect to call them, and alphabetically.
6. List of exhibits, keyed to the names of witnesses through whom they will be offered in evidence.
7. Abstract or digest of the expected testimony of each witness in narrative form and, where possible, in chronological order.
8. Separate facts which you expect to prove, naming the witnesses and exhibits in support thereof.
9. Separate facts which your opponent may try to prove, naming the witnesses and exhibits in opposition thereto.
10. Evidence, facts, and other material for cross-examination of anticipated opponent's witnesses.
11. Brief on the law, including authorities supporting your contentions and those refuting anticipated contentions of your opponent.
12. Expected requests to charge or instruct the jury.

This is but one set of possible contents for a legal brief. Each jurisdiction may have its own requirements for the brief. Similarly, the nature of the case can dictate the contents. The important thing to grasp is the general scope of the legal brief, recognizing how the human services professional can contribute to its contents.

Affidavits. Affidavits are similar in purpose to a legal brief. The human services professional may serve as an affiant (one who attests to something) on matters to which his or her expertise pertains, in order to establish a fact or premise for a legal action. That is, the professional may offer a "voluntary ex parte statement reduced to writing and sworn to or affirmed before some person legally authorized to administer an oath or affirmation. A mere affidavit, as distinguished from a deposition or the like, is made without notice to the adverse party and without opportunity to cross-examine" ("Affidavits," 1962, p. 380). The reference to "oath or *affirmation*" means that the affidavit will be acceptable even if the affiant does not take an oath. "An affirmation may be substituted for the oath where the person making the affidavit has conscientious scruples against taking an oath or where he does not believe in God" (Moore, 1964, p. 467).

An affidavit is not the same as a deposition, which "is limited to the written testimony of a witness given in the course of a judicial proceeding, either at law or in equity, in response to interrogatories, oral or written, upon notice and with an opportunity for cross-examination" ("Affidavits," 1962, p. 381). Depositions need not be voluntary; they can be compelled by statutorily prescribed notice or subpoena.

An affidavit can have a variety of uses. In judicial proceedings some of its uses may be "to verify a pleading, to prove the service of a summons, notice, or other process, in an action, to obtain a provisional remedy, an examination of a witness, [or] a stay of proceedings, . . ." (Moore, 1964, pp. 467–468). In the case of a human services professional offering an affidavit, it is his or her professional expertise and stature that casts authority on to the assertion.

The statutes of the given state typically prescribe the formal requisites for an affidavit, but most affidavits have certain features in common. That is, "every affidavit has, aside from the body of the instrument, certain component parts which may be either proper or absolutely essential, according to the law of the particular jurisdiction; they are usually designated as the caption or title, the venue, the signature of the affiant, and the jurat, which properly includes the authentication" ("Affidavits," 1962, p. 390). Moore (1964) cites the component parts of an affidavit as the title, venue, body, signature of affiant, jurat, and the signature, title, and seal of an officer. The "body" refers to the facts (generally not opinions or conclusions) based on positive knowledge (if knowledge is impossible, however, information and belief are permissible, especially for an expert opinion), and "jurat" refers to a certificate stating that the affidavit was signed and sworn to before a qualified officer (such as a notary public).

A human services professional might be asked to submit an affidavit to a judicial proceeding for various purposes. A psychologist, for example, might be asked to certify that a client with certain characteristics belongs in the "mentally retarded" classification; the attorney could then base a defense on the client's mental status. A social worker might be asked to attest to the effects of parental abuse on a child; the attorney then might be able to obtain a temporary order for a placement with other than the allegedly abusing parent. Or a behavioral scientist might be asked to assess the scene of an accident and assert the expected perception of a driver. Exhibit 2 (at the end of this chapter) shows a sample affidavit created for a child custody case. Certain facts (for example, names) have been changed to protect anonymity (even though an affidavit used in legal proceedings becomes public information), and some material that would ordinarily be included in an affidavit has been deleted (for the sake of brevity). Since, as mentioned previously, there is no single form to which an affidavit must be fitted, Exhibit 2 should be viewed only as an example, and adaptations should be made according to the statutory requirements and/or prevailing practices of the jurisdiction and to the characteristics of the contents being asserted, the nature of the case, and the affiant.

The affidavit should contain only those ideas that can, in fact, be supported by subsequent testimony. Once an affidavit is entered into the legal record, the affiant becomes a potential witness (such as by a subpoena requiring participation in the legal proceedings) and will then be available for cross-examination. Failure to substantiate assertions made in the affidavit will allow for the impeachment of the contents and/or testimony offered at another stage of the proceedings.

Finding Legal Sources. The walls of a law library, with their volumes in heavy, ornate bindings, can be awesome. After a reasonable orientation, however, the atmosphere can change and can bring on a sense of strength and support; for legal sources can give the human services professional invaluable information for buttressing contributions to legal proceedings.

It would be unrealistic to expect the human services professional to acquire the same facility at locating and understanding legal information as would be commonplace for the legal scholar. On the other hand, the human services professional can supplement his or her behavioral or health science expertise with legal ideas, albeit in a somewhat rudimentary fashion. The human services professional can achieve an adequate orientation by becoming familiar with the major types of legal sources. This fundamental orientation can be augmented by guidance from a professional legal librarian.

United States Supreme Court decisions are reported by official and unofficial reporters. The official reporter, created by statutory authority, is the *United States Supreme Court Reports* (cited as U.S.). The unofficial reporters, products of commercial publishers, are the West Publishing Company's *Supreme Court Reporter* (S. Ct.) and the Lawyers Co-operative Publishing Company's *Lawyers' Edition of United States Supreme Court Reports* (L. Ed. or L. Ed. 2d). All these editions are authoritative as to text, but the unofficial versions may also contain supplemental information (such as summaries of the attorneys' arguments or abstracts on specific legal points). If a Supreme Court case has not yet appeared in these publications, it might be found in *United States Law Week* (U.S.L.W.), a looseleaf service.

Decisions on cases from the U.S. Courts of Appeals appear in the *Federal Reporter* (F. or F.2d). U.S. District Court decisions appear in the *Federal Supplement* (F. Supp.) and *Federal Rules Decisions* (F.R.D.).

State court decisions (except in a few states) are disseminated by an official state reporter, such as *Michigan Reports* (Mich.) or *California Reports* (Cal., Cal.2d, or Cal.3d). There will also be a regional reporter, such as *Northwestern Reporter* (N.W. or N.W. 2d), which includes important cases from Michigan, Wisconsin, Minnesota, Iowa, North Dakota, South Dakota, and Nebraska.

Contrary to popular belief, not all court cases are published. That is, most cases at the federal level are published (especially those decided by the U.S. Supreme Court or a U.S. Court of Appeals); at the state level, most jurisdictions publish appellate decisions, but other cases (for instance, those decided at the trial level) may not be published unless they have special legal importance. Cases that are unreported elsewhere (as well as recent cases that have not yet appeared in the various reporters) may sometimes be found in separately paginated "advance sheets," in "looseleaf services" (such as the *Criminal Law Reporter,* the *Family Law Reporter,* or the *Labor Law Reporter*), or in legal periodicals.

Federal statutes appear, among other sources, in the *Statutes at Large* (these "session laws" are arranged in the order in which they are enacted); this source (cited Stat.) also includes congressional resolutions, select presidential proclamations, and treaties and other international agreements. The *United States Code* (U.S.C.) is published by the U.S. Government Printing Office and is the primary authority on final legislative law.

Federal administrative rules and regulations appear in the *Federal Register* (Fed. Reg.). The *Code of Federal Regulations* (C.F.R.) cites (by title and section) all federal administrative rules and regulations, except Treasury materials. Federal administrative decisions are published by various agencies, such as the Federal Trade Commission and the National Labor Relations Board.

State statutes—for example, the *Arkansas Statutes Annotated* (cited Ark. Stat. Ann.)—are published in bound volumes periodically. In between issues, a statute may be eliminated, amended, or added, and will be found in supplemental editions. It is always necessary to check in the back of a bound volume to see whether a "pocket supplement" reflects any revision of a statute.

Municipal and county ordinances appear in many forms but are usually confined to local distribution. The variations in form preclude detail herein. In general, however, these ordinances are similar in form to the statutes.

Legal research is blessed with encyclopedic sources. For example, the *American Law Reports* (A.L.R., A.L.R.2d, or A.L.R.3d) include selected cases and annotations on specific subjects, along with historical background, current law, and probable future developments. Similarly, the *Corpus Juris Secundum* (C.J.S.) series cites case authority, presents a researched summary of the law, and so on. *Words and Phrases* contains more descriptive and extensive definitions than the well-known *Black's Law Dictionary*.

An often-used legal research method is to "Shepardize" a case—that is, to use *Shepard's Case Citations* to follow the judicial history of a targeted case, learn the contemporary status of the case, locate other cases that have cited it, and acquire research leads (such as where to look in *American Law Reports*). The *Shepard* volumes are divided by jurisdiction. Statutes may also be researched in *Shepard's United States Citations*, and law review articles may be located in *Shepard's Law Review Citations*. Municipal charters and ordinances may be cited in *Shepard's Ordinance Law Citations*.

Legal materials follow a special referencing or citation system. For example, cases are cited as follows (with minor variations in type style used in different publications):

> *Tarasoff* v. *Regents of the University of California,* 17 Cal.3d 425, 551 P.2d 334, 131 Cal. Rptr. 14 (1976).
> ("Cal.3d" is the third series of *California Reports,* the state reporter for California Supreme Court cases; "17" is the volume where the *Tarasoff* case is reported, and "425" is the first page where the case appears. "P.2d" is the *Pacific Reporter,* the regional reporter for California state court cases; and, again, "551" is the volume number and "334" the first page where the case appears. "Cal Rptr." is *West's California Reporter,* an unofficial reporter for California court cases.)

> *Muller* v. *Oregon,* 208 U.S. 412, 415 (1908).
> ("U.S." is *United States Supreme Court Reports,* and "415" is the page where a specific quoted passage, presumably just cited in the text, appears. If the case has previously been cited, this citation may appear as *"Muller* v. *Oregon,* 208 U.S. at 415.")

> *Driver* v. *Hinnant,* 356 F.2d 761 (4th Cir. 1966).
> ("F.2d" is *Federal Reporter,* publisher of U.S. Court of Appeals cases; "4th Cir." indicates that the case was heard by the U.S. Court of Appeals for the Fourth Circuit.)

> *Greenberg* v. *Barbour,* 332 F. Supp. 745 (E.D. Pa.
> 1971).
> ("F. Supp." is the *Federal Supplement,* reporter for
> U.S. District Court Cases; "E.D. Pa." indicates that the
> case was heard by the U.S. District Court for the east-
> ern district of Pennsylvania.)

In addition, books, periodicals, newspapers, statutes, legislative materials, and other specialized materials are cited in prescribed ways. An authoritative source for learning legal citations is *A Uniform System of Citation* (12th ed., 1976), created by law review groups at Columbia, Harvard, Pennsylvania, and Yale (distributed by the Harvard Law Review Association, Gannett House, Cambridge, Massachusetts 02138).

The preceding information should provide the frame of reference needed for entering a law library. Law libraries are maintained by law schools and many local/state bar associations. Many university libraries and some municipal/county libraries will have the more important legal sources, such as the statutes or regional reporters; and most law firms will house a collection of basic legal sources.

The human services professional need not hesitate to embark on legal research. Law librarians exist to assist researchers, and not being an attorney will not ban the human services professional from the premises or the assistance. The adage "Ask and Ye Shall Receive" is the credo for approaching a law library.

Furthermore, attorneys themselves do not typically object to giving "free advice" for bona fide research efforts. An outside inquiring mind can brighten up an otherwise humdrum work day, even (especially?) for an attorney. Moreover, such contacts can promote new and improved interdisciplinary relations. The result may well be reciprocal benefits for both the attorney and the human services professional, such as working together on a case in the future.

Exhibit 1. A Sample Case Brief.

TARASOFF v. REGENTS OF UNIVERSITY OF CALIFORNIA
Sp. Ct. of Cal. (1974) 13 C.3d 177 [17 Cal.3d 425, 551 P.2d 334,
131 Cal. Rptr. 14 (1976)]

NATURE OF CASE: Action for wrongful death.

FACT SUMMARY: Doctors from the University of California (D) were aware that one of their outpatients intended to kill Tatiana Tarasoff but neglected to warn her of it.

CONCISE RULE OF LAW: "A doctor or a psychotherapist treating a mentally ill patient . . . bears a duty to use reasonable care to give threatened persons such warnings as are essential to avert foreseeable danger arising from his patients' condition or treatment."

FACTS: While a mental outpatient at a University of California (D) Hospital, Posenjit Poddar disclosed his intention to kill one Tatiana Tarasoff because she had spurned his romantic advances. The psychologist who learned of this intention, Dr. Moore, notified both the campus police and three staff psychiatrists; but, after a cursory investigation, it was decided that no action to confine Poddar was necessary. Tatiana was not warned of Poddar's intentions. Two months later, Poddar shot and killed Tatiana. At his trial, it was learned that Poddar had discontinued his treatment at the UC (D) hospital after the incident two months earlier. Tatiana's parents (P) thereupon filed this action against UC (D) alleging that the hospital's negligent failure to warn Tatiana of Poddar's intention had caused her wrongful death. This appeal followed. The Alameda County Superior Court found for the defendant in 1973. This appeal to the California Supreme Court followed. The case again was heard in 1976.

ISSUE: Are doctors under any duty to warn potential victims about known violent tendencies and intentions of their patients?

HOLDING AND DECISION: Yes. "A doctor or a psychotherapist treating a mentally ill patient . . . bears a duty to use reasonable care to give threatened persons such warnings as are essential to avert foreseeable danger arising from his patient's condition or treatment." There is no reason why the rule requiring doctors to take such action to prevent harm from physical illness should not be extended to mental illness situations as well. UC (D) contends that the burden of deciding which of the many threats which doctors hear should be taken seriously is too great; but, there is nothing improper in the law requiring a professional to exercise his professional judgment. UC (D) contends that requiring disclosure of such threats will destroy the confidentiality necessary to effective psychotherapy; but, the interest of society in protecting itself from physical violence must take precedence. The action may proceed.

EDITOR'S ANALYSIS: This case marks a diversion from the traditional attitude of the courts regarding the duty of a doctor to warn about threats made by a patient in confidence. As Justice Clark in his unreported (in the casebook) dissent pointed out here, there is nothing unusual in holding a psychotherapist liable for harm which results from the "negligent discontinuance" of psychotherapy. Pre Tarasoff, however, there was no precedent for predicating liability on a mere failure to disclose dangerous intentions. Note that this new rule is consistent with the psychotherapist-patient privilege since such privilege is expressly inapplicable in situations in which the safety or welfare of any individual is threatened.

Source: Reprinted by permission of Casenotes Publishing Co., Inc., from Casenote Legal Briefs, Torts, copyright © 1982.

Exhibit 2. A Sample Affidavit.

IN THE SUPERIOR COURT
IN THE COUNTY OF BRIDGEPORT

IN THE MATTER OF   Civil No. C-12345
JOE SMITH
D.O.B. 4/10/73   *AFFIDAVIT*
STATE OF NEBRASKA
                            SS.
COUNTY OF DOUGLAS

I, ROBERT HENLEY WOODY, Ph.D., Sc.D., being of lawful age and
first duly sworn upon oath, depose and state as follows:
    1. That affiant is a clinical psychologist engaged in the private practice
of clinical psychology with offices located at 1002 North 72nd Street,
Omaha, Nebraska, 68114.
    2. That affiant has satisfactorily completed all of the following educa-
tional programs and has earned and presently holds all of the following
degrees necessary to the practice of clinical psychology, to-wit:

[Omission: Degrees, etc., should be listed here]

    3. That in addition to the private practice of psychology which affiant
has been engaged in since 1967, affiant has had the following professional
employment since 1958, to-wit:

[Omission: Employment record should be listed here]

    4. That affiant presently holds licenses or certificates which are in good
standing from the following professional and/or government boards and
bodies, to-wit:

[Omission: Licenses and certificates should be listed here]

    5. That affiant is a member in good standing of the following profes-
sional societies and organizations:

[Omission: Professional memberships should be listed here]

    6. That affiant has authored or coauthored each and all of the profes-
sional publications described on Exhibit "A" attached hereto.

[Omission: Publications should be listed here or, if extensive, listed
on an attached exhibit]

    7. That the formal education and professional training of affiant has
included training and experience in the diagnosis and treatment of child-
hood emotional and behavioral problems; and has further included training

and experience in the evaluation of factors for child custody legal proceedings and has conducted nationwide research, which has been published in scholarly journals, on the criteria needed to meet the best interests of the child in child custody legal proceedings.

8. That affiant has conducted two clinical interviews with Thomas and Susan Jones, the latter the mother of Joe Smith, relevant to the psychological, social, and educational development of Joe.

9. That affiant has conducted a clinical interview with and administered the following psychological tests to Joe: the Bender Visual-Motor Gestalt Test; the Ammons and Ammons Intelligence Test; the reading portion of the Wide Range Achievement Test; the Callahan Anxiety Pictures Test; the Thematic Apperception Test (Boy Series, Cards 1-10 & 13MF); and the Children's Personality Questionnaire.

10. That as a result of the aforementioned psychological tests, the affiant interprets Joe's psychological status as encompassing: average (or higher) intellectual potential; perceptual errors (possibly due to anxiety, feeling of inferiority, and/or a maturational lag); reading problems that can adversely impact upon his educational achievement; and significant personal insecurity, with concomitants of mild depression, anxiety, and a seeming preoccupation with violence.

11. That as a result of these psychological findings and at the request of the mother, Susan Jones, the affiant reviewed and analyzed all of the clinical and test data relevant to Joe on file in the Bridgeport County Mental Health Services and interviewed B. F. Freud, Ph.D., the psychologist previously involved with the evaluation of Joe for child custody legal proceedings held in the Superior Court, County of Bridgeport.

12. That based upon my educational background and experience as a clinical psychologist and upon my review and study of the materials previously relied upon in the custody determinations for Joe Smith, affiant asserts that:

A. Psychological assessments have heretofore failed to include a comprehensive evaluation of mental abilities, such as the Wechsler Intelligence Scale for Children—Revised, as would be necessary to properly make professional recommendations for custody that would meet the best interests of the child;

B. A number of positive comments about placement with Thomas and Susan Jones were included in the Bridgeport County Mental Health Services' file but were not conveyed in the psychological reports therefrom to the Court;

C. Personality assessment from the Bridgeport County Mental Health Services failed to meet the prevailing standard of care, i.e., to "flesh out" a structure-oriented personality test (e.g., the Rorschach Ink-Blots Method) with a psychodynamic/interaction-oriented personality test (e.g., the Thematic Apperception Test), thereby allowing the expression of professional opinions about child custody placement without an adequate psychological data base;

D. B. F. Freud, Ph.D., did not interview Thomas and Susan Jones for purposes of fitting the social case history to the test data, thereby making interpretive professional opinions of suspect reliability and validity (i.e., this may also be viewed as a breach of the prevailing standard of care relevant to the use of the psychological tests relied upon for testimony to the court);

E. There have been no psychological assessments of any of the adults involved with potential placements for Joe, thereby negating a reasonable assessment of psychological parenting factors that could contribute to the best interests of the child; and

F. B. F. Freud, Ph.D., acknowledged in an interview with the affiant that there were significant emotional issues inherent to Joe's psychological makeup and that treatment attention was recommended.

13. That based on my educational background and experiences as a professional psychologist working with child custody determinations, affiant asserts that previous psychological, social, and educational evaluations of Joe Smith have been inadequate to allow a determination of what custody arrangements could fulfill the best interests of Joe.

14. That based on my educational background and experiences as a professional psychologist, affiant asserts that Joe Smith is a child with special psychological needs and that, therefore, a more comprehensive psychological, social, and educational evaluation is necessary.

15. Affiant asserts that the psychological tests support a change in psychological condition for Joe Smith since the previous custody determination by the Superior Court of the County of Bridgeport.

16. That based on my educational background and experiences as a professional psychologist, affiant believes that any subsequent evaluation for Joe Smith should include, among other actions, the following: psychological assessments of Thomas and Susan Jones and of Joseph and Helen Smith; a comprehensive appraisal of Joe's mental abilities, such as by the Wechsler Intelligence Scale for Children—Revised; a comprehensive personality evaluation, including the integration of the test data obtained by the affiant with other past and future data collected; interviews with school personnel and analysis of educational records; and a more thorough and more objective evaluation of the parenting conditions that could be provided by Thomas and Susan Jones versus those that could be provided by Joseph and Helen Smith.

FURTHER AFFIANT SAYETH NOT.

ROBERT HENLEY WOODY, Ph.D., Sc.D.
Diplomate in Clinical Psychology,
A.B.P.P.

SUBSCRIBED AND SWORN TO before me, a Notary Public, this _____ day of January, 1982.

Notary Public

Janet B. Porter   2

Criminal Law

Human services practitioners may work with criminal or juvenile law violators as probation or parole officers, court service workers, alcohol treatment counselors, residential workers, or school counselors. The goal of all these workers is to prevent the occurrence or recurrence of delinquent or criminal behavior. The challenge for the human services worker is to work successfully with a client who may not voluntarily seek services, since law violators are often coerced into securing treatment as a condition of a court order or to avoid incarceration.

In endeavoring to help the offender, many practitioners become frustrated with the criminal or juvenile justice system because they cannot come to grips with the sometimes irreconcilable differences between psychological or sociological rehabilitative goals and legal goals, which may only incidentally seek to rehabilitate the offender. To work effectively with juvenile and adult offenders and their families, administrators and practitioners in various social service agencies need a familiarity with the criminal laws in their state. Social service agency personnel have an obligation to assist in ensuring that offenders are aware of their legal rights and that rehabilitative goals comport with limitations imposed on offenders by the legal system.

Adult or youthful law violators come into the system because they have violated the legal norms of society. Although these norms may be found in constitutions and common law, today most laws with criminal penalties are codified in state statutes or municipal ordinances. Criminal and juvenile court statutes vary widely among the fifty states. Selected statutes and case law will be presented here, but human services workers should review the criminal and juvenile law in their own state.

A literal reading of a criminal statute or case will not always explain an action taken by a key actor in the system. For example, a statute may provide that an offender shall be granted bail except for a capital offense. A judge, in applying the statute, generally has broad discretion in its interpretation. Levine, Musheno, and Palumbo (1980, p. 276) quote a judge at a bail bond hearing: "I'm going to set $5,000 bail . . . Now, I'm leaving word that if bond is presented, the matter is to be sent back to me, and I'll tell you right now, if they put up $5,000 bail, I'll make it $10,000, and if they put up ten, I'll make it $25,000. I want these boys to spend one or two nights in jail." All key actors in the system make similar discretionary decisions in the daily performance of their duties. The police officer decides whether or not to arrest, the prosecutor decides whether or not to charge the offender, and the judge decides whether to impose a lenient or harsh sentence within the statutory limits. Differential enforcement and discriminatory application of the laws may result. Discretion by police, prosecutors, and judges can be justified, however, on the basis of the need for individualized justice, the fact that most laws are rather vague or not specific, and the desire to avoid inflexibility or rigidity in the enforcement of laws.

The police probably have the greatest discretion in the system. They can handle matters informally, so that there will be no further insertion of the law violator into the system. In fact, only a few of the reported crimes lead to an arrest. A police officer, thus, has the power to weigh social values in an individual case and to make a policy decision to seek an alternative to criminal processing, such as warning the parties involved, mediating between them, making a referral to a community agency, or doing nothing. Police practices involve low-visibility interactions with citizens and suspected law violators (with little review of an officer's final decision). Unless there is an arrest, there may be no record of what happened in the confrontation and subsequently little or no review of the officer's final decision (Davis, 1969).

Most discretionary decisions by police depend on such factors as political pressures in a particular community (Reiss, 1971); the personal values of the officer; department policies; the demeanor of the offender and/or the complainant; the type of law being broken; the relationship of the offender to the victim; the chances of getting a conviction; and the race, age, and sex of the offender or victim. Many of these same factors influence the decision of the prosecutor in deciding what (if any) charges should be filed against a law violator.

Because of alleged discrimination in the enforcement of criminal laws, recent administrative regulations, legislation, and judicial decisions have attempted to make decision making by key actors in the system less discretionary and more accountable. Civilian review boards, standard operating procedures, guidelines for plea bargaining and sentencing, and due process procedures for adult and juvenile law violators are examples of ways in which legislatures or courts have limited arbitrary discretion.

This chapter will consider substantive and procedural criminal laws as they relate to the law violator.

Substantive Criminal Law

The substantive criminal law in each state (and in the federal system) defines the conduct proscribed and the punishment imposed for inchoate (that is, partial or not completed) crimes; crimes against persons or property; crimes involving drugs and narcotics, gambling, fraud, family relations, or morals; offenses against the government; and miscellaneous other offenses. In early English and American history, judges declared certain conduct to be criminal; in modern times, however, the legislature enacts criminal laws. State criminal codes, rather than judge-made law, comport with an important due process principle requiring that an offender be given fair warning as to what conduct is proscribed by the government. Additional substantive law is found in constitutions. There are also a large number of administrative or regulatory laws that carry criminal penalties. In order to ensure enforcement of governmental regulations pertaining to health, safety, and the general welfare of the public (for example, traffic laws), the legislature has authorized criminal penalties for violation of those laws.

Although some criminal codes include archaic or unenforceable laws, many states have recently updated their criminal codes and incorporated sections of the 1962 and subsequent revisions of the American Law Institute's *Model Penal Code* (MPC). This code was written by outstanding lawyers and jurists throughout the country who reviewed criminal offenses in order to decriminalize some offenses, clarify the essential elements of crimes, and assign fair and proportional punishment. Legislatures can adopt all the provisions of the *Model Penal Code* when they enact new criminal codes, but most states include their own variations based on local conditions or political considerations. Congressional committees have been working on a new comprehensive federal criminal code for several years (see S. 1630, Criminal Code Reform Act of 1981; and H.R. 1647 and 4711, Criminal Code Revision Act of 1981). Political differences have led to an impasse, which has delayed passage of a revised federal criminal code.

Although juveniles are adjudicated in courts that have some attributes of civil rather than criminal courts, the petition (rather than an adult information or indictment) generally is based on a violation of the state's criminal code. (Separate juvenile court statutes include sections on delinquency, dependent and neglected children, and status offenders. See Chapter Three for a discussion of these offenses and protective statutes. State statutes also contain provisions relating specifically to youthful violations, such as Minor in Possession of Alcohol.)

Classification of Crimes. Crimes are classified in various ways (for example, *malum in se*, "evil in itself," such as murder; or *malum prohibitum*, "evil because prohibited by statute," such as driving without a license), but the principal classification divides crimes into felonies and misdemeanors. Felonies are punishable by fines or by imprisonment of one year or more; misdemeanors are punishable by a fine and/or a jail term of not more than one year. Statutory alternatives to imprisonment include, for example, probation. Failure to fulfill the court's conditions of probation will lead to revocation and, generally, incarceration. The following are examples of criminal offenses in the *Nebraska Criminal Code* (effective January 1, 1979):

> *Murder in the second degree;* penalty. (1) A person commits murder in the second degree if he causes the death of a person intentionally, but without premeditation.
>
> (2) Murder in the second degree is a Class IB felony [sec. 28-304].

> *Robbery;* penalty. (1) A person commits robbery if, with intent to steal, he forcibly and by violence, or by putting in fear, takes from the person of another any money or personal property of any value whatever.
>
> (2) Robbery is a Class II felony [sec. 28-324].

> *Assault in the third degree;* penalty. (1) A person commits the offense of assault in the third degree if he:
>
> (a) Intentionally, knowingly, or recklessly causes bodily injury to another person; or
>
> (b) Threatens another in a menacing manner.
>
> (2) Assault in the third degree shall be a Class I misdemeanor unless committed in a fight or scuffle entered into by mutual consent, in which case it shall be a Class II misdemeanor [sec. 28-310].

> *Burglary;* penalty. (1) A person commits burglary if such a person willfully, maliciously, and forcibly breaks and enters any real estate or any improvements erected thereon with intent to commit any felony or with intent to steal property of any value.
>
> (2) Burglary is a Class III felony [sec. 28-507].

> *Issuing a bad check;* penalty. (1) Whoever obtains property, services, or present value of any kind by issuing or passing a check or similar signed order for the payment of money, knowing that he has no account with the drawee at the time the check or order is issued, or, if he has such an account, knowing that the check or order will not be honored by the drawee, commits the offense of issuing a bad check. Issuing a bad check is:
>
> (a) A Class III felony if the amount of the check or order is more than one thousand dollars;

(b) A Class IV felony if the amount of the check or order is three hundred dollars or more, but less than one thousand dollars;

(c) A Class I misdemeanor if the amount of the check or order is seventy-five dollars or more, but less than three hundred dollars; and

(d) A Class II misdemeanor if the amount of the check or order is less than seventy-five dollars.

(2) For any second or subsequent offense under subdivision (1) (c) or (1) (d) of this section, any person so offending shall be guilty of a Class IV felony [sec. 28-611].

Essential Elements of a Crime. The essential elements of the crime (the necessary act and the culpable state of mind) and the penalty to be assessed on conviction are included in each criminal offense. In order to ensure that the penalties will reflect the seriousness of the crime and are proportional, most states have graded felonies and misdemeanors into several categories, ranging from the most severe penalty for conviction of a felony to the least severe penalty for conviction of a misdemeanor. As shown in Table 1, conviction of a Class I felony could result in the death penalty or life imprisonment, and in Nebraska this severe penalty is authorized only for conviction of murder in the first degree. In theft and bad check charges (see sec. 28-611), the penalty varies according to the amount of the theft or bad check. For example, if the bad check is more than $1,000, the penalty is a Class III felony, whereas a check of less than $75 is a Class II misdemeanor.

In order to convict a criminal defendant, the state must obtain evidentiary facts or proof (for example, eyewitness testimony, real evidence, or documentary evidence). The gathering of evidence begins during the investigatory stage, and a suspect is arrested when the police have probable cause to believe that he or she has committed the crime. However, the amount of evidence required for probable cause to arrest a suspect is substantially less than the proof necessary to convict a criminal defendant. The state has the burden of presenting relevant and competent evidence which will persuade the trier of fact (judge or jury) at the trial that the defendant is guilty beyond a reasonable doubt (that is, at least 90 or 95 percent certainty of guilt). In contrast, at a civil trial, guilt can be established with lesser de-

Table 1. Authorized Penalties for Various Crimes,
Nebraska Criminal Code.

	Felony				Misdemeanor		
Statutory Class	*Authorized Penalty*			*Statutory Class*	*Authorized Penalty*		
	minimum	*maximum*	*fine*		*minimum*	*maximum*	*fine*
I	———Life or Death———			I	0	1 yr	$1,000
IA	——————Life——————			II	0	6 mo	$1,000
IB	10 yrs	Life	NAᵃ	III	0	3 mo	$ 500
II	1 yr	50 yrs	NA	IIIA	0	7 days	$ 500
III	1 yr	20 yrs	$25,000	IV	NA	NA	$100–500
IV	0	5 yrs	$10,000	V	NA	NA	$ 100

ᵃNA = not authorized.

grees of certainty—namely, by "the preponderance of evidence" (about 50 percent certainty) or "clear and convincing evidence" (about 75 percent certainty).

Eighty to 90 percent of all felony defendants plead guilty to the criminal charge or to a lesser crime as the result of plea bargaining. Even a higher percent of misdemeanants plead guilty rather than go to trial. However, if a defendant chooses to proceed to trial, the prosecutor must prove the following essential elements: *mens rea* (bad state of mind), *actus reus* (a criminal act), concurrence of the bad act and bad state of mind, and causation (the social harm was the result of what the defendant did and not an intervening act).

It is a basic premise of substantive criminal law that there can be no liability unless there is a criminal act or a failure to act when there is a legal duty to do so. Proscribed behavior can thus include acts of commission and acts of omission. Sometimes the duty to act is imposed because of the relationship between the parties. For example, parents have a legal duty to provide necessary care and protection for their children. If they are unable to provide this care, parents have an obligation to seek assistance. Both parents must provide financial support for their unemancipated children. Failure to support one's family can result in criminal sanctions. The duty to act can also be based on an implied or express contract between the parties; for example, if a lifeguard at a public swimming pool leaves his or her post and someone in the pool drowns, the lifeguard might become criminally liable.

The criminal law seeks to punish people who are culpable or at fault. Various adverbs (such as "willfully" or "fraudulently") are used to describe the state of mind necessary to show criminal culpability. The MPC proposes four principal types of mental culpability: intention, knowledge, recklessness, or criminal negligence. The greatest fault is shown when a person injures another intentionally. The intentional act is particularly blameworthy if it is done with premeditation (most statutes differentiate murder in the first and second degree on the basis of premeditation or deliberation). The least blameworthy state of mind is criminal negligence. If a driver, knowing that his or her brakes are faulty but failing to repair them, subsequently injures someone, the law might infer that the driver is criminally negligent. The lifeguard leaving his or her post could also be considered criminally negligent. In substantive law proof of mental fault or culpability is shown by what a person does or says.

A recent national concern of citizens and legislators is to deter people from driving while intoxicated. Several states have passed criminal legislation providing stiffer penalties, such as jail sentences, for first-offense drunk drivers. Other statutes provide mandatory prison sentences where a person has been convicted for a third time of driving while intoxicated. The *mens rea* of the drunk driver would be recklessness, since the person who drives while intoxicated puts innocent persons at risk.

Motor vehicle, traffic, and pure food laws are examples of regulatory statutes that impose liability without fault. These statutes often do not include *mens rea* language at all; therefore, no fault is required in order to convict a wrongdoer. For example, exceeding the speed limit without *any* bad state of mind can result in criminal penalties (usually a fine). Many of us would not register our cars, keep within the speed limit, or obey other motor vehicle or traffic laws unless such criminal penalties were used as a stick to assure compliance.

Concurrence is an essential element because the *mens rea* must actuate the *actus reus* (LaFave and Scott, 1972). Substantive law requires that the perpetrator of a crime have the appropriate mental state for the crime charged. If a person intends to commit one offense, but inadvertently commits another requiring the *mens rea* of intent, that person should not be punished for the commission of the second offense. Felony murder is an exception to this general rule. Legislatures have determined that the intent to commit a dangerous offense (such as robbery, sexual assault, arson, or kidnapping), which then results in the death of another, is legally sufficient to show the requisite intent to kill.

Substantive law requires that the act committed by the wrongdoer be the cause of the social harm or bad result that occurs. In a relatively few cases, the bad result occurred in such an unusual way that the actor is not legally responsible for the result. A defendant is liable for any foreseeable result that he or she has set in motion. Only unforeseeable or abnormal results will exonerate the defendant. For example, it would be legally foreseeable that a gunshot victim would die from a disease contracted while that person is in the hospital receiving treatment for the wound.

It is apparent from the foregoing discussion that substantive law is very technical. Many wrongdoers are not brought to trial or are acquitted because the state has failed to meet its burden of presenting sufficient facts to prove the necessary elements of the crime. The burden is a heavy one because the judge or jury must be persuaded of the truth of these facts beyond a reasonable doubt.

Defenses to Criminal Charges. The defendant generally has to produce evidentiary facts that are a defense to a criminal charge. Even though a social harm has occurred (such as a death), the perpetrator contends that what he or she did was excusable or justifiable—because, for instance, he or she acted in self-defense or under duress.

The insanity defense is controversial today. A defendant may be so seriously mentally ill or have such a defect of reason that he or she will not be held legally responsible for a crime. The defendant raising the insanity defense has generally committed some notorious act—usually a bizarre killing. These events create headlines, and the public may believe that the defense is used frequently. Although insanity could be an issue in any case, the defense is generally raised only in capital offenses. For most crimes the offender might be better off receiving criminal sanctions because penal incarceration is for a foreseeable length of time. In most states persons acquitted by reason of insanity are subsequently hospitalized as a result of civil commitment procedures. This indefinite medical-custodial commitment may last a lifetime.

Once the issue is raised, the state has the burden of showing that the defendant was sane when the crime was committed. Since many of these defendants, if not insane, are weird or strange, the prosecutor does not have an easy task. Many times the issue of a defendant's sanity is raised prior to trial because the psychosis present when the crime was committed continues after the individual's entry into the criminal justice system. Due process would be violated if a person not legally responsible for his or her acts were tried, convicted, or punished.

The insanity defense is misunderstood because psychiatric testimony is usually essential to prove legal responsibility or lack of it. When two witnesses to a crime testify at a trial and present conflicting facts, the jury is usually able to decide which is more believable. When two or more psychiatrists, as expert witnesses in an insanity trial, present conflicting facts or conclusions, jurors become confused. A well-presented insanity defense can often create sufficient doubt to get either a hung jury or a verdict of not guilty by reason of insanity.

The jury's verdict in the *Hinckley* case is a good example of the confusion surrounding the insanity defense. The verdict of not guilty by reason of insanity for shooting President Reagan and three others has sparked demands for changes in the insanity defense. Congress and state legislatures have introduced or enacted laws to change the insanity defense in one of four ways: (1) abolishing the insanity defense altogether; (2) defining the term "insanity" more strictly; (3) shifting the burden of proving insanity to the defense; (4) creating a new verdict of guilty but mentally ill. Under this last approach, defendants would be sentenced under criminal law but would undergo psychiatric evaluation before beginning to serve their sentences. If found mentally ill or psychotic, they would be committed to a state hospital until they were determined to be capable of being returned to the state corrections facility to serve the remainder of their sentence.

Criminal Procedure

Figure 1 provides a comprehensive view of the processing of cases through the criminal justice system. The system consists of various complex components, each with its own functions. Basically, the system is structured into four major components: the police, the prosecutor, the courts, and corrections. Each component is dependent to some extent on the others, since a decision by one component will affect the others. For example, if a court dismisses a charge because of improper police conduct, a police officer may decide in a subsequent case to forgo arresting a particular law violator. If the violator is arrested, the prosecutor may choose not to file charges. If judges respond to public pressure to lock up all law violators rather than sentence them to probation or other community alternatives, prisons and jails will become overcrowded. Corrections officials may then have to defend lawsuits by prisoners who seek judicial relief for unconstitutional conditions of confinement.

When an individual enters the criminal justice system, a process begins whereby law violators can be exposed at various stages to all the components of the system. The first major component involves a suspect's contact with the police during a criminal investigation. One consequence is that the alleged offender may be arrested. This arrest may not lead to pretrial detention in jail, since the accused may be released on bail or on his or her own recognizance. The prosecutor decides whether the evidence warrants filing an information or seeking a grand jury indictment. Judges preside over various court hearings, such as arraignment, trial, and sentencing. Finally, a convicted offender may enter the correctional component of the system, which has as its goal to change deviant behavior. This change may not occur, and the offender may continue to violate the law and perhaps reenter the criminal justice system. The process then begins again.

At almost any stage in the process, the individual may be released through dismissal of charges or acquittal at trial. Large numbers of suspects may come into the system; but, as the process continues, cases "fall out," so that few persons suspected of committing crimes actually get as far as the corrections stage. According to a president's task force report (President's Commission . . . , 1967,

Figure 1. A General View of

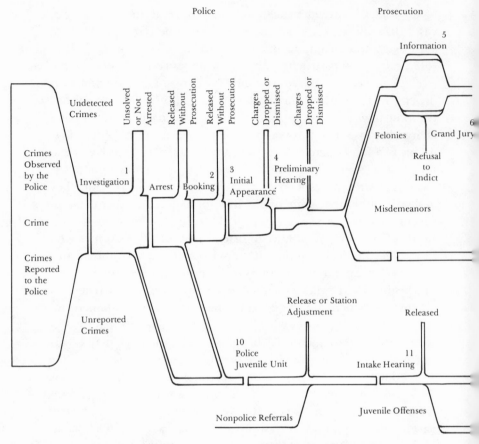

1. May continue until trial.
2. Administrative record of arrest. First step at which temporary release on bail may be available.
3. Before magistrate, commissioner, or justice of peace. Formal notice of charge, advice of rights. Bail set. Summary trials for petty offenses usually conducted here without further processing.
4. Preliminary testing of evidence against defendant. Charge may be re-

duced. No separate preliminary hearing for misdemeanors in some systems.
5. Charge filed by prosecutor on basis of information submitted by police or citizens. Alternative to grand jury indictment.
6. Reviews whether Government evidence sufficient to justify trial. Some states have no grand jury system; others seldom use it.

Source: Kamisar, LaFave, and Israel, 1980, pp. 26–27.

the Criminal Justice System.

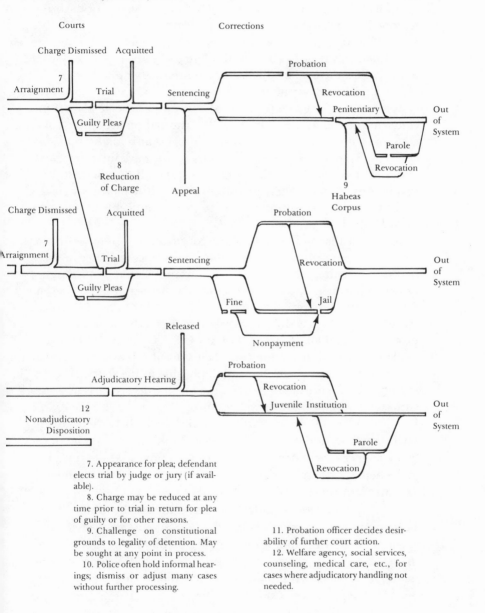

7. Appearance for plea; defendant elects trial by judge or jury (if available).

8. Charge may be reduced at any time prior to trial in return for plea of guilty or for other reasons.

9. Challenge on constitutional grounds to legality of detention. May be sought at any point in process.

10. Police often hold informal hearings; dismiss or adjust many cases without further processing.

11. Probation officer decides desirability of further court action.

12. Welfare agency, social services, counseling, medical care, etc., for cases where adjudicatory handling not needed.

p. 61), for one hundred cases reported, twenty-six arrests are made, six of which result in sentencing. Only about 2 percent of the original one hundred cases end with the perpetrator sent to prison.

Note in Figure 1 that there is separate nomenclature for juvenile law violators, who are processed through the juvenile justice system. For example, there is an adjudicatory hearing rather than a trial.

Under our system of government, there are restraints on the conduct of key "actors" as they deal with suspects, defendants, and convicted offenders. Procedures in the criminal justice system must comport with fairness in a democracy rather than a totalitarian government. To determine fair procedures, courts have interpreted federal and state statutes and constitutions as well as administrative regulations. Fundamental principles in the Bill of Rights in the United States Constitution have been made applicable to the states through the Fourteenth Amendment.

Until 1961 individuals whose constitutional rights were violated by the government in order to obtain evidence to prosecute them had to seek redress through civil or criminal actions or through a police department's internal disciplinary procedures. To the Supreme Court dissenters in *Wolf* v. *Colorado,* 338 U.S. 25 (1949), these remedies were largely illusory as a deterrent to police and prosecutor misconduct. In 1961 *Mapp* v. *Ohio,* 367 U.S. 643, overruled *Wolf* and made the exclusionary rule (the exclusion of relevant evidence at trial under certain circumstances) applicable to the states. (Unconstitutional evidence has been inadmissible in federal courts in prosecutions for violation of federal laws since *Weeks* v. *United States,* 232 U.S. 383 (1914).) Relevant evidence is excluded where there are unlawful searches and seizures, where police practices lead to involuntary statements or statements made in violation of *Miranda* rights, and where the government violates a defendant's right to counsel at a postindictment lineup.

The exclusionary rule has been criticized by Chief Justice Burger and other members of the U.S. Supreme Court, who argue that the rule does not deter illegal conduct by law enforcement officers and exacts a high price by excluding relevant and material evidence. Although the exclusionary rule has not been overruled, the Supreme Court has indirectly limited it in three major ways. First, the Court has limited the use of the federal writ of habeas corpus where a defendant has had his or her Fourth Amendment claims fairly litigated in state courts (*Stone* v. *Powell*, 428 U.S. 465 (1976)). The federal forum has been considered more sympathetic to a defendant's claims of unconstitutional government conduct than have state courts. Second, by changing the standing requirements (that is, the requirements an individual must meet in order to obtain "standing to sue"), the Court has made it more difficult for a defendant charged with a crime to challenge unconstitutional police investigative procedures (*United States* v. *Salavucci*, 448 U.S. 83 (1980); *Rawlings* v. *Kentucky*, 448 U.S. 98 (1980)). Not only does the person charged with an offense have to show an interest in the place to be searched or a possessory interest in the property seized, but he or she must have a reasonable expectation of privacy in the place searched. Even though property in a friend's home or car is used to convict a defendant, the defendant cannot get standing to raise the issue of whether the evidence was illegally seized unless he or she can show an expectation of privacy in that home or car. Third, the Supreme Court, while excluding unlawfully obtained evidence in the state's case in chief at trial (the point at which the state presents its evidence), has allowed that same evidence to be used to impeach a defendant who exercises the constitutional right to take the stand in his or her own defense. On cross-examination the government can challenge the defendant's credibility (believability) by introducing previously suppressed evidence as long as defense counsel has brought out testimony during direct examination and "opened the door" for such evidence (*United States* v. *Havens*, 446 U.S. 620 (1980)).

In addition to judicial action, states have also passed legislation to limit the exclusionary rule. In 1982, by 56 percent to 44 percent, California voters mandated a virtual end to the exclusionary rule as part of Proposition 8. Other broad statutory and constitutional changes were also enacted in this wide-ranging anticrime referendum.

Our system of justice is based on an adversarial, rather than an inquisitorial, system. The government has awesome power to investigate and prosecute an accused. This power is theoretically balanced in the scale of justice by a defendant who has some equivalent means to protect his or her rights. Procedural safeguards for persons who are to be formally processed through the criminal justice system include, in addition to the suppression of illegal evidence, the right to bail, counsel, speedy trial, jury trial unless waived, confrontation of the accuser, and privilege against self-incrimination.

The Right to Counsel. One of the most important procedural rights granted to defendants in criminal cases is the right to counsel. As stated in the Sixth Amendment to the U.S. Constitution: "In all criminal prosecutions, the accused shall enjoy the right to a speedy and public trial, by an impartial jury of the state and district wherein the crime shall have been committed, which district shall have been previously ascertained by law, and to be informed of the nature and cause of the accusation; to be confronted with the witnesses against him; to have compulsory process for obtaining witnesses in his favor; and to have the assistance of counsel for his defense." All these federal Sixth Amendment rights have been incorporated into the Fourteenth Amendment and are thus required in both state and federal prosecutions.

An understanding of criminal laws and procedures is essential if a suspect or defendant is to preserve his or her rights in the criminal justice system. In addition, guilt or innocence cannot be fairly determined unless the defendant's case is adequately presented. Defense counsel has been recognized as the key "actor" to protect the legal rights of persons in their dealings with the police, prosecutor, and courts. The system has historically permitted defendants to retain defense counsel if they could afford to do so. Not until 1963, however, did the Supreme Court unequivocally state that a fair system cannot discriminate between rich and poor defendants who need the assistance of counsel in order to present their claims adequately. In *Gideon* v. *Wainright,* 372 U.S. 335 (1963), the Supreme Court held that the right to counsel is so fundamental that counsel must be appointed for indigent defendants in state court felony trials. According to Justice Black, writing for the majority in *Gideon:* "From the very beginning, our state and national constitutions and laws have laid great emphasis on procedural and substantive safeguards designed to assure fair trials before impartial tribunals in which every defendant stands equal before the law. This noble ideal cannot be realized if the poor man charged with crime has to face his accusers without a lawyer to assist him" (at 344).

In *Powell* v. *Alabama,* 287 U.S. 68, 69 (1932), Justice Sutherland summarized the plight of the uncounseled defendant:

> The right to be heard would be, in many cases, of little avail if it did not comprehend the right to be heard by counsel. Even an intelligent and educated layman has small or sometimes no skill in the science of law. If charged with crime, he is incapable, generally, of determining for himself whether the indictment is good or bad. He is unfamiliar with rules of evidence. Left without the aid of counsel he may be put on trial without a proper criminal charge, and convicted upon incompetent evidence, or evidence irrelevant to the issue or otherwise inadmissible. He lacks both the skill and knowledge to adequately prepare his defense, even though he has a perfect one. He requires the guiding hand of counsel at each step in the proceedings against him. Without it, though he not be guilty, he faces the danger of conviction because he does not know how to establish his innocence.

Although the Supreme Court decisions of the 1970s and 1980s have eroded other constitutional rights of criminal defendants, the vitality of the constitutional right to counsel continues unabated as a shield to protect innocent persons. Once convicted, and particularly if sentenced to incarceration, defendants have fewer constitutional rights.

In 1972 the Supreme Court considered the consequences attendant on conviction of misdemeanors and petty offenses. In *Argersinger* v. *Hamlin*, 407 U.S. 25, the Court held that no person may be imprisoned for any offense—whether classified as petty, misdemeanor, or felony—unless he or she has been represented by counsel. In 1979, however, the Court limited the misdemeanor right to counsel to those cases where the judge *actually* sentenced an indigent defendant to a term of imprisonment (*Scott* v. *Illinois*, 440 U.S. 367 (1979)). In a 5-to-4 decision, the justices expressed concern that requiring counsel in all misdemeanor cases where incarceration was *authorized* by state statute would impose unpredictable and substantial costs on the state.[1] The *Scott* decision requires a judge to make a

[1]When the Supreme Court declares a procedure to be unconstitutional, it sets a lower limit or floor on those governmental practices. State legislatures or courts can grant defendants more rights under state constitutions, statutes, or case law. In fact, defendant Scott would have been entitled to appointed counsel in at least thirty-three of the fifty states at the time the case was decided.

pretrial, rather than a posttrial, decision whether to sentence a misdemeanant to incarceration. This puts the judge in a dilemma. The
trial may bring out facts that would cause a judge to incarcerate the
misdemeanant, but the judge cannot constitutionally do so unless
he or she had appointed counsel prior to trial. *Scott* is a good
example of the Court's attempt to balance or accommodate the
rights of the individual and alleviate possible financial burdens for
Illinois by not constitutionally requiring counsel in all misdemeanor cases where imprisonment was authorized.

The *Gideon* and *Argersinger* decisions were based on a concern about fair treatment for indigent defendants in the system. Two
rationales are involved. First, the government has an obligation to
treat all citizens fairly (a due process argument); second, it is unconstitutional to discriminate between rich and poor criminal defendants (an equal protection argument). As Justice Black observed in
Griffin v. *Illinois*, 351 U.S. 12 (1956): "There can be no equal justice
where the kind of a trial a man gets depends on the amount of
money he has." *Griffin* involved trial transcripts used for appellate
review. Illinois provided free transcripts only to indigents who had
been sentenced to death. The Supreme Court held that indigent
defendants had to be afforded as adequate an appellate review as
defendants who had money enough to buy transcripts. Since trial
transcripts in felony cases were essential to a meaningful appellate
review, states were constitutionally required to provide free transcripts.

The rationale of *Griffin* was equal protection. This equality
principle has been applied in other areas where an indigent defendant may be at a disadvantage—for example, in the payment of appellate filing fees. The Court also considered the state practice of indigents "working off fines" in two cases in the early 1970s. In
Williams v. *Illinois*, 399 U.S. 235 (1970), the Court held that a defendant who was unable to pay an imposed fine could not be constitutionally incarcerated beyond the maximum term of imprisonment
fixed by statute. If a statute provides a penalty of a fine only, an
indigent who cannot pay the fine may not be jailed to "work off" the
fine at, for instance, seven dollars per day (*Tate* v. *Short*, 401 U.S.
395 (1971); see also *Bearden* v. *Georgia*, 51 U.S. L.W. 4616 (1983)).

In 1963 the Supreme Court also required that indigents be appointed counsel for an appeal (*Douglas* v. *California*, 372 U.S. 353 (1963)). In almost every trial, evidence that is arguably improper under state statute, case law, or court rules is introduced. In order to obtain a meaningful appellate review of these trial errors, defendants need to be assisted by competent counsel. After considering the trial transcript and related documents, the attorney will write an appellate brief, setting out legal arguments (usually supported by cases in that jurisdiction) to show that reversible errors were committed during trial. The attorney may also make oral arguments before the appellate court to support the written brief. In *Douglas* counsel had not been appointed for the defendant's appeal. California had a rule that, on request by an indigent defendant, the appellate court would make an independent investigation of the record and determine whether the appeal had sufficient merit to warrant the appointment of counsel. The Supreme Court used the *Griffin* reasoning to hold that it would be an invidious discrimination to permit a state to grant appellate review so as to differentiate between defendants who could afford retained counsel and those too poor to do so.

Defendants dissatisfied with an appellate court's decision may want a second appellate court review of their conviction. (The government may also want to appeal from a ruling in favor of the defendant.) Assistance of counsel is important so that all legal issues may again be presented adequately. In *Ross* v. *Moffitt*, 417 U.S. 600 (1974), however, the Supreme Court decided that appointment of counsel for indigent defendants was not constitutionally required for a discretionary or second appeal. Justice Rehnquist, writing for the majority, used due process reasoning to conclude that unfairness by a state would result only if poor defendants were singled out and denied meaningful access to the system. The majority did not focus on the discriminatory classification of rich versus poor, which the *Douglas* precedent might have suggested. While the majority recognized that some procedures or services would benefit an indigent defendant, they held that due process is satisfied as long as there was adequate opportunity to present an appellate claim at least once.

In addition to counsel for misdemeanors (where a defendant is sentenced to incarceration), felony trials, and appeals, the Supreme Court has ruled that appointment of counsel is constitutionally required at other critical stages in the criminal justice process, such as arraignment, plea bargaining, preliminary hearing, postindictment lineup, and sentencing.[2]

Protections Against Unreasonable Search and Seizure. The seventeenth- and eighteenth-century immigrants to the United States recalled with resentment the power of the king and others in authority in England to order general searches of homes and property or seizure and incarceration of persons without due process of law. The Fourth Amendment to the U.S. Constitution (later made applicable to the states through the Fourteenth Amendment) is a logical outcome of that concern. The provisions of the Fourth Amendment restrain the government from intrusions affecting the liberty and privacy of American citizens: "The right of the people to be secure in their persons, houses, papers, and effects, against unreasonable searches and seizures shall not be violated, and no warrants shall issue, but upon probable cause, supported by oath or affirmation, and particularly describing the place to be searched and the persons or things to be seized."

In interpreting the provisions of the Fourth Amendment, the Supreme Court has given greatest protection to an expectation of privacy in one's home or premises not open to the public. Unless exigent circumstances or consent can be shown the Supreme Court has unequivocally declared that a search warrant based on probable cause is required prior to the search of a home.

Probable cause for a search warrant means that there is a substantial probability that unlawful items—such as contraband (for example, heroin), fruits of crime (a stolen television set), instrumentalities of a crime (burglars' tools), or evidence of a crime (a weapon)—will be found in a specific place. A police officer, while investigating a crime, may believe that illegal items or evidence of the crime will be found in a suspect's home. The officer will submit a sworn affidavit to a court, including facts that support the officer's

---

[2]Although a defendant may constitutionally act for himself (*pro se*) and effectively waive his right to counsel (*Faretta* v. *California*, 422 U.S. 806 (1976)), there is a presumption against waiver (*Johnson* v. *Zerbst*, 304 U.S. 458 (1938)). This means that the government has the burden of assuring that a defendant's waiver is knowingly and voluntarily made.

belief that these items will be found in the place to be searched. A neutral and detached magistrate evaluates the affidavit; if the magistrate determines that probable cause exists, a search warrant will be issued. Since information supporting the issuance of a search warrant may become stale, search warrants must be served promptly. State statutes often provide that they must be served within ten days, if not sooner. Search warrants usually are served by the police, who announce their purposes and show the warrant to the person on the premises. State statutes also authorize no-knock warrants, which permit the officers to enter the premises forcibly when there is a danger that evidence will be destroyed. No-knock warrants are used infrequently, since officers might be killed by residents intending to protect their homes from unknown intruders.

Facts to establish probable cause for a search warrant are usually based on observations by the police, a report by a witness or victim of a crime, or information supplied by a paid informant. Informants are used extensively in investigations of "victimless" crimes. In *McCray* v. *Illinois*, 368 U.S. 300, 303 (1967), the Supreme Court gave its approval to the use of informants by declaring them to be a "vital part of society's defensive arsenal." Informants are usually petty criminals or drug addicts who supply information to the police for money or some other benefit (such as the government's agreement not to prosecute them). In order to ensure that facts to support probable cause to search are not based on unfounded hearsay of informants, the Supreme Court has required that the affidavit must set forth the underlying circumstances, so that a judge may evaluate the validity of the informant's conclusion that the illegal items or evidence of a crime are where the informant said they would be. Sufficient detail must be given so that the magistrate can rely on more than a rumor of criminal activity or an accusation based on an individual's reputation. The affidavit must also include facts to show that the informant was credible or his information reliable (*Aguilar* v. *Texas*, 378 U.S. 108 (1964); *Spinelli* v. *United States*, 393 U.S. 410 (1969)). However, in 1983 the Supreme Court permitted the issuance of a search warrant on the basis of an anonymous informant's tip. According to Justice Rehnquist, writing for the majority, the two-pronged test of *Aguilar* v. *Spinelli*, if rigidly applied, would impede the work of law enforcement. An informant's veracity, reliability, and basis of knowledge were highly relevant in establishing probable cause for a search warrant, but they were not separate and independent requirements. Instead, they were to be evaluated in the totality of the circumstances so that a deficiency in one requirement could be compensated for by "some other indicia of reliability" (at 4714). The anonymous letter to the police gave a detailed description of alleged criminal activity and this persuaded the Court that the tip (later partially corroborated by the police) was sufficiently credible and reliable to establish probable cause (*Illinois* v. *Gates,* 51 U.S.L.W. 4712 (1983)).

Once the police have entered the premises lawfully (with a warrant or with consent or under exigent circumstances), the scope of the search may be expanded beyond the specific items in a warrant. Additional items in plain view which are found inadvertently and are of an incriminating character may also be seized without a warrant (*Coolidge* v. *New Hampshire,* 403 U.S. 443 (1971)).

Justice Powell, concurring in *United States* v. *Watson,* 423 U.S. 411 (1976), recognized that an arrest is probably a more serious intrusion than a search. Therefore, logic would dictate that arrests be subject to the warrant requirement, at least to the same extent as searches. However, the majority reviewed the history of common law arrests and concluded that arrest warrants are not constitutionally required.[3] The police, rather than the judiciary, make the initial determination of probable cause. Probable cause to arrest means that there is a substantial probability that a crime has been committed and that the person arrested committed that crime. A suspect arrested without a warrant cannot be kept in pretrial detention for an extended period without a judicial determination of probable cause (in many states at a preliminary hearing) (*Gerstein* v. *Pugh,* 429 U.S. 103 (1975)). Once a person is arrested for any offense, the police may do a full custodial search of his person, and any evidence found can be admitted at trial (*United States* v. *Robinson,* 414 U.S. 218 (1973)).

---

[3]For suspects arrested in their homes, however, an arrest warrant *is* constitutionally required unless the police can show an exigent circumstance (*Payton* v. *New York,* 445 U.S. 573 (1980)). In *Payton* the Court characterized entries to search and entries to arrest as fundamentally similar intrusions, which breach the privacy of one's home.

Stopping or detaining persons temporarily would be constitutionally permissible even where there is no probable cause to arrest. The quantum of evidence required for these governmental intrusions is reasonable suspicion. The leading case authorizing temporary detentions on less than probable cause is *Terry* v. *Ohio,* 392 U.S. 1 (1968). A plainclothes officer observed Terry and his companions engaging in suspicious behavior, as if they were reconnoitering a store prior to burglary or robbery. The officer stopped the suspects and, fearing that they might have weapons, patted down the outside of their clothing. A weapon was found, and Terry was subsequently convicted on a weapons charge. The Supreme Court held that this stop and frisk invaded Terry's Fourth Amendment right to privacy but was constitutionally reasonable. Reasonableness in this instance was determined by balancing the governmental interest (crime prevention or detection and protection of the officer) and the individual privacy interest invaded (characterized as a relatively minimal intrusion). An officer making on-the-spot observations and reasonably inferring, in light of his or her experience, that criminal activity is afoot may identify him- or herself, request identification, and make reasonable inquiry as to what a suspect is doing. If the officer then has reasonable grounds to believe that the suspect is armed and dangerous, the officer may do a protective frisk. The reasonable suspicion required for a stop and frisk can be obtained from information provided by an informant, as well as from observations by the police (*Adams* v. *Williams,* 407 U.S. 143 (1972)).

In *Michigan* v. *Summers,* 101 S. Ct. 2587 (1981), the Supreme Court permitted a temporary detention of a person in his home while the police executed a search warrant. Summers was descending the front steps of his house when the police came to execute a search warrant for narcotics. They temporarily detained him while searching the premises. After they found narcotics in the basement, they arrested and searched Summers. Several grams of heroin found on his person formed the basis for his conviction on the grounds of unlawful possession of narcotics. The majority of the Supreme Court found that temporary detention represents only an incremental intrusion on personal liberty where a valid warrant authorized the search. Since a thorough search of the premises for narcotics could be extensive and time-consuming, this temporary detention appears to exceed the scope permitted by *Terry*.

Until relatively recently courts have struggled with Fourth Amendment issues where the government seized words or private conversations. Seizure of words cannot be literally interpreted to mean seizure of persons or effects and, therefore, is not included within the language of the Fourth Amendment. In the early telephone or telegraph wiretap cases, seizure of private conversations was unconstitutional only if the wiretap device somehow intruded into a protected place, such as a home. Justice Brandeis considered the intrusiveness of telephone taps in *Olmstead* v. *United States*, 277 U.S. 438, 456 (1923): "Whenever a telephone line is tapped, the privacy of the persons at both ends of the line is invaded, and all conversations between them upon any subject, and although proper, confidential, and privileged, may be overheard. Moreover, the tapping of one man's telephone line involves the tapping of the telephone of every other person whom he may call, or who may call him. As a means of [governmental] espionage, . . . general warrants are but puny instruments of tyranny and oppression when compared with wiretapping."

Today, in addition to wiretaps, miniaturized microchip electronic devices can seize and record words from considerable distances and through walls. Laser beams can be used to bounce sound waves off closed windows. Beepers or transponders can be placed on cars, airplanes, packages, or persons and the signal picked up in another car or stationary point. The potential for governmental monitoring of citizens by means of sophisticated electronic surveillance equipment makes the privacy issue far more significant than could have been conceptualized by the framers of the Fourth Amendment. Justice Brandeis makes this point eloquently in *Olmstead:* "The makers of our Constitution . . . conferred [on its citizens] as against the government, the right to be let alone—the most comprehensive of rights and the right most valued by civilized men. To protect that right, every unjustifiable intrusion by the government upon the privacy of the individual, whatever the means employed, must be deemed a violation of the Fourth Amendment" (at 558).

The seminal case on protected areas and interests under the Fourth Amendment is *Katz* v. *United States,* 389 U.S. 347 (1967). Katz was convicted of transmitting bets over the phone in violation of federal statute. The government introduced evidence at trial of the warrantless seizure of his calls, made from a public pay phone, which were overheard by an electronic listening and recording device attached to the outside of the telephone booth. There was no physical intrusion of the device into the structure. The Supreme Court concluded that focusing on whether a given area was constitutionally protected deflected from the problem presented in the case. According to the majority, the Fourth Amendment protects persons, not places. If a person knowingly exposes something to the public, there is no Fourth Amendment protection. What a person seeks to preserve as private (even a conversation in a telephone booth where the person is visible) is constitutionally protected. The seizure of Katz's calls was, therefore, unconstitutional. Justice Harlan's concurring opinion has been repeatedly cited in later Fourth Amendment cases. He equated a telephone booth with a home, where, in contrast to an open field, a person has a constitutionally protected reasonable expectation of privacy. According to Justice Harlan, protection of people generally requires reference to a place.

Although the *Katz* opinion laid the foundation for scrutinizing the reasonableness of governmental invasions of personal privacy, later cases have focused on whether there was a search and whether the expectation of privacy was reasonable. For example, pen registers are mechanical devices that are installed in telephone lines by the police with the assistance of the phone company. Pen registers record any numbers dialed on a given telephone; no oral communication is overheard, nor is it known whether the call is completed. According to the majority in *Smith* v. *Maryland*, 442 U.S. 735 (1979), no search is involved by a pen register installation and recording; therefore, no warrant is required. Smith entertained no actual expectation of privacy in the phone numbers he dialed; even if he had, the Court concluded, his expectation would not have been legitimate. When dialing the phone, one has to assume the risk that the telephone company will reveal that information to the police.

In order to protect the privacy of wire and oral communications, Congress and state legislatures have passed statutes to supervise, monitor, and control governmental electronic surveillance. For example, with only a few exceptions, courts must issue warrants based on probable cause prior to the installation of wiretaps or electronic devices. Most of the electronic surveillance safeguards (for example, notification to the party whose phone is tapped) in Title III of the Omnibus Crime Control and Safe Streets Act of 1968, as Amended, have also been enacted into law in the various states.

Automobiles and the luggage, packages, or personal effects therein have been given less Fourth Amendment protection than other areas or interests. Where the police have probable cause to believe that a vehicle contains contraband, the Supreme Court has held that the police may "conduct a warrantless search of every part of the vehicle and its contents, including all containers and packages, that may conceal the object of the search. The scope of the search is not defined by the nature of the container in which the contraband is secreted. Rather, it is defined by the object of the search and the places in which there is probable cause to believe it may be found. For example, probable cause to believe that undocumented aliens are being transported in a van will not justify a warrantless search of suitcase" (*United States* v. *Ross,* 50 U.S.L.W. 4581 (1982)).

The court's decision in *Ross* relied heavily on the reasoning of *Carroll* v. *United States,* 267 U.S. 132 (1925), a prohibition case where federal officers had probable cause to believe that bootleggers were transporting illegal liquor. In the process of searching the car, the federal agents tore open the upholstery of a seat cushion and found sixty-eight bottles of gin and whiskey concealed inside. No warrant had been obtained for the search. In its decision in *Carroll,* the Supreme Court established the "automobile exception" to the Fourth Amendment warrant requirement. Given the nature of an automobile in transit, an immediate warrantless intrusion was necessary and not unreasonable.

Other warrantless searches of automobiles have been upheld without a showing of probable cause that the vehicle contains contraband. In *South Dakota* v. *Opperman,* 428 U.S. 364 (1976), the Supreme Court approved an inventory search of a car that had been impounded after being illegally parked in a restricted zone. When the car was brought to the impound lot, an officer observed personal property on the dashboard, back seat, and floor. Pursuant to standard police procedures, the automobile was unlocked and the contents inventoried. An unlocked glove compartment was opened and

marijuana found. Opperman was subsequently convicted of possession of marijuana. Chief Justice Burger, writing for the majority,
found that automobiles are effects within the Fourth Amendment
but that warrantless searches of cars are constitutionally permissible
in circumstances where searches of a home or office would not be.
Routine inventory searches are reasonable to protect the owner's
property, the police and public from potential danger, and the police from claims or disputes over lost or stolen property. Warrantless
inventory searches are justified because the mobility of automobiles
creates an exigent circumstance and there is less expectation of privacy in motor vehicles. Cars are subject to continuing governmental
regulation, such as requiring periodic inspections and licensing,
and are frequently taken into custody after accidents, when a car is
disabled on the highway, or for violation of parking ordinances.

The rationale justifying the automobile exception would not,
however, apply to permit a warrantless search of any movable container believed to be carrying an illicit substance that is found in a
public place—even when the container is placed in a vehicle (not
otherwise believed to be carrying contraband) (*United States* v.
Chadwick, 433 U.S. 1 (1977); *Arkansas* v. *Sanders*, 442 U.S. 753
(1979)).

The Fourth Amendment does, however, offer some protection
to motorists. In *Delaware* v. *Prouse*, 440 U.S. 648 (1979), the Supreme Court held that the police had to have a reasonable suspicion
that a driver or automobile was unlicensed or that other traffic laws
were being violated before they could stop a car to check the driver's
license or vehicle registration. This ruling struck down state statutes
that had permitted the random stopping of automobiles solely on
the basis of police discretion. Some patrol officers had a penchant
for stopping recreational vehicles and motorists with long hair or
other idiosyncratic characteristics. If an officer randomly stops
enough cars, something illegal may be found, and law violators may
be caught and convicted. An equally important consideration, however, is whether citizens in a free society should be arbitrarily
stopped when they drive their cars on the public highways.

Many people forgo or waive Fourth Amendment protections
by consenting to a search. Police often rely on consent searches
where probable cause is missing. The constitutional validity of con-

sents is tested by their voluntariness. A consent to search will be voluntary as long as it is not explicitly or implicitly coerced.

Although the U.S. Court of Appeals for the Ninth Circuit wanted a defendant's consent to be predicated on a warning that he or she was not required to consent, this approach was rejected by the Supreme Court in *Schneckloth* v. *Bustamonte,* 412 U.S. 218 (1973). Unlike the Sixth Amendment right to counsel, where there is a presumption against waiver, there is nothing constitutionally suspect in a person's voluntarily allowing a search. According to Justice Stewart, nothing in the Fourth Amendment should discourage citizens from consenting to searches that might yield evidence to ensure that a wholly innocent person is not wrongly accused. Justice Marshall, in his dissenting opinion, questioned whether one can voluntarily make a consent decision without knowing that he or she has a right to refuse consent. A decision made without knowledge of available alternatives may not be a choice at all.

People can validly consent to searches even though they are contrary to their own self-interest. In *United States* v. *Mendenhall,* 446 U.S. 544 (1980), the defendant consented to a search of her person, and heroin was found. The Supreme Court concluded that she had accompanied Drug Enforcement Administration agents from the airport terminal to their office in a "spirit of apparent cooperation" and that, "in the totality of the circumstances," her consent was voluntary. The defendant had been warned that she did not have to consent to the search. The fact that she was a young black woman without a high school education was relevant but not decisive. The Supreme Court specifically found that she had not been seized by the agents. Many federal courts have held that consent by someone in police custody would be invalid.

Sometimes the consent to search is obtained from someone other than the suspect. These are called third-party consents. For example, if premises are shared, effective consent can be given by a spouse or a roommate. As long as the third party possesses common authority over or sufficient relationship to the premises or effect to be searched, valid consent can be given (*United States* v. *Matlock,* 415 U.S. 164 (1974)).

Historically, the juvenile justice system has not emphasized the legal rights of children because all the adult "actors" in the systems are presumed to be working in "the child's best interest." Although young people do have Fourth Amendment rights and the exclusionary rule applies (at least to delinquents), very few cases have reached the appellate courts. State statutes permit police officers to take children "into custody" on grounds that would not authorize the arrest of an adult. In addition to law violations, children can be taken into custody where they are "in danger" or have "run away from their parents, guardian, or custodian."

The more limited expectation of privacy afforded children is based on their lack of legal responsibility. Since youth generally live in the home of parents, custodians, or guardians, most courts have permitted parents to consent to searches of their children's living quarters. Third-party consents have been upheld even if the youth refused to consent to a search. School officials have been permitted to search the lockers of school children because the officials are presumably acting in *loco parentis* or because the school maintains joint custody of the lockers (*Overton* v. *New York,* 249 N.E.2d 366 (1969)). Many schools print statements in student handbooks, putting young people (and their parents) on notice that their lockers may be searched. There may be some psychological, if not legal, merit in this practice.

Protections Against Self-Incrimination. Another important constitutional right of criminal defendants in a democracy is the privilege against self-incrimination. The Fifth Amendment to the U.S. Constitution reads: "No person shall be held to answer for a capital, or otherwise infamous, crime, unless on a presentment or indictment of a grand jury, except in cases arising in the land or naval forces, or in the militia, when in actual service in time of war or public danger; nor shall any person be subject for the same offense to be twice put in jeopardy of life or limb; nor shall be compelled in any criminal case to be a witness against himself, nor be deprived of life, liberty, or property, without due process of law; nor shall private property be taken for public use, without just compensation." With the exception of the grand jury indictment, all these provisions have been incorporated or made applicable to the states through the Fourteenth Amendment. The "witness against himself" clause means that a person does not have to speak out and incriminate him- or herself.

The individual interest in remaining silent in the face of police questioning is often in conflict with the governmental interest in solving crimes. In fact, an important police investigative tool is interrogation of suspects or others who may have important information about a crime. Evidence from interrogation is often decisive in proving the guilt of a defendant beyond a reasonable doubt. Most people respond to interrogation because of their perception about the authority of the police or the coercive atmosphere of the stationhouse. Cajolery, deception, persistent relay questioning, or even physical brutality have been used to make a suspect talk. During interrogation at the police station, the suspect is alone, in a strange or hostile environment, and surrounded by officers attempting to extract information that is likely to be detrimental to the suspect's interest. It is not surprising that suspects may believe that they will be held and interrogated until they speak. If an innocent person's will is overborne, damaging statements or confessions can be extracted and used to convict the person.

The first police interrogation cases to reach the Supreme Court were concerned with the voluntariness of a defendant's statements. The means by which police obtain evidence from a suspect is relevant because physical or psychological coercion will make the reliability or trustworthiness of the statements or confession suspect.

In *Brown* v. *Mississippi*, 297 U.S. 278 (1936), the defendants were admittedly whipped to obtain a confession. Physical violence or threats of it also pervaded later court cases.

In *Ashcraft* v. *Tennessee*, 322 U.S. 143 (1944), the Supreme Court considered the psychological pressures of prolonged, continuous interrogation. The Court disapproved of the police interrogation methods in obtaining a confession. Extended questioning raised a conclusive presumption of coercion.

In *Haley* v. *Ohio*, 332 U.S. 596 (1948), the Supreme Court held that a juvenile's involuntary confession had to be excluded. Haley was a fifteen-year-old youth subjected to incommunicado in-custody interrogation for three days. Neither his lawyer nor his mother was permitted to see him. The Court chastised the police for their callous attitude "towards the safeguards which respect ordinary standards of human relations."

In other cases trustworthiness of confessions resulting from physical or psychological abuse or threats became less important as a rationale for excluding confessions than due process principles that limit certain police practices, including coerced confessions, because they "offend the community's sense of fair play and decency" (*Rochin* v. *California*, 342 U.S. 164 (1952)).

From about 1940 the efficacy of the voluntariness test to restrain abusive police power in obtaining confessions began to be questioned. Voluntariness is evaluated in the "totality of the circumstances," including a consideration of the characteristics of a defendant (such as age and intelligence), as well as the way in which the interrogation was conducted. It was difficult to reconstruct what went on behind the closed doors of the stationhouse. The trial transcript would contain testimony by the defendant that his or her confession resulted from coercion; it would also contain police denials of improper conduct during the interrogation. In this "swearing match," state court judges would inevitably believe the police. Consider the facts in *Mincey* v. *Arizona*, 437 U.S. 385 (1978), wherein the state trial court found "with unmistakable clarity" that Mincey's statements were voluntary, but the United States Supreme Court did not: "A few hours before the interrogation occurred, Mincey had been seriously wounded . . . . According to the attending physician, Mincey had arrived at the hospital 'depressed almost to the point of coma.' At the time Detective Hust questioned him, . . . he was in the intensive care unit. Lying on his back on the hospital bed, encumbered by tubes, needles, and breathing apparatus, Mincey clearly and repeatedly expressed his wish not to be interrogated, but Hust continued to question him. Unable to speak because of the tube in his mouth, Mincey responded to Hust's questions by writing on pieces of paper, at one point writing: 'This is all I can say without a lawyer' " (at 385-386). The voluntariness test will result in exclusion of a confession only where there is egregious conduct by law enforcement officers and, by itself, does not provide sufficient constitutional protection for citizens in a free society.

In remedying the problem, the Supreme Court first restricted lengthy interrogation practices by federal law enforcement officers. Under its supervisory power of the federal courts, the Supreme Court required that a suspect be taken promptly before a committing magistrate, where his constitutional rights would be explained (*McNabb* v. *United States*, 318 U.S. 322 (1943)). In *Mallory* v. *United States*, 354 U.S. 449 (1957), the Court excluded a confession where the officers delayed taking a suspect before the magistrate for seven hours. The so-called *McNabb-Mallory* rule was not adopted by most state courts or legislatures. Moreover, since it was based on a federal rule of criminal procedure rather than the U.S. Constitution, the rule was not imposed on the states through the Fourteenth Amendment.

Appeals in state confession cases used right-to-counsel arguments to challenge police interrogation practices. In *Crooker* v. *California*, 357 U.S. 433 (1958), the defendant was charged with a capital crime and asked for his attorney prior to interrogation. This request was denied. On appeal, in a 5-to-4 decision, Justice Clark refused to bar the confession for failure to provide defendant with his or her retained counsel. He declared that requiring counsel prior to interrogation would have a "devastating effect" on police investigation because it would effectively preclude questioning until the accused called his attorney. Dissenting Justice Douglas insisted that right to counsel prior to interrogation is "often necessary to give meaning and protection to the right to be heard at trial."

The issue of when right to counsel begins was the basis for appeals during the late 1950s and early 1960s. The Supreme Court ruled that a person who has been formally charged by information or indictment has the constitutional right to retained counsel (*Spano* v. *New York* (concurring opinions), 360 U.S. 315 (1959); *Massiah* v. *United States*, 377 U.S. 201 (1964); see also *Brewer* v. *Williams*, 430 U.S. 387 (1977)). *Massiah* is an important case because the subsequently excluded conversations (rather than formal interrogation) had taken place outside the stationhouse. A codefendant agreed to cooperate with the police, who installed a radio transmitter in the codefendant's car. The recorded conversations included damaging statements that helped to convict Massiah. Justice Stewart, for the majority, excluded the statements and concluded that Massiah had been subject to an "extrajudicial" police-orchestrated proceeding designed to obtain incriminating statements from him.

In *Escobedo* v. *Illinois*, 378 U.S. 478 (1964), the Supreme Court held that a suspect's right to counsel begins even *before* the commencement of judicial proceedings. Before being questioned, Escobedo asked for his lawyer, and his retained counsel spent several hours trying unsuccessfully to talk to his client. In the absence of his attorney, Escobedo made damaging statements about his complicity in a murder; he was convicted, and then he appealed. According to the Supreme Court, "Once the process shifts from the investigatory to accusatory—when its focus is on the accused and its purpose is to elicit a confession—our adversary system begins to operate and . . . the accused must be permitted to consult with his attorney." The "focus on" test would be difficult to operationalize unless it was interpreted to mean that the police "focus on" a suspect when he or she is taken into custody.

Clearly, in confession cases since 1936, the Supreme Court was attempting to devise ways to protect persons from incriminating themselves because of what the police did during interrogation. The Court limited police practices by first relying on whether a confession was voluntary. When that curtailed only outrageous police practices, the Court required in the federal system that the defendant be promptly brought before a magistrate under the *McNabb-Mallory* rule. In state courts counsel was required during the interrogation stage when there was a shift from the investigatory to the accusatory.

The Fifth Amendment was not used as the rationale to limit police power in interrogation until 1964 (because historically that clause in the Fifth Amendment proscribed compelled statements). Since a suspect was not threatened with perjury for testifying falsely or with contempt for refusal to talk at all, the suspect was not compelled to be a witness against him- or herself. The Supreme Court leaped the inferential gap in *Malloy* v. *Hogan*, 378 U.S. 1 (1964), to hold that determinations of whether a confession was involuntary should be controlled by the Fifth Amendment.

Thirty years after *Brown*, the Supreme Court decided *Miranda* v. *Arizona*, 384 U.S. 436 (1966). It was a controversial decision, strongly objected to by prosecutors and law enforcement officials across the country. The opinion required that, prior to his in-custody interrogation, Miranda had to be warned that he had the right (1) to remain silent; (2) to an explanation that anything said can and will be used against him in court; (3) to have an attorney present at interrogation; and (4) if indigent, to have an attorney appointed to represent him. According to the majority, the presence of counsel at interrogation ensures that "the individual's right to choose between silence and speech remains unfettered through the interrogation."

Despite dire predictions that *Miranda* warnings would result in fewer confessions or convictions, there has been no breakdown in effective criminal investigations in this country. Subsequent *Miranda* cases have not been given an expansive reading by the Supreme Court. Justice Rehnquist called the *Miranda* warnings only "prophylactic standards" to reinforce the privilege against self-incrimination and thus denigrated their constitutional importance (*Michigan* v. *Tucker*, 417 U.S. 433 (1974)).

The Supreme Court continues to hear cases relating to the invocation and waiver of *Miranda* rights and the question of whether an in-custody suspect was interrogated. The decisions have generally given preference to governmental rather than individual interests.

Miranda rights are invoked once a person states explicitly or implicitly that he or she wishes to remain silent or asks for an attorney. In *Fare* v. *Michael C.*, 442 U.S. 707 (1979), a youth was taken into custody, given *Miranda* warnings, and interrogated at the police station. He asked to talk with his probation officer and was refused permission to do so. He made incriminating statements, which were used as evidence at trial, and he was convicted. On appeal his attorney argued that, by asking for his probation officer, the juvenile had invoked his *Miranda* rights, and interrogation should have ceased. The Supreme Court disagreed. In order constitutionally to invoke *Miranda* rights, an individual must ask for an attorney.

If a suspect invokes the right to silence, *Miranda* requires that the police must "scrupulously honor" that right. However, the Supreme Court has held that a suspect who invokes the right to silence may subsequently waive it. In *Michigan* v. *Mosley*, 423 U.S. 96 (1975), the defendant was questioned about some robberies and declined to discuss them. Two hours later Mosley was brought from jail, given *Miranda* warnings, and asked about a different crime. He made incriminating statements. In holding the statements admissible, the majority considered it significant that Mosley had not asked for an attorney, that another offense was involved, and that the second interrogation lasted only fifteen minutes.

Distinguishing *Mosley,* the Supreme Court in *Edwards* v. *Arizona,* 101 S. Ct. 1880 (1981), held that, once a suspect invokes his or her *Miranda* right to counsel, a valid waiver cannot be shown— even with another set of warnings. No further interrogation must occur until counsel has been made available or the suspect personally "initiates further communication, exchanges, or conversations with the police."

Miranda applies to suspects in custody. This generally means at the stationhouse or where the suspect is deprived of freedom of action in a significant way (for example, in a police vehicle where the suspect is handcuffed or otherwise restrained by the police). *Miranda* warnings are not required for on-the-scene investigations or where the person comes voluntarily to the stationhouse.

Lower courts have held that *Miranda* warnings are not applicable to misdemeanor or traffic offenses. This issue has not reached the Supreme Court.

Whether a person is interrogated within the meaning of *Miranda* depends on whether the police expressly question the suspect while he or she is in custody. Interrogation extends "only to words or actions on the part of police officers that they should have known were reasonably likely to elicit an incriminating statement" (*Rhode Island* v. *Innis,* 446 U.S. 291 (1980)). In *Innis* the suspect was being transported to the station in the back of a patrol car. Two officers riding in the front seat (who had been specifically told by their superior officer not to talk to the suspect) conversed with each other. One officer commented that it would be a shame if handicapped children in the area found the weapon purportedly used by Innis in a homicide. Innis interrupted and told the officer they "should turn the car around so he could show them where the gun was located." The Supreme Court found that the conversation between the officers was neither express questioning nor the functional equivalent to it and that the statement by Innis was admissible.

Police must give *Miranda* warnings to juveniles prior to in-custody interrogation. Most juvenile cases have been concerned with whether or not the suspect adequately waived the right to remain silent or to have appointed counsel. Courts are sharply divided as to whether a juvenile must consult with a parent or an attorney prior to waiver. Other courts look at such factors as age, intelligence, education, and experience with the police. Absence of the parents or attorney prior to waiver is one factor to be considered in the totality of the circumstances (*West* v. *United States,* 399 F.2d 467 (5th Cir. 1968)).

Miranda warnings were constitutionally required in order to protect persons against overbearing police conduct. Human services workers (for example, child protective workers) have generally not been required to warn parents that what is said to the worker during an abuse or neglect investigation may be used in either juvenile or, occasionally, criminal court. However, a recent case makes this still an open question (*Estelle* v. *Smith,* 101 S. Ct. 1866 (1981)). Even though the issue of competency was not raised at trial, a judge informally arranged a psychiatric examination of the defendant. The psychiatrist, Dr. Grigson, not only reported to the Court about Smith's competency to stand trial but testified (as the prosecution's only witness) at sentencing. On the basis of his pretrial examination, Dr. Grigson testified that Smith could be dangerous in the future (a factor to be considered by the jury in determining whether to sentence a person to death). Smith was sentenced to death and appealed. Dr. Grigson did not obtain permission from the defendant's attorneys to examine him, nor was the defendant warned that any statement could be used against him at sentencing. Attorneys for the state argued that, since the psychiatric testimony was not used to establish guilt and the communication was nontestimonial in nature, it was admissible. The Supreme Court disagreed and held that Smith's Fifth and Sixth Amendment rights had been violated by the use of Dr. Grigson's testimony at sentencing. Unless *Smith* v. *Estelle* is limited to the fact situation (death penalty cases have always merited special procedures because of the irreversibility of the penalty if a mistake is made), the case has implication for other governmental workers who ask incriminating questions (for example, probation officers obtaining presentence incriminating information that results in a recommendation of prison rather than probation).

Pretrial Release from Jail. Whether an arrested law violator can make bail or must remain in jail pending the outcome of the state's criminal accusation is an important initial consideration in processing offenders in the criminal justice system. If an accused remains in jail until trial, serious collateral consequences (such as the loss of a job) often result.

An accused can gain pretrial release from jail in the following ways:

1. *Release on personal recognizance.* A judge determines whether an accused can be released without monetary or property bail. Factors such as the seriousness of the offense, previous record, and community ties will be considered in order to predict whether an offender might flee the court's jurisdiction.
2. *Posting the full amount of the bail in cash.* When the defendant makes all court appearances, the money posted is returned to him or her. Most states also allow an accused or his or her relatives to use property in lieu of cash as collateral. Failure to appear means forfeiture of the money or property. If an accused "jumps" bail, he or she is considered a fugitive from justice, and an arrest warrant (or *capias*) will be issued. The defendant also is subject to a criminal charge of "jumping" bail.
3. *Posting 10 percent of the bail in cash.* This system is used in the federal system and in Pennsylvania, Illinois, Nebraska, and other jurisdictions. Cash amounting to 10 percent of the bond amount set is posted with the court. If the accused makes all scheduled court appearances, all but 10 percent of the bond (for administrative costs) is returned. Failure to appear results in a loss of the cash posted as well as liability to pay the remaining 90 percent of the original bond.
4. *Obtaining monetary bail from a bondsman.* A bail bondsman is a businessman who posts bail for an accused and charges a nonrefundable fee (usually about 10 percent of bond). Bondsmen weigh various factors (such as a defendant's previous criminal record, employment history, and family situation) in deciding who is an appropriate bail risk. If the defendant fails to appear at court hearings, the bondsman must pay the total amount of the bond. Many states, however, allow additional time for the bondsman to find the fugitive before the bond is forfeited. According to Neubauer (1979, p. 271): "In many cities, forfeited bonds regularly go uncollected . . . because of the discretionary power of judges to exonerate bondsmen from outstanding

bonds. . . . One [Dallas] newspaper estimated that $2 million in
bond forfeitures went uncollected."

Some jurisdictions allow the police to set the amount of bail
for misdemeanors (usually according to a schedule). Usually, however, the decision to grant bail is a judicial function. The prosecutor
affects the outcome because he or she is present at the bond-setting
hearing and offers facts about the strength of the government's case
and the prior criminal record (if any) of the accused. The police also
can influence the bail decision by inflating the initial charges
against an accused (making the person appear more dangerous).

The bail system is discriminatory against an accused who has
neither money nor property. Even if accused of serious offenses,
most defendants with financial resources do not remain in jail
awaiting trial. Although 10 percent bail is an important alternative
to dependence on the commercial bail bondsman, other reforms
have similarly reduced the number of pretrial detainees. For certain
misdemeanors a "citation" in lieu of arrest operates like the issuance
of a traffic ticket. Misdemeanants are summoned to appear in court
at a specific date and time. Kalmanoff (1975) reports that this system
has been successful in California, with only 4.5 percent of the defendants failing to appear. Various bail projects have added a support system, which sometimes affects a judge's willingness to release
the accused persons on their own recognizance. A project investigator interviews the accused about his or her family, job, and the like.
If the investigator concludes that the accused is a good risk, the
project will recommend to the court that the accused be released on
personal recognizance. Project personnel will make follow-up contacts to remind the accused about court hearings. Most projects will
not recommend persons accused of serious crimes, such as murder or
armed robbery (Baker and Meyer, 1980, p. 155).

Although the main purpose of bail is to ensure the appearance at various court hearings, the judge often lacks sufficient information to accurately assess risk of nonappearance. The severity of
the crime charged and the defendant's previous record are the primary factors considered by the judge in granting or denying bail.
Judges have denied bail in order to impose pretrial punishment ("to
teach a lesson") or to prevent further crimes by an accused. Imposi-

tion of pretrial detention for punishment would be unconstitutional. According to Justice Rehnquist in *Bell* v. *Wolfish*, 441 U.S. 520 (1979), punitive measures prior to a determination of guilt must be distinguished from regulatory restraints. The former may not be constitutionally imposed, but the latter may be. The distinction between penal and regulatory sanctions is not always clear, but a recent District of Columbia Court of Appeals concluded that pretrial detention is regulatory rather than penal (*United States* v. *Edwards*, 430 A.2d 1321 (D.C. 1981)).

The Supreme Court has not ruled on whether the Eighth Amendment's excessive bail clause (which states that excessive bail shall not be required, nor excessive fines imposed, nor cruel or unusual punishments inflicted) imparts a constitutional right to bail for all offenses. The issue is seldom raised on appeal because in serious felony cases, particularly where the defendant is a recidivist, judges usually make the bail so high that a defendant cannot pay it. For many poor defendants, paying a $500 bail bond is prohibitive. However, the *Washington Post* (May 6, 1981) has reported that drug traffickers have posted bonds as high as a million dollars.

Preventive detention has led to court cases challenging the validity of statutes and state constitutions that permit denial of bail (either for specific offenses or after a determination of dangerousness). Lower courts do not agree on the types of crimes and characteristics of defendants that would justify the denial of bail.

In *Blunt* v. *United States*, 322 A. 2d 579 (D.C. 1974), the judge denied bail, relying on a District of Columbia preventive detention statute. Although the defendant had an extensive criminal record, the decision was based on the defendant's potential to interfere with justice. The court emphasized that a defendant who had threatened a key government witness could be kept in custody, so that he would not interfere with witnesses or jurors. However, a Pennsylvania court refused to authorize preventive detention even though the state urged denial of bail to safeguard the well-being of witnesses and to protect the community from further criminal activity by the accused. Anticipated criminality alone was not proper grounds for the denial of bail (*Commonwealth* v. *Truesdale*, 296 A.2d 829 (Pa. 1972)). In another jurisdiction preventive detention was held improper in a case concerning a person suspected of having mailed a pipe bomb to

a police station where he had earlier been booked on other charges
(In re Underwood, 508 P.2d 721 (Cal. 1973)). A New York appellate
court held that the trial judge had erred in refusing to release a
person on bail on the basis of a psychiatrist's letter stating that there
would be a risk to the community if the accused were released from
custody *(People ex rel. Schweizer* v. *Welch,* 336 N.Y.S.2d 556 (1972);
see also a case that came to the opposite result, *United States* v.
Bond, 329 F. Supp. 538 (E.D. Tenn. 1971)).

Nebraska voters recently amended Article I, Section 9 of the
Nebraska constitution to include as offenses where bail could be
denied "sexual offenses involving penetration by force or against the
will of the person" as well as murder and treason. This amendment
was challenged in *Parker* v. *Roth,* 278 N.W.2d 106 (Neb. 1979) and
in *Hunt* v. *Roth,* 648 F.2d 1148 (8th Cir. 1981). The Nebraska
Supreme Court held that the amended constitutional provision was
constitutional—since neither the Eighth nor the Fourteenth
Amendment to the Constitution of the United States required that
everyone charged with a state offense must be given liberty on bail
pending trial. In *Hunt,* however, the U.S. Court of Appeals for the
Eighth Circuit struck down the sexual assault provision of the Nebraska constitutional amendment, reasoning that the constitutional
protections involved in the grant of pretrial release are too fundamental to be foreclosed by arbitrary state decree. Judge Murphy of
the Nebraska Supreme Court appealed this decision. When the case
was heard by the United State Supreme Court, the *per curiam* opinion (that is, by the entire Court rather than a single judge) concluded
that Hunt's claim to pretrial bail was moot once he was convicted,
and it did not reach the substantive issue of pretrial bail for sexual
assault *(Murphy* v. *Hunt,* 71 L. Ed. 2d 353 (1982)).

In *United States* v. *Edwards,* 430 A.2d 1321 (D.C. 1981), the
defendant was charged with armed rape. The government moved for
a denial of bail in accordance with the District of Columbia's preventive detention statute and in light of Edwards' extensive criminal
record. The motion was denied because the government failed to
produce the complainant for cross-examination. In another proceeding Edwards was charged with robbery, burglary, and sodomy.
This time the motion for preventive detention was granted. When
the case was appealed, Edwards argued that the District of Columbia

statute violated his Eighth Amendment and due process constitutional rights. The majority of the judges rejected these arguments and held that the preventive detention statute was not unconstitutional. Judge Mack dissented, reasoning that the state could not accurately predict which persons are dangerous. The utilization of the presumption of dangerousness would result in pretrial detention of persons who posed no threat to the community. Judge Mack cited a Harvard study (sponsored by the American Bar Endowment) on the rearrest rate of persons in the Boston area on bail during a six-month period in 1968:

> Using the District of Columbia preventive detention statute as a framework, the researchers focused on 427 released defendants charged with violent or dangerous crimes who would have been eligible for preventive detention had the District of Columbia law been in effect in Boston in 1968. Of the 427 defendants in the sample, 41 were rearrested and convicted of crimes committed during the pretrial period. Twenty-two of the 41 convictions were for violent or dangerous crimes as defined by the Act. [Using a dangerousness scale, the researchers] concluded that in order to prevent all 41 offenses it would be necessary to detain 376 persons. For every one recidivist detained, eight nonrecidivists would also have to be detained. Such a ratio amounts to little less than a dragnet [at 1343].

The legal issues relating to pretrial detention have not been resolved. It is misunderstood by the public and has been used as a rallying point for political conservatives. The Bail Reform Act of 1981 (S. 1554) modifies present federal law by permitting a judicial officer to consider the safety of any person or the community when making a determination relative to the release or detention of a person pending trial or pending sentence on appeal. The bill was reported out of committee on November 3, 1981, but there has been no further action to date.

Adults and juveniles have some of the same options to avoid pretrial detention (release on one's own recognizance and bail). The issue of bail for juveniles has not reached the U.S. Supreme Court. Most state statutes make juvenile bail decisions discretionary with

the judge. Since most children are released to their parents at detention hearings, the issue of bail for juveniles is seldom raised.

   Right to Trial by Jury. As shown in Figure 1, many decisions
made during the processing of a suspect or defendant result in
charges being dismissed or reduced through plea bargaining. In the
relatively few criminal cases that go to trial, the United States Constitution provides that a defendant is entitled to a trial by an impartial jury. In most states jurors are selected from voter registration
lists. There have been numerous state and federal cases challenging
the composition of a jury as nonrepresentative and therefore discriminatory. The deliberate exclusion of jurors because of race or
sex is clearly unconstitutional. However, as long as the method of
selecting jurors does not arbitrarily exclude any particular class or
group, courts have upheld the legal validity of the selection process.
In most jurisdictions jurors in criminal trials do not represent a
cross section of the community—particularly with regard to racial
composition.

   Social scientists—including psychologists, criminologists,
and sociologists—have been hired by attorneys to help analyze the
backgrounds and qualifications of persons selected as jurors. Community surveys, computerized profiles of the jurors, and analyses of
the potential jurors' courtroom behavior (for instance, their body
language and demeanor) during *voir dire* (a preliminary examination of prospective jurors by the prosecutor, defense counsel, and/or
judge) are the tools used by these experts.

   Most of the scientific jury selection has occurred in civil litigation with clients such as General Electric or Ford Motor Company. However, jurors for several well-publicized conspiracy cases
were also scientifically selected. Examples include the trials of Joan
Little, Angela Davis, the Attica prison rioters, and the Indians at
Wounded Knee. In all these cases, the defendants were acquitted
(Shell, 1980).

   The criticisms of scientific jury selection have ranged from
jury rigging to a more serious concern about the lack of empirical
evidence to validate its effectiveness. Several studies have concluded
that scientific jury selection may be unreliable and may also not
make a difference in the outcome of the trial. The evidence in a case
"has three to seven times more impact on the trial's outcome than
does systematic jury selection" (Shell, 1980, p. 54).

Supporters of scientific jury selection contend that *voir dire* in most cases is inadequate because attorneys have relied on intuition or hunches about jurors' prejudices and any system that collects and analyzes a variety of attitudinal or behavioral data cannot help but improve the selection of a fair and impartial jury.

Conclusion

Criminal conduct is proscribed and punished by a set of rules, usually codified in statutes or ordinances. In order for a person suspected of criminal activity to be charged with a crime, the state, as plaintiff, must prove essential elements, such as acting with a bad state of mind. Once a suspect enters the system, he or she is protected by various procedural safeguards guaranteed by federal and state constitutions. During recent years the United States Supreme Court has clarified the protections afforded by the Fourth, Fifth, Sixth, and Eighth Amendments to the United States Constitution. For example, the defendant's right to counsel has been expanded to offer protection at all stages of the criminal justice system. All the laws and procedures described in this chapter are administered by key actors in the criminal justice system, who generally have considerable discretion in applying these laws.

Administrators and human services practitioners make an important contribution to the system, both through working with offenders in various pretrial and posttrial rehabilitative programs and in empirically testing the efficacy of the criminal justice process. The professionalism of psychologists, social workers, teachers, and other human services workers helps to ensure the defendant's legal rights in the system, as well as protecting society from criminal behavior.

Juvenile Law

Children (defined in most states as youth up to the age of eighteen) who violate the law or who need the assistance or protection of the legal system are treated differently than adults. By the end of the nineteenth century, special laws and separate courts had been established to protect dependent or neglected children and to reform or change (rather than punish) youthful law violators. This chapter considers substantive and procedural laws pertaining to juvenile delinquents, status offenders, and dependent and neglected children. While the juvenile system is structurally similar to the adult system, different words are used to describe what goes on; for example, a child's sentence is called a disposition and a child is taken into custody by the police rather than arrested. (See Figure 1 in Chapter Two for a flow chart of the juvenile justice system.)

The adult criminal justice system will intervene or punish offenders to prevent them from committing criminal acts in the future, to separate dangerous persons from society, to deter others from committing criminal offenses, and because society deserves or requires that certain acts be punished (retribution or just deserts). Until recently, the juvenile justice system intervened in a youthful offender's life solely for rehabilitative purposes. Increasing numbers of statutory revisions include language to the effect that public safety as well as rehabilitation are proper concerns of the juvenile justice system.

The first juvenile courts, espousing the philosophy of *parens patriae*, concluded that children should be rehabilitated in an informal, nonadversarial climate. Legal safeguards were not important because everybody was acting in the child's best interest. In many states juvenile judges were human services practitioners rather than attorneys. Although the judge made the final decision about what would happen to a youthful offender, the judge relied heavily on background information and recommendations of psychologists, social workers, and school counselors.

Every case was assessed on its individual merits. Judges would review the psychological and sociological data available on each child or use their intuitive judgments to make a rehabilitative decision. In deciding the appropriate disposition for a troubled or troublesome youth, the judge would consider the least restrictive alternative. For most children this meant continued placement in their own homes with supervision by court workers.

Because youth were to be helped to "mature out" of delinquency or problem behavior, the juvenile justice system was and still is concerned about protecting the privacy of the child, so that the stigma of adjudication will not carry forward to adult life. Because of this concern for privacy, special procedures are generally required before a child can be fingerprinted or photographed; many juvenile courts are not open to the public; names of youthful offenders are not generally published by the media; and juvenile records are sealed or expunged, so that juveniles will not be burdened by the collateral consequences of a conviction record.

Juvenile Delinquents

The public is increasingly concerned about the juvenile offender and, in particular, the violent juvenile offender. According to the FBI's 1981 *Uniform Crime Reports*, juveniles accounted for 19.3 percent of all arrests for violent crime and 40.2 percent of all arrests for property crime, although they comprised approximately 14 percent of the total population. Juveniles accounted for 44.2 percent of arson arrests, 14.7 percent of aggravated assault arrests, and 9.3 percent of arrests for murder.

Waiver of Transfer of Juveniles to Adult Courts. Because of these statistics, a growing number of juvenile cases are tried in adult courts. In New York a juvenile at age thirteen who commits a serious felony may be tried as an adult. In many other states sixteen- and seventeen-year-olds are being tried in adult courts and receiving prison sentences after conviction. Even under the early juvenile court statutes, all states could impose adult sanctions on juvenile offenders through waiver or transfer statutes. In most states today, the juvenile court decides whether the juvenile should be tried in adult court. In Nebraska, county attorneys make this initial decision and the juvenile must bring a motion to have the case transferred to the juvenile court. Among the factors considered by the decision maker in waiver or transfer decisions are age, prior record, seriousness of the offense, and amenability to treatment through the juvenile court.

An especially important waiver/transfer case reached the Supreme Court in 1966 (*Kent* v. *United States*, 383 U.S. 541 (1966)). A fourteen-year-old juvenile came under the jurisdiction of the District of Columbia Juvenile Court in 1959 for housebreaking and attempted purse snatching. Two years later, while still on probation, he was arrested for burglary and rape. While detained, Kent was examined by two psychiatrists and a psychologist, who certified that he was a victim of severe psychopathology. By motion, Kent's counsel requested that the juvenile court retain jurisdiction and offered to prove that, with adequate treatment in a hospital, Kent would be a suitable subject for rehabilitation in the juvenile court. Counsel had also requested access to Kent's juvenile court file. The juvenile court judge did not rule on these motions, held no hearings, and made no findings. Kent was waived for proceedings in the adult court and was subsequently convicted. When the case was appealed to the U.S. Supreme Court, Justice Fortas delivered the opinion of the Court (footnotes and case citations within the case are deleted):

> Petitioner attacks the waiver of jurisdiction on a number of statutory and constitutional grounds.
> . . . We agree that the order of the Juvenile Court waiving its jurisdiction and transferring peti-

tioner for trial in the United States District Court for
the District of Columbia was invalid. . . . The issue to
be decided is the standards to be applied upon such
review.

We agree with the Court of Appeals that the
statute contemplates that the Juvenile Court should
have considerable latitude within which to determine
whether it should retain jurisdiction over a child or—
subject to the statutory delimination—should waive
jurisdiction. But this latitude is not complete. At the
outset, it assumes procedural regularity sufficient in
the particular circumstances to satisfy the basic requirements of due process and fairness, as well as
compliance with the statutory requirement of a "full
investigation." The statute gives the Juvenile Court a
substantial degree of discretion as to the factual considerations to be evaluated, the weight to be given
them, and the conclusion to be reached. It does not
confer upon the Juvenile Court a license for arbitrary
procedure. The statute does not permit the Juvenile
Court to determine in isolation and without participation or any representation of the child the "critically
important" question whether a child will be deprived
of the special protections and provisions of the Juvenile Court Act. . . .

We do not consider whether, on the merits, Kent
should have been transferred; but there is no place in
our system of law for reaching a result of such tremendous consequences without ceremony—without
hearing, without effective assistance of counsel, without a statement of reasons. It is inconceivable that a
court of justice dealing with adults, with respect to a
similar issue, would proceed in this manner. It would
be extraordinary if society's special concern for children, as reflected in the District of Columbia's Juvenile
Court Act, permitted this procedure. We hold that it
does not. . . .

Petitioner—then a boy of sixteen—was by statute entitled to certain procedures and benefits as a
consequence of his statutory right to the "exclusive"
jurisdiction of the Juvenile Court. In these circumstances, considering particularly that decision as to
waiver of jurisdiction and transfer of the matter to the
District Court was potentially as important to petitioner as the difference between five years' confinement

and a death sentence, we conclude that, as a condition
to a valid waiver order, petitioner was entitled to a
hearing, including access by counsel to the social records and probation or similar reports which presumably are considered by the court, and to a statement of
reasons for the Juvenile Court's decision. We believe
this result is required by the statute read in the context
of constitutional principles relating to due process and
the assistance of counsel [at 557].

Procedural Due Process. A year after *Kent,* the Supreme Court
again recognized that depriving a juvenile of procedural due process
was not necessarily rehabilitative. In *In re Gault,* 387 U.S. 1 (1967),
the Supreme Court required the following procedural safeguards at
the adjudicatory (trial) stage: notice of the charges, right to counsel,
right to confrontation and cross-examination, and privilege against
self-incrimination.

In *In re Winship,* 397 U.S. 358 (1970), the Supreme Court
required in delinquency adjudications that the government prove its
case beyond a reasonable doubt. Prior to *Winship,* since the juvenile
courts were considered civil rather than criminal courts, a lesser
standard of proof (proof by the preponderance of evidence) had been
used by most courts.

In these cases the Supreme Court regarded due process procedures as essentially the same for juveniles and adults. However, in
McKeiver v. *Pennsylvania,* 403 U.S. 528 (1971), the Court retreated
by holding that a jury trial for a juvenile delinquent was not constitutionally required. The plurality opinion expressed concern that a
jury trial would turn the juvenile proceeding into a "fully adversary
process and . . . put an effective end to what has been the idealistic
prospect of an intimate, informal protective proceeding" (at 545).

Disposition. Because there are few statutory guidelines concerning appropriate dispositions, juvenile judges may subjectively
decide penalties for various offenses. Consequently, although juveniles have most of the same procedural safeguards as adults at adjudication, the focus in juvenile courts on rehabilitation and acting in
the best interest of the child has often resulted in relatively harsher
dispositions and greater intervention in a juvenile's life.

The usual disposition of a case involving juvenile law violation is to put the youth on probation under court-ordered conditions. Both adult and juvenile probation orders carry conditions
forbidding future law violations and requiring that a person live in
a specific place and either obtain employment or attend school. In
addition, juvenile judges also attempt to reinforce parental authority over youth by specifying such conditions as completing certain
regular chores, complying with a curfew, and minding parents.
Since most juvenile cases are not appealed, juvenile court judges are
rarely challenged about their almost unlimited discretion in fashioning probation conditions.

Restitution is an increasingly important condition of probation for both adult and juvenile offenders. Adult offenders are usually ordered to make financial restitution to victims who have been
injured or lost property as the result of the crime. Although juvenile
conditions sometimes include the payment of money, restitution
through work assignments with community service agencies are
most common. Adult work restitution programs are also becoming
common in various sections of the country.

A juvenile judge will sometimes order placement out of the
home when the home is not conducive to the youth's rehabilitation.
The family may be disorganized, the parent hostile or antagonistic
to the child, or the parents may be unable to adequately control the
youth's behavior. The problem of lengthy out-of-home placements
will be discussed later in this chapter in the section on dependent
and neglected children.

The most severe sanction for the child is to take away his or
her liberty. This may occur at any of three stages in the juvenile
court process: as detention prior to adjudication, while awaiting an
out-of-home placement, or as incarceration after disposition. Most
communities do not have separate juvenile detention facilities.
Judges may use alternatives such as foster homes or they may detain
youth in separate sections of adult jails. One of the current priorities
of the Juvenile Justice and Delinquency Prevention Act of 1974 (as
amended) is to remove all youthful offenders from adult jails. The
latest amendments to the Act have retreated from an absolute ban on
detaining youth in adult jails because states with large rural popula-
tions often have no other kind of custodial facilities available.

All states have separate reform or training schools for incarcerating youthful offenders—usually after they have been adjudicated for committing a serious offense against a person or property or when they are repeat offenders. Training schools have been criticized for the failure of their programs and staff to effect behavioral changes in youthful law violators. In addition, most training schools are located in rural areas whereas many young offenders come from urban areas. The distance of training schools from large population centers tends to attenuate the youths' family ties during incarceration.

Right to Treatment. Since juveniles are supposed to be incarcerated for rehabilitative purposes, juvenile institutions have to provide treatment rather than punishment of youth. Important right-to-treatment cases for incarcerated juvenile offenders have reached the lower federal courts, wherein such practices as corporal punishment have been rejected either on statutory or constitutional grounds. Certain practices have been condemned as violating the Eighth Amendment prohibition against cruel and unusual punishment. This approach to ensuring adequate treatment is somewhat limited because, historically, it has ensured only a minimal standard of care. As a result, it falls short of a rehabilitative ideal for juveniles. The other principal constitutional argument is that inadequate care violates traditional due process under the Fifth and Fourteenth Amendments.

According to Kittrie (1969, p. 870), the right to treatment is founded on "a recognition of the concurrency between the state's exercise of sanctioning powers and its assumption of the duties of social responsibility. Its implication is that effective treatment must be the *quid pro quo* for society's right to exercise its *parens patriae* controls." (The reader may want to consult *Rouse* v. *Cameron,* 373 F.2d 451 (D.C. Cir. 1966). Although not a juvenile case, it is generally regarded as the leading right-to-treatment case for involuntarily confined persons.)

In *Martarella* v. *Kelley,* 349 F. Supp. 575 (D. N.Y. 1972), juveniles brought a suit to challenge the adequacy of treatment available and the mixing of status offenders (discussed later in this chapter) and delinquents in juvenile institutions throughout New York State. The court held that effective and humane treatment requires an adequate number of trained professionals who are knowledgeable about each child's particular problems. Expert witnesses agreed that a child/staff ratio of one to eight would be desirable. At one institution there were only four counselors for 135 children, and none of the staff had any specialized formal training. The court ruled that treatment at this institution was deficient in light of present knowledge and that lack of funds did not justify inadequate staff and facilities.

Nelson v. *Heyne*, 491 F.2d 352 (7th Cir. 1974), a civil rights class action, sought to enjoin the state commissioner of corrections and the superintendent of the Indiana Boys School from continuing unconstitutional practices. Specifically, guards at the Indiana Boys School, a medium security facility for boys twelve to eighteen years old, frequently disciplined the boys by beating them with fraternity paddles, and the institution routinely administered intramuscular injections of Thorazine and Sparine to boys who exibited excited behavior. The beatings were not governed by formal procedures, other than that two staff members were required to observe them. According to the court:

> [One] principle inherent in the cruel and unusual punishment clause is that a severe punishment must not be excessive. A punishment is excessive under this principle if it is unnecessary. The infliction of a severe punishment by the state cannot comport with human dignity when it is nothing more than the pointless infliction of suffering. If there is a significantly less severe punishment adequate to achieve the purposes for which punishment is inflicted, the punishment inflicted is unnecessary and therefore excessive. . . .
>
> There is nothing in the record to show that a less severe punishment would not have accomplished the disciplinary aim. And it is likely that the beatings have aroused animosity toward the school and substantially frustrated its rehabilitative purpose.
>
> We find [that] . . . (1) corporal punishment is easily subject to abuse in the hands of the sadistic and unscrupulous, and control of the punishment is inadequate; (2) formalized school procedures are at a minimum; (3) the infliction of such severe punishment

frustrates correctional and rehabilitative goals; and (4) the current sociological trend is toward the elimination of all corporal punishment in correctional institutions [at 356].[1]

The court also found that the administration of drugs for behavioral control, unless directed by a physician in each case, would violate the Eighth Amendment. Additionally, the court held that the right to treatment includes "the right to minimum acceptable standards of care and treatment for juveniles and the right to individualized care and treatment. Because children differ in their need for rehabilitation, individual need for treatment will differ. When a state assumes the place of a juvenile's parents, it assumes as well the parental duties, and its treatment of its juveniles should, so far as can be reasonably required, be what proper parental care would provide. Without a program of individual treatment, the result may be that the juveniles will not be rehabilitated, but warehoused, and that at the termination of detention they are likely to be incapable of taking their proper places in free society; their interests and those of the state and the school thereby being defeated" (at 360).

In addition to issues relating to corporal punishment, in *Morales* v. *Turman*, 383 F. Supp. 53 (E.D. Tex. 1974), the plaintiffs complained of the use of tear gas and other chemical crowd control devices in many of the Texas Youth Council (TYC) facilities.[2]

---

[1]In a 5-to-4 decision in 1977, the U.S. Supreme Court (*Ingraham* v. *Wright*, 430 U.S. 651) concluded that corporal punishment in the Florida public schools did not violate either due process or the Eighth Amendment. *Ingraham* is inapposite to *Nelson* v. *Heyne*, since children who are incarcerated would be protected under the Eighth Amendment. Considering that adult criminals are protected under the Eighth Amendment from corporal punishment in prison (*Jackson* v. *Bishop*, 494 F.2d 571 (8th Cir. 1968)), it would be paradoxical if, under the guise of rehabilitation, incarcerated children could be beaten and not receive constitutional protection.

[2]The decision was later vacated on the ground that a three-judge court should have heard the case. (535 F.2d 864 (5th Cir. 1976), reversed, 430 U.S. 322 (1977)). The appeals court remanded the case to the district court for further hearings in light of the changes that had occurred in the Texas Youth Authority. The appellate court also expressed doubts concerning a constitutional right to treatment, urging the trial court to rely on the Eighth Amendment as the constitutional basis for relief. (*Morales* v. *Turman* is also reported in 562 F.2d 993 (1977)).

Children were also placed in solitary confinement without statutory or administrative procedures on duration and intensity of confinement. These practices—along with children's being forced to maintain silence for purposes of punishment and to perform repetitive, nonfunctional, degrading, and unnecessary make-work tasks for many hours—were found to violate the Eighth Amendment. There were also procedural due process issues relating to the transfer of inmates to a maximum security unit, as well as First Amendment issues in censorship of incoming or outgoing mail and prohibiting or discouraging juveniles from conversing in a language other than English. The findings in the case depicted juvenile institutions that were not only antirehabilitative but repressive and brutal. The following are two examples:

> Complaints regarding physical abuse of TYC inmates at Mountain View and other institutions were supposed to be the subject of "incident reports," filed by all TYC inmates and personnel involved. Specific procedures vary from one institution to another, however, and falsification of reports by correctional officers, particularly at Mountain View, and by inmates under duress of the correctional officers is widespread. Many correctional officers forced an inmate to file a report that reflects that an injury was caused by a football game, for example, rather than by the use of force by the correctional officer. Moreover, many inmates testified to fear of reprisals by correctional officers for the truthful reporting of instances of physical abuse.
> Some Mountain View inmates are segregated from the general population on the basis of purported homosexuality and race. Two dormitories, referred to by TYC inmates and personnel as "punk dorms," are set aside for the smaller boys and those determined by the custodial staff, on the basis of nonclinical standards, to be homosexuals. One dormitory is for black inmates and the other is for Anglo and Mexican-American inmates. Experts testifying for both the plaintiffs and defendants and the various amici groups were unanimous in concluding that the permanent segregation of inmates on the basis of purported homosexuality was psychologically damaging [at 170-171].

Citing the Texas statute, the court held that each juvenile committed to TYC had a right to humane and rehabilitative treatment; that the due process clause of the Fourteenth Amendment also confers a federal constitutional right to treatment; and that the following TYC practices violated a juvenile's state and federal right to treatment:

> The segregation by untrained correctional officers of some inmates on the basis of suspected homosexuality. . . .
> Failure to allow and encourage full participation of family and interested friends in the program of a youthful offender. . . .
> The practice of withholding or neglecting to provide casework, nursing, and psychological or psychiatric services to juveniles confined in solitary confinement or secure facilities. . . .
> Failure to provide inmates of maximum security institutions such as Mountain View, which has a history of brutality, neglect, and intimidation, with access to a person who can hear their complaints and seek administrative redress for their grievances without fear of reprisals. . . .
> Confinement of juveniles in an institution in which a nurse is not available on the premises twenty-four hours a day. . . .
> The employment by the TYC of persons whose personalities, backgrounds, or lack of qualifications render them likely to harm the juveniles in their care either physically or psychologically, absent any attempt to administer the appropriate psychological testing or psychiatric interview [at 175].

Because the court found that the conditions of the TYC institutions were appalling, it ordered emergency interim relief, including restrictions on the use of physical force, the use of Mace and tear gas for disciplinary purposes, the practice of segregating suspected homosexuals, the use of solitary confinement, and mail censorship; increases in visitation hours and days; the appointment of an ombudsman; permission for inmates to speak non-English languages in the institution; and requirements that a nurse be present twenty-four hours a day and that new personnel be closely screened.

Other courts have reviewed state statutes and found that juveniles or involuntarily confined persons either explicitly or implicitly have a statutory right to treatment. The Supreme Court has yet to decide a constitutional right-to-treatment case. The issue was raised in *O'Connor* v. *Donaldson*, 422 U.S. 563 (1975), but the case was decided on other grounds. In 1974 the U.S. Court of Appeals for the Fifth Circuit had approved an instruction that a "person who is involuntarily civilly committed has a constitutional right to receive such treatment as will give him a realistic opportunity to be cured" (*Donaldson* v. *O'Connor*, 493 F.2d 507, 520 (5th Cir. 1974)). However, concurring Chief Justice Burger made it clear that a constitutional right to treatment was not given approval by the Supreme Court and was not binding on the parties.

If the right to treatment is to be effective in protecting incarcerated juveniles, adequate treatment guidelines must be formulated and a mechanism created for supervision of institutions, to ensure that they are in compliance. Formulating treatment standards will undoubtedly be difficult, since there is no agreement on what is required in order to rehabilitate a juvenile offender. Even if external criteria can be agreed on, there are still problems in trying to evaluate the effectiveness of treatment programs in institutions. According to Rothman (1973, p. 245): "Each institution will have a large staff of professionals, an elaborately designed program, and dedicated and articulate directors. And using these criteria the courts will turn away from constitutional attacks. From all past indications, judges will focus on performance, not on whether the institution actually does any good, but on external criteria, on the size of the staff and style of the directors, on whether the institution *promises* to do good."

Assuming adequate standards, effective ongoing supervision could probably be achieved through periodic institutional inspections and comprehensive yearly reports. If institutions failed to comply with judicially or statutorily imposed standards, courts could close them. While this action might provide a strong incentive to states to upgrade their institutions, a potentially dangerous youth could be returned to the community. Less drastic would be for courts to prohibit further assignment of juveniles to institutions that failed to meet minimum standards. One consequence of the *Morales* case (previously discussed) was that juvenile delinquents are no longer assigned to Mountain View. It is currently operating as a Texas women's prison.

While guaranteeing institutionalized juveniles a right to treatment is one step to ensure a rehabilitative milieu, there are inherent problems in juvenile treatment that is based generally on a medical model. The deviant juvenile is considered to be someone who can be "cured" through proper treatment. In point of fact, no one has developed a reliable treatment to cure the "disease" of delinquency. Moreover, it is a dangerous assumption that any type of treatment will benefit "sick" delinquents more than allowing them to mature without institutional intervention.

The juvenile justice system has been under recent attack because the system does not appear to rehabilitate. Some youths keep committing serious offenses and coming back into the system. A second criticism is that the system is unfair to youth. According to Schur (1973), the informality of the system and discretion by police, prosecutors, judges, and correctional workers result in punishment instead of treatment.

Status Offenders

One basic premise of criminal law is that people are responsible for their criminal acts. But can they also be punished because of their status? Can narcotics addicts and alcoholics, for example, be punished under the law just for being addicts and alcoholics, even if they do not commit a criminal offense? Can children be similarly punished if they commit an offense that would not be considered criminal if committed by an adult? *Robinson* v. *California*, 370 U.S. 660 (1966), is a leading case on this question. The plaintiff challenged a California statute making it a criminal offense for a person to be addicted to the use of narcotics. In holding this statute unconstitutional on Eighth Amendment grounds, the U.S. Supreme Court reasoned that addiction is an illness that might be contracted innocently or involuntarily. The Court emphasized, however, that states can punish such criminal *acts* as the sale, purchase, or possession of narcotics. A state also might legally detain noncriminals for compulsory treatment in order to protect society or the person; but detention for mere illness—without a curative program—would be impermissible.

Other courts followed *Robinson* in holding that it would also be cruel and unusual punishment to convict a chronic alcoholic for public drunkenness because such a person "is powerless to stop drinking" (*Driver* v. *Hinnant*, 356 F.2d 761 (4th Cir. 1966)). The *Driver* court also concluded that chronic alcoholism is a disease that causes the *in*voluntary act of public drunkenness. However, the U.S. Supreme Court rejected this conclusion in *Powell* v. *Texas*, 392 U.S. 5194 (1968). There was medical testimony that, when Powell was sober, the act of taking his first drink was a voluntary exercise of his will. Even though there might have been a strong compulsion to take the first drink, it was not completely overpowering. Neither Robinson nor Powell could have been punished for being an addict or an alcoholic (an involuntary status), but Powell could be punished for violating the criminal code on public drunkenness (characterized by the U.S. Supreme Court as a voluntary act). The Court was obviously concerned about weakening the principle of criminal responsibility and did not want to excuse narcotic addicts and chronic alcoholics from criminal acts or conduct related to their status or condition (for example, robbing someone to pay for drugs to avoid withdrawal symptoms).

Children as Status Offenders. Although drug addicts or alcoholics cannot constitutionally be punished for their status, children can be "punished" for such statutory offenses as running away from home or not minding their parents. A historical analysis of the parent-child relationship vis-à-vis the state is summarized in Table 1. In the first 175 years of our country's history, parents had enormous power over the conduct and behavior of children, with little interference by the state. Beginning with the Industrial Revolution, however, the state partially supplanted parental authority and intervened in the lives of children in order to correct deviant behavior, including acts that would not be criminal if committed by an adult. At the end of the nineteenth century, the establishment of a separate legal system based on a *parens patriae* philosophy further eroded parental authority. Within the last two decades, the juvenile court, as kindly parent, has been increasingly criticized. Justice Fortas in *Kent* v. *United States*, 383 U.S. 541, 556 (1966), concluded:

Table 1. Juvenile Justice Developments and Their Impact on Conceptions of Child, Parent, and State Relationships.

Period	Major Developments	Precipitation Influences	Child/State	Parent/State	Parent/Child
Puritan 1646–1824	Massachusetts Stubborn Child Law (1646)	A. Christian view of child as evil B. Economically marginal agrarian society	Law provides: A. Symbolic standard of maturity B. Support for family as economic unit	Parents considered responsible and capable of controlling child	Child considered both property and spiritual responsibility of parents
Refuge 1824–1899	Institutionalization of deviants, New York House of Refuge established (1824) for delinquent and dependent children	A. Enlightenment B. Immigration and industrialization	Child seen as helpless, in need of state intervention	Parents supplanted as state assumes responsibility for correcting deviant socialization	Family considered a major cause of juvenile deviancy
Juvenile Court 1899–1960	Establishment of separate legal system for juveniles—Illinois Juvenile Court Act (1899)	A. Reformism and rehabilitative ideology B. Increased immigration, urbanization, large-scale industrialization	Juvenile court institutionalizes legal irresponsibility of child	*Parens patriae* doctrine gives legal foundation for state intervention in family	Further abrogation of parents' rights and responsibilities
Juvenile Rights 1960–Present	Increased "legalization" of juvenile law—*Gault* decision (1966); Juvenile Justice and Delinquency Prevention Act (1974) calls for deinstitutionalization of status offenders	A. Criticism of juvenile justice system on humane grounds B. Civil rights movements by disadvantaged groups	Movement to define and protect rights as well as provide services to children	Reassertion of responsibility of parents and community for welfare and behavior of children	Attention given to childrens' claims against parents; earlier emancipation of children

Source: Smith and others, 1980, p. 29.

"There may be grounds for concern that the child receives the worst of both worlds; that he gets neither the protections accorded to adults nor the solicitous care and regenerative treatment postulated for children."

Today we have entered a legalistic era where children have legal rights to challenge procedures in the juvenile court and even parental practices that may be abusive or inhumane. Parents perceive that they have less and less power in making parental decisions about discipline, associations, and the like. This erosion of power and the uncertainty on the part of parents have been coupled with temptations and choices faced by adolescents today that were uncommon even three decades ago. It is not surprising that some parents feel beleaguered in trying to cope with adolescents who will not mind them, will not stay home, or will not go to school. They have sought the authority of the juvenile justice system to reinforce their parental influence. For some families social or family problems have become legal problems.

The following excerpts indicate the statutory language of recent juvenile codes in three states (Nebraska, Texas, and Wisconsin), therein describing acts or behavior that might bring children within the status offense jurisdiction of the juvenile courts in those states:

Revised Statutes of Nebraska
Who, by reason of being wayward or habitually disobedient, is uncontrolled by his or her parents, guardian, or custodian; who deports himself or herself so as to injure or endanger seriously the morals or health of himself, herself, or others; or who is habitually truant from home or school [sec. 43-247(3)(b) (1982)].

Texas Revised Civil Statutes Annotated
(b) Conduct indicating a need for supervision is: . . . (2) the unexpected voluntary absence of a child on ten or more days or parts of days within a six-month period or three or more days or parts of days within a four-week period from school; (3) the voluntary absence of a child from his home without the consent of his parent or guardian for a substantial length of time or without intent to return [art. 5103 (1977)].

Wisconsin Statutes Annotated
(6) who is habitually truant from school and evidence
is provided by the school attendance officer that school
procedures relative to truancy have been followed; (7)
who is habitually truant from home and either the
child or the parent, guardian, or a relative in whose
home the child resides signs a petition requesting jurisdiction and attests in court than reconciliation efforts have been attempted and failed [sec. 48.13 (1978)].

Although seven states include status offenses within their delinquency category, most states provide separate status offense categories in order to reduce the stigmatization of labeling. Two states
allow status offenders who commit a second status offense to be
reclassified as delinquent. Other states include status offenses within
the dependency category (Smith and others, 1980). Nebraska formerly had a separate jurisdictional category (in need of special supervision), but effective July 1, 1981, the neglect, dependency, and
status offense categories were combined (children in need of assistance). (Neglect and dependency are discussed later in this chapter.)
    Status offender statutes have been criticized because what pre-
cisely is forbidden is often unclear. Recently revised juvenile court
codes have attempted to be more explicit about the forbidden conduct. For school truancy Texas provides that a child must be absent
from school a specific number of days before a petition can be filed,
and Wisconsin requires certain procedures by schools before the
court will assume jurisdiction. Nebraska's is the least precise of the
three statutes. Before the state of Washington changed its code, a
status offender could be one who "frequents the company of reputed
criminals, vagrants, or prostitutes, is in danger of being brought up
to lead an idle, dissolute, or immoral life, [or] wanders about in the
night-time without being on a lawful business or occupation"
(Wash. Stat. Ann. sec. 48.13).
    Constitutional Attacks on Statutes. The constitutional argu-
ments in the drug addiction and alcoholism cases were based on the
Eighth Amendment's prohibition against cruel and unusual punishment. A major constitutional attack on the juvenile status offender statutes is that they are void for vagueness and therefore
violate due process. The United States Constitution and various

state constitutions provide that no person shall be deprived of his or her right to life, liberty, or property without due process of law. Just as there is no limitation concerning race or creed, there is no age limitation in the language of these constitutions. Juveniles are persons within the meaning of the Fifth and Fourteenth Amendments (*In re Gault*, 387 U.S. 1 (1967)). The "void for vagueness" test contains two elements: (1) The legislative language must be sufficiently specific that a person of ordinary intelligence does not have to guess at its meaning and application (*Connally* v. *General Construction Co.*, 269 U.S. 385, 391 (1926). (2) The legislative language must contain ascertainable standards to guide its enforcement (*United States* v. *Cohen Grocery Co.*, 255 U.S. 81, 89 (1921)).

What behaviors are required to show that a child is wayward? How many times must the behavior occur before it is considered habitual? In *Gesicki* v. *Oswald*, 336 F. Supp. 371 (S.D. N.Y.), affirmed without opinion, 406 U.S. 913 (1972), the New York "Wayward Minor Statute" was declared void for vagueness where it permitted the possible imposition of penal sanctions on minors who were "morally depraved" or "in danger of becoming morally depraved." Juvenile courts are sometimes called civil courts and do not carry the stigma associated with a criminal court. However, the Wayward Minor Statute was declared void despite express language that such an adjudication was not a criminal conviction. Due process requires that sufficient notice of acts prohibited be given prior to the commission of the act. The fact that allegations in a juvenile petition may be precise (absence from school for a specific number of days) does not cure the vagueness defect. The challenge is to the lack of specificity in the statute, not the petition. However, despite the strong arguments that many juvenile status offense statutes are so unclear that a reasonable person could not understand them, most statutes have withstood attack under the "void for vagueness" doctrine. Courts have generally concluded that the language is ambiguous and can thus be interpreted.

Intervention Problems. A minor's acts that are offenses under statutes regarding Persons in Need of Supervision (PINS), Children in Need of Supervision (CHINS), Juveniles in Need of Supervision (JINS), and Children in Need of Assistance (CHINA) may be justifiable in light of all the circumstances. Human services practitioners can attest that leaving a physically or emotionally abusive home may be an appropriate psychological response. Regardless of whether the actions involved are primarily the fault of the minor or of one or both parents, the minor is the one who is charged and who must suffer the consequences. Human services workers providing residential and nonresidential services for adolescent status offenders also report that these youth are often more difficult to work with than delinquents. One important reason is that status offenders are likely to be in conflict with their parents. Many parents are angry and want the child removed from their home and/or punished. When adolescents are brought into the juvenile justice system, they are often confused and frustrated because they do not believe they have done anything wrong or criminal. A fourteen-year-old girl, for example, will say "All I did was to stay over at my boyfriend's house."

For the status offender who is truant from home or school, the usual dispositional sequence is, first, placement at home under the supervision of a court officer. Since long-standing family conflicts are not easily resolved, the child continues the inappropriate behavior and violates the court order. After another court hearing, the child is placed in a foster or group home. Separated from friends and thrust into a strange environment, it is not surprising that the child's adjustment is poor, and he or she may run from the residential placement. Finally, the judge commits the child to a training school. Until recently 50 percent of the girls and 10 percent of the boys in training schools were status offenders. Even in an era of more permissive sexual norms, parents tend to impose stricter rules of sexual conduct on girls, and the system supports this differential standard. "More girls are locked up for status offenses than boys committing the same action. Girls on the average receive longer sentences for status offenses than boys do for criminal offenses" (Wooden, 1976, p. 119).

In the early 1970s, various documents described the often brutal and nonrehabilitative conditions in state training schools (see Wooden, 1976). Characteristics of Texas training schools found constitutionally statutorily deficient in *Morales* (previously cited) could also be found in other training schools throughout the country.

Promulgation of National Standards. Various organizations have proposed national standards relating to the status offender. Most state legislatures have adopted the jurisdictional standards proposed by the National Juvenile and Family Court Judges; this group recommends that the juvenile court retain jurisdiction over status offenders. The following reasons are cited to justify retention: children's judgments are immature, and they need special protection; troubled youth and families will not volunteer for services; school and parents need the court's jurisdiction when they have exhausted other efforts; and, without intervention, a status offense will escalate into delinquent behavior (Arthur, 1978).

Research is somewhat equivocal relative to the escalation theory. Thomas (1978) analyzed juvenile case records over a five-year period and found that many status offenders had been charged previously with delinquent offenses and that status offenders were more likely to repeat their offenses than delinquents were. On the other hand, Clarke (1978) reported exactly the opposite findings. Weis (1980) analyzed studies of self-reported delinquency (in which youths were asked whether they had ever engaged in behavior that violated the law). He concluded that status offenders and delinquents engaged in many types of illegal behavior, rather than specializing in one or the other; however, delinquents commit more serious crimes with greater frequency, whereas status offenders tend to commit petty offenses.

The most controversial standards relating to juvenile court jurisdiction over the status offender are those proposed by the American Bar Association and the Institute of Judicial Administration (ABA/IJA). The standards decriminalize status offenses by removing the jurisdiction of the juvenile court over this type of juvenile behavior. Those who support the standards argue that so-called rebellious youth are more appropriately treated as a social problem than through legal intervention. Arguments for decriminalizing status offenses are based on a concern for the punitive treatment accorded this category of youth and on the belief that the considerable court resources expended for status offenders would be better spent on the more serious or violent juvenile offender.

Maine, Washington, Utah, and California have juvenile codes that restrict juvenile court jurisdiction over the status offender:

"In Maine there is a jurisdictional abandonment of status offenses—if a juvenile does not commit an offense which would be a crime for an adult, the juvenile court does not have jurisdiction" (Weis, 1980, pp. 4–5).

Federal Response. The federal government, through the Juvenile Justice and Delinquency Prevention Act of 1974 (JJDPA), provided guidelines and funds that affected the states' responses to the status offender. Congress could have provided funds to decriminalize status offenses; instead, it provided guidelines and funds for diversion and deinstitutionalization. The congressional hearings focused on the bleak picture of status offenders in juvenile correctional institutions where children were abused and neglected. After 1974 most states received funds for community-based alternatives to correctional institutions based on formula grants. The goal was to deinstitutionalize at least 75 percent of accused and adjudicated status offenders within three years after submission and approval of a state plan, with complete removal of status offenders from detention and correctional facilities in a maximum of five years. The Act also sought to separate juveniles from adult offenders in detention and correctional facilities.

Numerous obstacles have hindered the states' achievement of full compliance with the JJDPA. The major obstacle is a paucity of appropriate community alternatives. In addition, attitudinal and philosophical differences among decision makers have resulted in ineffective programs and a lack of facilities in rural communities. Because of community resistance, juvenile programs could not be placed in certain neighborhoods. Some programs have been very costly, with little indication that they are effective. Many of the existing residential and nonresidential programs are inadequate to help youths solve their problems and return to their families.

The original purpose of the JJDPA has been further eroded by a recent amendment to the Act, effective July 1, 1982. It allows courts to jail status offenders "who violate a valid court order by running away from a court-ordered placement or other infractions" (*Criminal Justice Newsletter*, June 21, 1981, p. 5). Several states, using the court's contempt power, have jailed status offenders for violating court orders.

Throughout the country today, few status offenders are committed to the training schools. Like all reforms, however, this one has had unexpected results. More status offenders are coming under the jurisdiction of the juvenile court, and more status offenders are in residential care. When Nebraska passed legislation providing that status offenders could no longer be committed to the state training schools, judges were given an alternative whereby status offenders could be committed to the State Department of Public Welfare for suitable placement. When the bill was passed, there were thirty-three status offenders in the girls' and boys' training schools. Because no funds were allocated to the welfare department, it might be assumed that only thirty to fifty status offenders would be committed to the department each year. However, in June of 1982, the Department of Public Welfare reported that it was currently providing residential care for approximately four hundred status offenders.

Even though private placements may seem more humane than institutionalizing status offenders in correctional facilities, the unanswered question is whether taking the child out of the home restores family harmony. What appears to have happened is that status offenders become children without families once the juvenile court intervenes. Is it appropriate for the state under its *parens patriae* power to become a permanent parent (until majority) of adolescent youth?

Neglected and Dependent Juveniles

Besides delinquents and status offenders, the juvenile court has jurisdiction over cases where the petition alleges deficient parenting. Many social service agencies are called on to provide services for these parents and their children.

Allegations that a child is dependent (that is, in need of services that the parent cannot provide because the parent is mentally ill, mentally deficient, alcoholic, or in prison on charges unrelated to the parental role) focus on behaviors over which the parent has little or no control. A neglect petition, on the other hand, alleges that the parent has been at fault in failing to provide for the physical or mental well-being of the child—specifically, that the parent has abandoned the child or subjected the child to corporal punishment, sexual molestation, excessive confinement, an extremely unsanitary environment, or similar hazards. Some state statutes do not distinguish between neglect and dependency; instead, they simply list parental behaviors that will result in a child's being in need of protection or services.

Abuse-reporting legislation (requiring such professionals as doctors, nurses, school employees, or social workers to report incidents of abuse or neglect to a law enforcement agency or to a department of public welfare) has been passed in every state. Child abuse is also prohibited in specific sections of the criminal code (for example, assault or special child and disabled person statutes). Where a child is abused or neglected, criminal and juvenile court proceedings may be initiated separately or concurrently. Upon conviction, criminal courts punish law violators. Juvenile courts, as civil courts, intervene as *parens patriae* to act in the "best interest of the child." However, as Justice Fortas commented in *Gault* (previously cited): "The meaning of *parens patriae* is murky and its historic credentials are of dubious reference" (at 6).

A criminal conviction has direct consequences (most notably, incarceration) and collateral consequences (such as a criminal record, which can affect employment). The most serious consequences for an abusive or neglectful parent in juvenile court is that the child(ren) will be removed from his or her custody or parental rights terminated: "[The] forced dissolution of the parent-child relationship has been recognized as a punitive sanction by courts, Congress, and commentators," since it leaves the parent with no right to communicate with the child or participate in any important decisions about the child's development (Dissenting opinion, *Lassiter* v. *Department of Social Services of Durham County*, 452 U.S. 18, 39 (1981)).

Constitutional Attacks on Statutes. There have been constitutional challenges to dependency and neglect statutes because of the imprecise and unclear language regarding the parental conduct that is prohibited. In *Alsager* v. *District Court of Polk County, Iowa*, 406 F. Supp 10 (1975), parents challenged the constitutionality of a termination of parental rights statute on the ground that it was void for vagueness. Section 232.41(2)(b)(d) of the *Code of Iowa* allowed termination where parental conduct was "detrimental to the

physical or mental health of the child" or where the parent "refused
to grant the child necessary care and protection." In a neglect proceeding, the state had removed the Alsager children from their home
because the children were allowed to be outside in cold weather
without winter clothing, played in traffic, annoyed neighbors, ate
mush for supper, lived in a house containing dirty dishes and
laundry, and sometimes arrived late to school. The federal court
struck down the Iowa statute because it did not provide Mr. and Mrs.
Alsager with sufficient guidance to enable them to modify their
conduct in order to avoid termination of parental rights.

Although similar statutory language has withstood constitutional attack in other states, the *Alsager* case points up the legal
concern about appropriate criteria to establish what is or is not
adequate parenting. How bad does the parenting have to be before
the state should intervene in family life?

In an Oregon case, the court concluded that the alleged
neglectful conduct had to involve not just detrimental conduct but
seriously detrimental conduct. According to the court, "the circumstances of [this] family could be duplicated in hundreds of thousands of American families—transciency, incapacity, poverty, and
instability" (*State* v. *McMaster*, 259 Or. 292, 295 (1971)).

Courts and legislatures have emphasized the fundamental
right of family privacy. Initial government intervention (by the
police or the welfare department) should be based on objective
criteria rather than subjective value judgments about ideal
parenting.

Legal and Social Interventions. When an initial report or
referral is made to the police or the welfare department, there is not
always agreement about intervention. A law enforcement officer
may talk on the scene with parents but generally will file a complaint only where relatively dangerous conditions require immediate protective custody of the child or where there is probable cause
to arrest the parent for a violation of the criminal code. In contrast,
child welfare workers may consider intervention appropriate where
there is family dysfunction that can be ameliorated through appropriate social services. Most abuse and neglect cases are eventually
terminated by the welfare department after the acceptance of services
by the parent. Juvenile court intervention is sought in fewer than 10

percent of the reported abuse and neglect cases. Where assistance is provided to the family for a period of time without improvement in the parental conduct or behavior that led to the report or referral, the agency may seek juvenile court intervention to remove the children from the home or to support their rehabilitative efforts.

County attorneys (prosecutors) are often unwilling to file a petition to initiate the processing of the case through juvenile court. They may recognize that a dysfunctional family is likely to be deficient in adequate child-rearing skills, but they must also consider evidentiary issues such as whether there is sufficient evidence so that the court will make a legal finding of neglect or dependency.

Juvenile Court Responses. Few abuse and neglect cases reach the juvenile court, since most of them are handled informally or dismissed in the investigatory or prosecutorial stages. However, once a case reaches the juvenile court, the judge exercises enormous power in deciding what happens from intake through disposition and subsequent review. The judge's effectiveness in the *parens patriae* role will depend on his or her understanding of the complex social and legal issues involved in neglect or dependency cases, the evidence presented in court, and the resources available to assist the family after adjudication.

Initially, at a detention hearing, the juvenile judge determines whether a child should be temporarily removed from the custody of the parents. After a petition is filed, the judge may order the child, who is now a ward of the court, placed or continued in foster care, returned to the custody of the parent under court supervision, or placed with relatives. The child welfare worker and the court may not agree about a custody decision that returns the child to the parents pending adjudication. The case worker has usually been involved with this dysfunctional family for a period of time and wants out-of-home placement based on a more expansive view of what would be in the "best interest of the child." The judge, of course, is the legal decision maker.

Both criminal and juvenile court abuse cases are difficult to prove at trial or adjudication. They are often based on circumstantial evidence. The victim is usually too young or too frightened to testify, and often there are no other witnesses. The suspected abuser usually denies knowledge of the abusive incident. In the final analysis, neglect and dependency cases often depend on testimony from physicians, psychiatrists, psychologists, or social workers. In cases involving inadequate parenting other than physical or sexual abuse, it may be more difficult to obtain adequate legal proof. Generally, extreme deviation from appropriate parental conduct or behavior will be required. As one Nebraska court succinctly concluded: "This is not a messy house case [but] a situation involving consistently poor sanitary conditions and deficient personal hygiene which could and did work to the physical injury of the child" (*In re Interest of Souza-Spitler,* 283 N.W.2d 48, 52 (Neb. 1979)).

It often takes two or more days for presentation of the evidence in neglect or dependency adjudications. Police, medical personnel, school counselors, visiting nurses, and other human services workers may testify about incidents that they have observed. After adjudication the judge will deliberate and make findings. In most states, if there is insufficient evidence to sustain the state's burden of proof by the preponderance of evidence, the case will be dismissed and the jurisdiction of the court will terminate. If the evidence is insufficient to prove certain of the allegations in the petition, those counts will be dismissed. A court order will state the findings and indicate whether the child will remain in custody. The parties will also be told the date of the disposition hearing—since in most states adjudication and disposition hearings are heard separately. Court personnel, welfare workers, and the child's guardian *ad litem* may be ordered to prepare and submit an appropriate rehabilitation plan to the court.

At disposition the rehabilitation plan is presented and may be accepted, modified, or rejected by the judge. The court may consider all types of relevant and material testimony or exhibits, even if they violate the customary rules of evidence. Hearsay evidence, for example, ordinarily would not be admissible at adjudication but would be admissible at disposition. Parental rights usually are taken under advisement; in unusual cases, however, where the court is convinced that rehabilitation efforts will not result in appropriate changes in parental conduct or behavior, parental rights may be terminated. The court order following disposition will generally set a review date, so that the court can monitor the progress of the rehabilitation plan. If, after a reasonable period of time, there are grounds to believe that the parents will continue to be unable to discharge their parental responsibility, the state may file a motion or new petition for termination of parental rights.

Termination of Parental Rights. If parental rights are terminated in a juvenile court proceeding, a parent's legal rights to custody and decision making concerning the child are irrevocably lost. Since this is a serious and grievous loss, due process procedures are required—including notice, hearing, and opportunity to appeal the juvenile court decision. In many instances the parents' right to be heard and to defend themselves against allegations of neglectful conduct would be meaningless without counsel, since the juvenile court process is complex and incomprehensible to most parents. Therefore, some states, by statute or case law, have required that juvenile courts provide counsel for indigent parents in termination of parental rights proceedings.

In 1981 the Supreme Court had an opportunity to decide whether counsel should be required in all termination cases (*Lassiter* v. *Department of Social Services of Durham County*, 452 U.S. 18 (1981)). After weighing the private interest at stake, the government's interest, and the risk of an erroneous decision where there is inadequate procedural due process, the Court concluded that appointment of counsel is not required in every termination case. From the dialogue between the juvenile judge and Mrs. Lassiter in the trial transcript, it is clear that she was unable adequately to cross-examine the welfare worker who was the state's chief witness. However, after evaluating the weight of the evidence, the Court majority concluded that she lacked interest in her son's welfare. The evidence was sufficient to persuade the Court that assistance of counsel would not have made a difference in the outcome. A constitutional right to counsel in termination of parental rights cases is mandated only on a case-by-case basis after consideraton of the totality of the circumstances. The four dissenting justices balanced the relatively insignificant cost of providing counsel with the fundamental nature of the parental interest, the permanency of a termination, and the gross imbalance between the state prosecuting the case and the parent. They concluded that right to counsel in termination of parental rights cases is constitutionally required.

In 1982 the Supreme Court heard another case involving termination of parental rights. In *Santosky* v. *Kramer* (50 U.S.L.W. 4333 (1982)), the Court considered the quantum of proof necessary before a state could terminate parents' rights to their children. Thirty states, either by statute or case law, require clear and convincing evidence prior to termination of parental rights. Two states and the Indian Child Welfare Act of 1978 (25 U.S.C. sec. 1912(4)) require proof beyond a reasonable doubt. The New York Family Court Act (sec. 622) requires that only a preponderance of evidence support the finding for termination. The Supreme Court, in a 5-to-4 decision, held that the due process clause of the Fourteenth Amendment requires clear and convincing evidence before a state can completely and irrevocably sever the rights of parents. The Court reasoned that this standard of proof "reflects not only the weight of the private and public interests affected, but also a societal judgment about how the risk of error should be distributed between the litigants" (at 4335). Even though preponderance of evidence is the usual standard of proof in civil matters, in this case the interests at stake were more substantial than an award of money damages. According to the majority, in termination proceedings the "private interest affected is commanding, the risk of error from using a preponderance standard is substantial, and the countervailing governmental interest in favoring preponderance of evidence is slight" (at 4336).

If parental rights are not terminated, the juvenile judge will order the court staff, the welfare department, or other community agencies to continue working with the family to effect changes. In most cases improvement does occur, and the court will eventually terminate its jurisdiction in the case. Specific plans must be formulated, coordinated, and monitored by various caseworkers. Facts about the family and its progress must be carefully documented in the agency records. Periodic reports will be made to the court.

A few families do not respond to the rehabilitative efforts. In such instances termination of parental rights may appear to be in the best interest of the child. According to the one recent appellate court: "The right of a parent to maintain the custody of his or her child is a natural but not inalienable right and the public has a paramount interest in the protection of the child. . . . The first and primary consideration in any case involving the custody of the child is the best interests of the child" (*In re Interest of Spradlin*, 210 Neb. 734, 740 (1982)). If termination is considered, specific evidence must be gathered to persuade the prosecutor that this irrevocable step is necessary. If the allegation in the termination petition or motion is mental illness or deficiency on the part of the parent, diagnostic evidence (including prognosis) must be obtained from psychiatrists, psychologists, social workers, visiting nurses, and others to show that the parent's incapacity will continue for a prolonged, indefinite period. If the allegation is parental unfitness, evidence that the parent failed to respond to a structured treatment program or written agreements will show that reasonable efforts have failed to correct the parent's conduct or behavior.

Permanent Planning for Children. As previously noted, the juvenile justice system has been criticized for its intervention in American family life because of unclear or ambiguous statutory language and the resulting application of subjective values (often middle class) by various decision makers. Recently, legal writers have expressed concern that, after the court intervenes and removes the children from the custody of the parents, children remain in temporary foster care for long periods of time and thus lack the security that comes from permanency in a family. If a placement continues for longer than eighteen months, it is probable that the child will remain in foster care for the rest of his or her majority. Moreover, it has been statistically documented that a child in foster care will often be shifted from placement to placement; and, until recently, there has been inadequate monitoring and review of children placed in foster care (Mnookin, 1973).

Such monitoring and review are now provided by placement agencies or by courts or by citizen review boards. Placement agencies have developed administrative procedures to review every child in placement. Individual courts have set up monitoring procedures to require a periodic review of the progress being made to reunite the family, the effectiveness of the services being provided, and any additional services that may be needed. In New York, for example, the agency charged with a child's care must bring the case to the Family Court for review after the child has been in foster care for a continuous period of eighteen months (*Children's Rights Report*, 1977). Citizen review boards have been authorized in a number of states—

among them South Carolina, Delaware, Arizona, and Nebraska. Nebraska's Foster Care Review Act provides for a state board and local boards made up of citizens who will monitor a statewide register of all public and private foster care placements of delinquent and children in need of assistance (dependent, neglected, or status offenders). When a child has been in foster care for one year, the court having jurisdiction of the placement must review the dispositional order. Thereafter, the court must issue orders or conduct additional reviews of the foster care placement once every six months.

Conclusion

The juvenile justice system today is fraught with legal, psychological, and sociological problems. The medical model has been criticized because most juvenile law violators are not "sick" and the system has been unable to "cure" aberrant or illegal behavior. Despite juvenile court intervention, juvenile delinquents continue to commit crimes in disproportion to their numbers in the general population.

The contemporary critics of the juvenile justice system include people both from the political right and left who disapprove of the handling of juvenile offenders—but for different reasons. The political right wants the system to "get tougher" (for example, more incarceration or transfers to adult court), while the political left contends that many juvenile law violators receive neither the benefits of procedures mandated in the adult system nor any significant benefit from a *parens patriae* system with limited dispositional alternatives.

Juvenile offenders have been granted additional procedural rights in juvenile court since 1965, but so far neither courts nor legislatures have been willing to require significant substantive changes. Some changes are occuring in the system's response to the status offender. Although most states have not eliminated the jurisdiction of the juvenile court over status offenders, legislatures have clarified the language in the statutes so that people with reasonable intelligence can understand what is forbidden. Laws relating to neglected and dependent children are also more specific and less ambiguous.

R. Barry Ruback   4

Family Law

Over half of the civil filings in the United States involve some aspect
of family law, usually divorce (Hennessey, 1980). The decisions in
many of these cases are among the most difficult that judges are
called on to make because the major considerations are essentially
nonlegal and require the expertise of human services professionals
trained in mental health services. Because human services professionals are so important to the proper functioning of the family law
system, they need to understand the basic concepts of family law.

This chapter presents an overview of contemporary family
law in the United States. Such a summary is not easy to provide
because the law is in a state of uncertainty and change—as state
legislatures pass laws relevant to the family and to the breakup of
the family, the United States Supreme Court makes decisions about
family relations, and citizens themselves are unsure of the precise
nature and effects of their relationships. For example, the differences
between marriage and nonmarital cohabitation are no longer clear.
Thus, according to Weyrauch (1980, p. 415), "One cannot reliably
predict whether a particular set of facts constitutes engagement,
marriage, business partnership, sexual cohabitation, cotenancy,
employment, or something else."

Family law is, of course, much more complex than will be
presented here. States may have different rules and procedures than

those outlined in this chapter. For the law in a specific jurisdiction, the reader should consult that jurisdiction's statutes and cases. For the law relevant to a specific legal problem, the reader should consult an attorney. Much of the material for this chapter is drawn from more extensive summaries, the two most important being *The Law of Domestic Relations* (Clark, 1968) and *Family Law in a Nutshell* (Krause, 1977). For a more thorough discussion of family law, the reader is referred to these sources. Recent articles and cases are also discussed.

This chapter will focus on four aspects of family law: marriage, parent-child relations, separation and divorce, and child custody and child support after divorce.

Marriage

Under the English common law, marriage was a contract between a man and a woman that imposed on the parties legal duties defined by the state (Strickman, 1982). The precise nature of the contemporary marital contract and the role of the state in the fulfillment of that contract is currently undergoing change (Shultz, 1982).

Most marriages are ceremonial marriages. That is, there is a ceremony conducted by a civil or religious authority. In most states there is no required procedure for the ceremony, although most states do require witnesses to the ceremony (usually two) and require that the marriage license or certificate be recorded in the appropriate civil office. In most instances a marriage valid in the state of celebration is valid in all other states. There is some question, however, about the validity of marriage if the parties were married in a state that was not their domicile and if the only reason they were married in this other state was to avoid complying with the laws of their domiciliary state (Clark, 1968). For example, if two teenagers who are not old enough to be legally married in their home state get married in a state whose laws allow people of their age to marry, the marriage may not be legal in their home state.

A second type of marriage, less frequent than ceremonial marriages, is the common law marriage. This type of marriage grew out of the English ecclesiastical courts and was particularly useful on the frontier of the American colonies, where no religious or civil authority might be present. A common law marriage is, like a ceremonial marriage, a contract between two parties. In those states that recognize common law marriages, the courts require, in addition to the contractual agreement between the two parties, that the parties present themselves to the world as husband and wife. This additional requirement of publicly assuming the marital status was presumed to prevent a fraudulent claim of common law marriage (Clark, 1968).

Because a common law marriage was seen as a contract, the parties were required to have the legal capacity to make a contract. In contract law legal capacity encompasses such requirements as having reached a minimum age and having mental competency. Today statutory requirements for marriage in most states include being of minimum age (usually sixteen or eighteen) and having mental competency. In addition, many states require that the partners be tested for venereal disease and wait for a period of usually three days between issuance of the license and the marriage ceremony (Clark, 1968). A recent review of statutory restrictions on marriage (Strickman, 1982) suggests that such requirements, which delay but do not prohibit marriage, are not unconstitutional. However, a state requirement that prohibits marriage is subject to a much higher level of constitutional scrutiny. Thus, in *Zablocki* v. *Redhail*, 434 U.S. 374 (1978), the Supreme Court held unconstitutional a Wisconsin statute that required state residents who were under a court order to support minor children not in their custody to prove, before being permitted to marry, that the children were not likely to become public charges.

The Supreme Court has characterized a person's marital choice as a fundamental right: "The freedom to marry has long been recognized as one of the vital personal rights essential to the orderly pursuit of happiness by free men" (*Loving* v. *Virginia*, 388 U.S. 1, 12 (1967)). In *Loving* the Supreme Court held that Virginia could not prohibit interracial marriages between whites and members of other races because such racial classifications violate the equal protection clause of the Fourteenth Amendment and because marriage is an essential right: "Marriage is one of the 'basic civil rights of man,' fundamental to our very existence and survival [citations omitted].

To deny this fundamental freedom on so unsupportable a basis as the racial classification embodied in these statutes, classifications so directly subversive of the principle of equality at the heart of the Fourteenth Amendment, is surely to deprive all the state's citizens of liberty without due process of law. The Fourteenth Amendment requires that the freedom of choice to marry not be restricted by invidious racial discriminations. Under our Constitution, the freedom to marry, or not to marry, a person of another race resides with the individual and cannot be infringed by the state" (388 U.S. at 12)

Given that the right to marry is fundamental, a question arises as to the extent to which states may interfere with this right (see Strickman, 1982). Prohibitions against interracial marriages are unconstitutional (*Loving* v. *Virginia*), although prohibitions against bigamy are constitutional (*Reynolds* v. *United States,* 98 U.S. 145 (1879)). Less clear is the constitutional status of restrictions against homosexual marriages, even though every state that has considered this issue has ruled that such unions can be prohibited (see, for example, *Baker* v. *Nelson,* 291 Minn. 310, 191 N.W.2d 185 (1971), appeal dismissed, 409 U.S. 810 (1972)). There may also be constitutional questions regarding states' prohibitions against marriages between individuals who are related at a degree beyond that of the nuclear family (for instance, cousins, uncle-niece, aunt-nephew) and marriages between individuals who were formerly related by marriage within a certain degree (such as brother- or sister-in-law).

In *Griswold* v. *Connecticut,* 381 U.S. 479 (1965), the Supreme Court declared that there is a right of marital privacy deriving from the First, Third, Fourth, Fifth, and Ninth Amendments to the Constitution. At issue in *Griswold* was a married couple's right to use contraceptives. Upholding that right, the Court said: "We deal with a right of privacy older than the Bill of Rights—older than our political parties, older than our school system. Marriage is a coming together for better or for worse, hopefully enduring, and intimate to the degree of being sacred. It is an association that promotes a way of life, not causes; a harmony in living, not political faiths; a bilateral loyalty, not commercial or social projects. Yet it is an association for as noble a purpose as any involved in our prior decisions" (at 486). This right of marital privacy almost certainly comprises all procreative sexual activity, but courts disagree whether nonprocreative sexual activity is included (Strickman, 1982).

Because homosexual couples cannot legitimate their relationship by marriage, they are denied a number of advantages enjoyed by married heterosexual couples simply because they have the
status of being married (Weitzman, 1981). Included in this category
are governmental benefits (like Social Security benefits) that can be
given only to a legal spouse, the interspousal privilege with regard
to testimony in court (Schultz, cited in Weitzman, 1981), and certain
property rights (such as the law in some states that requires a widow
to get a share of her husband's property). Other advantages denied to
homosexual couples are insurance coverage for the partner, family
rates on travel, and "couple" rates for entertainment (Martin and
Lyon, 1972). Because of the problems concerning insurance policies,
pension plans, and acquiring a suitable residence, a twenty-two-
year-old male in New York sought and received permission to adopt
a twenty-six-year-old male with whom he lived and had a homosexual relationship (*Matter of Adoption of Adult Anonymous*, 435
N.Y.S.2d 527 (1981)). The court based its decision on (1) the two
men's testimony that they were not trying to create a quasi-marriage
through the adult adoption statute and (2) a decision of the New
York Court of Appeals holding unconstitutional a criminal statute
proscribing consensual sodomy between adults.

Prenuptial Agreements. According to Krause (1977), a prenuptial agreement is a contract made by a couple before their marriage in order to modify certain legal results that would otherwise
occur. Most states require that the prenuptial contract be in writing.
Generally, prenuptial agreements that concern the transfer of property before the marriage are considered valid, although there may be
federal tax consequences. Similarly, prenuptial agreements relating
to the distribution of property on the death of one spouse are also
usually valid, assuming there was full disclosure of the spouse's
financial circumstances at the time of the contract and the other
spouse is fairly provided for.

Prenuptial agreements often are used to spell out how the
property will be divided—if the couple divorce at a later time. Usually, in such a case, one partner has a great deal of property and is
using the prenuptial agreement to limit the amount of property the
other partner would receive in a divorce settlement and subsequent
support obligations. Such agreements relating to divorce are often
struck down by the courts as being against the public policy of the

state, since it is believed that such agreements encourage divorce. Moreover, some courts state that the agreement does not survive past the divorce, since arguably the divorce could be seen as modifying the earlier contract.

Another type of prenuptial contract concerns obligations and duties during the marriage. These agreements often deal with such issues as sexual practices, finances, and education of the children. This type of agreement is rarely enforced because courts are reluctant to intrude in ongoing marriages.

Cohabitation Without Marriage. Although the practice of living with someone of the opposite sex without being married is an old one, it appears to be a more common phenomenon today, both in the United States and in Europe (Glendon, 1980). Several reasons have been offered to explain this increase. According to Lavori (1976, pp. 14–15), these reasons include (1) "a desire to avoid the sex-stereotyped allocation of roles associated with marriage"; (2) "a feeling that marriage is unnecessary or irrelevant if no children are involved"; (3) "a lack of readiness to commit oneself"; (4) "a philosophical conclusion that you cannot predict what you will feel in the future and that you should not make promises you don't know you will be able to or will even want to keep"; (5) "a conscientious objection to marriage"; (6) "a desire to avoid the expense and involvement of a possible divorce"; and (7) "a belief that legal sanction of a relationship is irrelevant and meaningless." In addition, Bruch (1976) suggests that people today might be more likely to cohabit without marriage because they perceive shortcomings in traditional marriage that are not present with a private commitment and because nonmarital cohabitation is increasingly accepted by society.

Corresponding to this increase in the number of nonmarital couples living together has been a trend for individuals to go to court when the relationship ends to divide property that was obtained during the period of cohabitation (Crutchfield, 1981; Weitzman, 1974). For example, in *Marvin* v. *Marvin*, 18 Cal. 3d 660, 134 Cal. Rptr. 815, 557 P.2d 106 (1976), the California Supreme Court held that a cohabiting couple could make an express contract affecting their property rights, as long as sex was not part of the consideration for the agreement.. Not all states have followed this decision, however (see, for example, *Rehak* v. *Mathis*, 239 Gov. 541,

238 S.E.2d 81 (1977)). A general trend in this area is to incorporate concepts from other areas of the law to deal with the increasingly common fact of dividing the property obtained while the couple were cohabiting without being married. Such borrowed concepts include implied contract, implied partnership, and constructive trust (Douthwaite, 1979; Hennessey, 1980). A number of other legal areas are affected by nonmarital cohabitation, including employment, welfare, insurance, and tort liability (Douthwaite, 1979).

Another question currently being considered in the courts is whether unmarried couples have the same rights against third persons that married couples have. In particular, the issue raised in several courts is whether an unmarried partner has a cause of action against a third party for loss of consortium—a concept that includes sex, society, and services. It has been argued that consortium rights for unmarried couples should be recognized by the courts (Meade, 1981). Several constitutional arguments that would support this position have been presented elsewhere ("Fornication, Cohabitation, and the Constitution," 1978).

Spouse Abuse. The remedies available to an abused spouse are often quite limited (see Fleming, 1979). At the time of the assault, the abused spouse can call the police. However, because the abused spouse often later decides not to press charges, the police are understandably reluctant to arrest the abusing person. Recent training sessions for police, however, have increased their understanding of the problem and their willingness to make the arrest. If the abused spouse waits before calling the police, he or she will have to swear out a warrant for the arrest of the abusing spouse. Generally, the warrant must state the crime, the location of the crime, and the time the crime was committed. But even assuming that the case is eventually brought to trial, a severe punishment is very unlikely to be given. More common results are that (1) the case will be dismissed after the assaulting spouse promises not to beat his or her spouse again; (2) the court orders the assaulting spouse to stay away from the abused spouse; or (3) the abusing spouse is found guilty of assault and given a minor punishment, usually a fine (State Bar of Georgia, 1981). Rarely is a spouse abuser sentenced to serve time in jail. In sum, an abused spouse can seek aid through the criminal justice system, but such aid is likely to be of limited long-term value.

Another alternative for the abused spouse is to ask a state court to issue a protective order on behalf of the battered spouse. About three fourths of the states have passed legislation authorizing protective orders (Schechter, 1981). A protective decree orders the alleged abusing spouse to stop harassing, threatening, or beating the victim. This court order can be issued in many states on an emergency basis, without the presence of the alleged abuser at the hearing (*ex parte*), if there is a high probability of immediate danger. If such an *ex parte* order is issued, however, the alleged abuser is entitled to notice of a subsequent full hearing on the issue. According to Schechter (1981), the scope of these protective orders varies from state to state. In some states the victim must be a spouse, whereas in other states the victim may be a former spouse, another relative, or a nonrelated household member. In some states actual physical harm must have occurred before the order can be issued, whereas in other states a court can issue a protective order if there have been threats or attempted assaults. At the minimum, an abuser who violates the court order is in contempt and can be jailed for this violation, although the court may be reluctant to do so. About half of the states provide supportive services for battered spouses, usually in the form of emergency shelters for battered women (Schechter, 1981). Schechter argues that protective orders and emergency shelters are inadequate responses to the severity of the problem.

Of relevance to mental health professionals is their possible role as expert witnesses on the question of the "battered-woman syndrome." Recently, battered women charged with homicide of their mates have begun to claim self-defense even if the homicide did not occur as part of a battering incident. To support their claim that the homicide was self-defense, many of these women have called on experts on the "battered-woman syndrome." Lenore Walker (1979), probably the best known of the researchers on this question, characterizes the battered-woman syndrome as a cycle of three phases. In the first phase, the tension-building stage, minor battering incidents occur. In the second phase, the acute battering phase, the husband behaves in an uncontrollably violent manner. In the third phase, kindness and contrite loving, the husband is repentant and unusually attentive. In general, expert testimony is admissible (1) if it involves a subject that is "beyond the ken of the average layman";

(2) if the witness has sufficient skill, knowledge, or experience in that field or calling as to make it appear that his opinion or inference will probably aid the trier of fact in his search for the truth"; and (3) if "the state of the pertinent art or scientific knowledge" permits an expert to assert a reasonable opinion (Cleary, 1972, pp. 29–31).

The first case in which the testimony of an expert on battered-woman syndrome was permitted was *Ibn-Tamas* v. *United States* 407 A.2d 626 (D.C. 1979). In that decision the appellate court held that the testimony of the expert (Dr. Walker) would provide the jury with background information and would not deal with the ultimate issue in the case. Moreover, the court held that the testimony Dr. Walker would have given satisfied the requirements of expert testimony.

Decisions subsequent to *Ibn-Tamas* have not been consistent, with some state supreme courts allowing and other supreme courts disallowing the proffered expert testimony. One reason that courts may be reluctant to admit such testimony is that it may seem to be supporting homicide as a reasonable reaction to wife abuse (Cross, 1982). One commentator has suggested, however, that there are several safeguards against the abuse of such expert testimony, including the judge's discretion regarding the decision to admit or exclude the evidence and the opportunity of the prosecution to discredit the testimony of the expert (Thar, 1982).

Parent-Child Relations

Initiating the Parent-Child Relationship

According to Krause (1977), the creation of the parent-child relationship encompasses four topics: abortion, legitimacy, paternity, and adoption. These topics will be briefly discussed below. A fifth topic, surrogate parenthood, will also be presented.

Abortion. The most important case on the subject of abortion is the Supreme Court decision in *Roe* v. *Wade*, 410 U.S. 113 (1973), in which the Court examined the state's interests in regulating abortion. The Court held that during the first three months of pregnancy the mother's right to privacy is paramount and the state has no

compelling interest that outweighs this right; for the second trimester of pregnancy, the state has a compelling interest in the mother's health and therefore can establish reasonable regulations for the
abortion procedure; for the third trimester, the state has a compelling interest in safeguarding the life of the fetus. Thus, according to
the Supreme Court, the state can regulate and even ban abortion. In
Doe v. *Bolton*, 410 U.S. 179, rehearing denied, 410 U.S. 959 (1973), a
companion case to *Roe* v. *Wade*, the Supreme Court declared unconstitutional a Georgia statute that was too restrictive of abortion.
Among other things, this law required that abortions could be performed only in accredited hospitals and only after approval by a
hospital abortion committee. In 1975 the Supreme Court ruled that
a state could not prohibit advertising for abortions (*Bigelow* v. *Virginia*, 421 U.S. 809 (1975)). In a later decision, the Court decided
that consent from a woman's husband or parent is not required
before an abortion can be performed (*Planned Parenthood of
Missouri* v. *Danforth*, 428 U.S. 52 (1976)). In a more recent decision,
the Supreme Court held constitutional Utah's statute requiring
physicians, prior to performing an abortion, to notify the parents of
an unmarried, immature minor woman living with her parents (*H.
L.* v. *Matheson*, 450 U.S. 398 (1981)). The Court found several
significant state interests served by the statute, including encourag-
ing pregnant minors to seek advice from their parents, preserving
the integrity of the family, and protecting the adolescent.

    Legitimacy. A second topic relating to the establishment of
the parent-child relationship is legitimacy. A legitimate child is one
"who has a full legal relationship with both of its parents" (Krause,
1977, p. 119). Usually, marital status of the parents is the major
determinant of legitimacy. Because of the importance of legitimacy
and of stable family relations, the law presumes that a child born to
a married woman is the child of her husband.

    Until fairly recently, illegitimate children were denied sup-
port, inheritance, and wrongful death benefits that legitimate children received without legal problems. Although there is still some
discrimination, much of it was reduced by Supreme Court opinions
striking down legislation denying benefits to nonmarital children.
For example, in *Weber* v. *Aetna Casualty & Surety Co.*, 406 U.S. 164
(1972), the Supreme Court found no justifying state interest for deny-

ing workers' compensation benefits to the dead father's unacknowledged illegitimate children. In *Mills* v. *Habluetzel*, 102 S. Ct. 1549 (1982), the Supreme Court declared unconstitutional a Texas statute requiring that paternity suits must be brought before the child is one year old. The Supreme Court held that the statute denied illegitimate children the equal protection of the law, since it denied them the adequate opportunity to obtain support that legitimate children had. The relatively short time period of one year was held not to be substantially related to the state's interest in avoiding trials for fraudulent claims or claims that are weak because of the passage of time and the consequent loss of evidence. Although there are some questions about the current status of the law with regard to illegitimacy, "the fair conclusion to be drawn from the Supreme Court's decisions is that state and federal law may not discriminate between legitimate and nonmarital children in any significant substantive area, other than inheritance" (Krause, 1977, p. 134).

Paternity. States employ a variety of proceedings to determine the issue of paternity. In some states paternity is settled in a civil proceeding; in other states it is dealt with as an adjunct to a criminal proceeding. Because of the different proceedings, different standards of proof are used. In paternity suits a judgment that the man is the child's father usually includes an order for the father to pay periodic support for the child and may include an order for the father to pay the mother's expenses for the pregnancy and birth and her expenses in prosecuting the paternity suit (Krause, 1977).

Adoption. Clark (1968, p. 602) defines adoption as "the legal process by which a child acquires parents other than his natural parents and parents acquire a child other than a natural child." The rights and duties between the natural parents and the child are ended and replaced by rights and duties between the adoptive parents and the child. All states permit adoption of children and minors (Krause, 1977).

Most adoptions of children by nonrelatives take place through public and private adoption agencies, although private adoptions are legal in some states. In many states some contact with a public child welfare agency is required before a legal adoption can take place. The extent of the required contact with the agency varies. Some states require merely that parents notify the agency of the prospective adoption. In other states the agency investigates the prospective parents, and in still others it totally controls the adoption procedure. Criminal prosecution is possible if an adoption occurs in these states without the requisite agency involvement, particularly if the natural parent receives compensation beyond what is required for medical, legal, and appropriate administrative expenses (Krause, 1977).

In spite of the threat of criminal prosecution, there is an extensive black market in babies for adoption (Podolski, 1975). Moreover, in some states couples place advertisements in newspapers, stating their desire to adopt a child without going through adoption agencies ("Couples Place Want Ads. . . ," 1981). A shortage of "desirable" babies (usually meaning healthy, white children) is the reason for the increase in independent adoptions. In addition, it is often more advantageous for the natural mother to go through a private than a public adoption of her child. First, the procedure is often less demeaning in the private than in the public situation. Second, if the mother gives her child up through public adoption, she will not be reimbursed for her medical and living expenses, as is often the case with private adoptions. Finally, with a private adoption, the natural mother can meet the adopting parents, a practice that is usually impossible with public adoptions.

When feasible, courts prefer adoptions by parents who are of the same religious and racial group as the child (Simon and Altstein, 1977). Generally, such a view is seen as being in the child's best interests. Although most states permit adoption by single persons, courts prefer adoptions by couples, the presumption being that couples can provide a more natural environment for a child than a single person can (Krause, 1977). Moreover, courts probably prefer couples of child-bearing age to those who are older. However, these preferences in race, religion, marital status, and age are balanced against the court's desire to find homes for children who are difficult to place (for example, older, handicapped, or minority group children).

The law is presently not clear regarding the right of a nonmarital father in proceedings by others to adopt his children (Bedwell, 1979). In *Stanley* v. *Illinois*, 406 U.S. 645 (1972), the Supreme Court held that an unwed father was entitled to notice and a hearing concerning the disposition of his children. This decision may have resulted from the fact that the father had lived with the children in a *de facto* family unit (Krause, 1977). Many state courts interpreted *Stanley* to mean that an unmarried father's consent is needed for a valid adoption (Kern, 1979). Two more recent Supreme Court decisions, however, suggest that there are limits to the power nonmarried fathers have over the adoption procedure, if, for example, the unwed father had never had and had never sought custody or did not maintain frequent contact with his children (*Quilloin* v. *Walcott*, 434 U.S. 246, (1978); *Caban* v. *Mohammed*, 441 U.S. 380 (1979)).

Surrogate Parenthood. In recent years there has been an increase in the number of instances where only one member of the married couple is the natural parent of their child. In the case of artificial insemination of the mother from a donor who is not the husband, the child probably will be presumed to be legitimate, since it was born to a married woman. Although some courts have not reached this conclusion (see Krause, 1977), one court, at least, has held that artificial insemination does not constitute adultery if the husband consents to the procedure (*People* v. *Sorensen*, 66 Cal. Rptr. 7, 437 P.2d 495 (1968)).

A phenomenon of the past five years that is becoming increasingly more common is the use of a surrogate mother to bear the child of a father whose wife is infertile. The major obstacles to this procedure are the costs, the possible criminal penalties, and the unenforceability of the contracts between the parties. The costs are based on the surrogate mother's medical expenses (including prepregnancy medical and psychological screening) and on compensation to the surrogate mother for her pregnancy. Paying the surrogate mother for her services may make the procedure a crime, since most states have enacted statutes outlawing payments to parents for their consent to an adoption of their child. However, these statutes may well be invalid because they are vague and may violate constitutional guarantees of privacy (Handel and Sherwyn, 1982). The final obstacle facing the prospective parents is the possibility that the surrogate mother will decide to keep the child. To overcome this possible problem, lawyers have designed contracts signed by the prospective parents and the surrogate mother before the pregnancy

(Brophy, 1982). The best guess, however, is that these contracts are unenforceable (Handel and Sherwyn, 1982).

Parental Rights and Responsibilities

Generally, if the parents do not violate the state's neglect, dependency, and abuse laws, they have the right to custody of their children and the right to make decisions affecting the welfare of their children. Traditionally, most states statutorily placed the responsibility of child support on the father; the mother was liable only if the father defaulted or died (Krause, 1977), although most states now place responsibility on both parents (Foster and Freed, 1980).

Challenges to parental decision making regarding the welfare of the child have focused on issues of medical care (Hirschberg, 1980) and education (*Wisconsin* v. *Yoder*, 406 U.S. 205 (1972)). The difficult cases on medical care have been concerned with providing medical care to a child of parents who refuse on religious grounds to provide the needed treatment. For example, in cases where the child needs blood transfusions, a procedure opposed by members of certain religious sects, courts have appointed a guardian for the child. This guardian is ordered to consent to the blood transfusions and other necessary care (Krause, 1977). More difficult cases concern parental refusal to provide medical treatment that would be desirable for the child (for example, correcting a harelip) but that is not necessary to save the child's life. In a New York case in which this issue was raised, the court did not order the surgery (*In re Seiferth*, 309 N.Y. 80, 127 N.E. 2d 820 (1955); see discussion in Goldstein, Freud, and Solnit, 1979). Cases on parental decision making with regard to the child's education have concerned parents' rights to withhold their children from public schools after a certain age, in violation of states' compulsory attendance laws. In *Wisconsin* v. *Yoder*, the Supreme Court held that Amish children would not be required to attend public schools after completing the eighth grade. The decision was based on the parents' interests in providing religious training for their children, the preservation of the Amish religion, and the limited infringement on the state's interests. The Court did not consider, however, the children's interests and preferences on the issue, an omission noted by Justice Douglas in his partial dissent (Krause, 1977).

The major limitation on parents' treatment of their children are state statutes on neglect, dependency, and abuse. Neglect and dependency are defined as a failure to provide the necessary support, education, and medical care for the child. Usually, only the most acute cases are brought to the attention of the courts by child welfare agencies, so that generally there is little disagreement about the necessity of state intervention (Krause, 1977). Many of these acute cases concern child abuse. Child abuse is a major problem in the United States, with over 40,000 cases reported annually. A recent report by the U.S. Centers for Disease Control indicates that homicide is one of the top five causes of death in children aged one to seventeen; two thirds of the homicides are committed by parents or acquaintances and most can be classified as child abuse (Green, 1982). Most states have enacted statutes requiring certain professionals to report cases of suspected child abuse (Sussman, 1975). Originally, these statutes included only physicians. Later, however, other groups (including psychologists and social workers) were included, so that cases could be detected before the harm became so great as to require the services of a physician and so that the notion that all citizens have a duty to aid defenseless children would be reinforced (Gulley, 1977). Under these statutes reporters are generally granted immunity from tort actions for their good-faith reporting of suspected child abuse. Some make the failure to report suspected cases a misdemeanor offense, but there is some question about how effective these criminal statutes are (Schechter, 1981). One reason for the limited effectiveness of such statutes is that a therapist who learns of the abuse in a relationship protected by confidentiality is faced with a serious ethical problem (see Dickens, 1978).

If a court finds that a parent abused or neglected his or her children, several options are available to it (Krause, 1977). First, it may remove the children from the custody of the parents, temporarily or permanently. Second, it may appoint a temporary or permanent guardian (an individual or a state or private agency) who takes responsibility for the child's well-being. Depending on the facts of the case, the parent may or may not lose his parental rights, even with the appointment of a guardian. In severe cases of abuse or neglect, however, the state may initiate proceedings to terminate the parent's rights to custody of the children (see Browning and Weiner, 1979; Muench and Levy, 1979) and to permit the children to be adopted (Chemerinsky, 1979).

Before the state can permanently sever parents' custodial rights, however, the state must prove its allegations by clear and convincing evidence (*Santosky* v. *Kramer*, 102 S. Ct. 1388 (1982)). In *Santosky* the Supreme Court rejected New York's "fair preponderance of the evidence" standard in the termination proceeding because it denied the parents due process of law. The Court's belief in *Santosky* was that a fairly high standard of proof was necessary because the decision to end parents' custodial rights over their children is such an important one. In some cases of abuse or neglect, a criminal penalty may be imposed on the parent. For example, in *Jones* v. *Helms*, 452 U.S. 412 (1981), the United State Supreme Court upheld a Georgia law that made a parent's willful abandonment of a child a misdemeanor if the parent remained in the state but a felony if the parent left the state.

In child protective hearings in most states, children are represented by an independent agent (an attorney or a lay guardian *ad litem*) appointed by the court, who represents the child rather than the parents or the state (Perales, cited in Besharov, 1982). It is usually in the child's best interests for a court proceeding to take place, since prior screening will eliminate most of the cases that do not belong in court. But Besharov (1982) suggests that the child's interests might dictate a dismissal of court proceedings if (1) there is insufficient evidence of abuse or neglect, (2) the child is in no danger of further harm, (3) the parents voluntarily accept treatment services, (4) the harm from state intervention outweighs the dangers posed by the parents, or (5) a mature child asks that the petition be dismissed.

The Supreme Court has held that in proceedings to terminate custody indigent parents do not have a constitutional right to counsel under the due process clause of the Fourteenth Amendment (*Lassiter* v. *Department of Social Services of Durham County*, 452 U.S. 18, (1981)). The decision was based on a consideration of the private interests of the parent (total and irrevocable loss of parental rights), the state's interests (an accurate decision made as economically as possible), and the risk of error (an uneducated parent would not know courtroom procedure or the relevant evidence law). It was also based, at least in part, on the facts of this particular hearing: no expert witnesses testified; no particularly difficult points of law were involved; no allegations of abuse or neglect on which criminal charges could be based were made; and the parent in this case had not attended an earlier hearing, a fact that suggested a lack of interest in the care of her child. The Court concluded that whether indigent parents are entitled to the appointment of counsel must be made on a case-by-case basis by the trial court, subject to review by appellate courts. However, the Court did note and praise thirty-three states and the District of Columbia, which by statute provide for counsel in all parental termination hearings. Although on its face the *Lassiter* decision appears to reject indigent parents' right to counsel in termination proceedings, the decision can also be read as an expansion of the right to counsel in noncriminal proceedings (such as termination of custody), particularly in cases where severe abuse or neglect is alleged (Besharov, 1981).

The question of when the state should become involved in parent-child relations is a difficult one. Goldstein, Freud, and Solnit (1979) argue that the state should intervene only when there have been gross failures of parental care, since state intervention may make the situation worse. Gross failures would include disappearance without making provisions for the child's care, conviction of a sexual offense against the child, and inflicting or attempting to inflict severe bodily injuries on the child. Moreover, Goldstein and his associates argue that vaguely defined concepts such as "unfit home" and "emotional neglect" should not be used as bases for state intervention because such concepts do not give adequate warning to parents and provide little control over participants in the child placement process.

Legal Termination of Marriage

Not all marriages are successful. Indeed, recent statistics indicate that about 11 percent of all men and about 19 percent of all women who have ever been married are divorced or separated (U.S. Bureau of the Census, 1981). Although most unsuccessful marriages end by divorce, they may also be terminated by annulment. Moreover, often as a prelude to divorce, the parties may first undergo a legal separation.

Annulment. Annulment, which grew out of canon law, is a termination of marriage based on conditions existing at the time of the marriage that made the marriage invalid from the beginning (Clark, 1968). Common grounds for annulment include factors affecting the parties' ability to enter a legal contract (such as insanity, immaturity, fraud, and duress) and factors about the parties' marriage that are proscribed by law (such as incest; affinity, which refers to a relationship through marriage; and bigamy).

Legal Separation. Until recently, separation agreements have been looked on with disfavor by the courts (Sharp, 1981). Historically, courts opposed them because at common law the wife's identity was merged with that of the husband, and a person could not contract with himself. More recent judicial objections to separation agreements have concerned courts' reluctance to enforce an agreement made "in contemplation of divorce," since to enforce such agreements would encourage divorce and the state's policy is to encourage marriage. In addition, courts refused to enforce agreements that altered "the essential elements" of marriage, the most relevant being the husband's duty to support the wife. A separation agreement that attempted to remove the required duty to support was void (Sharp, 1981). In most states, according to Sharp, judicial hostility to separation agreements no longer exists. For example, the Supreme Court of Georgia in *Sanders* v. *Colwell*, 248 Ga. 376, 283 S.E.2d 461, (1981) overruled an earlier judgment by holding that agreements in contemplation of divorce and dealing with such issues as alimony, division of property, child custody, and child support are not invalid.

The laws regarding support during a legal separation are not uniform across the fifty states, since these laws have different origins (Krause, 1977). Some states continued the English notion of limited divorce ("divorce from bed and board"), which granted divorce without the right to remarry. In most cases the grounds for this type of divorce were the same as those for full divorce. In states that abolished divorce from bed and board, laws were passed providing for separate maintenance; that is, support for a spouse living apart from the other. Generally, these laws required specific reasons for the separation, and some provided that only "innocent" spouses were entitled to separate maintenance. A third group of states retained the concept of limited divorce and added a statutory separate maintenance, which did not require any specific grounds. Finally, some states abolished limited divorce, and the courts created an equitable remedy to enforce obligations of marital support when the parties did not live together. Because of the confusion surrounding separate maintenance and limited divorce, there have been calls for reform (Clark, 1968).

Divorce. There are over 1.1 million divorces annually, affecting approximately the same number of children (U.S. Bureau of the Census, 1981). In contrast to marriage, which is governed by relatively simple administrative procedures, divorce depends on more complex questions of fact and requires more complicated judicial mechanisms (Strickman, 1982). Although the Supreme Court has not yet considered the constitutionality of states' standards for granting divorces (see "Developments in the Law," 1980), it has considered the question of procedural access to divorce.

In *Boddie* v. *Connecticut,* 401 U.S. 371 (1971), the Supreme Court considered the constitutionality of fees for court costs and service of process in divorce cases. The case was brought by indigent plaintiffs who claimed that their inability to pay the required costs denied them due process. The court agreed. According to Strickman (1982, p. 311), there were two reasons for the Court's judgment: "the fundamentality of marriage" (and presumably the choice to dissolve it), and "unique procedural situation of divorce as the only private dispute not legally resolvable without the active intervention of state judicial machinery."

Under traditional divorce law, an innocent party could receive a divorce if he or she could prove that the other party was at fault. The original "fault" grounds were adultery and physical cruelty. Later, "fault" was expanded to include habitual drunkenness, willful desertion, mental cruelty, and conviction of a felony. Because divorce would be granted only if the complaining party was innocent of fault, divorce was barred if both parties were at fault. This reasoning, called the "doctrine of recrimination," was based on the notion that divorce was an action in equity requiring "clean hands." In a contested divorce, the party being sued had only to prove that the complaining party was also at fault in order to block the divorce action. Proof of collusion between the two parties was also sufficient to bar the action for divorce. This bar was based on the state's interests in protecting marriages.

One of the most significant trends in recent years has been the move from requiring fault in divorce actions to "no-fault" divorce (Hennessey, 1980). Some form of no-fault divorce is permitted in forty-eight states (Illinois and South Dakota are the exceptions), although many of the states also permit a divorce to be granted on traditional fault grounds (Freed and Foster, 1981). The trend toward no-fault divorce gained impetus with the Uniform Marriage and Divorce Act, a model Act by the National Conference of Commissioners on Uniform State Laws. Section 305 of this model Act proposed that a court could grant a divorce if it found that "the marriage is irretrievably broken." According to the commentary on Section 305, this finding was to be based on "the petitioner's reasons for seeking a dissolution of the marriage and the prospect that the parties may achieve a reconciliation" (National Conference of Commissioners on Uniform State Laws, 1971, p. 228). Most states that have adopted the "irretrievably broken" ground for divorce require evidence to support the court's finding (Freed and Foster, 1981). That is, mere consent of the parties is not sufficient.

There was initial opposition to no-fault divorces, because it was feared that the number of divorces would increase dramatically if divorces were relatively easy to obtain. To reduce the possibility of a large increase in divorces and to ensure that only those couples whose marriages were no longer viable would be granted divorces, many states enacted laws designed to slow down the divorce process. One such procedure, adopted in many states, is a mandatory minimum waiting period after the filing of the divorce action before the court is able to grant the divorce. A second procedure available in many states to minimize the number of hasty and possibly ill-considered divorces is court-ordered counseling and conciliation. Both the minimum waiting period and the required counseling are probably permissible under the Constitution because the state has an important interest in preserving marriages ("Developments in the Law," 1980). Although there were initial fears that no-fault divorce laws would increase the rate of divorce, a recent analysis found no systematic relationship between the two (Sepler, 1981).

The required counseling and conciliation sessions are conducted either by private counselors chosen by the parties or by counselors affiliated with the court system. For example, an Iowa statute allows judges to choose from a variety of possible counselors: "the domestic relations division of the court, if established, public or private marriage counselors, family service agencies, community health centers, physicians, and clergymen" (Iowa Code Ann. sec. 598.16 (West)). The major advantages of having the conciliation efforts attached to the court are that the judge generally can be assured that the counselors are competent and the couples are probably more motivated to give the conciliation effort a chance (Orlando, 1978).

Two successful reconciliation programs are the Los Angeles Conciliation Court and the Edmonton (Alberta) Family Court Conciliation Service. Both programs have a number of similarities (Scaletta, 1981): (1) they are of short duration (usually three sessions or fewer): (2) they are voluntary and free of charge; (3) they are integrated into the formal court system; (4) they are strictly confidential; (5) they are available at any time during the divorce proceedings; and (6) they are intended to supplement and augment existing services and the legal system. Conciliation services like those in Los Angeles and Edmonton may be valuable because they reduce rancor and perhaps restore some good feelings between the divorcing parties (Scaletta, 1981). This reduction in ill will might save money in the long run, for the clients and the court system, by reducing continued litigation (Orlando, 1978). Some individuals, however, have questioned the value of required conciliation given the expense, low probability of success, and shortage of trained personnel (see Krause, 1977).

State statutes that delay but do not deny access to divorce are almost certainly constitutional, assuming that the delay is reasonable and the state has legitimate interests protected by the requirements (Strickman, 1982). For example, in *Sosna* v. *Iowa*, 419 U.S. 393 (1975), the Supreme Court upheld Iowa's requirement of a one-year durational residency in the state for a divorce action on the grounds that the requirement could be justified in several legitimate ways other than budgetary considerations or administrative convenience (for example, making sure that the party seeking divorce had sufficient contact with the state before important questions such as child custody were decided by the state's courts).

Although most divorces are handled by lawyers for the two parties, the adversary role has been criticized as being counter to the ultimate interests of the clients and even the lawyers themselves (Steinberg, 1976). It has also been suggested (for example, by Haynes, 1978, and Saposnek, 1983) that much of the hostility accompanying a divorce could be reduced if a mediator, rather than two adversaries, were employed. Since lawyers are trained to be advocates in an adversary proceeding, they may have a tendency to heighten existing conflict—a tendency exacerbated by the fact that they receive information from only one side in the proceeding and by the fact that they generally receive higher fees when a long period of litigation is required (Kressel and others, 1978).

Mediation is a process in which a neutral party tries to help the divorcing couple solve specific problems through compromise (Irving, 1981, p. 77). Mediation can be conducted to resolve some or all of the couple's disagreements, although visitation, custody, and maintenance issues are usually the main focus. The two primary modes of mediation are through a court or through someone in private practice. Although the number of mediation services affiliated with courts is increasing, probably the best-known court-based mediation service is the one affiliated with the Los Angeles Conciliation Court. In general, the mediation consists of only a few sessions, usually five or six. Should mediation prove unsuccessful, the parties can choose advisory arbitration, binding arbitration, or the adversary system in the courts (Irving, p. 92). Evidence from Canadian courts suggests that the system can reduce the number of cases that go to trial. For example, Irving (p. 184) reports that in Toronto 70 percent of the families referred to mediation reached an agreement without consent and that, of these, 80 percent fully or partially kept the original agreement.

In court-based mediation the mediator is assigned to the couple; in private mediation the couple can choose their own mediator. The private mediator may mediate alone or with someone else. There may or may not be an advisory attorney present. One of the best-known private mediation systems is that of Coogler (1978), who founded the Family Mediation Association in Atlanta in 1975.

Coogler advocates what he calls structured mediation to resolve the issues of division of marital property, alimony, child custody, and child support. With structured mediation the husband and wife agree in advance about which issues are to be decided, how information will be collected and examined, and how impasses will be resolved. Coogler suggests that structured mediation is appropriate for individuals who want to be treated with respect and want their partner to be treated with the same respect, who have no investment in "winning" the divorce settlement, and who still care about each other. A couple who would like to enter structured mediation sign a contract with the mediation center. The following points are included in this contract: the appointment of a marital mediator, the obligations of the advisory attorney, and the deposit of a mediation fee (which covers the cost of ten hours of mediation time and the fees of the advisory attorney). The marital mediator, who is appointed from a panel of trained mediators, maintains control over the negotiations by deciding the order in which issues will be discussed and when the parties will move on to another issue. In addition, at the end the parties may call on the mediator to evaluate the fairness and workability of the settlement agreement. In most cases the mediator finds the agreement to be a fair one; but even if he or she does not, the parties can still accept it and be bound by it. The primary role of the advisory attorney is to draft the parties' agreement in terms that they can understand.

According to Coogler (1978), divorced couples who enter mediation are more likely to be committed to their decisions and the process is likely to be cheaper than the traditional adversarial divorce (see Winks, 1981). However, divorce mediation will not be satisfactory for every divorcing couple. As prerequisites for mediation, the couple must want to resolve the often unidentified issues between them, and the situation must be such that third-party intervention will be helpful (Charney, 1982). Charney has doubts about the usefulness of mediation if the parties are unable to agree about basic issues like child rearing. Moreover, Charney argues that a mediator trained only in the social sciences cannot adequately advise the parties about proposed property settlements and other financial arrangements. If the mediator were a lawyer, though, this problem would be overcome (Winks, 1981).

Exactly what role the family lawyer should take regarding family problems, particularly divorce, is not clear. Steinberg (1980) has suggested a "marriage" between lawyers and family therapists. According to Steinberg, such collaboration would be likely to lead to, among other advantages, timely referrals and increased professional creativity. Although there is a trend for family lawyers increasingly to counsel their clients on nonlegal matters (Hancock, 1981; Mussehl, 1977), some writers argue that attorneys, especially divorce attorneys, should limit their role to advocacy. For example, Callner (1977), in his defense of the traditional role of advocate, argues that attorneys usually are not professionally competent in psychological counseling; and, even if they were, they could not counsel both spouses, since to do so would be in violation of the *Code of Professional Responsibility* (American Bar Association, 1971). What emerges from this controversy is that the precise boundaries of the family lawyer's role are not clear.

Alimony. The concept of alimony was taken from the English ecclesiastical courts, which permitted married men and women to live apart but not to end the marriage ("divorce from bed and board"). Because the husband controlled the wife's property, the courts had to recognize the husband's duty to support the wife through alimony. The logic of adapting the English use of alimony support (which was used in situations where the couple were married but separated) to the United States (where it is used when the couple are no longer married) has been questioned, particularly in light of women's increased ability to find employment (Clark, 1968). Other commentators argue, however, that it is not unjust to require continued support from the economically stronger ex-spouse to the weaker ex-spouse (Krause, 1977).

In most cases the economically stronger ex-spouse is the husband. This fact is consistent with the common law concept that the husband had a duty to support his wife but that the wife had no reciprocal obligation to support her husband. This common law duty was extended to alimony; husbands but not wives had a duty to pay alimony. A few years ago, Alabama had a statute that essentially restated the common law regarding alimony. In *Orr* v. *Orr*, 440 U.S. 268 (1979), the Supreme Court held that this gender-based classification was unconstitutional because the state could easily provide individual hearings on the question of relative financial conditions rather than rely on this overbroad classification.

Although headlines are sometimes made by alimony awards, about 86 percent of all divorces do not involve alimony (U.S. Bureau of the Census, 1981). Moreover, the average amount of alimony awarded is relatively small (Weitzman and Dixon, 1980). Even among those that do involve alimony, many are settled by negotiation in separation agreements (Krause, 1977). Among those states that permit alimony (only Texas does not; see Connell, 1981), judges usually have no clear guidelines beyond considering the "wife's needs" and the "husband's ability to pay." Some statutory guidance for the amount of the alimony award is provided in thirty states, although no factor listed in these statutes is common to all the states (Connell, 1981). Section 308 of the Uniform Marriage and Divorce Act (UMDA) provides a general summary of these laws (National Conference of Commissioners on Uniform State Laws, 1971, pp. 233–234):

> The court may grant a maintenance order for either spouse, only if it finds that the spouse seeking maintenance:
>
> (1) lacks sufficient property to provide for his reasonable needs; and
>
> (2) is unable to support himself through appropriate employment or is the custodian of a child whose condition or circumstances make it appropriate that the custodian not be required to seek employment outside the home.
>
> (b) The maintenance order shall be in amounts and for periods of time the court deems just, without regard to marital misconduct, and after considering all relevant factors including:
>
> (1) the financial resources of the party seeking maintenance, including marital property apportioned to him, his ability to meet his needs independently, and the extent to which a provision for support of a child living with the party includes a sum for that party as custodian;
>
> (2) the time necessary to acquire sufficient education or training to enable the party seeking maintenance to find appropriate employment;

(3) the standard of living established during the marriage;

(4) the duration of the marriage;

(5) the age and the physical and emotional condition of the spouse seeking maintenance; and

(6) the ability of the spouse from whom maintenance is sought to meet his needs while meeting those of the spouse seeking maintenance.

The role that "fault" plays in the alimony award varies from state to state. Some completely prohibit it; others ban it in a more limited way (for example, prohibiting alimony only when the spouse seeking alimony has committed adultery); others consider fault as one of several factors in the question of alimony (Krause, 1977). In no-fault divorce states, the role of fault is often not considered in the determination of alimony. This position is consistent with Section 308 of the UMDA, which states that the award will be made "without regard to marital misconduct." In other no-fault states, the cause of separation is admissible with regard to alimony. One commentator in Georgia has suggested that the use of fault with regard to the determination of alimony means that the state has "gone full cycle from fault divorce and no-fault alimony to no-fault divorce and fault alimony" (House, 1982, pp. 3-7).

In their article examining the impact of no-fault divorce on alimony in California, Weitzman and Dixon (1980) reported a decline in the percentage of spouses awarded alimony (including token awards of $1 per month or per year), a decline in the percentage of awards to spouses in short marriages but much less of a decline in long marriages, a decline in the use of fault as a significant factor affecting the award of alimony, and a decline in the percentage of permanent or open-ended alimony awards (reflecting the belief that alimony should be used to obtain education and training leading to self-sufficiency). Contrary to their expectations, Weitzman and Dixon found a decline in the percentage of awards to mothers of young children, probably because these women tended to be younger, in shorter marriages, and married to men with lower incomes.

Generally, required alimony payments end with the death of the supporting ex-spouse, and in many states they end when the supported ex-spouse remarries. In some states alimony ends on proof that the supported ex-spouse is cohabiting with a person of the opposite sex.

Increasingly, the trend among the states has been away from alimony and toward a division of property. That is, alimony is being seen as a supplement to the division of property on divorce.

Division of Property. The division of property after a divorce is much too complex to be fully discussed here. In part, this complexity is due to the laws of marital property operating during the marriage. Two basic systems of marital property rights operate in the United States today, common law property and community property (Krause, 1977). In common law property states, each spouse owns separately the property that he or she brought into the marriage and that came to him or her during the marriage by gift, inheritance, personal income, or interest and dividends from separate property. Because the husband is more likely to work than is the wife and, even if the wife works, is likely to make more money than the wife, in most marriages in separate property states the husband is likely to have more separate property than does the wife. Problems can arise when property is bought during the marriage with money from both spouses but title is taken in the name of only one or when property is bought with money from only one spouse but title is taken in the name of both. On divorce, the courts often have difficulty deciding who owns which property, a question they attempt to answer by reconstructing the parties' intent at the time the property was purchased. To create a fair distribution of property after a divorce, courts use their power to divide joint marital assets and, in some states, the separate marital property of the two spouses. Alimony awards are another means of creating a fair property settlement.

As is true with awarding alimony, clear statutory guidance for judges is generally lacking for dividing marital property. Twenty-one states enumerate factors to be considered by the judge when deciding on the division of property. None of the factors are common to all twenty-one states. Most of the factors relate to an evaluation of marital assets (Connell, 1981).

In the eight community property states, the general rule is that all property that comes to the partners during the marriage belongs equally to the husband and wife. Thus, on divorce, the community property should be equally divided between the two spouses. In most cases, however, the courts are free to divide the community property as they see fit.

A recent development regarding the division of property on divorce concerns property that was, in some sense, earned during the marriage but not received during the marriage. Two such types of property can be considered: pensions and training, especially through a professional education. With regard to pensions, the trend, particularly in community property states, has been to give the spouse (usually the wife) a property interest in the husband's pension proportional to the amount of the pension earned during the marriage (Krause, 1977). An exception is made for military pensions. The Supreme Court has held that these pensions are controlled by federal law rather than state property laws (*McCarty* v. *McCarty*, 101 S. Ct. 2728 (1981)).

The second type of property "earned" but not received during the marriage is a professional degree, usually obtained by one spouse while the other works to pay for the education to support the couple. Several recent state court decisions have held that the spouse who worked (usually the wife) has an equitable interest in the value of the professional degree. For example, in *Reen* v. *Reen*, 8 Fam. L. Rep. 2193 (1981), a Massachusetts probate and family court held that a wife who sacrificed her own education and the prime years of her life to bear children in order to put her husband through dental school and orthodontic training was entitled to part of the value of the degree in orthodontia. Similarly, the Minnesota Supreme Court has held that a wife was entitled to restitution for her contribution to her husband's educational expenses (*DeLa Rosa* v. *DeLa Rosa*, 309 N.W.2d 755 (Minn. 1981)).

Child Custody and Child Support After Divorce

Some of the most difficult decisions judges are called on to make concern child custody and child support after a divorce. In this section legal issues involved in these determinations are discussed.

Child Custody

In most divorces with children involved, custody is not an issue initially because the divorcing parents agree that one or the other should have custody and the judge accepts this agreement. Problems with child custody often arise later, however, so that child custody is best seen as a continuing problem rather than a one-time determination.

Initial Custody Determination. In almost all child custody cases after divorce, the parties agree on a custody arrangement for the children (Woody, 1977). In about 85 percent of initial child custody determinations, primary custody is awarded to the mother, and visitation rights are granted to the father (Slovenko, 1973; Weitzman and Dixon, 1979). The father generally does not challenge the mother over custody of the children because, according to Slovenko, he realizes that the mother would be the better caretaker of the children; or because the children prefer to be with the mother; or because he recognizes that courts have a strong tendency toward awarding custody of the children to the mother (Foster and Freed, 1980).

This tendency to award custody to the mother is a vestige of a presumption called the "tender years" doctrine, which arose in the middle of the nineteenth century. Prior to that time, fathers were believed to be better caretakers because they were more likely to have property and, therefore, were more likely to be able to afford the expenses of the child (Weiss, 1979). Moreover, children were likely to be seen as the husband's "property." The tender years doctrine was an assumption that preadolescent children would benefit most from being with the mother, because only their mother could provide the needed care.

Since the late nineteenth century, mothers in the United States have generally been awarded custody of their children unless a judge considered them "unfit." The term "unfit" refers to moral fitness. It was (and is) generally an attack on the mothers' morals and was the only successful way of overcoming the tender years presumption. Children beyond their tender years were presumed to benefit most from being in the custody of their same-sex parent.

Thus, fathers were usually given custody of the boys and mothers were usually given custody of the girls. However, courts were reluctant to separate siblings (Krause, 1977).

Although the tender years doctrine has been superseded in most states by a policy of placing the "best interests of the child" above other considerations, judges still seem to have a bias that the child's best interests are served by granting custody to the mother. In a recent defense of the tender years doctrine, Klaff (1982) has argued that, when joint custody is not feasible, there should be a rebuttable presumption that the female parent should be given custody of the child. Klaff bases her argument on research from developmental psychology showing that a child needs continuity of care and attention. Since, according to data from the Census Bureau cited by Klaff, the primary care-giving parent is the mother in at least 90 percent of the cases, continuity of care can best be achieved by a presumption that custody should be granted to the mother. The presumption is rebuttable by evidence that the mother is not the primary care-giving parent or that other factors outweigh the importance of continuity of care. Klaff suggests that this rebuttable presumption focuses on the needs of the child rather than the social conduct of the parents, which is the basis of the "unfitness" standard of rebuttal.

In the past fifteen years, the tender years doctrine has been officially discarded by courts or legislatures in thirty-seven states (Freed and Foster, 1981) and replaced by the "best interests of the child" standard. The general guidelines encompassed in the best interests standard appear in Section 402 of the Uniform Marriage and Divorce Act (National Conference of Commissioners on Uniform State Laws, 1971, p. 241):

> The court shall determine custody in accordance with the best interests of the child. The court shall consider all relevant factors including:
> (1) the wishes of the child's parent or parents as to his custody;
> (2) the wishes of the child as to his custodian;
> (3) the interaction and interrelationship of the child with his parents, his siblings, and any other person who may significantly affect the child's best interests;

(4) the child's adjustment to his home, school, and community; and

(5) the mental and physical health of all individuals involved.

The court shall not consider conduct of a proposed custodian that does not affect his relationship with the child.

In addition to the five factors listed in this section, the judge may consider traditional presumptions, such as giving preference to a parent over a nonparent or giving preference to the custodian agreed on by the parties, as long as the decision is made in the best interests of the child.

There can be several problems in the application of the best interests test (Brosky and Alford, 1977). Let us deal with three problems.

First, regarding the wishes of the child, which are considered as a factor in about twenty states (Freed and Foster, 1981), the child may not want to express his or her wishes because to do so would offend the nonchosen parent. Moreover, the child may not necessarily be better off with the chosen parent (Weiss, 1979). To overcome some of the problems associated with the child's expressing a preference in open court, a majority of the jurisdictions allow the child to be interviewed in the judge's chambers, since the child is thereby "freed from direct participation in the traumatic courtroom struggle between his parents and is spared the pain and embarrassment of personally revealing his selection of one of them as his custodian" (Siegel and Hurley, 1977, p. 47).

A second problem in applying the best interests test is that many of the factors require judges to assess the quality of the child's interactions and adjustments and to decide how much weight should be attached to each of these interactions. Judges necessarily must be subjective, and their lack of professional training might cause them to make erroneous decisions. A third problem is that the test makes the conduct of the custodian irrelevant to the custody decision if such conduct does not directly affect the child's welfare. Nevertheless, it has been argued that circumstances indicative of fault in causing a marriage to break up may also be indicative of unfitness as a parent. That is, certain problems—such as habitual drunkenness, adultery, and gross immorality (for example, cohabitation without marriage)—which could lead to a divorce could also lead to poor parenting (Weiss, 1979).

According to one practicing family lawyer, most child custody decisions are based not on the substantive law, which is relatively simple, but on the presentation of facts and opinions about how the interests of the child can best be met (Girardeau, 1982)—specifically, facts and opinions about (1) the emotional ties, love, and affection between the child and the competing parties; (2) the ability and willingness of the competing parties to give the child love, affection, guidance, and, if relevant, a religious education; and (3) the ability and willingness of the competing parties to provide necessities such as food, clothing, medical care, and other remedial care. The judge has a great deal of discretion in making the child custody determination, and this judgment will be reversed on appeal only if it can be shown that there was an abuse of this discretion. Such abuse of discretion is difficult to prove, especially if conflicting evidence is offered to the court.

Because determining child custody after divorce is so difficult, judges often rely on the advice of experts (Litwack, Gerber, and Fenster, 1980). Expert testimony that the child's emotional needs can be better met with one parent rather than the other, particularly if the expert appears objective, can be very persuasive (Kazen, 1977). Often, therefore, parties who can afford them hire experts to testify regarding the child's best interests. Instead of using experts hired by the parties, some writers have suggested that the court should appoint a mental health professional to advise the court (Derdeyn, 1975; Henning, 1976), similar to the role of court-appointed legal representative (Bersoff, 1976). In some states the mental health professional is employed by the court to investigate the family and to make recommendations about custody (Gozansky, 1976). Although many experts favor the use of mental health professionals in custody proceedings, not everyone agrees that these experts are helpful (Litwack, Gerber, and Fenster, 1980; Okpaku, 1976).

Because a psychotherapist's testimony can be very important in the child custody decision, former patients may attempt to have such testimony excluded on the ground that its admission would violate the statutory psychotherapist-patient privilege (Guernsey,

1981). According to Guernsey, the psychotherapist's testimony is often admitted because five exceptions to the privilege have developed: (1) the requested information was obtained by an examination for a purpose other than diagnosis or treatment; (2) the party waived the privilege; (3) the therapist had an explicit statutory duty to report the information; (4) the party introduced his or her mental condition into controversy; and (5) the best interests of the child override the claim of privilege" (p. 964). Guernsey argues that there should be restrictions on the extent to which the psychotherapist-patient privilege is breached.

Instead of granting child custody to one parent and visitation rights to the other, eleven states now allow joint custody (Freed and Foster, 1981). California law goes so far as to presume that, since joint custody is in the best interests of the child, it should be awarded unless evidence indicates otherwise (Saposnek, 1983). Joint custody assumes "that the aims of custody adjudication should include achieving, as far as possible, the protection of the child's relationships with both parents, easy access to both parents, and the fostering of a relationship between parents in which each is supportive of the other's parental efforts" (Weiss, 1979, p. 335). Joint custody has been discussed a great deal recently (Folberg and Graham, 1979; Franklin and Hibbs, 1980; Miller, 1979; Roman and Haddad, 1978; Trombetta, 1981), but its effectiveness is still largely unknown. Anecdotal evidence suggests that it is effective, but for the most part, the research has examined only couples who have agreed to joint custody, rather than couples who were ordered by the court to have joint custody of their children.

The approach of Goldstein, Freud, and Solnit (1973) is exactly opposite to joint custody. They argue that only one parent should be granted complete custody and that the noncustodial parent ought not to have any rights regarding the child, including visitation rights. They assume that continued contact with the noncustodial parent may be harmful to the child, and they would leave all the decisions about visitation, whether and when, to the custodial parent. This view has been widely criticized and is contrary to studies showing that often the child desires a continued relationship with the noncustodial parent (Kelly and Wallerstein, 1977; Rosen, 1977).

Changes in Child Custody. In most states changes in child custody are permitted only if there have been substantial changes in the custody situation that affect the welfare of the child and that have arisen since the prior award of custody. By limiting custody changes in this way, states hope to reduce the number of cases taken to courts for a change in custody. In fact, however, acrimonious divorces are likely to cause continuing child custody disputes.

How children react to the divorce is relevant to the law in that any problems the children experience may affect judgments concerning modification of custody. A recent review of studies on children in families in turmoil suggests that there is a relationship between marital discord and behavior problems in children (Emery, 1982). These negative effects on the children seem to be due to a combination of factors, including separation from a parent (Bowlby, 1973); conflict between the parents (Hetherington, Cox, and Cox, 1976); change in discipline practices (Wallerstein and Kelly, 1980); and stresses caused by reduced economic resources and increased practical problems of day-to-day life, if, for example, the mother begins working at the time of the divorce (Hetherington, 1979). Since the mental health professional may be called on to counsel or to testify about children of divorce, he or she should be aware of the growing literature in the area of children's adjustment to divorce (see the recent reviews by Emery, 1982; Kurdek, 1981).

What constitutes evidence sufficient to justify a decision to change or not to change custody will vary from state to state. Moreover, as values change, what constitutes an "unfit parent" will also change. Thus, although a Georgia appeals court approved a change in custody because the mother was cohabiting with a man who was not her husband (*Sims* v. *Sims,* 243 Ga. 276, 253 S.E.2d 763 (1979)), in other states such behavior might not result in a change in custody. Another problem concerns the homosexuality of the custodial parent. Under traditional rules a parent's homosexuality was a bar to custody. More recently, before denying custody on the basis of homosexuality, courts have required evidence showing a connection between the parent's homosexuality and harm to the child (Guernsey, 1981).

Interstate Determinations of Child Custody. American society has become increasingly more mobile, as evidenced by the fact that about 47 percent of the population has moved at least once within the past five years (U.S. Bureau of the Census, 1981). One result of this increasing mobility is that divorced parents are increasingly likely to live in different states (Bodenheimer, 1981). Thus, for example, a parent who has moved from the original state and who believes that circumstances have changed may bring an action for custody in the second state, in effect overruling the judgment in the first state. Several states could be involved if, in addition to parents, grandparents or other relatives are seeking custody of the child.

Although interstate custody disputes may occur when the challenging parent is in legal custody of the children (as, for example, when they are in the second state visiting the parent under an agreed-on visitation arrangement), many of these interstate disputes result from behavior that violates the prior determination of child custody (*Uniform Laws Annotated,* 1979). Such behavior would include keeping the children after the visitation period had ended or snatching the children from their home in the first state, taking them to a second state, and bringing an action to change custody in the courts of the second state. If a court in the second state enters a judgment that conflicts with the judgment of the first, the legal custodian could be in the position of complying with one judgment while being in contempt of the other.

Until the adoption of the Uniform Child Custody Jurisdiction Act (UCCJA), it was fairly easy for the abducting parent to find a court in a second state that would not enforce the first state's custody decree. Three factors explain why a state would not have to enforce a custody decree from a second state (Katz, 1981b). First, the U.S. Supreme Court has not interpreted the Constitution as requiring that a second state give full faith and credit to the custody decree of another state. Second, jurisdiction over a child custody dispute can be based on so many different factors (the physical presence of the child, the domicile of the child, the domicile of one or both parents, and the court's having issued the original custody decree) that courts in more than one state could legitimately exercise jurisdiction over the same case (Clark, 1968). Third, child custody decrees are not final. That is, they can be modified on a showing by the noncustodial parent of changed circumstances, as long as the modification is in the best interests of the child. Presumably, a court in a second state with proper jurisdiction could make this judgment as well as the court that issued the original decree.

The UCCJA was designed both to reduce the amount of child snatching and to make the law in this area more uniform. The UCCJA has three major goals. First, it eliminates physical presence of the child as a requirement for jurisdiction. Second, with only a few exceptions, it prohibits a court from modifying custody decrees of courts in other states. Third, it requires a court to enforce out-of-state custody decrees. In cases of child snatching, the Act generally denies jurisdiction from courts in the second state and continues jurisdiction in the original state for six months after the removal of the child from the "home state" or the retention of the child in a second state after the child was to have been returned.

After a child has been taken to or retained in a second state in violation of the custody decree, the custodial parent can institute custody proceedings in the home state. The Act requires a reasonable attempt to give actual notice to the abducting parent, but it does not require that the custodial parent wait before filing an action until he or she learns where the abducting parent is living. If the custodial parent does not initiate an action within six months, technically jurisdiction in the home state is lost; regardless, the abducting parent would have difficulty bringing an action for custody in the second state, since to allow such an action would be supportive of child snatching, which is contrary to the intent of the Act.

Although two or more states could conceivably have jurisdiction over the initial child custody determination (for example, if one is the domicile of the child and the other has significant contacts with the child and the family), under the UCCJA only one state will make the final judgment, since one of the purposes of the Act is to prevent conflicting custody decrees in two or more states. To ensure that only one state makes the custody determination, the Act requires that the parties notify the courts of any pending custody proceeding in another state and that the courts involved resolve between themselves which is the more appropriate forum, so that the child custody determination will be made in only one of the courts. To prevent child snatching in one state by a parent who seeks to change a prior custody judgment, the Act provides that courts in other states must defer to the continuing jurisdiction of the first court. With few exceptions, only the first state can modify the custody decree. (An exception is made, for example, if an emergency requiring immediate action occurs.)

If a noncustodial parent does abduct his or her child, the custodial parent can seek one or more of the following remedies: criminal sanctions by the state, tort action against the noncustodial parent, civil contempt charges for violating a court's decree, and a habeas corpus action to reclaim custody of the minor child (Katz, 1981b; see also Katz, 1981a).

According to Katz, a state is unlikely to use criminal remedies for kidnapping by a parent before a final decree awarding custody to the other parent is issued, because, prior to the issuance of the final custody decree, both parents have an equal right to custody. A second factor limiting the effectiveness of criminal sanctions is that child stealing is often classified as a misdemeanor rather than a felony. Thus, by crossing into another state, the abducting parent can avoid prosecution, since misdemeanors are not usually extraditable offenses. To overcome this problem, some states have now made child snatching across state lines a felony, although concealing the abducted child within the state is still a misdemeanor. Finally, the effectiveness of criminal sanctions is limited because the penalties for child snatching imposed on a parent are rarely as severe as those imposed on a third party. Statutes that make kidnapping a felony do ensure that the abducting parent is subject to being extradited to the state where the kidnapping occurred. Although criminal sanctions against the abducting parent do not guarantee that the child will be returned to the custodial parent, in practice, according to Katz, the child is returned and the sanctioned parent is in a poor position to argue for custody both then and later.

The second remedy a custodial parent can seek against an abducting parent for child snatching is a tort claim for damages. Although such actions are not common, parents seeking to prove civil liability in tort have claimed a violation of a legal duty not to deprive the parent of lawful custody (see, for example, *Spencer* v. *Terebelo*, 373 So. 2d 200, writ denied, 376 So. 2d 960 (La. 1979)). According to Katz, the major advantage of a tort action, if it is available, is that it allows the custodial parent to recover actual damages (that is, the costs involved in retrieving the kidnapped child). Punitive damages to deter child snatching may also be awarded if the behavior was particularly egregious or if a violation of a statute occurred.

Civil contempt proceedings are an often-used third remedy by which a parent can seek to regain custody of the abducted child. Although a contempt citation is limited to the jurisdiction of the issuing court, courts in other states often enforce such citations under the principle of comity (that is, the principle supporting this kind of enforcement as a matter of practice rather than as a matter of law). According to Katz, however, the courts in the second state are reluctant to issue a contempt citation on their own initiative.

The fourth remedy a custodial parent may use against an abducting parent is the writ of habeas corpus. Assuming that the custodial parent can prove that he or she has a legal right to custody of the child, the court will order the abducting parent to bring the child before it. A habeas corpus action requires that the child be physically within a court's jurisdiction. A child custody habeas corpus action in a second state can also be brought by the abducting parent to modify a previous custody order. The abducting parent would argue that a modification of custody should be issued because the original court was wrong in its custody determination or because circumstances have changed since the issuance of the custody decree. Under the UCCJA a court in the second state should refuse to entertain the habeas corpus petition for a modification of child custody because the original court retains jurisdiction (Katz, 1981b). The intent of the Act is to limit the use of habeas corpus to enforcing the original judgment rather than to include modifying the custody decree, although a problem is certainly present if the noncustodial parent claims that the court in the second state should assume jurisdiction over the case because an emergency exists.

Child Support After Divorce

There are no clear guidelines governing child support awards after a divorce. The kinds of factors considered by judges, however, relate to the income, resources, and services of the two parties. Most of these factors are summarized in the Uniform Parentage Act (cited in Krause, 1977, p. 204):

> In determining the amount to be paid by a parent for support of the child and the period during which the duty of support is owed, a court enforcing the obligation of support shall consider all relevant facts, including
> (1) the needs of the child;
> (2) the standard of living and circumstances of the parents;
> (3) the relative financial means of the parents;
> (4) the earning ability of the parents;
> (5) the need and capacity of the child for education, including higher education;
> (6) the age of the child;
> (7) the financial resources and earning ability of the child;
> (8) the responsibility of the parents for the support of others; and
> (9) the value of services contributed by the custodial parent.

Child support awards can be modified upon a showing of a significant change in circumstances. Child support continues until the child reaches the age of majority, which must be the same for both males and females (*Stanton* v. *Stanton,* 421 U.S. 7 (1975)). There are still unresolved questions about the mandated inclusion of college education expenses as a part of a child support obligation, since the child of college age may have been statutorily emancipated as an adult. Moreover, if the courts can force a divorced parent to pay for his or her child's college education, there might also be an equal protection issue involved, since a child whose parents are not divorced cannot press such a claim (Krause, 1977).

Although the obligation of child support is difficult to enforce in an ongoing family except in cases of gross default, there are enforcement mechanisms available if the parties live apart (Krause, 1977). In some states failure to meet support obligations is a misdemeanor offense. More generally, support obligations can be enforced through contempt proceedings, either civil or criminal. In contempt proceedings the party seeking support must show that the supporting spouse has not complied with the support order and that this failure was intentional and without justification (Harp, 1982). Given that there is this evidence of willful contempt of the support order, the amount of money owed must be proved. The court will then order some method of repayment.

Although these remedies are available, it does not always make sense to impose a fine if the defaulting person could not make the original support payment. Nor is it always sensible to put the offender in jail, where he or she will be unable to earn the money needed to pay the support and will be costing the state money in addition to the money it might have to pay to support the family.

One of the real problems in enforcing child support obligations is that the supporting parent (usually the father) will often remarry and will thus be obligated to support a second family. The issue is whether the father's obligations to the children of the first marriage should be reduced because of his new obligations to the children of the second marriage. Courts generally have not found such changed circumstances to justify a reduction in previously ordered child support awards, and it is unlikely that a court's refusal to modify child support awards will ever be considered a violation of constitutional rights (Strickman, 1982). Generally, state courts have given priority to the children of the first marriage, although it has been suggested that all the children involved should be considered on an equal basis (Krause, 1982).

States generally will enforce support obligations from another state if there is a judgment for a specific amount of money for past-due installments or if the past-due installments could not be reduced retroactively in the original state. The primary means of enforcing out-of-state support obligations is the Uniform Reciprocal Enforcement of Support Act (URESA), which has been adopted in some form by all the states. Under URESA the party claiming support can bring an action in a court in his or her state of residence. This complaint is then forwarded to a court located in the obligor's state of residence, under whose law the case will be tried. The case is heard and a judgment is rendered and enforced at this second court. Monies collected under the judgment are sent to the first court, from which they are disbursed to the claimants.

The federal government recently has become involved in the problem of nonpayment of child support by a parent who resides in a different state or whose whereabouts are unknown. Under legislation passed in 1975, the Office of Child Support Enforcement was established as an agency operating within the Department of Health and Human Services. This agency helps states find absentee parents, establish paternity, and obtain child support from the absent individuals. In fiscal year 1980, the agency collected almost $1.5 billion, about half of which was obtained on behalf of welfare families (White, 1982).

Trends in Family Law

Family law is one of the fastest-changing areas of the law as society also changes. Hennessey (1980) has described several trends in family law, which he suggests are likely to continue: (1) a move away from fault in divorce actions; (2) an increasing emphasis on contract law, particularly with regard to nonmarital cohabitation; (3) the increasing constitutionalization of family law issues; (4) a move away from considering marital misconduct in awarding alimony and distributing property; and (5) a recognition of the nonmonetary contributions of spouses. Another apparent trend is the increased standardization of many laws across states (for example, the adoption of the UCCJA by forty-four states and of URESA by all fifty states). In addition, the federal government is taking a larger role in what have been traditionally the concerns of the states. For example, the Office of Child Support Enforcement has tools available to it that are not available to the states in order to reduce the number of parents who do not pay court-awarded child support. A final trend in family law is an increased reliance on mental health professionals to help judges deal with the difficult decisions they have to make in the family law area.

Ronald J. Palagi
James R. Springer   5

Personal Injury Law

Tort law is an area of law that is difficult to define, since any definition sufficiently comprehensive to cover all torts becomes too general and therefore nearly meaningless. However, the common element in all torts is that a person has sustained a loss or harm as the result of another person's act or failure to act. Stated more formally, then, tort refers to a civil wrong wherein one person's behavior causes a compensable injury to the person, property, or recognized interest of another and for which a civil remedy is sought (Kionka, 1977).

Tort law represents our legal system's recognition that society functions best when individuals are safe from indiscriminate harm. It is a complex system for compensating a person who sustains a loss as a result of another's behavior. It then aims to place the cost of such compensation on those and only those who ought to bear it. The complexities and nuances that give rise to modern tort law can best be understood by reference to actual cases. Accordingly, each section in this chapter will start with a brief introduction and be followed by selective representative fact patterns from landmark cases before concluding with analyses of the laws as they pertain to these cases. The cases have been chosen to provide a quick introduction to important issues of personal injury law as might be encountered by the human services professional.

Intentional Torts

Intentional tort law is the oldest of all tort liability law, having developed out of the writs proscribing breaches of the King's peace. These torts can be viewed as the civil side of criminal law and are necessary and basic to a well-ordered society.

In order to establish a prima facie case for intentional tort liability, three elements of proof are generally required: (1) an act, (2) an intention, (3) an injury. The following cases highlight these elements.

Example A

Two boys are climbing on a man's shed. He sees one of them and orders him off the roof. However, before the boy can get off the shed, the man throws a stick at him. The stick misses the first boy but strikes the second boy, whom the man did not see and did not intend to hit. The second boy sustains injuries and eventually loses one of his eyes. Is the man liable for the boy's damage? [*Talmage* v. *Smith*, 101 Mich. 370, 59 N.W. 656 (1894).]

Example B

A black man attends a business luncheon at a motor hotel. While he is standing in the buffet line, a hotel employee snatches his plate out of his hands, shouting that no Negro can be served at the club. The black man was not actually touched but was embarrassed and hurt by such conduct. Is the employee of the hotel liable for damages in a battery tort action? [*Fisher* v. *Carrousel Motor Hotel, Inc.*, 424 S.W.2d 827 (Tex. 1967).]

Example C

A woman is attempting to move out of her apartment when her landlord appears on the scene. The landlord has a gun and threatens to shoot the woman. The landlord never fires the gun, and the woman does not know whether the gun was loaded or not. Is the landlord liable for damages for assault? [*Allen* v. *Hannaford*, 138 Wash. 423, 244 P. 700 (1926).]

Example D

A student reports to the president of his university and makes wild accusations. The student is referred to the dean of men, who interviews him in the presence of a health service physician. The dean and the physician conclude that the student is hallucinating, and they trick him into being taken to the hospital by the campus police. The student is informed that he is being taken to the local law enforcement authorities, so that his views can be reported there. No judicial commitment was ever attempted. Will a cause of action against the physician for false imprisonment be held? [*Meier* v. *Combs*, 263 N.E.2d 194 (Ind. 1970).]

Example E

A man is working in his yard when two men drive up, get out of their car, and proceed to beat up the man. Unknown to the assailants, the man's daughter is watching the beating from a window in the house. As a result of what she sees, she becomes tremendously upset and suffers severe emotional trauma. An action for intentional infliction of mental distress is brought in the name of the daughter against the two assailants. Will they be held liable for her damages? [*Taylor* v. *Vallelunga*, 171 Cal. App. 2d 107, 339 P.2d 910 (1959).]

As mentioned previously, the first element of proof required for an intentional tort is an act—any volitional act on the defendant's part. Thus, if person Y, while having an epileptic seizure, strikes person Z, he has not committed a legal act because it was not a volitional act. The act must be volitional.

The second element, the requirement of intent, refers not only to the specific result but also to those results that are substantially certain to occur. Thus, if one shouts "Fire" in a crowded theater, intending only to scare his girlfriend, the action is nevertheless substantially certain to scare innocent patrons of the theater. Another aspect of intent is the doctrine of transferred intent. This doctrine applies where A, intending to commit a tortious act against B, somehow injures C. For example, A takes a swing at B; B ducks, and A hits C. The intent to commit the act against B is transferred, so that the elements for a case by C against A are present. In example

A, where the man threw the stick at the boy on his shed roof, the use of transferred intent was necessary to impose liability on the man. He had not even seen the second boy, so in no way could one say that he intended for the stick to hit the second boy. What was important to the court was that the man intended to inflict unwarranted harm on someone. Since that was the case, the fact that the injury resulted to another could not relieve the defendant of his responsibility. He was found liable for the boy's damages.

In intentional tort law, motive and intent are distinguished. Intent typically refers to the desire to act in a way that will bring about physical consequence; motive refers to the reasons prompting this desire. Intent, although a state of mind, is regarded by law as objective, since one is deemed to intend the consequences of his act, which he knows are substantially certain to result. If the result is intended or substantially certain to occur, the tort is intentional. The motive for the conduct—revenge, punishment, self-defense, or even a desire to help—may, in certain situations, aggravate or excuse the wrong but typically will not affect the person being held liable. Only the intent is relevant in establishing a prima facie intentional tort case.

The third element is the requirement of causation between the defendant's act and the harm caused to the plaintiff's interest. The act may be either a direct cause of the plaintiff's injury, or it may set in motion a chain of events that result in harm to the plaintiff. The causation requirement is met if the defendant's action is a substantial factor in bringing about the plaintiff's injury.

Keeping in mind the three general requirements of a prima facie case, we now examine the four intentional torts against the person: battery, assault, false imprisonment, and intentional infliction of mental distress.

Battery. Battery is the foremost of the intentional torts. In essence, a battery is the bringing about of a harmful or offensive contact with the person of another. Whether a contact is harmful or offensive is measured in accordance with the standards of a reasonable person of ordinary sensibilities (which eliminates the person of extreme sensitivity). The offensive contact may occur without the plaintiff's knowledge (for example, it may have been deserved by a third party); knowledge is not essential. Moreover, the contact need not cause physical harm to a person; it may be merely offensive to the person so contacted. The act need not be a direct cause of the injury, but may be indirect and set in motion a harmful or offensive contact. Also, the contact is not limited to the actual body of the plaintiff but may act on something closely connected to, or attached to, the plaintiff's body.

In example B, when the black man had the plate snatched out of his hands, there was no actual contact with his person. However, the court still found the requisite offensive contact, so that there was a battery. The court reasoned that the essence of an action for battery is the invasion of a person's inviolability and the resultant loss of dignity. Consequently, an actual contact is not necessary because the same loss of dignity is involved when contact is made with something closely associated with or attached to the plaintiff.

Assault. The intentional tort of assault is an action that is intended to and does cause reasonable apprehension of an immediate, harmful, or offensive contact with another person. The key element in an assault case is that there be apprehension. This apprehension must be reasonable under the circumstances at the time, and the contact must be perceived as imminent. Ordinarily, courts do not protect the person who has exaggerated fears. In order to satisfy the apprehension element of assault, one need only recognize that the harmful or offensive contact may occur. Human services professionals may be called by attorneys in these matters in order to help define "reasonable apprehension" versus exaggerated fears.

In example C, when the landlord pointed the gun at the woman, the woman had a reasonable apprehension of harmful contact. It was not necessary that the woman determine whether the contact could in fact occur; assault depends more on the apprehension of contact present in the assaulted person's mind than on the motives of the assaulting person.

Since the important inquiry is the mental state of the assaulted person, assault is different from battery in that the knowledge of the assault is a necessary element of proof. Obviously, a person cannot be apprehensive without knowledge of the actions taken by the assaulting person. The other important element of assault is that there be an apprehension of an immediate contact. Apprehension of contact in the future is not an assault.

Human services professionals employed in psychiatric hospital settings should be aware that if a mentally competent patient refuses to take medications for religious or other reasons, it is generally considered a form of assault or battery to force the taking of such medications. In a case involving such action, a woman was taken to a psychiatric hospital by a police officer when she refused to move to a different room in a hotel where she lived. She was reported to be dirty, unkempt, and initially unresponsive to questions. On admission to the hospital, she refused to allow the admitting physician to take her blood pressure, giving her Christian Scientist religion as her reason. Although she continued to object, she was given psychotropic medication for six weeks while in the hospital. She sued the physicians and the hospital, and the court allowed recovery, pointing out that the patient had never been found to be mentally ill or incompetent and that a medical patient suffering from a physical ailment would have been able to reject the medications (*Winters* v. *Miller,* 446 F.2d 65 (2d Cir. 1971)).

False Imprisonment. False imprisonment involves an act or omission by the defendant which confines the plaintiff in a specific, bounded area. Confinement of the plaintiff may occur in a variety of ways: use of physical barriers, use of physical force against plaintiff or a member of plaintiff's family, failure to provide a means of exit from an area that cannot otherwise be safely escaped from, and failure to tell plaintiff how he can resist any of these acts of confinement. Also, the length of confinement is not a factor in imposing liability, just the fact of confinement.

Threats of future harm and moral pressure are not sufficient acts of restraint to impose liability. Another important limit is that the area must have clearly staked-out boundaries. If the plaintiff could have gone in any direction to escape the bounded area, the action will not lie. However, the plaintiff must be aware of the means available to leave the bounded area; if he is not aware of the available direction of movement, then liability can be imposed on the defendant. Also, the means of escape must be safe.

In example D the student was confined to a bounded area (the hospital) and, in the process of being so confined, could not move at will. The element of trickery did not allow the student to understand his options, including the possible points of egress. The court held that a cause of action for false imprisonment existed against the physician.

A privilege to imprison is given to policemen when making felony arrests and arrests with a warrant. However, there is no privilege for nonfelony arrests made without a warrant. Therefore, policemen may be sued for false imprisonment. There also is a privilege given to shopkeepers to detain suspected shoplifters for investigation purposes. For the privilege to apply, the following conditions must be satisfied: (1) There must be reasonable belief that the theft occurred. (2) Detention must be conducted in a reasonable manner and with only nondeadly force used. (3) The detention must be only for a reasonable period of time and only for the purpose of making an investigation.

Intentional Infliction of Mental Distress. Tort liability for intentional infliction of mental distress arises when a defendant acts in an extreme and outrageous manner with the intent to cause severe mental distress to the plaintiff. Extreme and outrageous behavior is generally defined as conduct that transcends all boundaries of decency tolerated by society. This tort is something more than the daily abuses and jests many of us deal with on a day-to-day basis; therefore, language that is merely offensive or insulting is not subject to liability. Exceptions to this general rule do exist. One such exception pertains to common carriers and innkeepers, who are determined to owe a higher duty of care to their patrons and, therefore, may be held liable for conduct that is not outrageous. A second such exception occurs with people who have special sensitivities to particular words or actions. If a defendant is aware of these sensitivities, then the sensitivities of a particular plaintiff will be taken into account. As part of this exception is the case where a defendant causes physical harm to an individual, and emotional distress thereby results to a third person because of his or her relationship to the injured person. To establish intent and causation in such cases, the plaintiff must prove the following: (1) Plaintiff was present when the injury occurred to the other person. (2) Plaintiff had a close relationship to the injured person. (3) Defendant knew that plaintiff was present and knew of the relationship to the injured party.

In example E two of these three elements were present. The daughter who witnessed the beating obviously fulfilled the first two requirements. However, the assailants of her father were not aware of her presence. For liability to be imposed for intentional infliction of mental distress, the defendant must know or be substantially certain that such distress will occur. These assailants had no idea of the daughter's presence; therefore, they could not be held to have intended to cause her mental distress.

An element of this tort, unlike the other intentional torts, is the necessity of actual damages, harm, or injury. Plaintiffs no longer need to show an actual physical injury in order to recover. However, they must prove—often through the testimony of human services professionals—that they suffered severe emotional distress and the harm resulting therefrom.

Psychiatrists and psychologists are frequently asked to examine clients to assess the degree of emotional distress, the probable causative factors, and the prognosis for recovery. The issue of true emotional distress versus faking or malingering of symptoms invariably is explored, with counsel for both sides frequently offering conflicting psychological and psychiatric opinions regarding each of these elements. For the first time in the history of psychiatric nomenclature, a formal diagnostic entity has been given to describe emotional distress following trauma. The third edition of the *Diagnostic and Statistical Manual of Mental Disorders (DSM-III)* (American Psychiatric Association, 1980) specifically and behaviorally describes a disorder labeled "Post-Traumatic Stress Disorder," which has in the past been referred to in a variety of ways, including traumatic neurosis, acute neurotic reaction, industrial neurosis, post-accident anxiety syndrome, and accidental neurosis. The diagnostic criteria established for this disorder may prove to be helpful to human services professionals and courts alike in determining guidelines for severe emotional distress.

Negligence

Negligence is the central theory of personal injury law. To most nonlawyers the term "negligence" implies inadequate care rendered by someone who suddenly finds himself or herself in a lawsuit. Such a definition suggests forgetfulness or inattentiveness. In reality a lawsuit based on negligence theory is more complex. To establish a negligence case that can be submitted to a jury, a plaintiff's attorney must first prove that the defendant had a legal *duty* to do something or to refrain from doing something. The plaintiff must then prove that the duty was *breached* by the defendant. Next, there must be proof that the breach of that duty by the defendant was the "proximate cause" of the plaintiff's injury. Proximate cause is another elusive concept in the vocabulary of the law. Issues of proximate cause have little to do with proximity in time or place or causation. These issues deal more with proximity in the sense of justice and fairness; that is, the negligent act committed or omitted by the defendant must have been a significant contributing factor to the plaintiff's injury (*Morrow* v. *Greyhound Lines, Inc.*, 541 F.2d 713 (8th Cir. 1976); *Abrams* v. *B-Mark Pools, Inc.*, 616 S.W.2d 143 (Mo. App., 1981)). Finally, the plaintiff must show that he or she suffered an injury to his or her property or person.

Therefore, in order for a prima facie case of negligence to be established, the following four elements must be established by the plaintiff: (1) duty, (2) breach of duty, (3) causation, (4) harm or injury.

From the representative cases and the discussion that follows them, one can draw the general rule that negligence consists of a failure to use ordinary care to avoid injury to others. Ordinary care is a relative term, and the use of ordinary care requires precautions commensurate with the dangers to be reasonably anticipated under the circumstances (*Niemczyk* v. *Burleson*, 535 S.W.2d 737 (Mo. App., 1976)).

Example A

The driver of a car approaches an intersection and then stops the car for a stoplight; the driver looks left and right and, not seeing any traffic, proceeds through the intersection. The driver did not see the motorcycle that was halfway through the intersection. The car strikes the motorcycle, causing the driver of the motorcycle to be severely injured. Is the driver liable for the motorcyclist's injuries? [*Bonnes* v. *Olsen*, 197 Neb. 309, 248 N.W.2d 756 (1976).]

Example B

You give a party in your home. One of the guests is a young man with a reputation for violent, brutal behavior. You keep a loaded shotgun in a place where you know, or should know, that this young man is likely to find it. During the party the young man finds the shotgun and shoots another guest in the leg. A lawsuit is filed against you. Should you be liable for negligence because you kept the shotgun in a place where it was accessible to a person who was likely to use it? [*Scheibel* v. *Hillis*, 531 S.W.2d 285 (Mo. 1976).]

Example C

The owner of a swimming pool approximately 200 yards in length, with a mud and sand bottom, roped off one end of the pool where the diving boards were. A patron of the pool dives off the side of it within the roped-off section. He strikes his head on the bottom, sustaining serious injuries. Is the swimming pool owner liable for the swimmer's injuries? [*Boll* v. *Spring Lake Park Inc.*, 358 S.W.2d 859 (Mo. 1962).]

Example D

A woman goes to a grocery store to purchase a birthday cake. Upon entering the store, as she is walking down an aisle, she slips and falls. A bottle of liquid cleaner had shattered on the floor, making the floor slippery and covered with broken glass. The woman falls on her tailbone and sustains cuts. There is no evidence that the store had knowledge of the slippery floor. Is the store liable for injuries suffered by the woman? [*Vinson* v. *National Supermarkets Inc.*, 621 S.W.2d 373 (Mo. App. 1981).]

Duty. A plaintiff must establish that the defendant in the lawsuit had a duty to perform some act or to refrain from some activity which resulted in harm to the plaintiff. The basic standard of care used in negligence law to impose this duty is the "reasonable person" standard, which means that a jury must decide whether the behavior of the defendant comported with the behavior one would expect of a reasonably prudent person.

Example A, where the car struck the motorcycle in an intersection, involves breach of duty. Though the driver took reasonable action in checking traffic, the driver was negligent for failing to see the motorcyclist. The driver of a motor vehicle entering an intersection is obligated to look for approaching vehicles and to see any vehicle within the radius that denotes the limit of danger. If the driver fails to see a vehicle, that driver is guilty of negligence as a matter of law. In this case the driver of the car failed to see the cyclist; thus, she was negligent.

There are, however, several qualifications to this general standard of duty. In cases involving children, most courts decide whether a child's behavior is reasonable by comparing that behavior with the behavior of children of like age, education, intelligence, and experience. These characteristics are decided by a jury through a subjective evaluation of the factors involved. Human services professionals—particularly those with expertise in developmental psychology—may be called on to assist either the plaintiff or the defendant in determining what is reasonable for children at various ages.

Certain classes of defendants are expected to demonstrate a higher degree of care than the ordinary care expected from the reasonably prudent person. Common carriers—such as taxicabs, buses, trains, and airplanes—are held to a high degree of care in protecting their passengers. Because of the high degree of care imposed on them, these common carriers must use reasonable care to aid or assist their passengers in case of emergency or other peril. Those who profit from customers and other invitees are similarly bound to a duty of reasonable care to aid their guests and to prevent harm that might befall them as a result of the acts of third persons or artificial and unsafe conditions of the premises. Certainly, professionals in nearly all areas are expected, likewise, to demonstrate a higher degree of care than a lay person would exercise. A social worker would be expected to adhere to the standards of the reasonably careful and prudent social worker.

Generally speaking, no one is under a legal duty to perform any affirmative act to benefit another. In other words, there is no duty to rescue another person from danger or to aid an injured person. Here again, there are a number of important exceptions to the general rule. If a person is placed in peril as a result of the negligence of another, the person who created the peril must use reasonable care to help that person escape.

In example B, where you allowed the young man to have access to the shotgun, you would be liable for the injuries sustained by your guest. You had the duty of making your home reasonably safe for the people you had invited. As the appellate court noted in affirming the verdict against the hostess, "Where an instrumentality is rendered dangerous to a person rightfully in its proximity by the act of a third person, which act might have reasonably been anticipated by the person responsible for the instrumentality, failure to take appropriate precautions to avoid injury constitutes negligence. That is true whether the third person's act is innocent, negligent, intentionally tortious, or criminal" (*Scheibel* v. *Hillis,* 531 S.W.2d 285 (Mo. 1976)).

Another exception to the general rule that there is no duty to act to the benefit of another is the circumstance where someone, although under no duty to do so, comes to the aid of another person who may be in distress. Once this gratuitous aid is rendered, the person offering the help is under a duty to act as a reasonably prudent person would act under those circumstances. This is known, in legal parlance, as assumption of duty.

Finally, if someone has the authority and the actual ability to control the actions of third persons, a duty to do so may be imposed by the law. Thus, parents may be liable for the acts of their children, and employers may be liable for the acts of their employees. A human services professional, working in a setting where patient charts or records are reviewed by both professionals and paraprofessionals, must take caution to inform all staff members regarding rules and rights of confidentiality of patients or clients. The human services professional, who is the employer in such a case, could be held liable if a secretary or clerk were to release confidential information, even though the human services professional did not know exactly what information that employee might see in the context of his or her job.

Duties may also be imposed contractually or by laws requiring or proscribing certain kinds of behavior. Duty is imposed contractually when a party—for instance, a common carrier—agrees to provide certain kinds of services or benefits to another. In these cases, to establish that a duty is owed, a plaintiff must show that legislation dictates or forbids certain behavior or that the defendant assumed the duty via contract.

Breach of Duty. To establish the second element of a prima facie case of negligence, breach of duty, a plaintiff must prove that the conduct of the defendant has fallen short of the level required by the standard of care owed to the plaintiff. The jury, which is the trier of fact, must decide the factual question of whether the duty has been breached. In order for the jury to determine this breach, two separate stages of proof must be presented for its consideration: (1) proof that the injury actually occurred; (2) proof that the defendant acted unreasonably. The applicable standard of care to be required in a given case can be proved in a number of ways. Evidence of the customary practice or usage in a particular field may be introduced in order to establish that reasonably prudent persons in the same business or occupation as a particular defendant would act in a certain way. Once this customary conduct is established, the unreasonable behavior of the defendant may be shown.

Example C involved the liability of the swimming pool owner. A swimming pool owner has a duty to keep his or her pool reasonably safe and, for those dangers that cannot be protected against, to warn his or her patrons of potential danger. Here the pool owner had roped off the end of the pool where the diving boards were, giving the impression that the whole roped-off section was safe for diving. The swimming pool owner had a duty to warn his patrons that only a portion of the roped-off section was intended for diving. Warning signs indicating the various depths of the roped-off section would have discharged the pool owner's duty in this case.

Violation of a statute may be shown to the jury in order to establish a breach of duty. This is one of the clearest methods of proving breach, but it is not often seen in a trial because in such matters defendants generally choose to settle out of court.

One last major method of proving breach of duty is by *res ipsa loquitur* ("the thing speaks for itself"). If it is clear that the plaintiff's injury could not have occurred without negligence, and if the defendant is clearly connected with the negligence, *res ipsa loquitur* may apply. That is, the plaintiff must show that the occurrence resulting in an injury was such as does not ordinarily happen if a party in charge uses ordinary care; also, the instrumentality involved in the action must be under the management and control of the defendant. Finally, the defendant must possess superior knowledge or means of information concerning the cause of occurrence

(*Lent* v. *Lent,* 543 S.W.2d 312 (Mo. App. 1976); *Adams* v. *LeBow,* 160 S.W.2d 826 (Mo. App. 1942); *Lindsey* v. *Williams,* 260 S.W.2d 472 (Mo. 1953)).

A classic *res ipsa loquitur* case would be a lawsuit brought by a patient because a surgical instrument was discovered in his body after an operation performed by a single doctor. Only the doctor had control and management of the instrument. Obviously, he or she would have had superior knowledge or information concerning the occurrence. This type of injury would not happen if the doctor were to use ordinary care. Since the facts strongly indicate that the plaintiff's injuries were caused by the defendant's negligence, the jury, according to *res ipsa loquitur* reasoning, is allowed to infer that the defendant is negligent.

Causation. The third element in a negligence action is causation. In other words, the conduct of the defendant must be the proximate cause of the injuries suffered by the plaintiff. This concept is one of the most confusing in the legal profession. The usual but by no means universal test for proximate causation is known as the "but for" test. That is, the injuries suffered by the plaintiff would not have occurred "but for" the particular act or omission on the part of the plaintiff.

If, as in example D, a storekeeper negligently allowed a slippery surface on his floor to remain in a dangerous condition during a heavy shopping period, that negligent act would be the proximate cause of the injury suffered by the woman who stepped on the slippery surface and fell. If, on the other hand, the dangerous condition had been maintained for many months, it still would not be the proximate cause of an injury to someone who fell in another part of the store.

Even if the defendant is negligent, the negligent party may be absolved of liability if, through no fault of that party, a superseding force intervenes and thus breaks the causal connection between the original negligent act and the harm suffered by the plaintiff. For example, if a landlord were to leave an unvented can of flammable liquid next to a furnace in a building leased by tenants, he would be clearly negligent. However, if the furnace did not cause enough heat to ignite the liquid but a fire occurred nonetheless because someone threw a lighted cigarette on the liquid, there would be no proximate causation between the original negligence of the landlord and the fire. The cigarette would be considered a superseding, intervening force; and the chain of causation would have been broken.

The criminal acts of third persons are considered another category of superseding, intervening force. For example, if someone were to leave a loaded pistol lying around where a child could find it and the child actually did locate the pistol and take it home, the person who left the pistol could well be held liable for an accident if the child were to hurt himself or another person with the weapon. If, on the other hand, the child had found the pistol and taken it home, where a burglar or other intruder found it, the originally negligent person who left the pistol lying around would not be liable for harm inflicted with the gun by any criminal act of the burglar.

Harm or Injury. The fourth and final element of a prima facie case of negligence is the element of injury. Even if a plaintiff proves that the defendant owes him or her a duty, that the duty was breached, and that the breach was the proximate cause of the injury suffered by the plaintiff, actual harm or injury must be proved. This area is of great significance to the human services professional, who is frequently called on to testify to the presence or absence of psychological or emotional harm to an individual. Until recently courts have been reluctant to accept an injured person's right to freedom from emotional distress when the emotional distress has been presented as the only harm and not as an adjunct to damages for bodily injuries or other kinds of harm. However, many courts have come to realize that the intentional or reckless infliction of emotional distress that produces a severe and prolonged emotional response is cause for separate action. Psychiatrists and psychologists are frequently called on to evaluate plaintiffs to assess the degree of such distress. Consideration is given to the existence of a diagnosable mental disorder or condition. The presence of a diagnosable condition, plus testimony by the mental health professional that such disorder was caused by the negligence of the defendant, is essential. The extent of the harm or injury must also be measured by its consequences in such areas as permanency, loss of vocational role or status, disfigurement, need for treatment, loss of marriage or family, inconvenience, and loss of enjoyment. In the following representative cases, harm or injury of an emotional nature to the plaintiff was alleged, and liability was found against the defendant.

> A man drank from a bottle of a soft drink beverage and found an unpackaged prophylactic in the container. Thereafter he complained of emotional distress, including persistent nausea. The supreme judicial court of the state, in affirming a jury verdict for the plaintiff, held that there was a proximate causal relationship between this act of negligence and reasonably foreseeable mental suffering. The plaintiff was awarded $2,000 (*Wallace* v. *Coca Cola Bottling Plants Inc.*, 269 A.2d 117 (Me. 1970)).
>
> A woman was trying on clothing in a store when a wall collapsed. She experienced a personality change, along with severe and persistent leg, head, and back pains, although she was not struck by the wall and did not receive any physical injuries. Her doctor testified that her condition was caused by fright related to the collapsing wall and that her condition was permanent. The supreme court of the state affirmed the jury's decision for the plaintiff (*Okrina* v. *Midwestern Corp.*, 282 Minn. 400, 165 N.W.2d 259 (1969)).
>
> A woman used a hair care product that left resin in her hair. Since she could not remove the resin, she had to cut off her hair. For months she was too embarrassed and humiliated to leave her home. Although no permanent damage was done to the woman's hair, the defendant was found liable on breach of warranty, with damages provided for the emotional distress caused to the plaintiff (*West* v. *Alberto Culver Co.*, 486 F.2d 459 (10th Cir. 1973)).

In the above cases, emotional distress was not always inflicted intentionally. Nonetheless, through testimony related to the psychological nature of the injuries, plaintiffs were able to receive awards.

Defenses. There are two principal defenses for a defendant in a negligence case. The first is contributory negligence; the second is assumption of the risk. If a defendant is proved to have been negligent, he or she may still avoid the consequences of a verdict in favor of the plaintiff if, in spite of the defendant's negligence, the plaintiff was also negligent. The standard of care defining the plaintiff's actions as contributorily negligent is the same as the test for ordinary negligence. That is, the "reasonable person" standard is once again used. In a recent case, a widow brought an action against an electric utility for her husband's death, which occurred while he was operating a hydraulic boom mounted on a truck. The boom came in contact with an uninsulated electrical wire that was strung on a utility pole. The trial court held that the utility company had been negligent in maintaining an uninsulated overhead electrical wire in a populous residential area. However, the appellate court held that the operator of the boom was negligent as well, because he had not used ordinary care for his own protection in lifting the boom between electrical cables and allowing it to come in contact with a 7,200-volt wire. The appeals court therefore reversed the verdict awarded to the plaintiff by the trial court jury, and the widow received nothing for the death of her husband (*Tellis* v. *Union Electric Co.,* 536 S.W.2d 742 (Mo. App. 1976)).

As the *Tellis* case demonstrates, a plaintiff found to be contributorily negligent by the court is completely barred from recovering money damages in a lawsuit. Even if the defendant's negligence was much greater than the plantiff's, there is no recovery. The following case illustrates an unsuccessful attempt on the part of the defendant to use the defense of contributory negligence: An elderly hospitalized woman was told not to get out of bed. Her physician ordered a vaporizer to be placed in her room. She got out of bed against orders, touched the vaporizer, and subsequently burned herself. The court determined that there was no contributory negligence on the part of the patient because of her age and infirmities and that the hospital must safeguard such patients from danger (*Clark* v. *Piedmont Hospital,* 162 S.E.2d 468 (Ga. 1968)). Similarly, mentally ill patients who are not capable of understanding instructions or looking out for their own safety probably would not be found to be contributorily negligent.

Because the doctrine of contributory negligence often allows harsh (and perhaps even unfair) results to occur in cases where defendants are clearly negligent, a number of other doctrines, known as "escape doctrines," have been developed. One such doctrine is that of comparative negligence. Comparative negligence allows the plaintiff to recover even if he was contributorily negligent, as long as his negligence was, in the mind of the jury, no more serious than the defendant's negligence. The logic behind this doctrine is simple. If a plaintiff is found guilty of negligence to a degree less or no more than that of the defendant, it would be unfair to allow a negligent defendant to escape liability merely because, to an equal or lesser degree, the plaintiff was also negligent. This doctrine is the majority view in the United States and, where adopted, prevents the harsh result that often occurs in jurisdictions where contributory negligence is the doctrine applied by the courts. In some states the damages are apportioned on the basis of the percentage of negligent behavior by both parties.

The second major defense available to a defendant in a negligence action is the doctrine of assumption of risk. If the plaintiff knew of the risk created by the defendant's negligence and yet voluntarily assumed it, the plaintiff must be denied recovery for damages. The purpose behind this doctrine is to prevent a plaintiff from recovering when, even though the defendant was negligent initially, the plaintiff's own reckless action was itself the direct cause of the injury.

The assumption of risk may be express, as when an exculpatory clause in a contract insulates one party to the transaction from liability resulting from his or her own negligence. The courts are hesitant to enforce these kinds of exculpatory clauses and contracts, but most decisions hold that they are enforceable if they are knowingly agreed to by the party waiting his or her right to protection.

Generally, assumption of risk is implied by the facts of the case in question. The plaintiff must have known of the risk and voluntarily chosen to proceed with a given course of action in spite of that risk. The plaintiff must, of course, have some alternative to proceeding with that course of action. The following case example illustrates the doctrine of assumption of risk.

> An adult patient had had his ears washed out on several occasions because they had become plugged with wax. He came to the office of his physician without an appointment and, although told that the physicians who practiced in the office were at the hospital and that his ears would not be treated until they re-

turned, insisted that the nurse do it. She finally agreed to do so, but during the washing process both of the patient's eardrums were ruptured. The court held that the fact that the patient came to the office without an appointment and persuaded the nurse to perform the procedure was sufficient to support a finding that the patient had assumed the risk (*Brockman* v. *Harpole*, 444 P.2d 25 (Or. 1968)).

If a plaintiff encounters a danger created by the defendant's negligence and, on discovering the dangerous condition, is left with no alternative but to proceed, an "assumption of risk" defense by the defendant will not likely prevail. There are several other instances in which courts will not allow certain risks to be assumed. Common carriers and public utilities are not allowed to use disclaimers that limit their liability for personal injury resulting from a given kind of risk. In addition, when statutes or other ordinances are set up to protect certain classes of people, members of those classes are not allowed to assume any risk proscribed by the statute in question— for instance, such risks as those designed to be prevented by safety laws or other regulatory schemes. Also, under no circumstances does this defense apply to a negligence case. If the physician advises the patient of the risk of proper care and then provides improper care, he or she cannot defend him- or herself on the ground that the patient had assumed a risk (*Valdez* v. *Percy*, 217 P.2d 422 (Cal. 1950)).

Professional Negligence

An area of tort liability that has expanded over the last two decades is that of professional negligence. Although medical malpractice has received by far the most publicity, other professionals have also come under closer scrutiny. Lawyers, accountants, architects, human services professionals from all areas, and other professionals have all been subjected to liability for misfeasance in the performance of their duties. This section is concerned with standards of care as they apply to professionals. (A more detailed discussion of specific professional negligence issues as related to the human services professional is offered in Chapter Ten.)

Example A

A twenty-three-year-old woman complaining of nearsightedness consults two ophthamologists and is fitted with contact lenses. Several years later she consults them concerning irritation caused by the contact lenses. Over the next five years, she has numerous consultations until, after five examinations on successive months, they give her an eye pressure test. (This is nine years after her initial consultation.) The test reveals that the woman has glaucoma, which could have been effectively treated if detected sooner. The ophthamologists were following accepted practices in not administering the pressure test to someone under forty years old. Are they liable for medical malpractice? [*Helling* v. *Carey*, 84 Wash. 2d 514, 519 P.2d 981 (1974).]

Example B

An attorney is hired to draw up a will, which he apparently does. However, when the testator dies and the will is offered for probate, the will is not accepted as valid because the attorney had failed to have it properly attested. As a result of this failure, an intended beneficiary does not get a share of the testator's estate. In a suit brought by the intended beneficiary, will the attorney be liable for malpractice? [*Biankanja* v. *Irving*, 49 Cal. 2d 647, 320 P.2d 16 (1958).]

Example C

A patient under psychological care tells his psychologist that he intends to kill a woman who has spurned his romantic advances. The psychologist has the patient detained by campus police at the university hospital. Shortly thereafter a panel of three psychiatrists review the matter and recommend the patient's release from the hospital. Two months later the patient shoots and stabs the young woman. In a wrongful death action by the woman's parents, are the psychotherapists liable for the woman's death? [*Tarasoff* v. *Regents of the University of California*, 17 Cal. 3d 425, 551 P.2d 334, 131 Cal. Rptr. 14 (1976).]

The key to the professional negligence case is the higher standard of care imposed on the professional. He or she is not held to the standard of the reasonable man on the street but rather to the standard of a reasonable man in that profession.

One can see, then, that professionals are not required to be perfect, nor are they required to insure against all contingencies. However, professionals are required to perform their services competently and to the best of their abilities.

Keeping in mind the general principles of negligence applied to professional negligence cases let us now examine this area as it applies to individual professions.

Physicians. In order to find a physician liable for malpractice, courts require that the following elements be established by a preponderance of the evidence: (1) a physician-patient relationship (so that a duty is owed by physician to patient), (2) a physician's violation of the applicable standard of due care, (3) causation, and (4) injury to plaintiff (Belli, 1982).

A physician-patient relationship is a contractual relationship that occurs when the patient accepts the services of the physician for medical treatment. Both parties must knowingly accept the existence of such a relationship (*Tindlay* v. *Board of Supervisors of Inahove County,* 72 Ariz. 58, 230 P.2d 526 (1951)). The patient can end the relationship at any time, but the physician may not do so unless he or she gives proper notice to the patient. Consulting physicians, including psychiatrists who are asked to evaluate a patient upon referral of another physician, normally have not entered into a physician-patient relationship. Such a relationship occurs only when implied or expressed contracts are made for treatment or the treatment process itself begins. The presentation of a prescription for medications to the patient would imply treatment even if no other therapy is initiated.

Another important aspect of a medical malpractice case is violation of the applicable standard of care. A physician is expected to exercise the degree of care and skill expected of physicians with the same training and experience. This is a test of reasonable behavior under the circumstances and does not require the physician to guarantee results.

A doctrine historically used by the courts to assess the applicable standard of care is known as the locality rule. Under this doctrine expert testimony of a physician from the defendant's community was required in order to find the defendant negligent. Since it was often difficult to get doctors in the same community to testify against each other, many cases of medical malpractice were not rectified. However, this doctrine is falling into disfavor as more courts recognize that communities are no longer isolated islands and that medical technology flows freely across the country.

In determining a physician's standard of care, some courts require only that a physician follow "the practice of the profession." Most courts, however, continue the inquiry into other factors to determine whether the physician is negligent despite following practices of the profession. In example A the ophthamologists had followed accepted practices of their profession because the incidence of glaucoma under forty is small. Nevertheless, the court found the physicians negligent in not administering the eye pressure test. The court noted that the test is relatively simple and inexpensive to administer and that, if the profession were allowed to set its own standards, it might lag behind in the adoption of new and available techniques. Thus, in some situations the courts, for the protection of society, must impose a standard of care on a profession.

The last two elements of a medical malpractice case, injury and causation, are closely interrelated. In the flagrant medical malpractice case, where a surgeon cuts off the wrong leg or leaves a sponge in the patient, these elements are self-evident. It is clear that the patient suffered damages caused by the physician's negligence. However, in the typical malpractice case, injury and causation are not clear. Where a physician misdiagnoses a disease, a court must often determine whether the damages were indeed caused by the physician's negligence. It may be that the detection of the disease would not have stopped it from affecting the patient. Also, some courts are reluctant to impose liability on a physician because they recognize that the physician did not cause the patient to contract a disease.

Lawyers. As with the development of medical malpractice, legal malpractice is on the upswing. Originally there was some confusion as to whether the action arose out of contract or tort law. However, the modern trend is to proceed in tort. Since the issues in legal malpractice are the same as medical (duty, breach of duty, injury, causation), the use of tort simplifies the proceedings.

The standard of care for an attorney is similar to that of a doctor. The attorney must possess the skill and knowledge common to members of the profession and must exercise that skill in a reasonable, diligent, and prudent manner (*Spangler* v. *Sellers*, 5 F. 882 (S.D. Ohio 1881)). Circumstances play a part in determining the standard of care. The standard for an attorney called on to make a quick judgment is different from that imposed on the attorney who has time to reflect on the problem. Also, the type of work done by the attorney is important. Litigation—which, by its nature, depends more on subjective judgment and risk taking—is subjected to a different standard than, for example, examination of a title.

Typical cases of legal malpractice involve failure to meet filing deadlines or otherwise to act promptly on behalf of a client, failure to inform and counsel a client about an offer of settlement, and failure to avoid a conflict of interest with a client (for instance, by representing two clients in the same transaction or by accepting a case in which the attorney has an undisclosed interest in the outcome).

In example B, where the attorney failed to have a will properly attested, the court ruled in favor of the intended beneficiary even though he was not a client of the attorney. The court determined the attorney's failure to act promptly on behalf of the client (the deceased) resulted in foreseeable harm to the plaintiff and the correlation between the lawyer's conduct and the damage suffered was clear. In this case the damage was easy to identify (the share of the estate originally willed to the intended beneficiary); often in attorney malpractice cases the court's task of determining damages is more problematic. In such cases it is often difficult to show that the attorney caused the client's loss because, even had the case been tried, a jury might not have ruled in the client's favor. What often occurs in legal malpractice cases, then, is a suit within a suit. Only when the issues in the original action are determined can damages be assessed and causation established in the malpractice action.

Psychotherapists. Since psychotherapists are closely related to physicians in their practices, the principles applicable to medical malpractice are also applicable to psychotherapists. The most important development in this area is the change made by the courts in the standard of care a psychotherapist must exercise. Historically, the courts have recognized the contractual nature of the patient-psychotherapist relationship and the obligation that the psychotherapist owes to his or her patient. Most important, courts have recognized the need for strict confidentiality in this relationship. The confidentiality arises out of the patient's expectations, which are represented in the expressed or implied contract creating the relationship. Many courts have imposed damages when this confidentiality and trust have been breached (*Lockett* v. *Goodill*, 71 Wash. 2d 654, 430 P.2d 589 (1967); *Horne* v. *Patton*, 291 Ala. 701, 287 So. 2d 824 (1973); *Doe* v. *Roe*, 93 Misc. 2d 201, 400 N.Y.S.2d 668 (1977)). However, this recognition of the confidential relationship has been diminished somewhat in recent years. Some courts have imposed liability on a psychotherapist when his or her failure to breach confidentiality results in harm to a third person.

Example C represents a well-known California case where liability was imposed on the psychotherapist for the death of a young woman. The court held that the psychotherapist had a duty to warn the intended victim of the patient's violent tendencies. The court noted the confidential relationship of the psychotherapist with this patient. However, the ruling by the court in favor of the plaintiff requires the psychotherapist to breach confidentiality in favor of society's general interest and safety. (More details of *Tarasoff* v. *Regents of the University of California* are given in Chapter Ten.) When a psychotherapist determines that a patient may cause harm to a third person, he or she must warn or protect that third person or be liable for damages. If he or she is negligent in failing to detect the potential for violence in the patient, the psychotherapist will likewise be held liable for damages to a third person.

Other Liabilities

In addition to intentional torts and negligence, there are numerous other types of liabilities that the human services professional might encounter, although in more indirect ways. Three such types of liabilities are strict liability, products liability, and premises liability. The following three cases illustrate these types of liabilities:

Example A

You are the director of a daycare program for chronic psychiatric patients. On your premises you keep a dog as a source of pleasure, companionship, and constancy for your patients. On one occasion the dog bites an outpatient—the first such time the animal has been known to have bitten anyone. Are you or your center liable for the dog's action?

Example B

On the recommendation of a psychologist, a client purchases from a nationally known department store a piece of equipment that is supposed to help eliminate her child's problem with bed wetting. The directions for the equipment indicate an alarm will sound when the sheets become wet with urine, thereby waking the child. The power source for the unit consists of batteries. The equipment functions well for a while, but then the child develops a skin irritation, caused by the urine's interacting with the sheet that conducts the current. Evidently, when the batteries for the equipment get low, there is inadequate current to activate the bell. Instead, the current acts to electrolize the urine, causing what is diagnosed as "buzzer ulcers." Is it likely that the manufacturer of the equipment will be held liable for damages?

Example C

You and your colleagues have leased a section of a building for the private operation of a mental health clinic. You occupy half of the building, and a separate group leases the other half. Both groups share the hallway, the entrance area, and the parking lot. A client leaves your office and proceeds down the common hallway to the entrance area, where she stumbles on a protruding piece of ceramic tile, loses her balance, and falls into the glass door, breaking it and sustaining lacerations on her face and arm. Who is likely to be found liable for such damages?

Strict Liability. Strict liability is liability without fault. In contrast to negligence (which is based on the Judeo-Christian concept of fault, with the one who breaks the law or commandment being at fault), strict liability imposes liability on the defendant even though both parties may be at fault or both may be blameless. The rationale behind strict liability is the balancing of social equities in determining who is in the best position to bear the loss. This concept of liability first developed in cases involving unusually hazardous activities, such as keeping wild animals. Persons choosing to be engaged in such activities, it was reasoned, should bear the consequences of their choices. In such cases there are deemed to be extraordinary threats to the general safety of society, and those who create such threats must be responsible for any resulting harm. If society were only to require those persons to exercise due care, society would not be adequately protected from unusual hazards. The law then reasons that those who create the threats are in the best position to monitor the threats and bear the costs of damages resulting therefrom. In making decisions regarding strict liability, courts stress that the defendant is acting for his or her own purpose and may be seeking benefit or profit. Therefore, the potential benefactor is in a better position to bear the potential loss than is the innocent victim.

In example A, although you were the director of a program with a "therapy dog" that bit a patient, you would not be liable for damages unless the dog had previously bitten at least one other person or had shown propensities for violence. Owners of inherently nondangerous animals (such as dogs or cats) are not strictly liable for injuries these animals cause. Hence the phrase "Every dog is entitled to one free bite." (It should be noted, however, that in some states you would be held strictly liable if the dog proved to have dangerous propensities or dangerous characteristics, even though you had no prior knowledge of them.) Had the animal been a pet lion or other animal with known dangerous propensities, you would undoubtedly have been held strictly liable. In determining which activities are abnormally dangerous, courts will consider the following questions: (1) Does the activity involve a high degree of risk of grave harm to personal property—risk that cannot be eliminated by the use of reasonable care? (2) Is the activity one that is not commonly engaged in by the community? (3) Is the activity inappropriate to the place where it occurs? (4) Is the acvitity of little or no value to the community?

Products Liability. In recent years there has been a tremendous growth in the number of claims for product-caused injuries; more than one million claims per year have been filed regarding products liability, with nearly half of those claims involving litigation (Kionka, 1977). The current underlying philosophy of products liability law is that anyone who makes and markets a defective product is responsible to the ultimate user and consumer. When harm to plaintiffs or their property is causally related to the unsafe condition of a product, the plaintiffs may have a cause of action against those who designed, manufactured, or furnished that product. In most jurisdictions a products liability lawsuit may be based on negligence, breach of warranty, and/or strict liability.

There are a variety of ways in which the designer, manufacturer, distributor, or retailer of a product may have negligently created an unsafe condition. The design of the product itself could have been unnecessarily dangerous. Negligence may have occurred during the manufacturing process itself—for instance, by the use of defective materials. The product's packaging or container might also be inadequate, as might the warnings or directions for use of the product. In short, liability for negligence might be found if a defendant failed to exercise the care of a reasonable person under the given circumstances. The focus is on the negligent conduct of the defendant in designing, manufacturing, or selling the product.

Warranties are certain kinds of express or implied promissory representations of fact which are made by the manufacturer or seller as part of the sales transaction. *Implied* warranties require that the product be fit for the typical purposes for which it was sold. A plaintiff who sues for breach of one of these warranties need not prove negligence or other fault.

The focus of *strict* liability in products liability cases is on the unreasonably dangerous nature of the product—not on the conduct of the defendant. Strict liability is a response to modern marketing techniques, which produce goods that cannot be adequately inspected by the typical consumer. In order to establish liability, then, the plaintiff must show that the product is unreasonably dangerous. To determine the unreasonably dangerous nature of the product, the court will typically consider the following factors: (1) the usefulness and desirability of the product; (2) the availability of other and safer products to meet the same needs; (3) the likelihood of injury and its probable consequence; (4) the obviousness of the danger; (5) common knowledge or abnormal public expectation of danger; (6) the avoidability of injury by care in use of the product, including the effect of warnings and instructions; and (7) the ability to eliminate danger without seriously impairing the usefulness of the product or without making it unduly expensive. Regardless of which theory the injured party uses, a causal relationship between the product's defect and the harm suffered must be proved. In example B, a hypothetical case, it appears that a defect in the design of the equipment has allowed the urine to interact with the electric current without ringing the bell. A causal relationship between this defect and the resulting harm can be shown. The manufacturer of the equipment probably would be found liable in a products liability case; it is unlikely, however, that the psychologist who recommended the product would be found liable.

Because of the increasing frequency of use of technical equipment and instruments in fields employing human services professionals, more products liability cases may in the future be filed against these professionals. Biofeedback equipment, computerized testing stations, aversive conditioning devices, and other equipment powered by either alternating or direct current, while seemingly safe and relatively free from products liability suits thus far, increase the potential for damages in the professional fields employing these devices. In order to decrease the likelihood of products liability suits, manufacturers are increasingly employing human factors engineers, who study the relationship between the human being and the product or machine. The use of these specialists reflects the post-World War II dramatic increase in the use of complex machines and the need for these pieces of equipment to fit the human being. Human factors engineers apply principles of psychology, physiology, and engineering to show how machines can be designed so that, in their normal operation, injuries will be avoided. In attempting to design safe products, the human factors engineer uses three basic approaches that are recognized by safety groups: (1) Design out the dangerous characteristics. (2) If you cannot design out the dangerous characteristics, then find a way of guarding or protecting the human from the hazards. (3) If you can do neither of the above, then warn, direct, and instruct the potential users of the products—adequately and effectively.

Premises Liability. Human services professionals who own buildings for their own practices, who lease part of their buildings for the use of others, or who themselves occupy leased space should be aware that certain duties and responsibilities accompany each of these roles. The general rule is that the owner of property owes no duty to protect one outside his land from natural conditions existing on the land unless the dangers on the land extend onto adjacent properties (for instance, a dilapidated building hanging over the boundary of the land) or affect persons traveling on public ways adjacent to the owner's land. (The term "owner" applies to the person who occupies the land or, if it is unoccupied, to the actual owner.)

The owner's duty to those on the premises depends on the legal status for those persons to be on the premises. The principal statuses of the visitors to the land include trespassers, licensees, invitees, and tenants.

A landowner owes no duty to trespassers (those who come on the land without permission) except that the owner must exercise ordinary care to warn the trespasser of hidden artificial dangers, such as excavation operations or covered holes in the ground, that involve a serious risk of bodily harm. However, the owner will be liable for injuries to child trespassers if the dangerous condition on the land is likely to cause injury to children and the owner knows that children do frequent the land. This is known as the "attractive nuisance" theory and applies to abandoned automobiles and refrigerators, woodpiles, elevators, railroad terminals, and other potentially dangerous settings (*Sioux City and Pacific Railroad Co.* v. *Stout,* 84 U.S. 657 (1873)).

Licensees are those who enter the land with the permission of the owner for purposes other than the owner's benefit. Firemen, social guests, and strangers who are allowed to enter the property are among those classified as licensees. The duty owed to licensees is simply to warn them of dangerous conditions if known to the owner.

Invitees are similar to licensees in that they too enter with the owner's permission. Invitees, however, enter for some purpose related to the owner's business, and some economic or other benefit must accrue to the owner in connection with the visitor's entrance. The health service professional's clients or patients would be classified as invitees. The owner owes a greater legal duty to this classification of visitors. There is imposed, by common law, a general duty to use reasonable and ordinary care in keeping the property reasonably safe for the benefit of the invitee. Over and above this duty, the law expects the owner to make reasonable inspection to discover and repair hazardous conditions (such as slippery floors or holes in the floors) that threaten the safety of the invitee. Warnings may also suffice. Any invitee may, however, exceed the scope of his or her invitation and thereby lose the status of invitee. If, for example, a client in a mental health office should enter the staff coffee room (in an area marked "Restricted to Staff Only") and burn himself on the coffee pot, the courts may hold the patron to be a trespasser and thus attach no liability for the harm on the part of the defendant.

Landlords' liabilities to tenants vary greatly from jurisdiction to jurisdiction, but the general rule of common law is that a tenant who leases an entire building must maintain it so as to avoid unreasonable risk of harm to others. If only portions of the premises are leased, the tenant is charged with this duty for the leased portions only. The landlord remains responsible for the liability associated with areas over which he or she maintains control. Common areas or those areas on the premises not used exclusively by any tenant—areas such as hallways, approaches, entrances, stairwells, and elevators—typically remain the responsibility of the leasor. In example C liability for injuries to the woman who stumbled on the tile and fell into the glass door would likely remain with the leasor unless specific details of the lease agreement dictated otherwise.

Workers' Compensation

Workers' compensation laws developed in the 1900s as an attempt to provide satisfactory means of handling occupational disabilities, which had been increasing in volume as America became more industrialized. Prior to the enactment of these laws, common law principles held that negligence must be shown before a worker could be compensated for injuries or harm sustained at work. While injured employees had the right to initiate actions against employers who were negligent, the accepted common law defenses of contributory negligence, assumption of risk, and negligent acts of fellow servants resulted in few favorable decisions for the injured workers. Disabled workers who did sue employers often found the process slow, costly, and, at best, uncertain.

In 1911 the first workers' compensation laws were enacted, and by 1920 all but eight states had adopted such laws. Today each of the fifty states has a workers' compensation law.

The social philosophy that is the basis for workers' compensation is the belief that society should provide financial and medical benefits for injuries arising out of the employment situation without regard for any fault involved. Resulting economic losses are considered costs of production; thus, the ultimate source of payment is the consumer of the product.

The publication *An Analysis of Workers' Compensation Laws* (Chamber of Commerce of the United States, 1981), lists the basic objectives underlying these compensation laws:

1. Provide sure, prompt, and reasonable income and medical benefits to work-accident victims, or income benefits to their dependents, regardless of fault.
2. Provide a single remedy and reduced court delays, costs, and work loads arising out of personal injury litigation.
3. Relieve public and private charities of financial drains—incident to uncompensated industrial accidents.
4. Eliminate payment of fees to lawyers and witnesses as well as time-consuming trials and appeals.
5. Encourage maximum employer interest in safety and rehabilitation through an appropriate experience-rating mechanism.
6. Promote frank study of causes of accidents (rather than concealment of fault)—reducing preventable accidents and human suffering.

The following cases are representative of those seen in litigation regarding workers' compensation:

Example A

A man employed to load pulp wood onto trucks by hand felt a pain in his back as he was working. When the pain worsened later in the day, he reported it to his superior and received medical attention. One month later he was admitted to the hospital, and a herniated disc was removed from his back. The work done by the employee was not dangerous, nor was the employer negligent in having the worker perform such work. Is the worker entitled to workers' compensation benefits? [*Matthews* v. *R. T. Allen and Sons,* 266 A.2d 240 (Me. 1970).]

Example B

A social worker, while driving from his home to his office, was fatally injured in a single-car accident. As part of his employment, the employer required that he have a car at work. Is the family of the social worker entitled to workers' compensation benefits? [*Smith* v. *Workmen's Compensation Board,* 69 Cal. 2d 814, 447 P.2d 365 (1968).]

Example C

A thirty-seven-year-old man had a known service-connected disability of asthma and neurosis. He was hired as an attendant-nurse for a cottage in a home for the mentally retarded. When one of his patients died as a result of injuries, the ensuing investigation resulted in newspaper, television, and radio publicity. This nurse-attendant was one of those questioned by the media. He committed suicide during the course of the investigation, following a "personality change" and depression noticed by those around him. Is his widow entitled to workers' compensation benefits? [*Trombley* v. *Michigan,* 366 Mich. 649, 115 N.W.2d 561 (1962).]

Example D

A bus company employee had been under treatment for hypertension. While he was loading the baggage compartment of the bus, he suffered a heart attack and subsequently died from it. The autopsy revealed that the employee had atherosclerosis, which increased the risk of heart failure. Will the widow's claim for death benefits be granted? [*Chrisman* v. *Greyhound Bus Lines, Inc.,* 208 Neb. 6, 301 N.W.2d 595 (1981).]

Example E

The employee was a foreman at a steel plant that had unionized despite management's efforts to stop it. When friction developed between the union and management, the foreman was caught in the middle—between the production demands of management and the job quality standards of the union. He became disabled as a result of chronic anxiety mixed with depression. The condition developed over a period of years. Is the foreman entitled to a compensation award? [*Albanese's Case,* 79 Mass. 1171, 389 N.E.2d 83 (1979).]

Although workers' compensation laws vary from state to state, several themes and aspects are common to nearly all. The intent of all these laws is to award employees certain benefits when they suffer injuries arising out of and in the course of employment. Negligence and fault are generally irrelevant; negligence by the employee does not lessen the employee's rights or benefits, nor does an employer's freedom from negligence lessen his liability. Coverage is limited to persons having the status of an employee—as distinguished from an independent contractor.

The benefits to which one is entitled under workers' compensation laws also vary, although, once again, common themes run among jurisdictions. Cash-wage benefits generally amount to two thirds of the worker's previous average weekly wage, with minimum and maximum amounts of benefits determined on a state-to-state basis. Monies received via workers' compensation benefits are generally not considered to be subject to federal income tax. In the case of death, benefits for dependents are provided in all states.

Hospital and medical expenses *related to the compensable injury* are provided to those found to be entitled to workers' compensation benefits. These expenses typically include but need not be limited to doctors' fees, emergency room costs, hospital care, physical therapy treatments, medications, prosthetics and other therapeutic devices, nursing care, special equipment or supplies to reduce pain and discomfort, and, in the case of work-related emotional disturbances, psychotherapy and other types of psychological, psychiatric, and behavioral treatment.

Employees receiving workers' compensation benefits are also entitled to services that will assist in their rehabilitation. The premise behind this benefit is that it is cost-effective to retain or otherwise rehabilitate injured workers, so that they can eventually return to vocationally gainful activities. Such a return reduces cost to the employer and the insurer and is also beneficial to the injured worker. Some states allow for the continuance of benefits to injured workers until they are able to equal or exceed the wages earned on the job at which the injury incurred. Rehabilitation services may be directed by state agencies, private rehabilitation firms hired by the workers' compensation insurance carrier, or by rehabilitation specialists working directly for the insurance carrier or the company being insured. Workers' compensation recipients participating in such programs typically continue to receive regular wages plus any additional travel or other costs incurred as part of the rehabilitation.

In return for these benefits, injured employees and their dependents give up the right to sue the employer for damages related to any injury covered by the workers' compensation law. They do, however, retain the right to sue third persons whose negligence caused the injury to the employee. If such liability actions result in favorable actions for the plaintiff, amounts recovered may first be applied to reimburse the employer for workers' compensation benefits, with the balance going to the employee.

The right to workers' compensation benefits generally depends on one test: Is the injury connected to work? That is, did the injury occur "in the course of employment," and did it "arise out of the employment"? Again, negligence is not an issue. Accordingly, then, even if the employer's conduct is faultless and the employee's conduct negligent, the employee will receive benefits if the injury arises out of and in the course of the employment. Conversely, the employer might have little respect for the safety of his or her workers and require them to perform dangerous acts, while the worker's conduct is faultless. The injured worker receives the same award. Thus, the test is the relationship of the injury-producing event to the employment. Such a determination is a matter not of assessing the blame but of marking out boundaries.

Example A, where the worker injured his back, is a classic workers' compensation case. The injury resulted from the performance of job functions. The work was not necessarily dangerous, nor was it likely to cause injury; the employer did not make unreasonable demands on the employee, nor was the worker performing his job improperly. Nonetheless, since the injury occurred in the course of a work-related activity, the worker was awarded full benefits under the applicable workers' compensation act.

In workers' compensation cases, unlike tort cases, the only injuries compensated are those that produce disability and, therefore, adversely affect earning power. Thus, some injuries that might produce large money verdicts at common law result in minimal awards under workers' compensation. The workers' compensation system, unlike the tort recovery system, does not pretend to restore to the claimant what he lost; instead, it gives him a sum that—when added to his remaining earning ability, if any—will presumably enable him to exist without having to resort to public aid.

Since the amount of compensation is not an issue, the primary question in most workers' compensation cases is whether the injury was indeed work related; that is, did it arise out of and in the course of employment? This test has been subject to a great deal of legal interpretation in various jurisdictions. In general, however, the courts define "arising out of" as "caused by" or "resulting from" and "in the course of employment" as "on the work site"—not traveling to or from work. This rather strict definition of "in the course of employment" has been eased by various exceptions. Example B, regarding the social worker involved in an auto accident on his way to work, illustrates one such exception. In this case, even though the worker had not yet begun his workday, the court awarded death benefits to his widow. The court held that the employer's rule requiring this social worker to have a car at work made this particular accident compensable. If the employer had not required the worker to take the risk of driving his car, the widow would not have been entitled to the death benefits.

The injury "arising out of" employment may be either physical trauma, emotional trauma, or some combination thereof. All that is necessary is that the injured worker be able to identify an event or series of events that are work related and result in disabling injury. The injury need not be a major physical trauma; the courts have recognized that different workers react in different ways to various injuries. What might appear to be a slight injury to one could result in disability to another.

In example C, where the employee was known to have preexisting physical and mental conditions prior to employment, the issue was whether the injuries (and ultimate death) were those "arising out of" employment. The employer argued that the emotional injuries and the ultimate death were caused by preexisting conditions that were, therefore, not compensable. The appeal board of the workers' compensation commission found that the investigation did precipitate a personality change and significant depression in the worker and that the eventual suicide during the course of the investigation was an uncontrollable impulse caused directly by the investigation. The court awarded his widow death benefits on the grounds that the suicide was induced by a work-related mental disorder.

In spite of preexisting physical or mental conditions, employers must accept employees with personal susceptibilities and weaknesses and must provide workers' compensation insurance for those employees just as they would be provided for all other employees. When a worker becomes disabled with personal injuries arising out of employment, that worker is entitled to workers' compensation benefits regardless of underlying biological, social, or psychological weaknesses. A recent case in Michigan involved a bakery worker who had previously been diagnosed as suffering from a "bipolar disorder, manic." He found work in a bakery and, although not a model employee, managed to maintain his employment as a general laborer and sanitation worker for four years prior to having a manic episode while at work. Just prior to the psychotic episode, which required hospitalization, he had complained to supervisors and co-workers of feeling "hassled." In addition, he complained that he was given unpopular jobs and was unfairly criticized. He was involved in a shoving and name-calling incident with his supervisor just days before his manic episode. The case was settled out of court, with the workers' compensation insurance carrier for the bakery voluntarily paying workers' compensation benefits. In this case it was clear that the employee's underlying mental illness clearly predisposed him to react to life stresses (the daily pressures of competitive work, job duty changes, and conflicts with supervisors) with psychological symptoms that reached psychotic proportions. The testimony of the evaluating psychologist was instrumental in the employer's decision to pay workers' compensation benefits without further litigation. The patient returned to work at the bakery some months later.

In some states a disabled worker who honestly, even though mistakenly, perceives that the injuries resulting in the disability occurred in the course of employment may be awarded benefits. Such were the facts in the case of Mary, a former waitress who claimed that she had to discontinue her work in the restaurant because of continued harassment from supervisors and co-workers. She claimed that she had been threatened and ridiculed and felt as if other employees were staring at her, making faces at her, occasionally bumping into her, and flaunting higher tips in front of her. She claimed that as a result of this harassment, she suffered fatigue, anemia, depression, sleep disturbances, and loss of appetite. She was diagnosed as having a paranoid disorder. She was awarded workers' compensation benefits.

Workers' compensation claims involving psychiatric and cardiac conditions have been particularly difficult ones for courts to decide. These two types of claims have a number of common characteristics, not the least being that the subjective history given by the patient is important to the eventual outcome of the litigation. The majority of cases involving both heart and emotional symptoms also involve significant issues related to preexisting conditions or predispositions. The employment factors in each may extend over long periods of time, and therefore the employment may not appear to be the immediate precipitating cause of the disability. Proof of causation may be quite difficult in each case and may ultimately hinge not only on the true facts of the case but on the skills and believability of the expert witnesses from the fields of medicine and the human services called on to testify for both the worker and the employer. In addition, it is difficult to determine where the stresses of daily nonoccupational living (for example, marital, family, or financial stresses) stop and where the stresses of employment start.

Example D illustrates a claim for death benefits involving a cardiac condition. In this case the employee had a heart attack while loading a bus and subsequently died. The work done by the employee was not considered unusual for his employment. Also, the hypertension and atherosclerosis made the employee susceptible to heart attacks whether on or off the job. The court held that the widow was not entitled to death benefits under the workers' compensation laws because there was no unusual stress or exertion involved in the job and because the particular injury was not the result of an accident.

A landmark case involving compensation to an employee for a psychiatric disability not associated with any physical injury, accident, specific event, or unusual stress is that of *Carter* v. *General Motors Corp.*, 106 N.W.2d 105 (Mich. 1960). James Carter worked on an assembly line at General Motors, where his job involved his taking a hub assembly from a nearby table to his own workbench to remove burrs, grind out holes, and place the assembly on a conveyor belt. He was unable to keep up with the pace of the work unless he took two assemblies with him at a time, but he was told repeatedly not to do so because the assembly parts became mixed up on the line. Twelve days after starting this work, he suffered an emotional breakdown variously described as paranoid schizophrenia and schizophrenic reaction, residual type. He filed a claim for workers' compensation benefits for disability and was awarded such benefits by the referee. The award was later affirmed by the workers' compensation appeal board. The Supreme Court of Michigan, on appeal by General Motors, decided that the condition was not permanent but did affirm the award of damages for temporary disability. The court noted that the diagnosed psychosis and disability did not result from a single event or injury but, instead, from emotional pressures encountered by Carter in the daily performance of his work.

Example E represents another case where the mental trauma extended over time. The anxiety experienced by the foreman developed over a number of years of being stuck in the middle between management and the union. The court recognized that this type of emotional disorder was a personal injury just like any other. This disorder was also accidental even though the accident stretched over a period of years. Since there was a causal relationship between the disability and work-related activities, the court ordered a compensation award. (This claim would not be uniformly granted in all states, since several states still require some physical cause of injury. Other states will find that the mental stresses did not constitute an accident but may view them as part of an occupational disease.)

The involvement of human services professionals in workers' compensation cases may be varied and extensive. Psychiatrists and psychologists are now routinely asked—often by the attorneys for both parties—to evaluate plaintiffs to determine the presence of emotional disability and to shed professional light on the role that work might have had in 'he development of any diagnosable psychological or psychiatric conditions. In *Carter* v. *General Motors,* the plaintiff was evaluated by only one mental health professional. The defendant did not offer expert psychiatric or psychological testimony to refute Carter's claims or to rebut the testimony of the psychiatrist who evaluated Carter. Thus, the psychiatrist's findings were accepted by the court. Such actions today would be unusual and unexpected. In fact, as the following case illustrates, mental health evaluations completed by psychologists and psychiatrists evaluating the same patient can reveal obvious discrepancies and differences in thinking.

The patient was a fifty-four-year-old female who was injured at work while operating a press break. A co-worker was attempting to repair the machine when a monkey wrench being used flew out of the machine and struck the worker on the neck and back. She was treated in an emergency room and later by numerous physicians for shoulder, neck, and back pain; paresthesia of the lower left extremity; headaches; and sleep disturbances. She was referred for a psychological evaluation by the attorney representing her in a workers' compensation claim and for a psychiatric evaluation by the attorney for the workers' compensation insurance carrier.

The psychologist diagnosed a conversion disorder and a dependent personality disorder. In his report he commented, "The disturbance is clearly not under voluntary control and cannot be explained by any physical disorder or known pathophysiological mechanism." Regarding the role of work in the establishment of the disorder, he stated, "It is clear that the incident involving her being struck with a monkey wrench served as a precipitant for the original pain." The psychiatrist diagnosed and concluded the following: "She does not exhibit any symptoms of a psychiatric illness; ergo, her complaints, which are bizarre and variable, must be construed to constitute malingering. In the absence of manifest anxiety and tension, the proposition of conversion mechanism is untenable." This illustration is given to show the disparity between two independent evaluators—one receiving a referral from the attorney for the plaintiff, the other from legal counsel for the defendant—not to draw conclusions about the accuracy of the diagnosis. (At this time the case is still pending.)

In addition to claims based on psychiatric disability alone, other—more numerous—cases for evaluation will claim some form of emotional disorder as secondary to physical injury or harm. A psychiatrist-attorney (Shlensky, 1978, p. 40) has commented, "Any serious illness or injury has psychological dimensions," and a psychiatrist (Blinder, 1979, p. 84) has added, "There is probably never a personal injury without some measurable psychic trauma or functional overlay." Many workers' compensation attorneys—when filing petitions for hearings with workers' compensation boards, commissions, or bureaus—now routinely add phrases such as "and functional overlay as a result of a documented work-related injury" to claims for organic injury or illness. In these cases the mental health experts serving as evaluators typically are asked to determine whether a worker is malingering or has a diagnosable mental condition. Psychiatrists, specifically, have been singled out for their failure to diagnose malingering in personal injury cases. Slovenko (1973, p. 306) has commented, "It appears that medical specialists in fields of the most objective empirical orientation, [for example,] neurosurgery, tend to see malingering as being much more prevalent than do those in the most subjective specialty, psychiatry. Perhaps the reason for this disparity lies in the psychiatrist's greater appreciation of the unconscious factors surrounding complaints of injury, an appreciation which seems to militate against the diagnosis of malingering."

Damages

When the actions or omissions of one party cause injury to the person or property of another, the basic (and often only) remedy for the detrimental injury or loss is monetary damages. In personal injury cases, damage refers to a sum of money awarded to the injured person.

Kionka (1977) sites three fundamental ideas of common law rules for damages: (1) The plaintiff is owed the right to be restored, to the extent possible, to his preinjury condition with money. Not only economic losses but loss of physical and mental well-being should be reimbursed. (2) It is possible to translate most noneconomic losses into monetary figures. (3) When a plaintiff sues in tort for an injury sustained, he must recover all damages arising from that injury in one sum and in a single lawsuit.

In tort there are three major categories of damages: nominal, compensatory, and punitive. These categories are not mutually exclusive, however, and one or more categories may be recoverable by any injured person. For example, an injured party may recover both compensatory and punitive damages. The amount of damages to be awarded to a person is not a question of the law. Rather, in a tort action, the actual amount of damages is a question to be resolved by the jury.

Nominal Damages. Nominal damages are awarded to an injured party when there is no substantial loss or injury to be compensated but, instead, merely a technical invasion of the injured party's legally protected rights. As the name implies, nominal damages exist as damages in name only; the amount of the award is generally unimportant. The current practice for nominal damages is to award one dollar; historically, nominal damages were for thirty cents— stemming from the thirty pieces of silver for which Judas sold out Christ. No allegation or proof of the loss need be shown by the plaintiff to receive an award of nominal damages. Such awards are sometimes seen in intentional torts, such as trespass to land, or in cases where the plaintiff proves actual damage but is unable to establish the amount.

An award of nominal damages will typically have the following results: (1) It may determine disputed property rights. (2) The plaintiff's reputation may be vindicated, as in an action for slander. (3) If a judgment is in favor of the plaintiff, he or she may be able to shift costs to the defendant.

Compensatory Damages. The most common type of damage, compensatory damage, is awarded to compensate the plaintiff for an actual loss or injury sustained; that is, to restore the plaintiff to the position he or she was in before the injury or loss. Compensatory damages, unlike nominal damages, require proof of actual loss before an award can be made.

Compensatory damages generally fall into the two subdivisions of general damages and special damages. General damages are awarded for harm and loss that are natural and usual consequences of the injury asserted in the statement of facts constituting the claim for tort. For example, general damages may be awarded for pain and suffering, past and future; loss of enjoyment of life; embarrassment and humiliation; and diminished earning capacity. These damages may be awarded without proof of pecuniary loss and may include compensation for bodily harm and emotional distress.

Special damages are actual damages that flow as a natural and proximate consequence from the defendant's wrong. These include medical expenses, past and future; cost of prescriptions and corrective supports; loss of earnings, past and future; property damage; and damages for unusual effects of the injury.

The determination of which items are general and which are special depends on the tort itself and the injuries alleged. Typically, general damages are more abstract than special damages. For example, loss of enjoyment of life is much more abstract than $4,000 in hospital bills. General damages cannot be reduced to an exact, straightforward mathematical figure; therefore, there can be no fixed standard for which such damages can be measured. Also, in personal injury cases, it has become common to refer to all economic losses as special damages; noneconomic losses then reflect general damages.

The issue of pain and suffering and its monetary value has continued to perplex attorneys, psychologists, and physicians as well as juries. Some states allow the attorney for the injured party to explain pain and suffering by reducing it into time segments of days, hours, and minutes. These time units then have a dollar value set on each unit, with a total monetary product resulting. For example, if it is established that a fifty-five-year-old man with a life expectancy of 20.8 years will suffer pain for the rest of his life, and if the man evaluates the pain and suffering at $10 per day, his attorney will argue for $75,920 for pain and suffering (20.8 years equal 7,592 days at $10 per day).

The injured party is also entitled to be compensated for the reasonable cost to repair property damage, or, if the property was totally or almost totally destroyed, to be awarded damages for the fair market value of the property at the time it was destroyed.

Generally, damages are not reduced or mitigated by reasons of benefits received by the plaintiff from other sources, such as health insurance, sick pay from an employer, Social Security benefits, disability insurance, or public aid. Attorney's fees, however, are not recoverable as damages in tort cases.

Punitive Damages. Punitive or exemplary damages are awarded to punish the defendant for aggravated, willful, wanton, or outrageous acts and to deter him from similar conduct in the future. These damages are awarded in addition to nominal and/or compensatory damages. In determining an award for punitive damages, a jury will consider the following elements: the character of the defendant's conduct; the seriousness of the loss or injury to the plaintiff; the defendant's financial status; and the expense of the litigation and attorney's fees to the plaintiff.

Consequential Damages. In addition to damages awarded to the plaintiff for losses or injuries, third parties who have suffered because of the injury may initiate a separate cause of action for "consequential damages." Such actions are typically limited to spouses, parents, and employers of the injured person. "Loss of consortium" refers to the loss of love, companionship, sexual relations, material services, conjugal fellowship, and other factors typically related to the loss or a partial loss of a spouse (Belli, 1980). Loss of consortium may be seen as a type of mental suffering associated with these losses related to the injury of a spouse. A modern case regarding such a loss (*Rodriguez* v. *Bethlehem Steel Corp.* 12 Cal. 3d 382, 525 P.2d 669, 115 Cal. Rptr. 765 (1974)) resulted in an award of $500,000 for the wife. Belli (1980, p. 73) has commented, "It may well be malpractice for an attorney to fail to become informed as to the marital status of a client and not advise the noninjured spouse of his or her loss of consortium rights." Employers historically had a property interest in the services of an employee sufficient to support a cause of action against a defendant whose tort removed such services. While a few states have preserved such action, most courts have refused to allow employers to be compensated. Children also have been denied such action for loss of the care, support, love, and nurturings of a parent, although some states allow the parents to recover for loss of services, companionship, and affection of the children.

Conclusion

The human services professional may be helpful to the court in the establishment of damages in a given case. The loss of consortium may represent an area where these professionals may offer testimony about the nature of the relationship and the significance of such loss. The whole issue of pain and suffering tends to be viewed as more of a psychological than a physical process and therefore falls more into the expertise areas of psychologists and other mental health workers. Testimony by these professionals can be extremely helpful in informing jurors of the individual responses and losses associated with personal injuries, pain, and loss of psychological and intellectual equilibrium. The neuropsychologist, in particular, can now provide strong and convincing data and testimony regarding the loss of intellectual ability secondary to trauma and pain (Woody, 1979).

As personal injury law continues to grow and expand in its attempts to safeguard citizens in their pursuit of health and freedom, the roles for human services professionals should similarly expand. Psychologists, psychiatrists, social workers, and other human services professionals can be expected to be called on more and more frequently to express their views on the safety of the environment and its natural and manufactured products, the nature and cost of pain and suffering, the value and resulting losses pertaining to work-related injuries, the need for sound physical and emotional environments, and, undoubtedly, a variety of other areas associated with personal rights, freedoms, and liberties.

Roger A. Rapaport

6

Employment Discrimination Law

❧❧❧❧❧❧❧❧❧❧❧❧❧❧❧❧❧❧❧❧❧❧❧❧❧

In our society, where employment constitutes a major ingredient of human life, the successes or failures of employment will significantly influence the individual's overall satisfaction with living. It is therefore essential that human services professionals be effective in helping their clients and patients properly integrate employment into their strategies for living.

The employment relationship has become increasingly subject to legal sanctions and restrictions. For the most part, these are intended to safeguard the interests of workers, but they reach to the very essence of the business enterprise. Neither the employer nor the employee is exempt from the mandates of the law. Employment relations law encompasses the legal tenets that apply to the conditions and interactions relevant to the employer and employee. The focus of this chapter is on employment discrimination.

Discrimination is a psychosocial entity. It is, simply stated, unjust treatment or the denial of equal treatment to all employees or job applicants (Miner and Miner, 1979, p. 6). In reviewing the law of discrimination, one should note that activities not involving current discrimination may, nevertheless, be contrary to law if they have an "adverse impact" on the employee or the job applicant. In *Griggs* v. *Duke Power Co.*, 401 U.S. 424 (1971), the Supreme Court of the United States held: "The objective of Congress in the enactment of

Title VII [of the Civil Rights Act of 1964] is plain from the language of the statute. It was to achieve equality of employment opportunities and remove barriers that have operated in the past to favor any identifiable group of white employees over other employees. Under the Act, *practices, procedures, or tests neutral on their face,* and even *neutral in terms of intent,* cannot be maintained if they operate to "freeze" the status quo of prior discriminatory employment practices" (pp. 429–430, emphasis added).

Many of the services performed in the employment context by human services professionals are vulnerable to discrimination, either intentional or unintentional—particularly in the areas of original employee selection and subsequent employee evaluation. To optimize human services for employment, the professional involved in the selection and evaluation process needs to understand how the law must be accommodated in these activities.

Historical Perspective

Perhaps the best way to understand the present laws regarding discrimination in employment is to perceive them against the background of change that has occurred since the turn of the century. These changes have affected both business and government and their relationships with their employees.

In the early 1900s, the business sector was small, locally owned, and locally controlled. The normal business enterprise was based in a small locality, and ownership was centralized in a single family or a small organization. These companies had very limited social impact. Only the local community was directly affected by the policies of the company. The governing philosophy was one of laissez-faire. This, in effect, granted the owner total and complete freedom to operate the business as he or she saw fit. Under the doctrine of laissez-faire, only economic factors needed to be considered in business decisions. Such factors as cost of raw materials, cost of transportation, cost of production, wages, and the market price of the product were the business owner's only considerations. When a business decided on a course of action, the social impact of that business policy was either not considered or, if considered, simply ignored.

At the turn of the century, government interference in or control of business was almost nonexistent. Although a few small agencies regulated very specific areas, in general the entire governmental philosophy was opposed to the regulation of industry on a national scale. Over the past eight decades, this philosophy and its application have changed to such an extent that today, in the 1980s, government has vastly increased in size and influence. This growth of government was necessitated by (1) the growth of business, which expanded beyond the local community; (2) the advent of two world wars; (3) the societal results of the Depression of the 1930s. In response to these factors, the federal government was forced to turn its back on laissez-faire and to develop policies of protection for selected special-interest groups.

With the abandonment of its laissez-faire attitude, the federal government used its power to counter the financial and organizational power of large manufacturing concerns as workers sought to organize labor unions. The right to organize was granted to workers by the government support through legislation. Court decisions enforced this policy and brought about the labor-management relationship as it is known today. The National Labor Relations Act, 29 U.S.C. sec. 151 *et seq.*, was enacted in the 1930s. This original Act regulating the workplace had only two purposes: first, to protect workers in their organizational efforts and union acvitity; second, to provide for the peaceful resolution of industrial disputes through collective bargaining. The National Labor Relations Act was not intended to rectify problems of racial, sexual, or religious discrimination. Even with no specific language on the point, however, the courts have applied the Act to provide substantial protection for the traditional victims of discrimination. The clear trend has been a steady increase in the number of government-protected groups. This has resulted, of necessity, in a spectacular increase in the size of government.

Today policy has shifted all the way from laissez-faire to affirmative action. No longer do national and state governments merely protect; they now act as advocates for certain groups. The underlying objective has been to force the business sector to take into account the social ramifications when policy decisions are being made. Today the business community is charged with a duty to correct the harmful effects of not allowing certain groups into the American economic system.

Evolution of Present Law

One major area of governmental intrusion into the private sector is in the area of employment discrimination. Surprisingly, the legislation in this area is not designed to eliminate employment discrimination. Rather, the purpose of such legislation is to ensure that discrimination is based only on real business considerations and qualifications rather than on social prejudice. In the 1980s, if a person is not hired, it must be because she or he does not fit the job or is not the most qualified. No longer may an individual be precluded from employment because of an employer's prejudices.

One of the first government attempts to regulate private employment was the 1926 Railway Labor Act, 45 U.S.C. sec. 151 *et seq.*, which protected employees of railroads and airlines from interference by employers and gave employees the right "to engage in concerted activities for mutual aid or protection." The Act forbade employers from discriminating against employees because of their "membership in any labor organization." Nine years later Congress passed the National Labor Relations Act to provide the same protection for all employees engaged in interstate commerce. Under the Act labor unions were given the exclusive right to represent employees; that is, only one union would represent all the workers in an occupation at a given factory or business.

While a union may be the exclusive bargaining agent for an employee, a duty of fair representation was imposed in *Steele* v. *Louisville & Nashville Railroad Co.*, 323 U.S. 192 (1944). This case involved a union that was certified to bargain for a contract with the employer. The negotiated contract called for the firing of all black union members and for the promotion of white union members. The Court ruled that, because the union had exclusive representation rights, it also had the implied duty to represent all its members fairly. The Court concluded that the union, by discriminating against blacks, had not properly represented the black employees.

The Supreme Court expanded this opinion in *Vaca* v. *Sipes*, 386 U.S. 171 (1967), stating that the union was obligated "to serve all members without discrimination toward any and to avoid arbitrary conduct." The Court defined arbitrary conduct as including discrimination based on race, sex, country, national origin, or religion.

The Fair Labor Standards Act, 29 U.S.C. sec. 201 *et seq.*, passed in 1938, consisted of amendments to existing legislation. Under this Act, which expanded employee protection and regulated working conditions, children were given favored treatment. Their hours were regulated, and they were not allowed to work at certain jobs. The Act also, for the first time, gave veterans the guaranteed right to return to their premilitary jobs. It also established minimum wages for some employees and required time-and-a-half payments for overtime work.

In 1959 Congress passed the major piece of legislation that regulates discrimination by a labor union against its members. The Labor-Management Reporting and Disclosure Act, 73 Stat. 519 (the Landrum-Griffin Act), protects the members from arbitrary discipline by the union itself. Under Landrum-Griffin union members are protected from discipline for exercising their First Amendment rights to free speech. The Act does not, however, contain language regulating discriminatory practices.

In 1963 the Equal Pay Act, 29 U.S.C. sec. 206 *et seq.*, an amendment to the Fair Labor Standards Act of 1938, was passed. The Equal Pay Act regulates minimum wages, overtime, and child labor. It requires that an employer "engaged in commerce" not discriminate "between employees on the basis of sex by paying wages at a rate less than the rate at which he pays wages to employees of the opposite sex for equal work on jobs requiring equal skill, effort, and responsibility and which are performed under similar working conditions" (sec. 206(d)). Some of the notable exceptions to this Act are seniority systems, merit systems, and systems in which earnings are measured by quantity or quality of work.

The term "equal work" has been defined to mean "substantially equal" in duties actually performed (*Schultz* v. *Wheaton Glass Co.*, 421 F.2d 259 (3d Cir. 1970)). Job titles or descriptions will not be controlling in determining equality. In other words, if two jobs have the same name, the court will not necessarily consider them to be the same jobs; conversely, if two jobs have different names but the work is identical, they will be considered equal. Jobs will be considered equal only if all the elements of the definition of "equal" are shown to exist for them. These elements are skill, effort, responsibility, and similarity of working conditions.

"Skill" refers to the individual employee's "experience, education, training, and ability" and must relate to the performance of the job. In *Brennan* v. *City Stores, Inc.*, 479 F.2d 235 (5th Cir. 1973), the court ruled that, even if male and female salespersons use different selling skills, the degree of skill is equal. In *Hodgson* v. *Brookhaven General Hospital*, 470 F.2d 729 (5th Cir. 1972), male orderlies and female nurses were ruled to have equal skills because the general nature of their jobs was the same.

"Effort" is defined as the "physical and mental exertion needed for the performance of jobs." In *Hodgson* v. *Daisy Manufacturing Co.*, (317 F. Supp. 538; affirmed in part, reversed in part, 445 F.2d 823 (8th Cir. 1971)). The court ruled that "effort" includes both the mental and physical effort involved in a job. The court held that the physical exertion of male workers could be balanced by the mental efforts of female workers. In other words, a court may hold that the efforts expended by a man and a woman in different types of work are equal.

The term "responsibility" is concerned with the "degree of accountability required in the performance of the job." A key element in determining whether responsibilities are equal is whether the employee is ultimately responsible for the consequences of his or her actions. In *Brennan* v. *Victoria Bank & Trust Co.*, 493 F.2d 896 (5th Cir. 1974), the court ruled that a teller who handled exchanges of cash with the public had greater responsibility than a teller who dealt with exchanges not involving cash. The court reasoned that a mistake by the teller dealing in cash would be costly and difficult to correct, while a mistake by the teller involved in a mere paper transaction would be less expensive and less difficult to correct. Once the court ruled that the responsibility accorded the two tellers was not equal, the bank was under no obligation to provide them with equal pay. Similarly, in *Kilpatrick* v. *Sweet*, 262 F. Supp. 561 (M.D. Fla. 1967), the bookkeeper authorized to expend company funds was considered to have greater responsibility than another bookkeeper not so authorized—because, again, the ultimate consequences of their actions was different.

The expression "similar working conditions" includes not only the physical surroundings but also the job hazards to which the employee is exposed and incidentals such as ventilation, heat, and light. In *Corning Glass Works* v. *Brennan,* 417 U.S. 188 (1974), the Supreme Court held that the mere working of different shifts did not constitute differing working conditions. The Court reasoned that a person working in the daytime, all other factors being equal, has the same working conditions as a person working at night.

One of the most important and significant legislative acts relating to employment discrimination is Title VII of the landmark Civil Rights Act of 1964, 42 U.S.C. sec. 2000e *et seq.* Title VII forbids discrimination in employment by making it illegal for an employer to "fail or refuse to hire or to discharge any individual, or otherwise to discriminate against any individual, with respect to his [or her] compensation, terms, conditions, or privileges of employment, because of such individual's race, color, religion, sex, or national origin." The second part of the Act makes it illegal for an employer to "limit, segregate, or classify employees or applicants for employment in any way which would deprive or tend to deprive any individual of employment opportunities, or otherwise adversely affect his status as an employee, because of such individual's race, color, religion, sex, or national origin."

The coverage of the Act extends to all areas of the economy. Employers include individuals, corporations, labor unions, partnerships, trusts, state or national governments, and educational institutions. To be included under the Act, employers so defined must "be engaged in an industry affecting commerce" and have fifteen or more employees. This language has been interpreted to provide the broadest possible protection against discrimination. Under the Act employment agencies are considered persons "undertaking to procure employees for an employer." Newspapers that run help-wanted ads are considered to be employment agencies. Professional certification boards, however, have been held not to be employment agencies and thus are not covered by the Civil Rights Act. Labor organizations that deal with employers concerning wages, labor disputes, and grievances and that affect commerce are included in this Act and, like employers, cannot discriminate on the grounds of race, sex, national origin, or religion.

The protection of the Civil Rights Act extends to all individuals but not to all types of discrimination. Forbidden factors of selection are race, color, national origin, religion, and sex. Factors not covered by the Act include political association, physical condition, age, and private morality.

Educational and vocational testing are areas that have accounted for between 15 and 20 percent of all litigation under the Civil Rights Act of 1964. The Act provides, in Section 703(h): "It shall not be an unlawful employment practice for an employer to give and to act upon the results of any professionally developed ability test, provided that such test, its administration, or action upon the results is not designed, intended, or used to discriminate because of race, color, religion, sex, or national origin."

In fact, nothing in Title VII precludes the use of tests or other selection procedures (see *Griggs* v. *Duke Power Co.,* 401 U.S. 424 (1971)). In *United States* v. *Chicago,* 573 F.2d 416 (7th Cir. 1978), however, the court held that a selection procedure which excludes persons protected by Title VII (for instance, a procedure that has a racially or religiously unfair impact) will be considered an unfair employment practice unless (1) the selection procedure can be demonstrated to be a reasonable measure of job performance or (2) the use of the selection process is required by a business necessity. If there is such a disadvantageous impact, and if neither exception is met, then the selection process is illegal even if there was a lack of intent to discriminate in administering the test. Such a test would still be illegal even if similar tests are in general use (see *United States* v. *Enterprise Association of Steamfitters Local 638,* 360 F. Supp. 979 (S.D. N.Y.), remanded on other grounds, 501 F.2d 622 (2d Cir. 1974)).

Another piece of legislation that expanded the scope of forbidden discrimination is the Age Discrimination in Employment Act of 1967 (ADEA), 29 U.S.C. sec. 621 *et seq.* The wording of the Act is identical to that of the Civil Rights Act of 1964, except that the word "age" is used in place of "race, color, religion, sex, and national origin." Protection against age discrimination in employment is not blanket; it covers only those individuals "at least forty years of age but less than seventy years of age." The Act permits discrimination on the basis of age when the individual involved is under the age of forty or over seventy. The purpose of the ADEA is to protect an older worker within the protected age group from being discriminated against *in favor of* a younger worker. The key requirement is that the discrimination be based on age. The ADEA even protects a worker from discrimination in favor of a younger worker in the protected age group (see *Polstroff* v. *Fletcher*, 452 F. Supp. 17 (N.D. Ala. 1978)).

The ADEA does not prohibit discriminatory decisions and practices that relate to "bona fide occupational qualification(s)" (sec. 623(f)) or to certain types of employee benefit and retirement programs (sec. 623 (f) (2)) or that are based on factors other than age (sec. 623(f)(1)).

Advertising is affected by the Age Discrimination Act if it indicates a preference based on age. Certain types of advertising are clearly forbidden. For example, use of words such as "boys," "girls," "students," or "recent graduates" has been ruled illegal by the secretary of labor (29 C.F.R. sec. 860.92(b)).

The Rehabilitation Act, 29 U.S.C. sec. 794, passed by Congress in 1973 and amended in 1974, prohibits discrimination solely on the basis of handicap. To quote from the Act: "No otherwise qualified handicapped individual in the United States . . . shall, solely by reason of his handicap, be excluded from participation in, be denied the benefits of, or be subjected to discrimination under any program or activity receiving federal financial assistance." The Act is aimed at employers having contracts with the federal government over $2,500. It requires employers to take action to hire handicapped workers.

A "handicapped person" is defined as any person who has a mental or physical impairment that substantially limits one or more major life activities, has a record of such impairment, or is regarded as having such impairment (34 C.F.R. Part 104).

In addition to the various legislative acts discussed, the courts have invoked the constitutional protections of the Fifth and Fourteenth Amendments in the area of discrimination. The Fifth Amendment states: "No person shall be . . . deprived of life, liberty, or property without due process of law." The Fifth Amendment, as it applies to discrimination in employment, has been interpreted to include due process requirements of procedural fairness. The Fifth

Amendment requires that laws affecting life, property, or liberty must be rational and valid. The courts have consistently held that laws, rules, or regulations based on a racial or sexual discrimination policy are not fair or valid and thus must be struck down as unconstitutional. Property was defined in *Perry* v. *Sindermann,* 408 U.S. 593 (1972), to include the right to employment. This implies that an employer who deprives someone of employment because of unfair procedural processes is violating that individual's Fifth Amendment rights.

The Fourteenth Amendment to the United States Constitution states: "All persons born or naturalized in the United States, and subject to the jurisdiction thereof, are citizens of the United States and of the state wherein they reside. No state shall . . . deprive any person of life, liberty, or property without due process of law; nor deny to any person within its jurisdiction the equal protection of the laws." The Fourteenth Amendment expands the Fifth Amendment and applies it to state private action, which may be regulated. The Fourteenth Amendment does not apply to federal actions.

Executive Order 11246, signed in 1965, expanded on previous executive orders regulating discrimination. The previous orders—issued in 1941, 1943, and throughout the 1950s—had prohibited racial discrimination by companies doing business with the government. The executive order of 1965 was set up in three parts. Part I forbids discrimination within the government itself. Parts II and III impose contractual obligations on employers performing contracts with the United States government for a dollar value in excess of $10,000. Both the prime contractor and subcontractors are affected. By this order the federal government requires that discrimination based on race, color, religion, sex, or national origin must be ended and that contractors are charged with the duty to pursue affirmative action in order to provide employment to individuals in those classifications who had previously been discriminated against. The contractor must provide information to the secretary of labor showing compliance with regulations propounded pursuant to the order. The order also forbids discrimination in advertising as disseminated by the contractors.

In addition to the legislation enacted between 1927 and 1960, legislation passed prior to the turn of the century has been reconsidered and reapplied to bar discrimination in employment cases. Notably, the Reconstruction Civil Rights Act of 1866, 72 U.S.C. sec. 1981, provided that all citizens shall have the same rights "enjoyed by white citizens to inherit, purchase, hold, and convey property." This has been held to mean that all persons have the same rights to make and enforce contracts. In *Waters* v. *Wisconsin Steel Workers of International Harvester Co.*, 427 F.2d 476 (7th Cir. 1970), and again in *Johnson* v. *Railway Express Agency*, 421 U.S. 454 (1975), the federal courts considered this legislation and held that the right to employment is a contractual arrangement. Apparently, however, the Act can be construed only in favor of blacks. In *Rowser* v. *Miller,* 631 F.2d 433 (6th Cir. 1980), a federal appeals court held that whites are not protected from discrimination in favor of blacks. In *Waters* v. *Hueblein, Inc.,* 8 Empl. Prac. Dec. 908 (N.D. Cal. 1974), the court involved held that women do not fall within that classification of individuals afforded protection under the 1866 Act.

Another piece of legislation from the Reconstruction Era, the "Ku Klux Klan Act" of 1871, 42 U.S.C. sec. 1985(3), forbade any conspiracy to deprive a person or group of persons of equal protection under the law. Under modern law a person is guilty of conspiracy if he or she agrees with another person that they will engage in conduct that constitutes a crime or in an attempt or solicitation to commit crime or if the person agrees to aid other persons in the planning or commission of crime. In order to prove that a conspiracy exists, the prosecutor must prove that the persons intended to commit a crime and that two or more persons were involved (see *Cole* v. *University of Hartford,* 391 F. Supp. 888 (D. Conn. 1975); *Coley* v. *M & M Mars, Inc.,* 461 F. Supp. 1023 (M.D. Ga. 1978)).

Enforcement of Antidiscrimination Laws

In order to understand how the various legislative acts, executive orders, rules, and regulations are enforced, one must consider the legal process involved, how courts function and, more specifically, how discrimination suits are tried by the courts. To file a discrimination suit under Title VII, one must meet rigid requirements. First of all, a charge of discrimination must be made in writing, and the document must be signed and sworn to. It must indicate the name of the person bringing the charge of discrimination, the name of the party charged, and the nature of the discrimination.

A discrimination charge must be filed with the local state enforcement agency if the state has fair employment laws. As an alternate, the charge may be filed both with the state enforcement agency and with the Equal Employment Opportunity Commission (EEOC). Even if the state has an enforcement agency, the charge may still be filed only with the EEOC; this is not a favored policy, however, and the practice is not encouraged. In states where there is no state employment commission, charges of discrimination must be filed directly with the EEOC.

Under Title VII a discrimination charge can be filed by any "aggrieved" individual, by a person acting on behalf of an aggrieved individual, or by a member of the Equal Employment Opportunity Commission (42 U.S.C. sec. 2000e–5(b)). Title VII prohibits certain forms of job discrimination against "applicants," "individuals," and "employees." Because the Act allows charges to be filed by any "person claiming to be aggrieved," a charging party need not be an "applicant," "individual," or "employee" in order to be an aggrieved person (see *Schoeppner* v. *General Telephone Co.,* 417 F. Supp. 453 (W.D. Pa. 1976)). Labor organizations (*International Chemical Workers Union* v. *Planters Manufacturing Co.,* 259 F. Supp. 365 (N.D. Miss. 1966)), employers (EEOC Compliance Manual sec. 201.5(b)), retired pensioners (*Hackett* v. *McGuire Brothers, Inc.,* 445 F.2d 442 (3d Cir. 1971)), and even the spouse of a deceased employee (*Mixson* v. *Southern Bell Telephone Co.,* 334 F. Supp. 525 (N.D. Ga. 1971)) have been held to be proper charging parties.

To pursue a discrimination case, one must follow rigid time requirements. The EEOC enabling legislation provides for—in fact, encourages—amicable settlement between the parties. If the matter is unresolved after sixty days at the local level, the charges may be filed with the EEOC (42 U.S.C. sec. 2000e–5(c)). After the charge is originally filed with the state agency, there will be a sixty-day hiatus while the parties attempt to resolve matters prior to a lawsuit.

The statute of limitations for a discrimination charge is very short. The time limit for the filing of a charge varies, depending on the circumstances, from thirty to three hundred days after the alleged discrimination act. In no event may a charge be filed after three hundred days (29 C.F.R. sec. 1601.19 (a)).

Even those areas with no local enforcement agency, or in those situations where the charge is originally filed with the EEOC, the commission will still wait sixty days before beginning its investigation.

If the charge is not resolved at the state level, and if the charge is brought within three hundred days, then the EEOC will begin its investigation (42 U.S.C. sec. 2000e-5(b)). The investigation will be comprehensive and will include, if necessary, the use of subpoena power to determine whether there is reasonable cause to suspect that the law has been violated. Traditionally, EEOC investigations are very broad in scope. The investigation will cover not only the unlawful employment practice alleged in the charge but also practices "like or related" to the alleged charge. The investigation will include practices affecting not only the aggrieved party but all other employees as well (42 U.S.C. sec. 2000e-9).

After the commission investigates the charge, it must, "so far as practicable, not later than one hundred and twenty days from the filing of the charge," issue its determination (*Kelly* v.*Equal Opportunity Employment Commission*, 468 F. Supp. 417 (D. Md. (1979)). The determination must state whether the commission believes the charge is true and accurate.

The investigation must result in one of three possible findings. The commission may determine that there is no cause of action, and no further action will be taken (EEOC Compliance Manual sec. 125.2). In this situation, the government simply concludes that nothing happened or that nothing can be proved. Under different circumstances the commission will choose not to sue but will issue what is called a right-to-sue letter, permitting private legal action in federal court by the aggrieved individual. If the EEOC determines that discrimination exists, attempts at conciliation will be made (42 U.S.C. sec. 2000e-5(b)). If conciliation fails, the commission may institute a civil action against any private respondent named in the original charge (42 U.S.C. sec. 2000e-5(f)(1)).

Under Title VII there are actually four statutorily granted ways for a court case to be instituted:

1. If the preliminary investigation indicates that immediate judicial action is necessary, the commission may apply to the federal courts for injunctive relief (42 U.S.C. sec. 2000e-5(f)(2)).

2. If the EEOC and respondent cannot negotiate a conciliation agreement, the matter may be filed in court (42 U.S.C. sec. 2000e–5(f)(1)).

3. When the EEOC has reasonable cause to believe that an entity is engaging in a pattern or practice of resisting any rights secured by Title VII, and where the pattern or practice is of such an egregious nature as to deny the full exercise of the rights set forth in Title VII, the EEOC will initiate a suit (42 U.S.C. sec. 2000e–6(c)).

4. If the commission dismisses the charge, the aggrieved individual may sue (42 U.S.C. sec. 2000e–5(f)(1).

The court process, to be understood, must be seen in the abstract. The system itself is based on an adversary method to shape the outcome of the lawsuit. It consists of opposing parties contesting with each other, both sides seeking a decision favorable only to their side. Conflicting assertions will be resolved in favor of one or the other side. The current legal system seeks winners, not mediation. The trial judge or jury must decide which of the two conflicting views has the greater validity and must enter an award for that "side." The findings and conclusions in the trial court are not, however, final. A U.S. District Court decision may be appealed to a U.S. Court of Appeals, and the appellate court's decision may be appealed on to the U.S. Supreme Court.

As with any adversary system, the charges set forth by the complaining party must be proved. The person filing the suit must show that a violation of law has occurred and that he was damaged by that violation of law. The plaintiff has what is called the "burden of proof"; in other words, the person bringing the charge must prove that some wrong has been done to him or her and that the person charged did the wrongful act. For the plaintiff (charging party) to prevail, he or she must establish by a "preponderance of the evidence" that the charged violation occurred. A preponderance means that more evidence must be presented to show that a violation occurred than is presented to show that no violation occurred. If the person bringing charges (plaintiff) cannot prove that the law has been violated, the suit ends with the charges being dismissed. If, on the other hand, the plaintiff provides evidence that a violation of law has occurred, then the burden of proof shifts; and the person charged will have to prove that a violation of law did not occur, or that the violation of the law did occur but the defendant (the person charged) is not to blame or that a violation did occur and the defendant caused it but has a good excuse and should not be punished (*Franks* v. *Bowman Transportation Company*, 424 U.S. 747 (1976)). The plaintiff in most discrimination suits attempts to prove the case through the use of statistics. The first type of proof is disparate rejection rates, showing that the number of those in a protected group who pass an employer test is lower than the pass rate for members of a nonprotected group who take the same test (*United States* v. *Enterprise Association of Steamfitters Local 638*, 360 F. Supp. 979 (S.D.N.Y. 1973)).

According to the federal government's guidelines for employee selection, an employer will be regarded as discriminatory if its selection rate for any subgroup is less than 80 percent of the rate for the highest group (43 Fed. Reg. 38290; 29 C.F.R. sec. 1607.2B). The selection rate can be computed by dividing the number of successful minority applicants by the total number of minority applicants, and then comparing this figure with the figure arrived at by dividing the number of successful nonminority candidates by the number of total nonminority candidates. When the percentage of minority candidates who are successful is divided by the percentage of successful nonminority candidates and the result is less than 80 percent, proof, or at least strong evidence, of discrimination exists (43 Fed. Reg. 38290; 29 C.F.R. sec. 1607.2B). As a further example, if one hundred blacks take an employment test and only ten pass, while one hundred whites take the same test and eighty pass, the difference is simply too great. When the test, on its face, or based on the end result, discriminates against a minority group, then a suit may be brought alleging that the test is discriminatory.

Under guidelines established by the EEOC, tests may be validated in three ways:

1. The employer may use *criterion-related validation* by establishing identifiable criteria that indicate successful job performance and then matching the test scores with the job performance ratings for the selected criteria (*James* v. *Stockham Valves & Fittings Co.*, 559 F.2d 310 (5th Cir.), certiorari denied, 434 U.S. 1034, 98 S. Ct. 767, 54 L. Ed. 2d 781 (1977)).

2. The employer may use *construct validation* by identifying the general mental and psychological traits believed necessary for successful job performance and then fashioning a qualifying examination to test for the presence of such general traits (*Bridgeport Guardians Inc.* v. *Members of Bridgeport Civil Service Commission*, 482 F.2d 1333 (2d Cir. (1973)).
3. The employer may use *content validation* by establishing a test or selection process that closely duplicates the actual duties to be performed on the job. (see *Pennsylvania* v. *Glickman*, 370 F. Supp. 724 (D. Pa. 1974), and *Bridgeport*).

Statistics also are used to compare the percentage of a minority group in the general population with the percentage of minorities in the work force. To perform such a comparison, one first divides the number of minority employees by the total number of employees and then divides the number of nonminorities in the geographical area by the total number of people in the same area. If the population is 50 percent black and only 5 percent of the work force is black, this will be considered evidence of discrimination.

An individual who sues may establish discrimination by proving the elements of the legal definition of discrimination: (1) An individual belongs to a minority group. (2) The employer was seeking applicants for the job. (3) The minority candidate applied. (4) The applicant was qualified. (5) The applicant was rejected. (6) The job remained open. (7) The employer continued to seek applicants. (8) The applicants sought had the same qualifications as the rejected applicant (*McDonnell Douglas Corp.* v. *Green*, 411 U.S. 792 (1973)). The employer need not do anything overtly discriminatory; the employer need only refuse to hire a qualified minority and continue to look for applicants.

An employee's suit will be denied if he or she fails to show any of the requisite elements: (1) Title VII class membership, (2) qualification for the position (*East Texas Motor Freight System, Inc.* v. *Rodriguez*, 431 U.S. 395 (1977)), (3) adverse action by the employer (*Thompson* v. *Sun Oil Co.*, 523 F.2d 647 (8th Cir. 1975), or (4) an indication of discriminatory animus (*Larkin* v. *United Steelworkers of America*, 409 F. Supp. 1137 (D. Pa. 1976)).

Once charged, an employer may challenge the facts as presented by the plaintiff. That is, the employer may say (1) that the information was incorrectly gathered; (2) that the statistics were arrived at by incorrect arithmetic methods; or (3) that the information gathered did not apply to him (*Equal Employment Opportunity Commission* v. *Data Point Corp.*, 570 F.2d 1264 (5th Cir. 1978), rehearing denied, 575 F.2d 300, remanded to 457 F. Supp. 62 (W.D. Tex.)).

Under certain circumstances an employer can admit the facts but argue justifiable excuse. One excuse that is acceptable to the courts is the "business necessity" test. In *Robinson* v. *Lorillard Corp.*, 444 F.2d 791 (4th Cir. 1971), the court required that the defendant establish one of three elements in order to prove that the discrimination was excusable. The employer was required to show a "manifest" relationship between the job and the qualifications. For example, a truck company's minimum height requirement will be upheld as a valid rule if the employer can demonstrate that persons shorter than the height required cannot see over the dashboard or touch the floor pedals of a truck.

The discriminating company may further demonstrate that the reasons for upholding the discriminatory rule are important enough to justify the resulting discrimination. In *Spurlock* v. *United Airlines, Inc.*, 475 F.2d 216 (10th Cir. 1972), the requirements of a college degree and minimum flight time were upheld, since these qualifications were found likely to reduce the risk to life and property. United Airlines convinced the court that hiring minority candidates with less than the required qualifications would endanger the lives of passengers on the aircraft because of the lack of skill of these candidates. The court held that this was a legitimate reason for discrimination.

A third alternative is that the discriminatory rule in question may be shown to be the least discriminatory of the various alternatives. In *Green* v. *Missouri Pacific Railroad Co.*, 523 F.2d 1290 (8th Cir. 1975), the court held that blanket discrimination against persons previously convicted of crime could not be excused by the need to ensure honesty among employees because such a test was broadly discriminatory and much less discriminatory practices were available. In *Wallace* v. *Debron Corp.*, 494 F.2d 674 (8th Cir. 1974), however, the court suggested that discrimination against repeat offenders might be justified based on the demonstrated higher likelihood of dishonesty among members of this group. The court determined this to be an alternative of minimal discrimination.

In the area of sex discrimination, the employer may prove that the discrimination is proper by using the "bona fide occupational qualification" test (*Weeks* v. *Southern Bell Telephone Co.*, 408 F.2d 228 (5th Cir. 1969)). When raising this defense, the employer must show that unique qualifications are necessary for the job. This is, of course, difficult to do—except for very specialized jobs, such as sperm bank donor or wet nurse, French cook in a French restaurant, or employee in a religious organization (where employment may justifiably be limited to members of that religion).

The government is involved in all stages of the employment process, including the recruiting stage and the selection stage (which, in turn, includes education, interviewing, and testing) (*Boston Chapter NAACP* v. *Beecher*, 504 F.2d 1017 (1st Cir. 1974)). Testing involves college tests, aptitude tests, and physical ability tests.

In the case of *EEOC* v. *Detroit Edison Co.*, 515 F.2d 301 (6th Cir. 1975), the court held that a recruitment program limited to referrals from a work force that was predominantly white was discriminatory. A situation in which a black worker would have very little chance of being recruited because of his color is prohibited. Even recruiting by means of radio broadcasts when all the stations used are owned by the same company would be considered a violation of Title VII (EEOC Decision No. 70-158 (1969)).

Recruitment by word of mouth that favors friends and relatives of union members when union membership is predominately white was held to be discriminatory in the case of *EEOC* v. *Local 14 International Union of Operating Engineers*, 553 F.2d 251 (2d Cir. 1977). The court found this practice in violation of the spirit and intent of Title VII, determining that it would discriminate against minority people simply because of their minority status.

Legal action often calls for the selection process to be justified, especially when the process involves educational requirements. In *Griggs* v. *Duke Power Co.*, 401 U.S. 424 (1971), the Supreme Court outlined the issues involved in testing and educational discrimination and the proof required of both. The Duke Power Company required a high school diploma as a condition of employment. It also required passing scores on two tests. One test, called the Wonderlic Personnel Test, measured general intelligence; the other, the Bennett Mechanical Comprehension Test, measured mechanical aptitude. Passing scores were the average scores that would be made by most high school graduates. Many black applicants were denied jobs because they lacked the necessary diploma and/or failed to score high enough on the two tests. After being denied employment, a black man named Griggs filed suit claiming discrimination. Both the district court and the appeals court held that no violation of Title VII had occurred. Both held that Griggs had failed to show that Duke Power Company had intended to discriminate against blacks and in favor of whites. The courts also held that the tests had been applied equally to all applicants. Griggs appealed to the United States Supreme Court, which agreed to hear his case and which reversed the findings of the lower courts.

The Supreme Court rejected the notion that motive to discriminate must be proved: "The Act proscribes not only overt discrimination but also practices that are fair in form but discriminatory in operation" (401 U.S. at 431). The Court noted that the high school diploma requirement and the passing of the two tests disqualified a greater percentage of black than white applicants. Thirty-four percent of white males in the state had diplomas, but only 12 percent of black males had high school diplomas. Thus, the power company was recruiting from two different population bases. The evidence also established that 58 percent of white males passed the Wonderlic and Bennett tests, compared to 6 percent of the blacks. In the Supreme Court's view, the difference between the two rates showed that some discrimination was occurring.

The Court examined the purposes of the tests given by Duke Power Company and concluded that they were discriminatory if they had the effect of excluding a particular class and could not be shown to relate directly to job performance: Congress did not intend that less qualified be preferred over better qualified but placed on the employer the burden of showing that any given requirement must have a manifest relationship to the employment in question. "The touchstone is business necessity. If an employment practice which operates to exclude Negroes cannot be shown to be related to job performance, the practice is prohibited" (at 432). In regard to employment testing, the Court added: "The facts of this case demonstrate the inadequacy of broad and general testing devices as well as fixed measures of capability" (at 424).

Most important among the many significant interpretations of the law announced in *Griggs* v. *Duke Power Company* was the Court's emphasis on the consequences of hiring policies. Lack of evil intent was not enough to justify a hiring policy. Companies were expected to change the results of years of prior discrimination.

The precedent set by *Griggs* was followed in *Johnson* v. *Goodyear Tire and Rubber Co.*, 491 F.2d 1364 (5th Cir. 1974), where the appellate court struck down another high school diploma requirement. In that case, Goodyear had adopted a policy of requiring all new employees to have a high school diploma and pass written tests. This policy applied to all new employees, except those hired into the labor department. Any tenured employee wishing to transfer out of this department had to meet the new criteria. However, any employee who was able to meet the qualifications and transfer out of the labor department also lost his accumulated seniority upon transfer. In striking down such requirements, because they had the effect of locking in labor department employees, the court explained that "it had the invidious effect of unduly limiting those black employees hired into the labor department without a high school diploma who subsequently wished to transfer to other sections in Goodyear's plant" (at 1372).

A case where educational requirements were upheld, *Spurlock* v. *United Airlines, Inc.*, 475 F.2d 216 (10th Cir. 1972), concerned a black male who challenged United Airlines' requirements that trainees for flight training must have a college degree and at least 500 hours of flight time. United, in this case, demonstrated the connection or correlation between possession of a college degree and graduation from flight training. The court held that the risk to life of unqualified pilots justified the requirements, however discriminatory they might be.

In *Hicks* v. *Crown Zellerbach Corp.*, 319 F. Supp. 314 (E.D. La. 1970), the Wonderlic Personnel Test and the Bennett Mechanical Comprehension Test were ruled invalid and discriminatory because of the low passing rate for black as compared to white applicants. In *Boston Chapter NAACP* v. *Beecher*, 504 F.2d 1017 (1st Cir. 1974), a multiple-choice examination used to select trainees for fire fighter training was ruled discriminatory. The court reasoned that the test was improper because it was not professionally developed. It further reasoned that the use of arbitrary cutoff scores not related to actual scores was improper. In addition, there was no correlation between the test and the performance of persons either in the school or on the job.

Achievement tests, which seek to measure a person's ability to learn from past performance, have also been challenged. In *Albemarle Paper Company* v. *Moody*, 422 U.S. 405 (1975), the question of relating various tests to job performance arose. Employees wishing to be advanced had to pass a group of tests, including the Personnel Test and the Revised Beta Examination. The paper company attempted to defend the use of the tests by showing that high scores on the tests were later matched by high scores on the job. The Supreme Court ruled that the testing practices were, in part, discriminatory because the job performance test—in which foremen at the factory used an arbitrary system to rate employees and were given no training or instruction in measuring job performance skills—was not objective. The Supreme Court also noted that scores on some tests did not match scores on tests given later on the job, so that the tests themselves did not seem to be measuring anything significantly related to the employment. The third objection of the Court was that the testing done at the paper company was not performed within the guidelines issued by the EEOC.

Another area of challenged criteria involves physical aptitude. Aptitude tests may be challenged when the requirements of the test exceed the standards of the job or when an employer refuses to hire because of the applicant's physical handicap (*Dorcus* v. *West Vaco Corp.*, 345 F. Supp. 1173 (D. Va. 1972)). In *Gurmankin* v. *Costanzo*, 556 F.2d 184 (3d Cir. 1977), the appellate court held that blindness did not disqualify an applicant from teaching English. An employer can, however, reject a job applicant who does not pass a physical examination or physical aptitude test if the physical requirements are actually related to the job in question (*Batyko* v. *Pennsylvania Liquor Control Board*, 450 F. Supp. 32 (W.D. Pa. 1978)). If physical strength is a bona fide job necessity, an employer may give a test that measures strength (*Dothard* v. *Rawlinson*, 433 U.S. 321 (1977)). Such a strength test would satisfy the standards of Title VII (if it is administered fairly), because it would measure the applicant *for the job* and not in the abstract (*Smith* v. *Olin Chemical Corp.*, 555 F.2d 1283 (5th Cir. 1977)).

In the area of sex discrimination, employers have had great difficulty in proving bona fide occupational qualifications. Title VII provides both men and women with protection against discrimination on the basis of sex. Limiting a job to a certain sex is prohibited unless the sexual requirement is, indeed, a bona fide occupational qualification. This is an extremely narrow exception. Title VII mandates that the employer judge both men and women on the basis of individual capacities to perform the particular job (EEOC Decision No. 71-1103 (1971); *Jurinko* v. *E. L. Wiegand Co.*, 331 F. Supp. 1184 (W.D. Pa. 1971)). A requirement that an employee be a man is not considered a bona fide occupational qualification for employment if the requirement was instituted (1) because the employer assumes that the job turnover rate is higher for women (29 C.F.R. sec. 1604.2(a) (1) (i)); (2) because the employer believes that the job is too dangerous (*Dothard* v. *Rawlinson*, 433 U.S. 321 (1977)) or too physical (*Rosenfeld* v. *Southern Pacific Co.*, 444 F.2d 1219 (9th Cir. 1971)) for a woman; or (3) because there are no restroom facilities for women (EEOC Decision No. 70-558 (1970)).

The EEOC and the federal courts also have held in violation of Title VII employers who refused to hire a man because they considered men less capable of assembling intricate equipment (29 C.F.R. sec. 1604.2(a) (1) (ii)) or because the jobs were those "traditionally" held by women, such as nurse (*Wilson* v. *Sibley Memorial Hospital*, 340 F. Supp. 686 (D.D.C. 1972)) or airline flight attendant (*Diaz* v. *Pan American World Airlines*, 442 F.2d 385 (5th Cir. 1971)).

In *Phillips* v. *Martin Marietta Corp.*, 400 U.S. 542 (1971), a company rule against hiring women with school-age children was not considered a bona fide qualification because it did not relate to the job and the company could not demonstrate that children would adversely affect the women's job performance. In *Weeks* v. *Southern Bell Telephone Co.*, 408 F.2d 228 (5th Cir. 1969), the telephone company failed to prove that only men could meet the test of lifting thirty pounds safely. The court held that some women can lift thirty pounds safely and that, in any case, lifting thirty pounds was not even part of the job.

Marital status requirements must also be job related to be held valid. In *Sprogis* v. *United Airlines*, 444 F.2d 1194 (7th Cir. 1971), a rule prohibiting the hiring of married women as flight attendants was challenged. Spragis was qualified in all respects except that she was married. She filed suit alleging discrimination. The court awarded her the position, saying that "passenger preference for single stewardesses" was not a bona fide reason for the requirement. After *Spragis* it is clear that customer preference is not sufficient reason for giving preference to one class of applicants as opposed to another.

General physical standards that automatically exclude too many members of a protected group must be job related or will be held to be discriminatory (29 C.F.R. sec. 1606.1(b)). In *Dothard* v. *Rawlinson*, 433 U.S. 321 (1977), a woman was refused employment because she could not meet the minimum height requirements and was under the minimum weight requirements. These requirements excluded 33.3 percent of all women but only 1.3 percent of all men. The employer was unable to prove that the requirement had "a manifest relation to the employment in question."

Height requirements that disproportionately affect women and Spanish-surnamed or Oriental males have been held discriminatory (EEOC Decision No. 71-1529 (1971)). Likewise, weight restrictions (or minimums) will be held to be unlawful discrimination when they disproportionately affect women or Hispanic and Oriental males (*Meadows* v. *Ford Motor Co.*, 62 F.R.D. 98 (D. Ky. 1973)).

The interview process is also regulated by Title VII, because casual interviews may be used to discriminate against protected classifications. An employer will have problems when different groups have different rejection rates (29 C.F.R. sec. 1607.13)). An employer violates the law both by awarding "points" for subjective and non-reviewable reasons in interview (*United States by Mitchell* v. *United Association of Journeymen & Apprentices*, 314 F. Supp. 160 (D. Ind. 1969)) or by failing to interview members of any minority group (*Gillin* v. *Federal Paper Board Co.*, 479 F.2d 97 (2d Cir. 1973)). In *Rowe* v. *General Motors*, 457 F.2d 348 (5th Cir. 1972), workers challenged ratings based only on interviews because the employees were given verbal, rather than written, instructions and the standards by which workers were to be evaluated were not made clear or exact. The court, in reviewing the situation, summed up the findings about subjective ratings: "[They constitute] a ready mechanism for discrimination against blacks, much of which can be covertly concealed." The court concluded that the interview process in question discriminated on the basis of race.

United States v. *Hazelwood,* 433 U.S. 299 (1977), involved the use of interviews in the hiring of teachers. The Court found that the criteria used were so vague that "each school principal possessed virtually unlimited discretion in hiring teachers for his school. The only general guidance given to the principals was to hire the 'most competent' person available and such intangibles as 'personality, disposition, appearance, poise, voice, articulation, and ability to deal with people' counted heavily" (at 302).

King v. *New Hampshire Department of Resources and Economic Development, Hampton Beach Meter Patrol,* 420 F. Supp. 1317 (D. N.H. 1976), concerned discriminatory intent. A woman applying for a parking meter–patrolling job was asked whether she could swing a sledgehammer, and she was not hired. Since the court could see no relationship between the question and the job, it held that the question showed an obvious intent to discriminate against the woman.

A reading of all pertinent legislation coupled with the court's interpretation of that legislation will give both the employer and the employee sufficient instruction to determine whether a certain practice constitutes improper discrimination. The best recommendation that can be made to the employer is to avoid overtly discriminatory acts and to limit tests and interviews to the qualifications of the applicant for the actual job opening (*Griggs* v. *Duke Power Co.,* 401 U.S. 424 (1971)).

An employer can guard against a discrimination suit by issuing a written equal employment policy and an affirmative action commitment statement. This process is equally applicable to the large, small, and medium-sized business. Every employer should designate one individual to review hiring and to ensure that no discrimination takes place. If an employees's sex, age, race, color, size, or physical disability does not affect his or her ability to do the job, then such factor must not be considered (42 U.S.C. sec. 2000e–2(e)(1); 29 C.F.R. secs. 1604.2(a) and 1606.1(a)).

The employer should publicize its policies in the area of affirmative action (*United Steelworkers of America* v. *Weber*, 443 U.S. 193, remanded to 611 F.2d 132 (5th Cir. 1979)). Internally, the employer should also survey minority, female, and age employment and should develop programs intended to promote and further utilize minority and female employees. Most important perhaps, in regard to testing and applications, a review of the employment system itself should be undertaken.

As has been noted, requirements used by companies may be challenged by minority groups for a number of reasons, including the lack of opportunity for minorities to participate in the educational system; inferior opportunity when they do participate (*Griggs* v. *Duke Power Co.*, 401 U.S. 424 (1971)); and the fact that the educational requirements are not related to the job (*Watkins* v. *Scott Paper Co.*, 530 F.2d 1159 (5th Cir. 1976)). In fact, all levels of educational requirements have been challenged in the courts: high school requirements, requirements for some college courses, the requirement of a Bachelor of Arts degree, or even the requirement for advanced degrees (*Kutska* v. *California State College, Department of Education*, 410 F. Supp. 48 (W.D. Pa. 1976)).

The testing policy of an employer may be challenged, and any employer that does test employees (or potential employees) should take great care to validate the given test when it is used and to make certain that it is supervised by a professional person (*Kirkland* v. *New York State Department of Corrections*, 374 F. Supp. 1361 (S.D.N.Y. 1974)).

A number of methods exist to validate tests (29 C.F.R. Part 1607). One method, as mentioned, is by way of a criterion validity study. Such a study establishes the predictive validity of a test by requiring that applicants be tested but that the actual hiring be done without reference to test scores (*Pennsylvania* v. *Glickman*, 370 F. Supp. 724 (W.D. Pa. 1974)). The test scores are then later compared with job performance scores. If a company can demonstrate that the test relates to job performance, the test is considered to be reasonably valid. Another method of criterion validity testing is concurrent validity (see EEOC Decision No. 73-0499 (1973)). This method requires that a present worker be tested with the same tests given to applicants and that the test scores for present employees be compared with job performance scores of these employees. This is not as highly recommended as the other type of criterion validity testing (*United States* v. *Chicago*, 573 F.2d 416 (7th Cir. 1978)). Content validity of any test given can be determined when the work is analyzed in terms of the skills needed and the specific performances required by the job (*Bridgeport Guardians, Inc.* v. *Members of Bridgeport Civil Service Commission*, 482 F.2d 1333 (2d Cir. 1973)). The performance is, in fact, the test. In other words, if a job requires typing, the test would be a typing test.

Whenever validity studies are carried out, the company should take great pains to document them (29 C.F.R. sec. 1607.14B). All the dates and times of data collection must be documented, and the names, titles, and publishers of any tests used must be listed. Whenever a job performance test does not concern the work actually performed, the reason for choosing the performances tested must be documented (29 C.F.R. sec. 1607.4A). A company must explain how the criterion skills were measured and why a particular group of employees was chosen as a sample (29 C.F.R. sec. 1607.4B). The statistical methods used to gather and analyze the data, the statistical results, and the statistical adjustments should be indicated. The company should be able to explain how the tests were used and how cutoff scores were chosen (29 C.F.R. sec. 1607.15B–D).

In the area of content validity, the employer should take care to document why each performance was chosen (*United States* v. *Buffalo*, 457 F. Supp. 612 (W.D.N.Y. 1978)); which specific tests were used; how the tests relate to the job; and why the cutoff scores, if any were used, were chosen (*Washington* v. *Davis*, 426 U.S. 229 (1976)).

When conducting interviews, an interviewer must take care that the questions asked will be considered fair and not discriminatory (*Equal Opportunity Employment Commission* v. *Detroit Edison*, 515 F.2d 301 (6th Cir. 1975)). An unfair inquiry on the topic of age, for example, would be a question that stresses any preference for a person under forty years of age (EEOC Decision No. LA7-5-210 (1969)). In the area of arrest information, there simply are no fair questions. In fact, any and all inquiries relating to arrests are considered unfair and potentially discriminatory (EEOC Decision No.

71-7970 (1970)). In regard to convictions, an interviewer may ask whether the conviction has been secured within seven years of the interview and whether this conviction would relate to job fitness. It is unfair, however, to ask a question about convictions that happened more than seven years before the application date or that concern activities unrelated to the job (EEOC Decision No. 75-103) (1974)).

In the area of citizenship, it is fair to ask whether the immigration status of the applicant would prevent lawful employment, but it is unfair to ask whether the applicant is, in fact, a citizen (*Espinoza* v. *Farah Manufacturing Co.*, 414 U.S. 86 (1973)).

Questions about family affairs are considered fair if the employer is concerned about family duties or activities as potential interferences with jobs, but questions concerning the spouse or children of the applicant—especially any specific inquiries related to income or employment of the spouse—would be unfair and potentially discriminatory (*Phillips* v. *Martin Marietta Corp.*, 400 U.S. 542 (1971)).

In the area of physical handicaps, it is fair to ask whether a handicap exists and whether it may affect the job (*Smith* v. *Olin Chemical Corp.*, 555 F.2d 1283 (5th Cir. 1977)). However, questions regarding health that are unrelated to job performance would be considered unfair. Height and weight concerns are fair where the job relates to certain height and weight standards but unfair if simply a general question about physical condition (29 C.F.R. sec. 1606.1(b)).

In the area of marital status, apparently there are no fair nondiscriminatory questions and such should not be included in the interview (EEOC Decision No. 70-1102 (1970)).

In regard to military history, questions asking for any military experience or detailing military experience are fair. Questions that relate to the type of discharge are considered unfair (*Bailey* v. *DeBard*, 10 Empl. Pract. Dec. para. 10389 (D. Ind. 1975)).

The name of the applicant may be solicited, of course, especially if the name is requested to determine whether the applicant has worked for the company under different names or whether the references would know the person by a different name (for example, maiden name, family name if changed, and the like). If the question is intended to divulge national origin of the applicant, then it would be considered discriminatory (29 C.F.R. sec. 1606.1(d)). Questions regarding national origin are fair if the employment concerns the need, for example, to speak a foreign language. However, if it is asked simply to determine the ancestry of the applicant, the question would not be considered a fair one. The interviewer may ask about an applicant's membership in organizations—but not with the intention of choosing or eliminating an applicant because of the types of organizations belonged to (29 C.F.R. sec. 1606.1)(b)).

Questions about pregnancy are fair if they are asked to determine whether absences may be anticipated (42 U.S.C. sec. 2000e(k)), but questions regarding pregnancy which are simply an exploration of the medical history of the applicant are considered unfair (*Holthaus* v. *Compton & Sons., Inc.,* 514 F.2d 651 (8th Cir. 1975)).

In the area of race, there are no fair questions (EEOC Decision No. 72-0979 (1972)).

Regarding relatives, a fair questions would be to request the names of relatives employed by the company, but questions designed to elicit the names of any relatives not employed by the company are definitely unfair (*Lea* v. *Cone Mills Corp.,* 438 F.2d 86 (4th Cir. 1971)).

Questions are not permitted with regard to religion (EEOC Decision No. 71-1471 (1971)).

Residence, of course, may be solicited when the company needs to contact the applicant (*Detroit Police Officers Association* v. *Young,* 446 F. Supp. 979 (D. Mich. 1978)).

As can be seen from both the statutes and the case law, the watchword for both employer and employee is "performance." If an individual is able to perform the job duties, she or he may not be discriminated against. As a practical matter, one can say that common sense should apply. If the skills tested, interview questions asked, or physical qualifications required do not impair job performance, then the employer will be found to be engaging in unlawful discrimination if the applicant is discriminated against.

It is recommended that the prospective employer plan to process employee selection carefully. The interview form should be carefully thought out, so that it relates only to the job position offered. All tests should be unbiased and, once again, related to job performance. While the federal and state rules and regulations regarding discrimination in its various forms probably occupy thousands of pages, one need not spend a lifetime reading the law to avoid discrimination. As a general rule, the statutes and the courts do not attempt to "trick" the unwary. All that is asked is that all employees have the same opportunity to obtain employment and that, once employed, the employees' continued employment be based strictly on job performance.

Thomas J. Reed

7

Capacity to Make Contracts and Wills

𝒯𝒯𝒯𝒯𝒯𝒯𝒯𝒯𝒯𝒯𝒯𝒯𝒯𝒯𝒯𝒯𝒯𝒯𝒯𝒯𝒯𝒯𝒯

This chapter is concerned with two subjects: the legal basis for invalidating a transfer of property on account of the transferor's mental condition, and the types of mental disorders that may affect a person's ability to make a transfer of property. Traditionally, the courts have been concerned with analytical legal standards for invalidating transfers. The disparity in outlook between the legal profession's point of view and that of professionals who treat mental disorders apparently grows wider each year.

Individuals are deemed legally unable to make a contract if they are unable to know and appreciate the consequences of their actions. This standard is also employed by courts to determine whether a person should be placed under a court-appointed guardianship. It occasionally arises as a legal standard to evaluate a contract made during life and after the death of the contracting party. The rationale for this standard is that a person should not be forced to honor any consensual undertaking when the person making the agreement cannot comprehend the duties or undertakings accepted. The appellate court decisions construing this legal standard suggest that courts resort to a rationalistic, voluntarist standard for contractual capacity and do not regard the notion of diminished functional mental capacity as a sliding scale to be applied to contracts of different complexity.

229

The mental ability required to make a will has been traditionally described as a state of mind of the person making the will (the testator in legalese)—a state of mind that permits the testator (1) to know the persons who are his or her kindred or the natural objects of his or her bounty; (2) to know the nature and extent of his or her property; and (3) to form a rational plan for disposition of his or her property by will (Reed, 1979, p. 445). A similar legal standard is applied to evaluate the effectiveness of deeds and trust indentures or declarations executed by persons of diminished mental capacity (American Law Institute, 1959, secs. 18, 20, 22; Patton, 1952, sec. 12.69). This standard, called testamentary capacity, was invented by the courts to deal with an elderly person who makes a will, deed, or trust while suffering from arteriosclerotic brain disease or senile psychosis. It has been extended to cover a wide range of organic and functional mental disorders, without regard to changing medical and psychological theory about mental disorders and diminished responsibility, which have been applied in criminal cases.

Additionally, persons who execute wills, deeds, or trusts arranging for postdeath transfer of assets must also be free from what the law calls "undue influence" exerted by a person importuning for benefits at death. Undue influence is an insidious substitution of the free will of an importuning beneficiary for the free will of the person making postdeath distribution plans. In Freudian terminology, it is a legal repudiation of transference as inappropriate (Shaffer, 1970b, pp. 197–204). The evil that the law tries to avoid is the transfer of property by a person because of inappropriate feelings of the kind existing between patient and therapist, in which the transferor misperceives the transferee as an object of feelings properly directed toward others. The law of undue influence is not so well defined as that of testamentary capacity and is in closer touch with the more recent findings of behavioral theorists than is the law of testamentary capacity.

Finally, a will, deed, or trust procured through fraud, a distinct legal category resembling but not identical to that of undue influence, will not be enforced by the courts. Unlike lack of capacity and undue influence, fraud may be perpetrated on persons whose mental capacity is undiminished. An ordinary lifetime contract can be vitiated by fraud, as well as a lifetime transfer. The avoidance of a contract, will, deed, or trust on the ground of fraudulent procurement or inducement is based on a standard that does not take into account the mental capacity of the victim. Instead, the law of fraud concentrates on a peculiar element, known to law as *scienter*—the conscious intent of the person working the fraud to deceive the victim with materially false declarations of fact. The law has not dealt with susceptibility to fraudulent importuning or the means by which confidence operatives use well-known psychological means to manipulate the behavior of victims.

This chapter will analyze the legal theories of capacity to contract, testamentary capacity, undue influence, and fraud, so that the human services professionals working with lawyers on capacity cases can understand the lawyer's point of view. The chapter also describes the common organic and functional disorders that may affect a person's ability to transfer property by contract, deed, will, or trust instrument. Organic disorders can be classified as (1) long-term psychoses arising from organic causes, such as arteriosclerosis, tertiary syphilis, alcoholic ingestion or ingestion of other toxic substances (such as mercury) that attack and destroy brain cells, and traumatic brain damage at birth or by later incidents; and (2) temporary disorders produced by phenomena such as fever, intoxication, and traumatic shock. Legal scholars do not distinguish between temporary organic disorders and long-standing psychotic behavior patterns induced by organic disorders. In the portions of this chapter devoted to the law of capacity, these conditions will be reviewed as a source of understanding the medical and psychological evidence for a finding of diminished mental capacity. Since the rules about testamentary capacity were made with the person suffering from senile psychosis or arteriosclerotic brain disease in mind, this discussion is particularly relevant.

Functional mental disorders, whose etiology is unknown, also can curb mental acuity. The law has a rule—called the "insane delusion" rule—that is intended to cope with property transfers made by persons exhibiting certain types of psychotic behavior. This legal rule was worked out in cases involving the transferor's apparent paranoia and was not designed to deal with the responsibility of schizophrenics, manic-depressives, or involutional psychotics. The "insane delusion" rule could have been expanded into a rule that invalidated transfers upon proof of significant impairment of mental functions, as a sliding scale to be applied to the relative difficulty of the mental tasks required. However, this rule has not been used as a vehicle for evaluation of this type. In describing the legal rules about capacity, undue influence, and fraud, we will note the relationship between legal rules, especially the rules of evidence affecting proof of mental disability by expert opinion, and functional mental disorders.

Capacity to Make Contracts

Normally, the law considers the making of a contract to be the free act of two or more individuals who comprehend the subject matter and the terms of their agreement. The contract represents the memorial of the parties' assent, or "meeting of minds" on the terms of the agreement. When one of the parties to the contract is mentally incapacitated, so that his ability to reason is impaired, meeting of minds does not occur and there is no contract (American Law Institute, 1981, sec. 12). Consequently, when an individual attempts to make a contract after he or she has been adjudicated mentally incompetent and placed under guardianship, it follows that the attempted contract is not a binding agreement. Persons who are put into a conservatorship or committee because they are physically incapable of taking care of their business are, in many states, permitted to make contracts, and other parties to the contract are permitted to enforce the agreement against the person subject to conservatorship (*Board of Regents* v. *Davis*, 14 Cal. 3d 33, 120 Cal. Rptr. 407, 533 P.2d 1047 (1975); see also Regan, 1972, p. 569).

The usual judicial test of mental capacity to make a contract has been generally stated as whether or not, on the facts, the contracting party whose acts are at issue had sufficient mind and understanding to be able to comprehend the character and effect of the actions involved in making that particular contract ("Mental Illness and the Law of Contracts," 1957, pp. 1026–1032).

The courts universally agree that, in order to invalidate an instrument, a plaintiff must prove by direct or circumstantial evidence that the contracting party was mentally incompetent at the exact moment of execution of the contract (*Hall* v. *Crouch*, 341

S.W.2d 591 (Ky. 1960; *Lynn* v. *Magness* 191 Md. 674, 62 A.2d 604 (1948)). The courts also apply a uniform standard to organic and functional mental disorders affecting contracting parties, as well as to the present effects of intoxication or drug-induced states of euphoria (American Law Institute, 1981, sec. 16). Over the past seventy years, the main judicial controversy over the contracts of mentally incapacitated persons has been whether to hold them void or voidable. A contract is voidable if at the time it is made the contracting party is unable to understand in a reasonable manner the nature and consequences of the transaction (American Law Institute, 1981). A void contract in legal terminology is wholly unenforceable; and, in order to end their obligations under the contract, the parties may not be required to restore each other to the economic position they were in when the contract was made. A voidable contract, however, is enforceable unless the party who has the option to void the contract first makes a claim that the contract is unenforceable and offers to restore the other party to the position he or she was in when the original bargain was made. If restoration is not feasible, the innocent party is permitted to introduce equitable defenses to termination of the contract, such as lapse of time and change of position in reliance on the agreement. Six states (Alabama, Arkansas, Colorado, Missouri, Nebraska, and Oregon) and the District of Columbia hold that the contracts of mentally incompetent persons are void. Twenty-eight states (Arizona, California, Connecticut, Delaware, Florida, Georgia, Hawaii, Illinois, Indiana, Iowa, Kansas, Kentucky, Maryland, Michigan, Minnesota, Mississippi, Missouri, New Hampshire, New Jersey, North Carolina, Ohio, Oklahoma, Pennsylvania, South Carolina, Texas, Vermont, and West Virginia) hold that the contracts of mentally incompetent persons are voidable. The remaining states have taken no stand on the issue.

Although the law reporters contain hundreds of cases construing the mental capacity of persons who make wills, deeds, or trust instruments, relatively few cases have dealt with the capacity of an individual to make a contract. Those few have generally dealt with the capacity of persons to make "life care" contracts with relatives or friends in return for the deed to a personal residence (*Weller* v. *Copeland,* 285 Ill. 150, 120 N.E. 578 (1918)) or a change of beneficiaries to an insurance policy (*Olsen* v. *Hawkins,* 408 P.2d 462

(Idaho 1965)), or to make debt obligations such as promissory notes (*Holman* v. *Stockton Savings & Loan Bank,* 49 Cal. App. 2d 500, 122 P.2d 129 (1942)), although no cases involving the assignment of leases have been reported (*Hanks* v. *McNeil Coal Corp.,* 114 Colo. 578, 168 P.2d 256 (1946)). Many of the issues raised in contests over the wills, deeds, or trusts of incompetent persons are not raised in the contract capacity cases (for example, the "Dead Man Act," which bars any proof of an oral claim against the estate of a dead person, does not arise because all the contracts sued upon have been in writing; therefore, they fit within an exception to the "Dead Man Act" which permits proof of a written contractual claim against the estate of a dead person); and the judicial standard for mental capacity to make a contract is more rigorous than that required to make a will, deed, or trust. The only reason for suggesting that a different standard should apply to contracts would be that, since contracts are usually bilateral agreements, more rationality is required for contract making than for the unilateral execution of a deed or will. This distinction seems to be without logical force, however.

One other possible reason for the difference in the test for capacity to contract and capacity to make a will, deed, or trust is that contracts are the fibre of commercial transactions, and a higher standard of mental performance may be required of persons engaging in gain-seeking activities than would be demanded for the act of giving away assets by will or by deed. Even this distinction seems to be forced, and full of unproved assumptions. The most probable explanation for the difference is that different English courts decided cases involving contracts and cases involving wills or deeds. The Court of King's Bench enforced contracts that were broken, while the Prerogative Court enforced wills relating to personal property, and Chancery enforced the provisions of deeds and trusts. This historical diversity of source law seems to be the reason for a different standard for mental capacity to make a contract.

Types of Incompetents

Since setting aside a contract for mental incapacity is a matter of factual determination by the courts, an examination of the relevant types of contracting parties whose agreements are attacked as lacking in capacity may clarify the legal standards at issue. Essentially, the courts routinely see four types of incompetents: the senile party, the drunken or drugged party, the organically impaired party, and the insane party.

The Senile Party. In *Hanks* v. *McNeil Coal Corp.*, 114 Colo. 578, 168 P.2d 256 (1946), the conservator of the estate of Lee A. Hanks, an incompetent, sued to cancel an assignment and deeds to mineral rights. In 1920 Hanks had executed a coal lease to his farm for a twenty-year term, and several hundred thousand tons of coal had been removed. In 1931 Hanks had mortgaged the farm and lost it at foreclosure sale, only to redeem it by means of two new mortgages and notes to his judgment creditors. He also assigned the coal lease to them. A dispute arose between Hanks and the McNeil Coal Corporation over the company's use of a haulage way across Hanks's land. The coal company agreed to purchase Hanks's mineral rights and a fee simple title to his land for $5,000 cash, which was much less than the fair market value of the mineral rights and the land. The coal company also agreed to assume and pay Hanks's oustanding mortgage, and to lease the land back to Hanks for a five-year period. In 1940 Hanks was committed and adjudicated legally insane. His son was appointed his conservator and filed an action to cancel the contract of sale and the deeds on the ground that Hanks was incompetent to make the contract in July 1937, two and a half years prior to his adjudication of insanity.

At trial a psychiatrist testified that Hanks was suffering from senile dementia and paranoia, which were long-term progressive illnesses. When Hanks was examined in 1940, he was hallucinating and experiencing delusions, which in the psychiatrist's opinion might have made him incompetent as early as 1937. Hanks's son testified that he believed his father was incompetent in 1940, when he instituted the conservatorship for him, but had suspected several years earlier that his father was unable to handle his affairs. Other lay witnesses (including a bank president) who had had business dealings with Hanks between 1936 and 1939, testified that in their opinion he was of sound mind during those years.

The Colorado Supreme Court began by stating the old proverb that the contracting parties were presumed sane. It held that the burden of proving lack of sanity was on the party seeking to upset the contract. The court admitted that Hanks had an "insane delusion" connected with the medical value of a horse liniment he had concocted out of brick dust, glass, and other items, but it squarely held that the law does not recognize degrees of insanity. The court concluded that the plaintiff had failed to show that Hanks was incapable of understanding the nature and effect of the agreement at the time it was drawn up. Therefore, the court affirmed the trial judgment for the defendant as sustained by the evidence.

In *Brannon* v. *Hayes,* 190 Ind. 420, 130 N.E. 803 (1921), the Indiana Supreme Court sustained the cancellation of a "life care" contract made by an elderly widow who exhibited many signs of senile psychosis. Eliza Pratt, the party whose capacity was at issue, developed "senile dementia" and lost the sight of one eye around 1914, while living with a daughter in Chicago. She went home to Crown Point, Indiana, to live in the Pratt family homestead as a life tenant. Her two daughters, who lived in Chicago, sent her money to survive on. A third daughter, Mrs. Brannon, somehow procured a "contract" from her mother, turning over most of her mother's property to her in return for life care. This contract was made on Columbus Day, 1915. Mrs. Brannon agreed to invest her mother's money, manage her property, pay her medical expenses and funeral expenses, in return for transfer of all of Mrs. Pratt's property. Mrs. Pratt died in 1918, and the Chicago daughters attacked the contract as the product of an unsound mind. There was abundant evidence that Mrs. Pratt was senile, irritable, and hallucinatory during the years from 1914 to 1918. She became a recluse, refusing to let her family into her home. She hid her laundry from her daughters, so that it could not be washed; habitually talked and mumbled to herself; and made extravagant plans for disposing of her property at her death. The trial court, after hearing the evidence, canceled the life care contract, effectively reducing Mrs. Brannon's share to one third of her late mother's estate. The state supreme court held that the evidence clearly supported the lower court's finding that Mrs. Pratt did not have the ability to understand and act with discretion in the ordinary affairs of life when she made the life care contract.

In *Brannon* the plaintiff, who had the burden of overcoming a presumption of capacity on the part of Mrs. Pratt, provided sufficient lay evidence of mental impairment to avoid the instrument. In this case the court was not hampered by any doctrinal requirements to comply with the *Greenwood-Baker* rule for testamentary capacity (discussed in the section headed "Testamentary Capacity"). It was free to evaluate the contracting party's conduct to determine whether the contract was the product of Mrs. Pratt's mental condition. Unlike the *Hanks* court, it did not equate capacity to contract with capacity to make a will, and so fall into the legal Slough of Despond created by the doctrinal law on testamentary capacity.

The Drunken or Drugged Party. *Shotwell* v. *First National Bank of Omaha*, 126 Neb. 377, 253 N.W. 416 (1934), illustrates the judicial treatment of the contracts of chronic alcoholics. William Hoagland had been a chronic alcoholic and drug addict for more than two decades before he shot and killed himself on December 9, 1931. On November 20, 1931, Hoagland had executed a nonnegotiable promissory note for $50,000 in favor of Margaret B. Shotwell, payable six months from date at 6 percent interest. This note was presented as a claim against Hoagland's estate by Mrs. Shotwell. Mrs. Shotwell was not a relative and apparently had a "childlike crush" on Mr. Hoagland for many years and had paid a great deal of attention to him during his last years. The estate resisted payment, claiming that Hoagland was incompetent to execute a contract when he made out the note.

The evidence at trial showed that William Hoagland had been an alcoholic since about 1912. He would come home with a supply of whiskey and gin, go to bed, and then drink almost continually for up to three weeks. These periodic drinking bouts continued until 1929, when Hoagland became addicted to morphine. His attending physician testified that Hoagland was a victim of Korsakoff's psychosis and that a half grain of morphine, administered three times a day in the months prior to his death, was required to control his behavior. The jury returned a verdict for the defendant, finding that the promissory note had been executed when Hoagland was not mentally competent.

The plaintiff's appeal was grounded on the defendant's use of an alienist, Dr. Neuhaus, a Creighton University professor of medicine and an expert in mental disorders. The defense attorney had read a four-page hypothetical question to Dr. Neuhaus and asked whether Hoagland "had such memory, judgment, intelligence, and understanding relative to that transaction as would enable him to understand the nature and effect of his act in connection therewith." Dr. Neuhaus answered that Hoagland was not competent to judge the nature and effect of his acts at the time the note was signed because ingestion of large quantities of alcohol over a long period of time had produced permanent organic changes in his brain. Although the report of the case did not state explicitly, the plaintiff apparently argued that the hypothetical question had assumed facts not in evidence, and did not raise the claim that Dr. Neuhaus had testified on the ultimate issue of fact for the jury in the lawsuit. The Nebraska Supreme Court affirmed the trial court verdict and judgment, as supported by sufficient evidence.

Conversely, in *Olsen v. Hawkins*, 408 P.2d 462 (Idaho 1965), the Idaho Supreme Court reached an opposite conclusion under similar facts. Hobart Turner, a Union Pacific railroad conductor, had a $3,500 life insurance policy on his life. When Turner's wife died in 1956, he changed the beneficiaries on his life insurance policy to his stepson, Marvin Olsen, and his stepson's wife. This change took place January 9, 1957. In March 1960 Turner made a second change of beneficiary in favor of Charles Hawkins, the station agent at Ashton, Idaho, who had become a friend of Turner's from 1958 until his death in 1962. Turner had asked Hawkins to keep up the payments on the group insurance policy, so that when he died he could be buried next to his wife at Pocatello. Turner told Hawkins that he had asked his stepson to take care of the policy but that the stepson could not be trusted.

After Turner's death, the Olsens brought suit to cancel the second change of beneficiary form as the product of Turner's alcoholism. The record at trial showed that Turner turned to drink after his wife's death and that in May 1957 he was hospitalized as a chronic alcoholic in the Lava Springs State Alcoholic Hospital. Turner remained in the hospital until May 1, 1958, when he was discharged. Lay witnesses who knew Turner at Ashton testified that he had no apparent drinking problem in March 1960. The Olsens produced evidence that Turner had clearly lapsed into alcoholism only a few months after executing the change of beneficiary forms. On this record the trial judge entered judgment for the plaintiffs, setting aside the second change of beneficiary. The Idaho Supreme

Court reversed, holding that the testimony of the people in Ashton who witnessed the change of beneficiary signature for Turner in March 1960 could not be totally disregarded. There was insufficient evidence to sustain the court's finding that Turner made the change of beneficiaries while mentally incompetent.

The plaintiffs in *Olsen* did not produce expert medical testimony to describe the effects of chronic, acute alcoholism on the brain or the resulting bizzare behavior that would indicate alcoholic psychosis. If the Olsens had done so, they might have tipped the scales in their favor, since they had no direct or indirect evidence that Turner was under the influence of alcohol at the time he made out the second beneficiary change. In *Shotwell* the jury had extensive and detailed testimony from an attending physician and an expert on mental disorder, which tied the effects of long-term alcohol abuse to mental competency.

The Organically Impaired Party. Although contests have been waged over the wills of epileptic persons, no contractual capacity cases have involved epileptics. A few old decisions have held that a person who is deaf, dumb, or blind is prima facie unable to make a contract (*Griffin* v. *Collins*, 122 Ga. 102, 49 S.E. 827 (1904)). A number of courts have held that old age and feebleness of bodily condition are not enough to invalidate a contract (*Pontes* v. *Pontes*, 40 Hawaii 620 (1954) (canceling mortgage); *Children's Home of Rockford* v. *Andress*, 311 Ill. App. 446, 36 N.E.2d 596, affirmed in part, reversed in part on other grounds, 380 Ill. 452, 44 N.E.2d 437 (1942)). However, only a very few contractual capacity cases have invalidated a person's contract on the grounds of physical infirmity alone.

In *Collins* v. *Trotter*, 81 Mo. 275 (1883), the Missouri Supreme Court sustained the refusal of a trial judge to enforce a promissory note against two deaf mutes who had apparently signed as sureties to the maker of the note. The record is not clear on whether these individuals were also mentally retarded. In *Longley* v. *McCullough*, 68 R.I. 395, 27 A.2d 831 (1942), the Rhode Island Supreme Court affirmed the trial court's refusal to void notes and mortgages executed by Ronald S. Longley, who had been mentally deficient from youth. Longley had inherited a great deal of money from his father. The money had been originally put in trust but was released to him by his mother in 1922. Longley attempted to run a diner and to buy and sell cars without much success. In 1929 he was approached by Willard Sweet to lend his signature to some promissory notes that Sweet and an associate had made to finance a car dealership. Sweet had obtained a loan from a man named Joseph McCullough on the strength of the suretyship of Longley. Longley agreed to act as surety and endorsed each note accordingly. When the notes came due in 1931 and Sweet failed to make payments when called by McCullough, McCullough persuaded Longley to give him two notes of $4,000 each, plus a mortgage on Longley's diner and on real estate owned by him. A few days after the notes and mortgages were executed, Longley was placed under guardianship. Ten years later his guardian sued to set aside the notes and mortgage as the product of an unsound mind, although the guardian had paid the interest payments without protest. The guardian produced testimony that Longley had been considered mentally retarded from birth. An expert physician testified that Longley suffered from a congenital brain condition that impaired his rational faculties, although a person dealing with him might not perceive his impairment. The trial judge decreed that the notes and mortgages were enforceable obligations. Longley was held mentally competent to give the obligations in 1931, despite his retardation. The court took into account evidence that Longley had dealt with Sweet through O'Meara, his legal adviser and eventual guardian, who had honored the obligations for ten years before protesting them as acts of an incompetent.

Jiminez v. *O'Brien,* 117 Utah 82, 213 P.2d 337 (1949), is the most interesting case involving an organically impaired person's ability to contract. Jiminez sued O'Brien for personal injuries arising out of an automobile accident that occurred on July 6, 1945. Jiminez suffered a severe brain contusion (bruised nerve tissue in brain) and was unconscious for two to two and a half weeks. An insurance adjuster named Duncan visited the hospital frequently and secured a release of liability from Jiminez on August 13, 1945, for $1,708.40, representing all medical expenses and $1,000 for damages.* The release was pled as an affirmative defense. Jiminez main-

---

*A "release" is a contract made by any party who has a claim for damages against another party, giving up that claim in return for money or a promise of some type. An "affirmative defense" is a defense made to a

tained that he was still suffering from traumatic brain injury at the time he signed the release and that he had no recollection of signing. At trial Jiminez called his attending physician, who testified that his patient was unable to reason normally at the time he signed the release. The trial court let the case go to the jury; it awarded Jiminez $5,000 damages, deducting the payment that he had already received from the award. The Utah Supreme Court reversed on the ground that Jiminez had failed to produce clear, unequivocal, and convincing evidence that he lacked the capacity to contract when he signed the release.

The court doubted Jiminez' good faith in asserting that the release was signed when he lacked mental capacity—probably because, after signing the release, he had visited a lawyer about suing the people who had hit his car. The court also discounted the evidence of abnormal mental functioning produced by Jiminez' attending physician by a doctor who had treated Jiminez for posttraumatic mental disorder in the fall of 1945; and it excluded medical opinions from two physicians who had treated Jiminez for other disorders, so that those opinions were not sent to the jury in support of the verdict.

The Insane Party. Any attempted contract made by an individual after he or she has been adjudicated insane would be void or voidable under prevailing legal theories ("Mental Illness and the Law of Contracts," 1957, pp. 1020, 1043, 1054–1055). Contracts made by the insane person prior to adjudication may also be set aside. Thus, any adjudication of insanity occurring before or after the time of contract making would be relevant and admissible in an action to avoid the contract (*Jefferson Standard Life Insurance Co. v. Cheek,* 258 Ky. 621, 80 S.W.2d 518 (1935)). Since the cases do not always differentiate between functional mental disorders (such as schizophrenia and manic-depressive psychosis) and more common organic psychoses (such as psychosis due to alcoholism), two cases involving the mental capacity of functionally disturbed individuals illustrate

---

plaintiff's complaint in which the defendant sets up and is obliged to prove some issue. If the defendant pleads "release," the defendant must prove that the release contract exists and is enforceable. Consequently, the defendant in this case must prove that the plaintiff had the mental capacity to make the contract.

the kind of treatment the law accords persons who make contracts while insane.

In *Weller* v. *Copeland*, 258 Ill. 150, 120 N.E. 578 (1918), Ann Odell, an aged and mentally unbalanced woman, brought suit through her fiduciary conservator, Weller, to cancel a life care contract and an accompanying deed to her house in Pontiac, Illinois, on the ground that she was incompetent to make the agreement. W. A. Copeland, a thirty-four-year-old auto salesman and mechanic, had agreed to take care of Ann Odell for her life, and to pay off a $900 mortgage on her house, in return for a gift deed to the house. Miss Odell was seventy-six when she made her arrangements with Copeland. The trial record abounded with testimony describing Ann Odell's irrational and implausible fantasies about marrying a younger man. She believed that Copeland would marry her if she gave him her property, and she repeated this sentiment to other people whenever she had an opportunity. She consulted with the spirits of the dead, and she reported seeing little boys and girls being cut up with knives in a park across from her home. Her dress and hairdo were also bizarre. As it turned out, she had earlier importuned a handyman named D. B. McKinney, who came to build an addition to her house. She had promised to give McKinney her house and to get him an automobile if he married her.

Miss Odell took much the same tack with Copeland, a man whom she did not know before she began importuning him to marry her. She tried to get Copeland to rent rooms from her; when that failed, she gave him a tie pin for Christmas and otherwise importuned the young man. Copeland finally agreed to pay off her mortgage and to look after her; once or twice he took her uptown in his car for a ride and ran errands for her. After these incidents the contract was concluded.

The trial court set aside the contract and deed as the product of an unsound mind, even though Miss Odell herself urged that the suit be filed and even though she was not adjudicated insane. The Illinois Supreme Court agreed that the evidence supported a finding that Miss Odell had an "insane delusion or monomania" about marrying Copeland, so that she could not be rationally persuaded not to give Copeland all she owned in return for his marriage to her. It affirmed the decision.

In *Mahin* v. *Soshnick,* 128 Ind. App. 342, 148 N.E.2d 852 (1958), a quarrel over the assets of the estate of Mrs. Bertha Mahin was resolved by a compromise of will contest filed by Mrs. Marshall, a daughter of the decedent. Mr. Soshnick, the lawyer who was the executor of Mrs. Mahin's estate, had offered this compromise settlement and had obtained the releases of all heirs and legatees, including that of the plaintiff, Glenn Mahin. The signatures to the releases were obtained on December 8, 1952, and a hearing was set for March 19, 1953. In the meantime, Glenn Mahin began to behave so strangely that his wife had him put into custody under insanity process; and on March 21, 1953, he was adjudicated insane and packed off to the Madison State Hospital for the Insane. He spent ninety days in the hospital and was then released. The record did not disclose his underlying mental problems. After his release, Mahin sued to set aside the release that he had given to his mother's executor, on the ground that he was insane when he gave the release.

At trial Mahin's petition for insanity process signed by his wife was introduced under the public records exception to the hearsay rule. It showed that Mahin had no signs of mental illness prior to January 1953. Since the compromise had been reached a month before his aberrations were manifested, the trial court dismissed Mahin's suit. On appeal, the Indiana Court of Appeals affirmed, standing by the traditional rule that, as long as Mahin could understand the nature and effect of his action in making the release in December, the contract would stand, despite his later insanity.

It would have benefited the plaintiff's case to set aside the release if he had produced psychiatric expert witnesses to explain to the court the nature and insidious process of most mental illnesses severe enough to become psychotic. Since the *Mahin* record is devoid of testimony describing the type of mental illness suffered by Mahin, the court's entry of judgment for the estate was justifiable.

Evidence of Mental Incapacity to Make a Contract

The critical issue in contract capacity cases is whether the alleged incompetent contracting party had mental capacity to know and understand what he or she was engaged in at the moment of execution of the contract. Since the ultimate issue is a question of law and fact, the acts and conduct of the contracting party both before and after the execution of the contract are relevant to determining what sort of mental capacity he or she had at the magic moment of assent (*Page* v. *Prudential Life Insurance Co. of America,* 12 Wash. 2d 101, 120 P.2d 527 (1942)). In particular, prior and later adjudications of insanity are relevant to the determination of want of contractual capacity (*Timberman* v. *Timberman,* 229 Iowa 835, 295 N.W. 158 (1940)). The courts usually hold to a presumption of capacity to contract, which places on the attacking party the burden of overcoming the presumption by greater than a preponderance of evidence (*Rath's Committee* v. *Smith,* 180 Ky. 326, 202 S.W. 501 (1918)).

Statements of the alleged incompetent made at or near the time of the execution of the contract are also admissible as state-of-mind exceptions to the hearsay rule, which excludes out-of-court statements made by witnesses to events, repeated at trial by persons who heard the out-of-court declaration (*Deanes* v. *Tomlinson,* 54 So. 2d 474 (Miss. 1951)). Written notations on a contract by the alleged incompetent, while also hearsay, are likewise admissible as evidence of the state of mind of the incompetent party (*Timm* v. *Schneider,* 203 Minn. 1, 279 N.W. 754 (1938)).

The usual strategy pursued by the party seeking to set the contract aside is to call as witnesses all persons who saw and observed the bizarre behavior of the incompetent, at a time not too remote from the date of making of the contract. After describing the behavior to the judge and jury, each witness is permitted to express an opinion on the mental competency of the party, carefully formulated by lawyers something like this: "Please tell the court and jury whether—based on your personal observation of Mr. X on the last time you saw and observed him prior to the date of execution of the contract in this case—Mr. X was able to know and appreciate the consequences of his actions." This formula is approved by the legal commentators for the eliciting of lay opinions on mental competence (Wigmore, [1913] 1940, vol. 3 (Chadbourn Revision), secs. 1933, 1937, 1938).

After eyewitnesses have testified about the acts and conduct of the incapacitated party, lawyers usually will call one or more experts who are professionally qualified to interpret data and to diagnose mental disease—in most instances a psychiatrist, although psychologists and neurologists may be just as useful, depending on the nature of the underlying disease process. The approved method for conducting the examination of the expert is to present the expert with a previously prepared written hypothetical question, summarizing all the relevant data to the judge and jury. The expert, who has usually helped prepare the hypothetical question and sometimes advises the attorney on what to ask lay witnesses in order to put proof of each assertion in the hypothetical question into the record, then responds by giving his or her opinion on the mental capacity of the alleged incompetent party (*Kemmerer* v. *Kemmerer*, 139 N.E.2d 84 (Ohio App. 1956)). Unless the alleged incompetent has been confined to a psychiatric treatment center or has been under psychiatric care, no treating physician is usually available to testify. In some courts expert testimony given by response to a prearranged hypothetical question is discounted and given very little weight (*Jiminez* v. *O'Brien*, 117 Utah 82, 213 P.2d 337 (1949)).

The defendant in a contractual capacity case uses much the same ammunition to rebut the attack of the party trying to upset the contract: a parade of lay witnesses giving their version of the acts and conduct of the incompetent, followed by opinions on competency; then the calling of expert witnesses for the defendant, who will testify, in response to a defense-oriented hypothetical question, that in their opinion the alleged incompetent was competent at the time the contract was made ("Mental Illness and the Law of Contracts," 1957, pp. 1046–1051). This type of trial too often results in confusion for the jury and judge.

Testamentary Capacity

The judicial test for testamentary capacity comes from two English decisions, *Greenwood* v. *Greenwood*, 163 Eng. Rep. 930 (K.B. 1790) and *Harwood* v. *Baker*, 13 Eng. Rep. 117 (P.C. 1840). In *Greenwood* Lord Kenyon charged the jury in a will contest with the following: "The inquiry and the single inquiry in this cause is whether he was of sound and disposing mind and memory at the time when he made his will: however deranged he might be before, if he had recovered his reason at that time, he was competent to make his will. . . .If he had a power of summoning up his mind so as to

know what his property was and who those persons were that then
were the objects of his bounty, then he was competent to make his
will" (at 943).

This jury charge stated the first two elements of the judicial
test, ability to recall property and to recollect the natural objects of
one's bounty. In *Baker,* a case sent to the Privy Council after the
Prerogative Court had approved the probate of a will made by a man
dying from encephalitis, Lord Erskine added the third element of
the capacity formula—the ability to make a rational plan for
disposition:

> But their Lordships are of opinion, that in
> order to constitute a sound disposing mind, a Testator
> must not only be able to understand that he is by his
> Will giving the whole of his property to one object of
> his regard; but . . . must also have capacity to com-
> prehend the extent of his property, and the nature of
> the claims of others, whom, by his Will, he is exclud-
> ing from all participation in that property . . . and
> therefore, the question which their Lordships propose
> to decide in this case is not whether Mr. Baker knew
> when he was giving all his property to his wife, and
> excluding all his other relations from any share in it,
> but whether he was at that time capable of recollecting
> who those relations were, of understanding their re-
> spective claims upon his regard and bounty, and of
> deliberately forming an intelligent purpose of exclud-
> ing them from any share of his property [at 120].

This judicial standard was applied to American cases within a few
years after its final synthesis in *Baker.* It appeared in *Delafield* v.
Parish, 25 N.Y. 9, 29 (1862), one of the leading early American will
contests, as the rule for decision. This test, then, is called the
Greenwood-Baker rule (Reed, 1979, pp. 456–463).

The first element in this test, natural objects of bounty, refers
to the persons who would take the testator's assets at death by operation of law—persons normally described as next of kin or heirs. The
expression "knowing the natural objects of one's bounty" seems at
first glance to deal with recall and perceptual function, or some
form of orientation. However, the legal standard is founded on a

sense of moral obligation, the presumed duty to favor one's relatives according to blood kinship over strangers and to prefer one's closest relatives to more distant relatives. The duty to prefer one's kinfolk to persons not of the blood and to distribute such favor to the closest kin of the same blood is medieval in character. "Knowing the natural objects of one's bounty," then, means something other than the ability to perceive them when present or to recall their names when absent. It means that the testator is supposed to render to these "natural objects" (those closest to the testator in kinship) their due—a due presumed to exist by reason of kinship.

Although no such thing as a psychology of property exists, a tentative psychological explanation for this standard can be tendered. If property serves as a means of extending one's ego in space and time, as it clearly does in postdeath transfers, then the use of this instrument allows the ego to alter the behavior of others during life and after death of the ego. In that sense, depriving the kinship circle of property in a significant way, or violating the taboo against transferring property from close kin to those more distantly related to the giver, represents a form of retribution which the ego takes on those whom it perceives as enemies. If the testator is confused, disoriented, and unable to recognize this primitive set of cultural and psychological guideposts and transfers property despite the limits of the intrakinship system of justice, the testator lacks knowledge of the natural objects of his bounty.

"Nature and extent of one's property" appears to refer to a simplistically conceived psychology of recall: During the will-making process, was the testator's brain stimulated by electrochemical stimuli so as to revive an electrochemical action originally "patterned" by stimuli received through the sensory apparatus? The original "pattern" would be the change wrought in the testator's brain by sensing his or her immediate family and property. If the electrochemical mechanism affecting this retrieval system were impaired by neural damage, or by some functional disorder such that the "circuits were down" or "busy," then no recall could take place. In a fumbling sort of way, the second element of the *Greenwood-Baker* rule for testamentary capacity follows this kind of thinking (Krech, Crutchfield, and Livson, 1969, pp. 466–472). The courts do not require that the testator be producing a sensate recall image of all his or her property when the will is signed; they require only that the testator be able to recall at that time if required to do so (*Yarbrough* v. *Moses,* 223 Ark. 489, 267 S.W.2d 289 (1954)).

"Ability to form a rational plan for disposition of property," the third pole of the traditional *Greenwood-Baker* rule about testamentary capacity, seems to deal with impaired ego functioning and postulates an individual who is disoriented in some way. Some courts have held that this element is the primary constituent of a testamentary capacity (Reed, 1979, pp. 460–463). For several decades most American courts have inconsistently required greater orientation for people making ordinary contracts than for those making wills. The ability of a person to integrate functional recall of assets and the relative distributive justice of one's kinspeople is generally considered less mentally taxing by judges than the making of a simple sales contract in a store.

Types of Impairments

Organically Impaired Testators. In the old days, many will contests dealt with people whose mental functioning was assessed as retarded, or under the now-disused classifications of idiots, morons, and imbeciles (Page, 1960, vol. 1, sec. 12.25). The wills of mentally retarded individuals have been struck down when the court has found that the retarded person simply did not appreciate the consequences of his or her actions (*In re Glesenkamp's Estate,* 378 Pa. 635, 107 A.2d 731 (1954)); similarly, such wills have been supported and ratified by the courts when the mentally retarded individual seemed to know and appreciate the consequences of his or her actions (*In re Teels' Estate,* 14 Ariz. App. 371, 483 P.2d 603 (1971)). In those few cases where appellate courts have dealt with the wills of retarded persons, the principal inquiry seems to have been related to the judicial standard for imposing a guardianship on the testator, and not to the *Greenwood-Baker* rule. The courts have not yet reviewed the wills of mentally retarded persons with a view of clinical assessment of brain damage and its effect on recall or on sensory perception.

Cases involving the wills, deeds, and trusts of persons who suffered from some infirmity while they were making postdeath distribution plans have been treated as mental competency cases by the courts. A surprising number of will contests have been filed against the wills of people who were blind, deaf, or ill at the time a will or deed was made out. The wills of persons afflicted with Parkinson's disease or locomotor ataxia have been dealt with by the courts as a problem for assessment of traditional testamentary capacity. In reality, unless some underlying brain condition is disclosed, as in the case of epileptics, such cases have simply demonstrated the physical feebleness of the testator.

In *Lynn* v. *Ada Lodge*, 389 P.2d 491 (Okla. 1965), the testator suffered from an unknown seizure disorder, which led his mother to commit him to a mental hospital. After his release the testator, erroneously believing that the local Odd Fellows Lodge had worked to get him released from the mental hospital, made a will leaving his estate to the lodge. The Oklahoma Supreme Court upheld his will, although his mother contended the will was the product of the testator's insane delusion about the reasons for his release from the mental hospital. Organic conditions such as that present in the *Lynn* case raise serious questions about the victim's state of mind at the time of making a will, deed, or trust, since the disease process may actually affect both recall and orientation. This is especially true of Jacksonian epilepsy. Nonetheless, the courts traditionally have not gone into the issue of whether an epileptic person's will was made during or shortly before or after a seizure. None of the reported cases make a distinction between physical illness that affects the brain and sensory system and those conditions that do not. For example, in *Nowlin* v. *Spakes*, 250 Ark. 26, 463 S.W.2d 650 (1971), the testator suffered from Parkinson's disease. His will was challenged on the ground that he lacked capacity because of this condition. It was eventually sustained, the appellate court finding the grounds for contest baseless.

Senile Testators. The largest number of cases filed in court to challenge postdeath property distribution plans are those dealing with individuals who are quite elderly and exhibit one or more of the symptoms of what was once called "senile dementia." In reality, there are two conditions, one organic and one functional, that strike a number of elderly individuals and impair their orientation and functioning. Arteriosclerotic brain disease is an organic condition caused by the accumulation of fatty deposits in the large and small blood vessels supplying blood to the brain; these vessels then ossify, creating blood clots and resulting in the death of nonregenerative nerve and brain cells. This condition is detectable by a number of symptoms, some of which are marked behavioral changes (Frankel, 1970, vol. 3, sec. 17.9). These changes include impairment of orientation, memory, judgment, and other mental functions (including comprehension, calculation, knowledge, and learning) and instability of emotional reactions. At times these symptoms may be accompanied by vivid auditory or visual hallucinations or both. Senile psychosis is a functional mental disorder that produces similar behavioral changes in elderly persons. Both conditions are lumped together in legal thinking and were the principal object of the *Greenwood-Baker* rule establishing the legal test for setting aside postdeath distribution plans.

The courts have long held that the wills of persons who are elderly are not invalid for that reason alone (*In re Washburn's Will*, 248 Wis. 467, 22 N.W.2d 512 (1946)). On the other hand, people who exhibit memory loss or childish behavior patterns may be questionable mentally, and their postdeath distribution plans may be attacked on that basis.

Two relatively recent will contests may help to illustrate the point. In *Zawacki* v. *Drake*, 149 Ind. App. 270, 271 N.E.2d 511 (1972), Frances Andrewjewski, the testator, had disinherited her adopted children in favor of Daniel Zawacki, a brother. A severely depressed recluse, Mrs. Andrewjewski lived in squalid and cluttered surroundings and was incoherent in her infrequent contact with outsiders. Her physician testified that she suffered from partial memory loss and disorientation in space and time and was not of sound mind at the time she made her will. Most of the lay evidence at the trial consisted of family members of neighbors describing Mrs. Andrewjewski's physical filthiness and the condition of her house. The jury entered a verdict for the party wishing to set aside her will, and against the legatee under her will. The Indiana Court of Appeals affirmed the decision, concluding that the verdict was supported by sufficient evidence to show Mrs. Andrewjewski's lack of capacity to make a will.

In *Cubbage* v. *Gray,* 411 S.W.2d 28 (Ky. 1967), the daughter of an elderly man attacked her father's disinheriting will as the product of his senility. John Clark made his will at eighty-two. At that time he professed to know that the mountain behind his house contained gold; in order to find the gold, he conversed with sticks and other inanimate objects. The daughter proved at trial that she and her husband had tried to stop her father from digging for gold and that the old man then decided that they were out to kill him. Persisting in this belief, he made a will that disinherited his daughter. This will was set aside at trial, and the Kentucky Court of Appeals sustained the verdict of the lower court as supported by the weight of the evidence.

The *Zawacki* and *Cubbage* cases are typical of the handful of successful will contests lodged against senile testators. The will of a senile testator has about a 70 percent chance of being sustained after attack by disinherited relatives; 80 percent of the wills of persons legally placed under guardianship and adjudicated incompetent to make an ordinary contract are sustained on appeal (Reed, 1979, Appendix, Table V). The usual judicial attitude toward will contests of this type is highly negative.

Cases such as *In re Scoville's Estate,* 149 Neb. 415, 31 N.W.2d 284 (1948), are much more typical of the results usually obtained in such cases. The testator was survived by his wife and three daughters. In September 1942, Scoville made a will leaving his 160-acre home farm to his eldest daughter, Mrs. Flossie Wensky. He left an 80-acre tract to her son, Robert, and made cash gifts of $1,000 each to his daughters Jessie Arthur and Orpha Cross. Mrs. Wensky was residuary legatee. In July 1943, Scoville made a second will. He left the home farm to Mrs. Wensky, the 80-acre tract to Mrs. Cross, cancelled the cash gift to Mrs. Cross, and cancelled Mrs. Wensky's status as residuary legatee.

Scoville made a third will in August 1943, when he was eighty-three years old. In it he left the home farm to Mrs. Cross, as well as the 80-acre tract given to her in the second will. Mrs. Arthur received a $1,000 cash gift and the residue of Mr. Scoville's estate was left in trust for the benefit of his widow, Mrs. Arthur, and Mrs. Cross. Mrs. Wensky was cut off with a $5.00 gift. Mrs. Wensky filed an action to contest the probate of the August 1943 will. At that trial a number of lay witnesses testified that Scoville had acted strangely. He had accused his grandchildren of stealing his tools. He had wanted all the turtledoves shot around his homestead. He threatened to shoot some family members he was not fond of. He quarreled with Flossie Wensky and her husband, who were managing his farm for him and living in his house, threatening to kick them off the farm and then begging and pleading with them to stay. The contesting party's major witness was the dead man's physician, who testified that Scoville suffered from senile dementia and could not have understood what he was doing when he made his last will, in 1943. The trial court refused to submit the issue of capacity to the jury, holding as a matter of law that the will was not infirm. On appeal the Nebraska Supreme Court sustained the trial court, despite the fact that in Nebraska the courts had already classified "senile dementia" in guardianship cases as the equivalent of a medical opinion of insanity. The Nebraska Supreme Court held that an insane person is not prevented from making a will, assuming that the *Greenwood-Baker* test for capacity could be sustained at the precise moment the testator signed his will. Since the contesting party had not shown that Scoville was actively insane at the "magic moment," there was no issue for the jury to decide.

The *Greenwood-Baker* rule seems to permit persons who are incapable of managing their own affairs to make wills, deeds, and trusts transferring property at trust. The legal standard for capacity, in the case of persons who may have arteriosclerotic brain disease or senile psychosis, is a laissez-faire standard. The social policy represented by this standard is against setting aside postdeath transfers of property when those transfers are executed with the formalities required by law and all instruments and execution ceremonies are run by lawyers.

Drugged Testators. The *Greenwood-Baker* rule also permits the wills of drug addicts and alcoholics to be probated, even when substantial medical evidence at trial shows that the will-making party was disoriented and otherwise chronically ill from drug or alcoholic poisoning. The judicial standard for avoiding these kinds of postdeath transfers has traditionally been confined to the requirement that the contesting party prove that the testator was actually drugged or intoxicated when the will, deed, or trust declaration was signed (*Lewis* v. *Roberts*, 207 Va. 742, 152 S.E.2d 144 (1967)). In many instances the only people qualified to testify on the issue were the lawyer who prepared the document and the secretary who witnessed its execution. This standard ignored the possibility of long-term psychotic changes produced by chronic addiction, such as perceptual alteration; death of brain cells, producing a condition similar to arteriosclerotic brain disease; and alteration of motivation. It is not surprising that four of five wills made by persons exhibiting alcoholism and nine of ten wills made by drug addicts or persons under heady medication are sustained (Reed, 1979, Appendix, Table V).

Two cases illustrate this point. In *Deery* v. *Hall*, 96 Ind. App. 683, 175 N.E. 145 (1931), Oria Dolan, the testator, died of nephritis and pneumonia in St. Vincent's Hospital, Indianapolis. In his will, made at the hospital the day before his death, he left his substantial estate to several Catholic charities, excluding his own family members. His family challenged the will, claiming that Dolan was an alcoholic and unable to comprehend what he was doing when he made his will. An expert witness, a physician, testified that Dolan died of a long-term side effect caused by chronic alcoholism; the physician also stated that, in his opinion, Dolan lacked the ability to know and recognize his family or to recall his property when he made his will. Lay testimony about Dolan's bizarre behavior and his history of drinking was counterbalanced by evidence that Dolan had gone "on the wagon" some time before his death. The jury returned a verdict for the contestant, which the Indiana Court of Appeals set aside as the result of prejudicial error in propounding the hypothetical question to the expert. Dolan was very ill from his long-term alcoholism when he made his will. The court simply refused to recognize the overwhelming strength of the medical evidence showing the destruction of Dolan's mental competency by chronic alcohol abuse.

Appelhans v. *Jurgeson*, 336 Ill. 427, 168 N.E. 327 (1929), concerned the will of Christine Hagenow, a chronic alcoholic who had disinherited her sister and her nephews in favor of a male boarder at her home. A parade of lay witnesses described her intoxication on almost every occasion (for example, on visiting her dentist a year before she made her will and at a bowling alley ten years prior to the date of the will), clearly sustaining that Mrs. Hagenow was an alcoholic up to the time she died. Her attending physician did not believe she had the mental capacity to make a will. The trial court set her will aside; but the Illinois Supreme Court reversed, holding that—since the contesting parties had not shown that Mrs. Hagenow was actually drunk when she signed her will—there was insufficient proof to sustain the jury verdict.

The instances in which the wills of alcoholic and addicted people have been set aside are so few that virtually no "pure" examples can be found, since the cases for the contesting parties were also often based on undue influence by a beneficiary. One of the few "pure" cases is *Swygart* v. *Willard,* 166 Ind. 25, 76 N.E. 755 (1906), decided by the Indiana Supreme Court in 1907. The record of trial was filled with eyewitness testimony on the testator's bizarre behavior and heavy drinking day after day during the period his will was made, partially disinheriting some of his children. The contesting party competently proved that Swygart's mind was deranged from long-term use of alcohol. The court found the trial verdict for the contestants supported by the evidence. There was enough circumstantial evidence in the *Swygart* case to permit the inference that the testator was actually drunk when he signed his will, though no direct proof existed that he was intoxicated at the time.

The key to the successful challenges to the wills of alcoholics and addicts appears to be the medical evidence adduced to show the long-term effect of drug abuse on the individual whose will, deed, or trust is under attack. In most of the cases reported, only superficial lay opinion was offered as evidence on the state of the decedent's mind; evidence provided by medical experts was incomplete or inadequate. Since most of the cases predate the widespread acceptance of psychologists as expert witnesses, no cases have been found in which a psychologist testified as a contestant's expert.

Functionally Impaired Testators. A person whose mental processes are impaired by such diseases as paranoia, manic-depressive disease, or schizophrenia is functionally rather than organically impaired. By definition, the mental diseases enumerated are not caused by organic damage to the brain, as in the case of senile psychosis, which arises when brain cells die because of decreased blood supply to the brain. A person who has a functional mental impairment may not be able to form the legal intent to make a contract, commit a crime, or transfer property. While a test for criminal intent has evolved that would preclude the conviction of any person suffering from a mental disease that affects his or her ability to form a purposeful act (*Durham* v. *United States,* 214 F.2d 862 (D.C. Cir. 1954), there is no corresponding doctrine in the civil law of contracts and property transfer. The law has, however, long recognized that an individual's will, deed, or trust can be set aside if it is the product of an "insane delusion" (*Dew* v. *Clark,* 162 Eng. Rep. 419 (Prerog. 1826)). Anglo-American law is committed to dealing with intentional acts of parties; and required intent is part of the law of contracts, criminal justice, and the transfer of property.

If a deceased testator is unconsciously laboring under some delusion about the conduct or fidelity of the natural objects of his or her bounty when executing the dispositive instruments before death, and makes a will with that delusion present, the will is invalid because it is the product of an insane delusion (*American Seaman's Friend Society* v. *Hopper,* 33 N.Y. 619 (1865)). The judicial definition of an insane delusion about one's kinsmen has been variously put as "a fixed belief in something which no rational person would believe in" (*Jackman* v. *North,* 398 Ill. 90, 75 N.E.2d 324 (1947)) or as a "false and fixed belief not founded on reason and incapable of being removed by reason" (*Hall* v. *Mercantile Trust Co.,* 332 Mo. 802, 59 S.W.2d 664 (1933)). In other words, a person making post-death distribution plans operates under an "insane delusion" if he or she accepts a phenomenon as actual when it is not actual and—in contemplation of the illusory phenomenon, delusion, or hallucination—alters his or her postdeath distribution plans (Reed, 1979, p. 491).

Taxonomically, the "insane delusion" cases are divided into two major groups: the "they're-out-to-get-me" cases and the "crank" cases. The judiciary has been willing to set aside postdeath plans in both situations, on the theory that a person having testamentary capacity may nonetheless have made an invalid distributive plan because he or she was operating under an insane delusion (Reed, 1979, p. 492). An example from both classes may make the legal notions about "insane delusions" a bit clearer.

In *Dumas* v. *Dumas*, 547 S.W.2d 417 (Ark. 1977), the Arkansas Supreme Court acquiesced in the voiding of a will of Wray Dumas, who had exhibited a number of startling behavioral changes within a few years of his death. In the late 1950s, Dumas had had an affair with a woman and became obsessed that everyone in his church congregation knew of it and were out to get him. He had been committed by his daughter to the state hospital, where he was diagnosed as a involutional paranoid, unable to relate to reality and suffering from delusions of persecution. Dumas was let go after an observation period and then returned to his home town. He divorced his wife and made a will disinheriting his daughter and a deed of gift transferring his assets to his brother. As evidence developed in the trial between Dumas's daughter and his brother over the estate, Dumas had a delusion that the members of his church were out to get him, and he singled out his daughter and wife for retribution because they were church members and did not stop going when he did. The staff psychiatrist from the state hospital testified for the contestants and repeated his earlier diagnosis. The jury gave a verdict for the contestants and set aside both deed and will as the product of an insane delusion. The Arkansas Supreme Court concurred in the finding, the evidence being overwhelming. These types of cases generally tend to be decided in favor of the contesting parties, once clinical evidence and expert opinion establish that the postdeath transferor was suffering from a delusion about his or her family.

The "crank" cases are much more difficult to rationalize within the conceptual framework of the law of postdeath transfers. The usual "crank" case involves an attack on the will, deed, or trust of a dead person who was reputed to hold unacceptable religious or political opinions during life. On the basis of these supposed "irrational" beliefs, the disappointed kinsfolk attack the dead person's transfers as the product of an "insane" delusion. Many of these cases are from the turn of the century, when the spiritualist movement was at its height. In *Owens* v. *Crumbaugh*, 228 Ill. 380, 81 N.E. 1044 (1907), the will of an eighty-three-year-old retired banker and farmer living in central Illinois was attacked as the product of his "insane delusion" about spiritualism. After providing for his wife, Crumbaugh left the balance of his estate to the local spiritualist church and endowed a library for the little town of Leroy, Illinois, for the purpose of teaching spiritualism. His nieces and nephews filed a will contest, alleging that the decedent had an insane delusion that his dead son, now a spirit guide named "Bright Eyes," appeared and talked to him about various concerns, including his own safety. Crumbaugh had been very attached to his son, who had died as a small child. The trial jury set his will aside, but the Illinois Supreme Court—holding that, as a matter of law, a belief in spiritualism does not amount to an insane delusion—dismissed the original complaint and ordered a retrial. On retrial the jury entered a second verdict for the contestant. The Supreme Court again reversed and ordered judgment entered for the proponents of the will. After this long and costly series of trials and appeals, Crumbaugh's estate was reduced considerably by expenses and lawyers' fees but was still directed toward his cherished charitable object, the spiritualist library in Leroy.

In *McReynolds* v. *Smith,* 172 Ind. 336, 86 N.E. 1009 (1909), however, a belief in communication with spirits of the dead, coupled with other bizarre or strange behavioral patterns involving family members, did lead to the voiding of a will as the result of an insane delusion. The decedent, an ardent Swedenborgian, was convinced that he could talk with the spirits of the dead. He also informed his friends that he had traveled to Jupiter and Mars. His will disinherited his son and daughter and left his wife a life estate, the balance of his assets being given to the Swedenborgian church. The decedent claimed that his will had been dictated to him by the spirit world and was sacred and unchangeable. The court set aside this will, and the decision was sustained by the Indiana Supreme Court as supported by the manifest weight of the evidence.

Also set aside have been the wills of persons who believed in witchcraft (*Schildnicht* v. *Rompf,* 4 S.W. 235 (Ky. 1887)), faith healing (*Spencer* v. *Spencer,* 221 S.W. 58 (Mo. 1922)), charismatic religious experience (*In re Tritch's Will,* 165 Pa. 586, 30 A.1053 (1895)), or divine revelations (*In re Murray's Estate,* 173 Or. 209, 144 P.2d 1016 (1944)).

Most of the "insane delusion" cases, whether of the "delusion of persecution" type or "crank" type, are quite old. This ground for setting aside postdeath transfers has fallen into disuse. It did not evolve a general doctrine for setting aside a postdeath transfer as the product of mental disease, thus opening up a line of communication

between the medical and psychological professional and the bench
and bar on the presentation of evidence on the issue of mental capacity. The attempt to squeeze modern medical psychiatric and psychological knowledge into an antique model of the *Greenwood-Baker*
rule usually results in such distortion of the relevant data base as to
make the expert testimony of physicians and psychologists misleading or contradictory.

Evidence of Want of Capacity in Court

The law has defended for many years a "magic moment"
theory of the law of testamentary capacity. If, at the precise instant of
execution of will, deed, or trust, the person whose capacity is questioned met the threshold test of the *Greenwood-Baker* rule and the
"insane delusion" rule for capacity, the entire scheme is regarded as
sound, despite evidence that before the magic moment, during the
planning process, the person's mental capacity was questionable.
Most courts invite only direct evidence of infirmity on the execution
date and time; they disregard all circumstantial evidence, other than
testimony by medical and psychological experts concerning the
mental capacity of the transferor at time of transfer (*In re Martin's
Estate*, 270 Cal. App. 2d 506, 75 Cal. Rptr. 911 (1969)). This general
judicial bias probably springs from unfamiliarity with the onset and
progress of organic and functional mental disorder and the implicit
faith in the appearance of "lucid moments," in which the transferor
suddenly recovers total mental functioning. However, a jury is free
to draw inferences from testimony about the conduct of the transfer-
or prior to the actual moment of execution. Such evidence then becomes relevant to proof that the transferor did not possess capacity.

Verbal Statements, Behavior, and Written Documents. The
usual contest is supported by profuse lay testimony describing the
acts and conduct of the transferor shortly before execution of the
will, deed, or trust. John Henry Wigmore, a noted authority in trial
evidence, states: "Any and all conduct of the person is admissible in
evidence. There is no restriction as to the kind of conduct. There can
be none" (Wigmore, [1913], 1940, vol. 2, sec. 228). The only outside
limitation on lay testimony about behavior observed is that of re-
moteness in time from the magic moment of will execution.

The sort of behavior that the law considers "acts and conduct of the testator" includes both verbal and nonverbal behavior. Normally, many of the verbal statements of the transferor will be admissible despite being "hearsay," since these statements will fall into two well-worn exceptions to the bar to hearsay evidence. First, much of what the transferor said during life will be directed to proof of state of mind of the transferor, and admissible as an exception because "state of mind" is the primary issue in the average will contest. Second, those few out-of-court statements that do not fit the state-of-mind exception to the hearsay rule are relevant to explain the series of transactions involved in the transfer process and thus are called by lawyers *res gestae* and admissible (*Nowlin* v. *Spakes*, 250 Ark. 26, 463 S.W.2d 651 (1967)).

The various transactions in postdeath transfer, reduced to writing and available in documentary form for examination by court and jury are also generally admissible in challenges to capacity. The intrinsic evidence of the dispositive documents themselves are further "verbal acts" of the transferor and admissible to show state of mind (*Embry* v. *Beaver*, 192 Ind. 471, 137 N.E. 55 (1922)). The internal evidence of the instrument under attack, showing what the courts have described as an "unnatural" disposition, is relevant to show that the transferor had or did not have mental capacity to make a transfer (*In re Sturdevant's Appeal*, 71 Conn. 392, 42 A. 70 (1889)).

The courts also permit lay witnesses to express an opinion, based on personal observation of the transfer, about the transferor's mental capacity to execute a will, deed, or trust instrument when they last saw the individual (Wigmore, [1913] 1940, vol. 7, secs. 193–199). This doctrine, of course, permits attesting witnesses to deeds, wills, or trusts to give an opinion, perhaps based on a few minutes' contact in a superficial manner, on the mental capacity of the transferor (*Wheat* v. *Wheat*, 156 Conn. 575, 244 A.2d 359 (1958)). If the attesting witness was the testator's lawyer, the opinion is entitled to very great weight in some states (*In re Fordyce's Estate*, 130 Ill. App. 755, 285 N.E.2d 886 (1971)).

Testimony by Expert Witnesses. Finally, the courts permit the employment of physicians and other specially qualified individuals as witnesses for either side in the contest over capacity. These individuals, tagged "expert witnesses" by the law, may be called to testify for either side or for the court (Fed. R. Evid. 705 (1975)) in order to aid the court and jury in understanding the difficult factual situations presented by capacity cases. Generally, there are two types of expert witness testimony. First, the treating physician, psychiatrist, or psychologist may testify on what he or she learned by firsthand examination of the testator. Second, a nontreating medical or psychological professional may be called to give a hypothetical opinion on mental condition based on facts put into the record from other sources.

There are special problems about the use of treating physicians as witnesses at trial. First, in nearly every state, matter communicated by a patient to a physician in the course of examination or treatment is privileged; it is not admissible in court unless the patient waives his or her privilege to exclude the matter (Uniform R. Evid. 503 (1974)). In a will contest based on lack of testamentary capacity, most states hold that the testator's physician may testify on the testator's mental condition even though the testator could have claimed that information communicated to his or her physician was privileged. These courts hold that in an action attempting to set aside a will on account of mental condition of the testator, any privilege relating to physician-patient communications or examinations is waived. A minority of states do not accept this doctrine but insist that the proponent of the will alone has control over the introduction or exclusion of the testator's medical history from the testator's physician (*Pence* v. *Meyers,* 180 Ind. 583, 101 N.E. 716 (1913)). A similar rule applies to cases in which a deed, trust instrument, or contract is under attack on account of the mental condition of the person executing the deed, trust, or contract. In such cases most courts hold that the physician-patient privilege has been waived (*Newkirk* v. *Rothrock,* 155 Ind. App. 505, 293 N.E.2d 550 (1973)).

The observations and opinions of an attending medical or psychological specialist would be strong evidence either for or against mental capacity in any contest and, were it not for a judicial discounting factor, probably would determine the outcomes. The hostility shown by lawyers and judges to medical experts who testify in will contests is difficult to explain. It seems to come partly from the recognition that there will be little left for the legal professional to do if medical experts take over the burden of inquiry in such cases (*In re Powers' Estate*, 375 Mich. 150, 134 N.W.2d 148 (1965)).

The parties are always free, however, to call alienists who will reply to a hypothetical question concocted by the examining attorney—structured with data already put into the record of the proceedings by other witnesses, from which the expert may assume what happened and draw a conclusion about mental competency.

Until quite recently an expert witness called at trial was required to testify only in response to a hypothetical question based only on evidence put in record at trial prior to the witness's being called. The expert, after being qualified professionally by the lawyer and accepted as an expert by the court, then listened to the hypothetical as read by the lawyer and responded to it by giving an opinion on mental competency on the relevant date. The expert was then permitted to give an explanation of the basis for his or her opinion. This had some aspects of a sterile and boring ritual, which failed to highlight important testimony and consumed a good deal of trial time (Wigmore, [1913] 1940, vol. 5, secs. 555–571).

In the past few years, with the adoption of the *Federal Rules of Evidence*, both by federal courts and by twenty-two states, this ritualism has been loosened. It is now possible for an expert to give an opinion based on data in the trial record and on data that are not in the record but are regularly used by similar professionals and are available to the expert before trial. The matter need not be fed to the expert through a hypothetical question detailing each assumed fact (Fed. R. Evid. 701–705 (1975)). This simplifies the task of the expert on direct examination.

However, all experts may be cross-examined by opposing counsel. This procedure, a form of intimidating tactics, is based on the general notion that truth is best ascertained if the party who is hostile to the witness's testimony is able to put suggestive questions to the witness, preventing the witness from falsification and fabrication. The cross-examiner is permitted to use medical, psychiatric, and psychological books to cross-examine professionals. These books may be cited to the professional, who may be asked whether he or she uses the treatise or would consider it an authoritative treatise. If the professional agrees that the material is authoritative, the lawyer may read any portion of the treatise and ask whether the expert agrees with the extract. This procedure may continue until the expert contradicts his or her own testimony on direct or until a point of disagreement is reached between the text described as authoritative and the expert's own opinion. Such a tactic is called impeachment and is commonly used in trials. It works for both sides in a dispute over mental capacity.

Undue Influence

The English Statute of Wills contained no provision for avoiding wills made under undue influence. Canon law had no maximum that applied to the conduct of importuning beneficiaries. The doctrine appeared to emerge out of nowhere in the late eighteenth century in the case of *Mountain v. Bennet*, 29 Eng. Rep. 1200 (Ex. 1787), in which the will of a sane individual was attacked by his family. The evidence showed that Mr. Bennet was excessively devoted to women. He had been fond of a neighbor named Mrs. Hartford, and he married her secretly after her husband died. Later he made out a will leaving her all his property. Although Bennet was fond of drink and women, he satisfied the *Greenwood-Baker* rule for testamentary capacity and had no insane delusions about his relatives. Nonetheless, they insisted that the will should be voided. Lord Chief Baron Eyre agreed, at least, that the plaintiffs' case held legal water: "If a dominion was acquired by any person over a mind of sufficient sanity to *general purposes*, and of sufficient soundness and discretion to regulate his affairs in *general;* yet if such a dominion or influence were acquired over him as to prevent the exercise of such discretion, it would be equally inconsistent with the idea of a disposing mind. . . . On a general view of this case, it must turn on one or another of these grounds: namely either on the general capacity of Mr. Bennet to act for himself . . . or on the ground of a dominion or influence acquired over him by the women with whom he had most unfortunately connected himself" (29 Eng. Rep. at 1200–1201). The case was taken from the jury because the plaintiffs failed to show that Mrs. Bennet had importuned Bennet for the marriage and for his property. In fact, the evidence showed that Bennet had importuned Mrs. Hartford for a quick marriage. The rule of *Mountain* v. *Bennet* stated that a will might be avoided, even if made with testamentary capacity, if it were procured by a beneficiary who importuned the testator for favors at the expense of other natural objects of his bounty.

In the early-nineteenth-century case of *Casborne* v. *Barsham*, 44 Eng. Rep. 1108 (Ch. 1839)), another footnote was added to the growing law on undue influence by beneficiaries. The suit was to set aside a deed by Dennis Chandler to his solicitor, Barsham, of property to satisfy an antecedent debt due. The plaintiff, Casborne, was a creditor of Chandler's who claimed that Barsham had exercised undue influence in obtaining the deed against other creditors of Chandler, including the plaintiff. Although the case did not fit the law for cancellation of fraudulent conveyances, and was not an unlawful preference by Chandler, Casborne sought to show at trial that Barsham controlled Chandler's mind and had secured the deed by substituting his own interest for that of his client. The Chancellor's Court set aside the deed. The petitioner appealed, but the Lord Chancellor affirmed, holding that the evidence showed that Barsham's habitual exercise of power over Chandler constituted undue influence, depriving Chandler of freedom of will.

Mountain v. *Bennet* and *Casborne* v. *Barsham* indicate that a will, deed, or trust declaration can be avoided if one party has a confidential relationship with another person, exercises dominion over him, and importunes him for favors—thereby depriving him of free will in making transfers. The *Mountain-Casborne* rule crossed the Atlantic and was influential in several early-nineteenth-century American will contests, notably *Gardner* v. *Gardner*, 22 Wend. 526 (N.Y. 1839), and *O'Neill* v. *Farr*, 1 Rich. 80 (S.C. 1844). However, the standard for setting aside a will, deed, or trust as the product of undue influence exerted by a beneficiary refused to be neatly defined for many years.

Perhaps the most acceptable test for undue influence was generated by *In re Falk's Will*, 246 Wis. 319, 17 N.W.2d 423 (1945). A claim to set aside a will, deed, contract, or trust instrument for undue influence arises when a person who is susceptible to undue influence by others, by reason of mental or physical infirmity, establishes a confidential relationship with a person who uses that confidential relationship to manipulate the transferor in order to force

the transferor to change his or her postdeath distribution of property
in favor of the influences or an accomplice, provided the results of
the change are socially unacceptable.

"Susceptibility to influence" is present in nearly all successful contests to set aside wills or deeds as the product of undue influence. The transferor in such cases is usually described as senile,
weak, easily led, and the like (*In re Willeson's Estate,* 251 Iowa 1363,
105 N.W.2d 640 (1960)). Courts that have refused to set aside a
transfer on the grounds of undue influence often describe the transferor as a person of "strong mind" or stubborn character. Almost all
undue influence cases also set up proof that the transferor had a
peculiar dependence on the alleged influencer (*Starr* v. *Starr,* 293
Ala. 204, 301 So. 2d 78 (1974)). The courts characterize a dependent
relationship as "confidential," loosely including within that umbrella the relationship between attorney and client (*Kozacik* v. *Fass,*
134 Ind. App. 557, 241 N.E.2d (1968)); doctor and patient (*In re
Falk's Will,* 246 Wis. 319, 17 N.W.2d 423 (1945)); nurse and patient
(*Gerrish* v. *Chambers,* 135 Me. 70, 189 A. 187 (1937)); agent and
principal (*Bank of America* v. *Saville,* 416 F.2d 265 (7th Cir.), certiorari denied, 386 U.S. 1038 (1969)); parent and child (*McCartney* v.
Rex, 127 Ind. App. 702, 145 N.E.2d 400 (1957); and brother and
sister (*Fiumara* v. *Fiumara,* 258 Pa. 340, 427 A.2d 667 (1981)). If
someone who enjoys this type of relationship with a transferor importunes the transferor to make a change of distribution plans and
the change takes place, then the courts generally find undue influence. If there was no change of disposition as a result of importuning by a potential beneficiary, then the courts do not find undue
influence present.

"Unconscionability" is the legal word used to describe a
transfer that the courts consider contrary to social policy objectives
of fairness. The courts refuse to define "unconscionability." However, they have held "unconscionable" the act of a person who
willed all his property to an extramarital sex partner (*Brelsford* v.
Aldrich, 42 Ind. App. 106, 84 N.E.2d 1040 (1908)); and they have held
"not unconscionable" the act of a man who disinherited children by
a first marriage as a result of the importuning of a second wife, who
got all his estate by will or deed (*Crane* v. *Hensler,* 196 Ind. 341, 146
N.E. 579 (1925)). Giving all one's property to one's lover is, or was,

considered socially unconscionable; but distribution of all to one's second wife, in preference to children, is not considered unconscionable.

Types of Undue Influence Cases

The phenomenon of beneficiary importuning is a little easier to understand if the types of contests in which undue influence is alleged are described as a taxonomy of undue influence cases.

Husband-Wife Undue Influence. One of the most commonly filed actions to avoid a deed, will, or trust for undue influence is an action brought by disappointed children of a first marriage against their parent's transfer of substantial assets to a new marriage partner.

In *Workman* v. *Workman*, 113 Ind. App. 245, 46 N.E.2d 718 (1943), for example, an elderly, mentally weakened man gave most of his estate to his second wife, a much younger woman, whom he had met while cruising bars in the company of a lawyer named Herbert Lane. The three children of his first marriage alleged that the transfer was the result of undue influence over the old man exerted by his new wife and his lawyer/drinking companion. At trial the contestants put in much evidence describing Workman's drinking, his "trips" with Lane, and the way in which Lane prepared a new will disinheriting the old man's children. The will was signed by Workman in the hospital, away from his family, and it was unclear that Workman understood what he was doing. The trial court set aside Workman's will, and the verdict was sustained by the Indiana Court of Appeals as supported by the evidence.

Most husband-wife undue influence cases go in favor of the importuning spouse. For example, in *Snell* v. *Seek*, 363 Mo. 225, 250 S.W.2d 336 (1952), the Missouri Supreme Court sustained probate of the will of Damaris S. Seek, which left essentially all her estate to her second husband, Joseph E. Seek, in preference to the two children whom he and her first husband, John Summers, had adopted and raised until marriage. Summers, a Missouri farmer, died in 1939 and left land in Texas to his adopted children and the residue of his estate to his wife. She married Joseph Seek, ten years her junior, in 1941. Seek was a minister of the Christian Union Church and a part-time coal miner and paperhanger. On June 17, 1949, he took some handwritten notes to a lawyer in Excelsior Springs, Missouri, indicating that his wife wanted to make out her will according to the notes. The will gave essentially everything she owned to her husband. The next day the lawyer took the drafted will out to the Seek farmhouse and interrogated Mrs. Seek on its provisions. Satisfied that Mrs. Seek understood the will and its effects, including disinheritance of her children, he had the will executed by the testatrix and two witnesses. Mrs. Seek was in bed at the time the will was signed.

The usual parade of lay witnesses varied on their opinion of Mrs. Seek's mental capacity at the time of execution. Witnesses testified that Mr. and Mrs. Seek were a warm, affectionate, and caring couple; that Mr. Seek took care of writing checks for her; and that the couple eventually merged their assets into a single joint account. The trial court found this evidence sufficient to set aside the will as the product of Mr. Seek's undue influence, since Mr. Seek had gone to the lawyer with a set of notes in handwriting not shown to be his wife's and had managed her affairs for some time prior to making the will. The Missouri Supreme Court reversed. It held that, although Mr. and Mrs. Seek enjoyed a confidential relationship as husband and wife and Mr. Seek managed Mrs. Seek's property for her, there was no evidence showing that Mr. Seek used undue influence to benefit from his second wife. Since Seek had never said a derogatory word about Mrs. Seek's children, the court felt that there was no evidence of an unconscionable action on his part in securing benefits under the will. It also said that a wife who left her estate to her husband in preference to her children did not behave unnaturally, inferring that there was nothing unconscionable in Mrs. Seek's will.

Undue Influence by Children. Many lawsuits over undue influence on individuals involves alleged manipulation of a parent by one child to gain favor from the parent through a deed or will. In some instances the "favorite" child provided a home for the elderly parent and performed a number of useful services, in return for which the parent left that child all or a disproportionate share in the parent's estate. In other instances the "favorite" is a "prodigal son" who returns home to ingratiate himself or herself with the parent after a long separation. In return for reconciliation, the parent leaves that child a disproportionate share of his or her estate at death.

The kind of intersibling undue influence case that results in a verdict and judgment setting aside the parent's dispositive plan is illustrated by *In re Gelonese Estate*, 36 Cal. App. 3d 856, 111 Cal. Rptr. 833 (1974). Rosa Balassi Gelonese immigrated to the United States from Italy before World War I. She married a man named Balassi and had five children, Robert, Lena, Rosie, Charles, and Peter. Mr. Balassi died in 1935. Mrs. Balassi, after an unsuccessful second marriage, married Antonio Gelonese in 1950. Mrs. Gelonese made a will in 1960, giving a specific bequest of $1,000 to Robert Balassi and his wife and dividing her assets equally among her five children. Her third husband died in 1966, and Mrs. Gelonese suffered a stroke shortly after his death. Robert Balassi and his wife took their mother into their home and cared for her from that date until her death in 1971. In 1966, after Mr. Gelonese's death, Mrs. Gelonese visited a lawyer and requested that a new will be drawn up. The lawyer sent his law partner, Petersen, to Mrs. Gelonese's house to draw the will, accompanied by a priest and by an unknown physician selected by the lawyer. After seeing Mrs. Gelonese, the physician and priest advised Petersen that Mrs. Gelonese lacked the capacity to understand what she was doing. Petersen refused to write her will. Mrs. Gelonese then went to a real estate broker named Angelo Penitenti and asked him to translate her will from English to Italian and to make some changes in the will. Mrs. Gelonese went to her doctor's office with Lena Belassi and received a doctor's certificate of competency. Meanwhile, Robert procured witnesses for his mother's will. The will, redrafted in Italian, was executed in Mr. Penitenti's office. One of the attesting witnesses noted that Mrs. Gelonese said nothing and that her son and daughter did all the talking for her.

The new will divided her substantial estate equally among Robert, Lena, and Peter, leaving Rosie Balassi Del Grosso and Charles Balassi with $1,000 specific bequests each. After the new will was executed, Charles and Rosie testifed that Peter, Lena, and Robert had prevented them from visiting their mother. Witnesses also testified that, after making the 1966 will, Mrs. Gelonese told people that Charles already had enough property from Mr. Gelonese's will and that Charles and Rosie had betrayed her. Charles had a life estate in a trailer court, together with his mother, and had sued Robert and Lena for committing waste on his life estate in the trailer park.* There was strong circumstantial evidence that Robert, Lena, and Peter had turned against their brother and sister as a result of this lawsuit and had infected their mother with the notion that Charles and Rosie had deserted her and did not care for her. The trial court entered a judgment on a jury verdict setting aside the will as the product of Robert, Lena, and Peter's undue influence over their mother. The California Court of Appeals sustained the judgment of the trial court, finding that—since the relationship between parent and child was considered a confidential relationship under California law—a presumption arose that the 1966 will was the product of undue influence exerted by Robert, Lena, and Peter, because they assisted their mother in procuring her new will by taking her to the real estate agent's office and dictating the terms to him, as well as by providing the witnesses.

The kind of intersibling undue influence case that results in the will's being sustained after attack is represented by *In re Rheay's Estate*, 249 Minn. 123, 81 N.W.2d 277 (1957). Thomas Rheay, a widower, died June 28, 1955, survived by one son, Arthur, and two daughters, Clara and Mabel. His will left $1,700 to his two daughters, payable by his son out of his share of the estate. Arthur received the family farm and cash, valued at $38,000. Clara and Mabel had both left home and moved away after marriage. Arthur, the eldest child, stayed home and worked the family farm. He built a small house on the farm in which he initially lived until 1962, when he exchanged houses with his father. After Mr. Rheay turned seventy, he did very little work on the farm, leaving the maintenance and upkeep to his son. Arthur's wife did his laundry and prepared his meals. Mr. Rheay freely told his friends that Arthur had been a good boy who had not received much from running the farm all those years and that, as a result, he was leaving him the farm.

---

*Waste is a legal term denoting unlawful abuse or destruction of real estate by a person in possession who does not own full legal title in fee simple to the land. An example of waste is the pulling down of a house by a tenant without the landlord's permission.

Arthur took his father to see a lawyer to make a will and was in the same room with him when his father gave the lawyer directions on what to put in the will. The lawyer testified in court that Arthur said nothing and that Mr. Rheay gave him all the details of the will without help. There was also evidence that Mr. Rheay, in his eighties, still drove his own car, made visits to his daughter and to friends over long distances, and handled all his own finances. More important, the 1953 will was essentially the same as a 1950 will, which had also given Arthur the farm. It was conceded that Arthur did not assist in procuring the earlier will at all. The only importuning traceable to Arthur was a request made to his father that he be given more time to pay the cash legacies to his sisters. The trial court found that the 1953 will had not been procured by Arthur's undue influence. On appeal the Minnesota Supreme Court sustained the trial court. It found that the sisters who attacked the will did not prove that Arthur exerted undue influence by clear and convincing evidence. In fact, the evidence tended to show that Arthur exercised no particular influence over his father's will at all, although Arthur was certainly aware that he was to receive the balance of his father's estate at his death.

The difference between *Gelonese* and *Rheay* can be seen in light of the behavior of the alleged influencer. The three Balassi children who lived in the same city as their mother tried to prevent the two children who lived away from home from seeing their mother. They also poisoned their mother's mind by insinuating that the other children stayed away through indifference or hatred. In *Rheay* the evidence showed that Mr. Rheay was not estranged from his daughters and in fact went to visit them quite frequently. His choice was by way of compensating an eldest son for minding the farm for more than twenty years for him. Mrs. Gelonese, on the other hand, was mentally weak (whereas Mr. Rheay was said to be mentally vigorous) and dependent on her children for advice and direction. She was also mistaken about the intentions of Charles and Rosie, and their feelings for her, whereas Mr. Rheay was not mistaken.

Collateral Relatives Influence. A fair number of contests over postdeath transfer have involved the importuning of brothers, sisters, nieces, nephews, or cousins of the transferor. In many instances these cases involve the disinheritance of a spouse or children in favor of a collateral relative, a situation almost certain to bring on a contest between the children or spouse and the collateral.

In *Gurley* v. *Park,* 135 Ind. 440, 35 N.E. 279 (1893), Mary B. Park, a widow, had lived essentially by herself from the date of her husband's death until her own death. Mrs. Park had a son, who was in some degree of actual want, having a large family and small income. She was said to be "unbalanced" and unable to manage her own affairs well. At various times she told friends that she would leave her estate to her son, and at other times she indicated that she would leave her estate to other individuals. Eventually she became seriously ill, and on her death bed she made a will in favor of her brother's children, at the insistence of her brother. The trial jury set aside Mrs. Park's will as the product of undue influence on her brother's part. The Indiana Supreme Court sustained that finding, on the strength that the jury's verdict was supported by ample evidence that Albert N. Gurley, the brother, had engaged in undue influence by importuning his mentally unbalanced sister for benefits for his children. This case is typical of those in which the contestant is able to show a will or deed procured by undue influence. As in *Gurley* v. *Park,* the courts seem inclined to find an injustice in the transfer of property away from children to a collateral.

The type of case in which the contestant is usually unsuccessful is represented by *In re Glass's Estate,* 85 Wis.2d 126, 270 N.W.2d 386 (1978). Hazel Glass was survived by her sister, Celeste Halvorsen; a brother, Glenn Odegard; and Anders Birkleand and Gordon D. Odegard, two nephews. Mrs. Glass had been a widow since the 1960s and had cancer. She lived in Milwaukee, as did her nephew Gordon Odegard. Her other relatives lived in different communities. Mrs. Glass's will had originally divided her estate equally between Anders Birkleand and Gordon Odegard, excluding her brother and sister entirely. After becoming ill with cancer, Mrs. Glass or Odegard contacted Paul C. Konnor, an attorney, who came to the hospital to discuss the contents of a new will. The will was prepared and executed on November 4, 1975, at the hospital, and was witnessed by Konnor and a nurse. This will left all her estate to Gordon Odegard. Before going into the hospital, Mrs. Glass had told a friend that she planned to change her will and leave her estate to Gordon Odegard alone.

Mrs. Glass died November 30, 1975, and Gordon Odegard's petition to probate her new will was opposed by Anders Birkleand. A jury trial was held, in which the jury found that Gordon Odegard exercised no undue influence over Mrs. Glass and enjoyed no confidential relationship with her. The trial court found that Odegard had done nothing to procure the will, despite Konnor's testimony that Odegard may have called him.

The Wisconsin Supreme Court affirmed the trial court's verdict for Odegard, even though the November 1975 will was a dramatic shift in Mrs. Glass's testamentary plans, disinheriting one nephew without cause and excluding her brother and sister entirely. The court also found, on the basis of the evidence, that Mrs. Glass was a woman of strong and independent mind and not subject to influence from others. She was characterized as "stubborn" by her friends who were called as witnesses for the contesting party. The court therefore held that she was not susceptible to undue influence, despite testimony of John Griest, a psychiatrist, who offered a professional opinion that Mrs. Glass was more susceptible to undue influence in the hospital while dying than at home.

The difference between the two cases really lay in the perceived antisocial result in *Gurley* v. *Park*. In that case the contestant was the only son of the deceased testatrix. He was in want, and his mother surely knew of his need for money. Instead, she yielded to the demands of her brother on her death bed, who practically forced her to make a will favoring his children at the expense of her own son. In *Glass* the elderly testatrix chose to concentrate her estate on a single nephew rather than to spread it between that nephew and another whom she had not seen for a good while. The rationality of the latter choice was much easier to defend, and the results were not deemed antisocial by the court.

Influence by Helping Professionals. The courts are likely to take a very careful look at wills, deeds, or trusts that transfer property to a nonfamily member in preference to the family— particularly in cases where a helping professional receives a legacy or an *inter vivos* transfer (a transfer "between two living people") from a patient or client. In the past several decades, many such contests have been filed by family members attempting to set aside transfers of property to doctors (*In re Satterlee's Will,* 281 A.D. 251, 119 N.Y.S.2d 309 (1963)), nurses (*Gerrish* v. *Chambers,* 135 Me. 70,

189 A. 187 (1937)), lawyers (*In re Powers' Estate*, 375 Mich. 150, 134 N.W.2d 148 (1965)), and other professionals, on the ground that the professional exercised undue influence over the decedent. The insidious process of influence is easier to see in a case where the helping professional gradually appropriates the management of the transferor's business and financial affairs until the transferor readily accepts the professional's dictation of such instruments as deeds or wills without question. Weakness, physical or mental, and the other indications of undue influence, usually convince courts to set aside such nonfamilial transfers.

The kind of activity by a helping professional that can lead to a jury verdict against a will or deed as a product of undue influence is illustrated by *In re Satterlee's Will*. In 1947 the testatrix was referred to Sol A. Rosenblatt, an attorney, who took care of her divorce in 1948 and was also her agent by power of attorney to handle her business affairs. He became the beneficiary of Mrs. Satterlee's first will, made in 1948, which left him her residuary estate under precatory language (expressing a request or wish but not a command) telling him to give the estate to charity. Mrs. Satterlee made two more wills. The last one was drawn up in February 1949 by a lawyer whom Rosenblatt had recommended—his own partner's brother-in-law. In this 1949 will, Rosenblatt became her absolute legatee, with an understanding that he would convey a portion of his legacy to her physician, Dr. Hoffman. Mrs. Satterlee had first gone to Hoffman for her medical problems around the time of her divorce and had become irrationally infatuated with him, although he was a married man. She told her friends that she was in love with Hoffman and wanted him to marry her. After Mrs. Satterlee's death, her sister contested her last will, in which she left her estate to Rosenblatt.

The trial judge excluded testimony from Rosenblatt and Hoffman, called as adverse witnesses for the contestant, on the ground that their testimony would have been privileged communications. The contestant had already adduced some evidence that Rosenblatt and Hoffman had conspired to get Mrs. Satterlee's property away from her. The trial court entered a judgment admitting the 1949 will to probate, and Mrs. Satterlee's sister appealed. The New York Supreme Court, Appellate Division, ordered a retrial and denied the 1949 will legal effect until Hoffman and Rosenblatt could be examined by the contestant. In this instance the reviewing court held that, in a contest over the validity of Mrs. Satterlee's will, the facts communicated to her lawyer and physician concerning the making of that will would not be privileged after her death.

The kind of contest that results in a jury verdict and judgment for the proponent of the transfer instrument is represented by *Frye* v. *Norton*, 148 W. Va. 500, 135 S.E.2d 603 (1964). Mabel Tarrer died June 6, 1961, leaving a will giving most of her estate to her lawyer, Wilbert Norton. Mr. and Mrs. Tarrer had run a restaurant in Huntington, West Virginia, for many years before Mr. Tarrer's death in 1952. Norton had been their attorney for thirty-five years. The Tarrers had no children, and Mrs. Tarrer had no close relatives. Mrs. Tarrer decided to have Norton appointed her trustee to manage her affairs if she became incompetent and to make him her residuary legatee. He correctly advised her to consult another lawyer, and she set up an appointment with the president of the county bar association, who made out her will and trust. These instruments were executed two years after her husband's death. Her cousins challenged her will in 1961, claiming that Mrs. Tarrer was an alcoholic and unable to comprehend what she was doing in 1954, and was also under the domination of her lawyer, Wilbert Norton. The contesting parties induced the trial judge to read an instruction to the jury stating that, if the jury believed that Norton procured the will in which he was beneficiary, the jury would presume that Mrs. Tarrer's estate had been obtained by fraud or undue influence by Norton, laying on him the burden of disproving any complicity in obtaining the will. The jury promptly returned a verdict setting aside the will, which the proponent appealed to the West Virginia Supreme Court.

The supreme court first held that Mrs. Tarrer's addiction to alcohol was not tied to the date when she made out her will and trust and was not sufficient proof that she lacked capacity to make a will. The only witness who claimed that Mrs. Tarrer was intoxicated on the day she made her will contradicted his earlier statement in a deposition when he said that he couldn't remember anything about Mrs. Tarrer's condition on February 25, 1954, the date she signed her will. The court also held that the trial judge gave an improper instruction to the jury on undue influence, since there was no evidence that Norton had anything to do with procuring the will in his favor and, in fact, had sent his client to another lawyer to make her will when she mentioned a desire to make him a beneficiary. The West Virginia Supreme Court sent the case back for a new trial, instructing the trial court not to use the instruction on presumed undue influence if the parties chose to retry the case.

The difference between the two cases again lay in the conduct of the party who was the principal beneficiary under the will. In *Satterlee* the beneficiaries, Rosenblatt and Hoffman, were shown to have worked in concert to acquire their victim's estate. In *Frye* the lawyer-beneficiary did not seek to get any property from his client and sent her away when she began to suggest that he should take a share of her estate. In both cases the beneficiaries were aware that the transferor wanted to share the estate with them. In the first the beneficiaries cultivated that irrational desire. In the second the beneficiary "let it happen" and did not actively discourage his client from making a will in his favor.

Influence by Friends. In a number of contests over wills, deeds, or trusts, the alleged undue influencer is a friend of the family, who receives a legacy or property at the expense of family members. These family friends are not helping professionals and are not subject to the same suspicions that surround lawyers or physicians who are the object of a client or patient's will. Nonetheless, courts are suspicious of such transfers, and a good number are set aside as the result of undue influence.

Typical of this kind of case is *In re Westfall's Estate,* 74 Ariz. 181, 245 P.2d 951 (1952). Elise Westfall was an elderly, frail woman who suffered from a number of ailments, including arteriosclerosis of the brain and heart. She advertised for a housekeeper and on March 20, 1950, interviewed Marie Proctor. Mrs. Proctor agreed to come in from 8 a.m. to 4 p.m. six days a week for $30 a week, later increased to $50 a week. She and her husband immediately began to campaign for Mrs. Westfall's entire estate. On April 8 they took her to a lawyer to draw a power of attorney in their favor. On April 11 Marie Proctor contacted another lawyer about drawing a will for Mrs. Westfall. On April 12 this individual came to Mrs. Westfall's home and presented Mrs. Westfall with a will that left all her estate to Mrs. Proctor. The will was torn or damaged during execution, and the lawyer came back the next day with a clean copy, which was then signed by Mrs. Westfall with an X, she being unable to sign her name.

Mrs. Westfall had made an earlier will leaving her estate to Naoma Anderson and including specific bequests to four other individuals. Shortly after her 1950 will was executed, she was placed under guardianship at the behest of her bank. After her death the bank and Mrs. Anderson contested her 1950 will on the grounds of want of capacity and of undue influence exerted by Mrs. Proctor. At trial the judge found that Mrs. Westfall had testamentary capacity, although she was frail and arteriosclerotic in 1950. The trial court also held that the will had not been procured by undue influence. The contestants appealed, and the Arizona Supreme Court reversed the case.

The supreme court held that all the facts surrounding the making of Mrs. Westfall's will suggested that Mrs. Proctor actively procured the will. Since she had contacted the lawyers in order to have the will drawn, and even told one that she expected to be "paid" for her services by a deed to all Mrs. Westfall's real estate and by a bequest in her will, she clearly had procured the will. She also quit Mrs. Westfall's employment eight days after becoming her residuary legatee. The trial court had evidently been under the illusion that the burden of disproving the will's validity for undue influence was much heavier than the law actually required. Although the Arizona Supreme Court agreed that properly executed wills are presumed free from undue influence, the presumption disappears as soon as credible evidence is offered to show that the will was procured through the activities of the beneficiary. It reversed the trial court and ordered that the will be excluded from probate.

The kind of case in which undue influence is rejected is represented by *In re Comegys' Estate*, 204 Or. 512, 284 P.2d 758 (1955). Felix Comegys, an eighty-two-year-old bachelor, had a married sister, Ida Doneen, who came to live with him in 1953, when her husband died. Ida fell and broke her hip in February 1951 and was a bedfast invalid thereafter. After hospitalization Ida went back to her brother's house for a few weeks before being taken to her son's home in Washington. At his sister's suggestion, Comegys had hired Margery Ann Mischel, a distant relative, as a housekeeper while his sister was in the hospital and had retained her afterward to look after the two old people. Margery Mischel's husband was a commercial photographer studying in New York. The Mischels had been friends of the two old people for a number of years, had driven them various places, and had taken them to visit relatives. The husband took a job with a studio close to Comegys' farm, and the Mischels went to live and care for Comegys. No particular arrangement was made for paying the couple at the time.

On January 2, 1952, Comegys had Mr. Mischel drive him to a lawyer's office. On the way Comegys told him that the Mischels were to have his entire estate at his death. Mischel went into the lawyer's office with Mr. Comegys and sat in on the will interview with the lawyer but took no part in the discussion. Two weeks later he drove Comegys back to the lawyer's office to execute the will. Comegys told Mischel to say nothing to anyone about the terms of the will. On Comegys' death, his sister filed objection to the probate of the 1952 will, charging that her brother lacked testamentary capacity and that the Mischels had exercised undue influence over the old man. The trial jury returned a verdict for the Mischels, upholding the will's validity, and Ida Doneen's appeal was turned down by the Oregon Supreme Court.

The supreme court described Felix Comegys as "a friendly, gregarious man who enjoyed life and lived it fully almost to the very end." He had in fact appeared as a rider in the Sheridan, Wyoming, Phil Sheridan Day parade only a few months before his death. Comegys had a pool table in his home and enjoyed shooting pool and playing cards with fellow old-timers. Furthermore, Margery Mischel had, as a girl, been raised on a neighboring farm. She was an accomplished horsewoman and had gone riding with Comegys, a superior horseman, many times. There was nothing in the evidence at trial suggesting that Comegys had consulted the Mischels on any business affairs or had involved them at all in his plans for making a will. Although Mischel had gone with Comegys to the lawyer's office, he took no part in the will-making process and was simply a chauffeur. The contestant's allegations of error were dismissed by the court as immaterial, and probate was ordered.

The difference between these two cases again had to do with the conduct of the beneficiary. In *Westfall* Mrs. Proctor and her husband had sent for the lawyers to make Mrs. Westfall's will. They had admitted dictating to Mrs. Westfall that she "pay" them for Mrs. Proctor's services by deeding over her real estate and willing over her personal property to them, in addition to wages. They also quickly left her employ when Mrs. Westfall had transferred all her property to them. In *Comegys* the Mischels had played no active role in Felix Comegys' change of testamentary plans. They neither solicited him for a bequest nor had anything to do with his financial affairs. As housekeepers and companions, they were simply friends. In both instances a strong emotional dependence on the beneficiaries appeared from the record. In *Comegys* the bequest to the Mischels was let stand because Felix Comegys was a strong-minded, independent man who consulted no one about his financial affairs. In *Westfall* the victim was characterized as weak and susceptible to influence (Shaffer, 1970b, pp. 218–226).

Evidence of Undue Influence in Court

Undue influence is a charge that must be proved by the party attacking a will, deed, or trust, since the courts routinely find that properly executed instruments are presumed to be made by people free from undue influence (*In re Farmer's Estate*, 385 Pa. 468, 123 A.2d 630 (1956)). Many courts grant a countervailing presumption to contestants who prove that the transferor and the alleged influencer had a confidential relationship and that the transferor changed his or her disposition in favor of the influencer. In such situations the courts may find that a presumption of undue influence arises, which shifts to the party under attack the burden of disproving undue influence or of rebutting the presumption with credible evidence of lack of influence (*Reed* v. *Shipp*, 293 Ala. 632, 308 So. 2d 705 (1975)).

As in cases challenging a transfer for want of capacity, the acts, declarations, and conduct of the transferor are admissible to prove that the transferor acted under undue influence in making the transfer (Wigmore, [1913] 1940, vol. 7, sec. 1738). The actual verbal utterances of the transferor should be admissible as state-of-mind exceptions to the hearsay rule, since the degree of influence asserted by the beneficiary of the transfer is critical to the determination of the case. However, a minority of courts have excluded the actual statements of the transferor about the nature of his or her acts on the basis that the statements are hearsay and that an undue influence claim does not pertain to the state of mind of the transferor (*Robbins* v. *Fugit*, 189 Ind. 165, 126 N.E.2d 321 (1961)).

The opinions of lay witnesses about mental capacity would seem to be as admissible on the issue of undue influence as on the issue of capacity alone, since the state of mind of the transferor is at stake. However, only Georgia permits lay persons to express an opinion, rooted in firsthand observations, on the susceptibility of a transferor to undue influence (*Thompson* v. *Ammons*, 1606 Ga. 866, 129 S.E. 539 (1925)). All other states reviewing the admission of lay opinion evidence on undue influence have rejected such opinions without much elaboration on the reason for rejection (*Ferguson* v. *Ferguson*, 169 Va. 77, 192 S.E. 774 (1937)). The logic for excluding such evidence, given the general admissibility of lay opinion evidence on mental competency, is obscure.

Former wills, deeds, or other dispositive instruments indicating a different distribution pattern are logical proof of undue influence because they substantiate a change of disposition. In most instances former dispositive documents are admissible to prove undue influence (*Ofstad* v. *Sarconi*, 126 Colo. 565, 252 P.2d 94 (1952)).

Physicians, psychiatrists, and psychologists may give professional opinion evidence on a person's susceptibility to undue influence at trial (*Smeak* v. *Perry*, 175 Md. 73, 199 A. 788 (1938)). Such evidence is, of course, limited by the concept of physician-patient privilege, which prevents disclosure of matter communicated to a physician or psychologist in the course of treatment unless the patient waives the privilege at trial or unless it is waived by operation of law. Since most states hold the privilege waived in will or deed contests, attending physicians or treating psychologists may testify directly from their own clinical records and firsthand observation of the transferor on susceptibility to influence (Levitt, 1970, p. 83; Lassen, 1964, p. 239). Many courts have already approved of clinical psychologists as experts (*Indianapolis Union Railway* v. *Walker*, 162 Ind. App. 166, 318 N.E.2d 579 (1979)). An expert responding to a hypothetical question taken from facts already in evidence at trial would also be able to express an opinion on the extent of susceptibility of the transferor to undue influence.

The human services worker must reckon with the way in which the judiciary deals with undue influence. Since not all forms of importuning for favors from a transferor are suspect, the human services worker needs to be able to determine when importuning and pressuring for a change of will has passed the bounds of allowable intrafamilial squabbling. Thankfully, at least one authority has tried to sort out this typology, using the phenomenon of transference as a guideline. Shaffer (1970b, p. 197) has classified undue influence cases into four types:

1. "Conscious manipulation" cases, in which the influencer knows that he is the object of transference by the transferor and uses the relationship to extract pecuniary benefits from the transferer.
2. "Let it happen" cases, in which the undue influencer is aware that the transference is occurring and does nothing to stop the transferor's irrational love for him or her or to impede receipt of pecuniary benefits from the transferor.
3. "Unconscious opportunism" cases, in which the undue influencer is not aware of having awakened strong positive and inappropriate feelings of love in the transferor and does not anticipate a pecuniary reward.
4. "No-manipulation" cases, in which no transference relationship exists.

Under Shaffer's classification system, the most clearly perceived early signs of conscious or unconscious manipulation of another person through a transference relationship would be the type of romanticism associated with "falling in love" directed toward an inappropriate object for such feeling—for example, one's physician, lawyer, or business adviser. In *In re Kaufman's Will*, 20 A.D.2d 464, 247 N.Y.S.2d 664 (1964), affirmed, 15 N.Y.2d 825, 205 N.E.2d 864, 257 N.Y.S.2d 914 (1965), which Shaffer used as an illustration, a note found in Kaufman's safety deposit box along with his will was introduced as evidence. The note, written by Kaufman, exhibited irrational and romantic tendencies toward his business adviser, Mr. Weiss. Again, the simple dictate of informed judgment when one spots such a psuedoromantic relationship existing between two persons, where none would usually be, is to note the situation and prepare to deal with later inquiries into the mental state of both parties. As a matter of professional ethics, intervention in such an instance would be extremely difficult to justify.

Fraudulent Procurement of Postdeath Transfer

So far this chapter has examined the mental state of the transferor of property and has not examined the mental state of the beneficiary. In contests where property is transferred as a result of fraud perpetrated on the transferor, the mental state of both parties is at issue.

Fraud, an ancient grounds for setting aside a contract, deed, or will, is a species of legal wrong called a tort, a private injury resembling a criminal act. Fraud can arise in several different ways in a contest to set aside a transfer. First, the transferor's signature could have been forged to dispositive documents, making them invalid instruments (*Fryer* v. *Gibbs,* 139 Ind. App. 77, 231 N.E.2d 251 (1967)). Second, the actual change of disposition might have been carried out by the transferor in reliance on the acts and conduct of a beneficiary, which acts and conduct were intended to deceive the transferor and thus to obtain property under false pretenses.

Only a handful of American will, deed, or contract contests have been tried on this issue. Perhaps the most illustrative is the strange case of *Orth* v. *Orth,* 145 Ind. 184, 42 N.E. 277, rehearing denied, 145 Ind. 184, 44 N.E. 17 (1895). Godlove Orth had willed all his property to his second wife, Mary Ann. The will was accompanied by a letter in which Orth stated that Mary Ann was to "act justly toward yourself and toward all my children. . . . Then, what is left give to all the children alike." It was apparent that Godlove Orth expected his widow to make a will distributing his substantial estate equally among the children of both marriages. Mary Ann's will excluded Orth's children by his first marriage. These people immediately brought suit to cancel the will as the result of fraud by Mary Ann Orth on her husband. The trial court dismissed the suit, and the dismissal was affirmed by the Indiana Supreme Court. The court stated that, if Mary Ann Orth had procured the estate by fraud on her husband, the court would have imposed the legal remedy of placing a "constructive trust" on the assets that Mrs. Orth received from her husband, in favor of all four children of both marriages.

However, the court found no evidence that Mary Ann Orth had persuaded her husband not to make a will splitting the estate at his death into shares for his children, so that active fraud did not cause the distribution to her of all Godlove Orth's assets.

Since fraudulent procurement of property by will or deed is simply a subspecies of the common law tort of deceit, the legal standard for setting aside a transfer of assets on account of fraud is really derived from the tort of deceit. If a person makes a material representation of past or existing facts to another person, with the knowledge that the representation is false or with reckless disregard of the truth or falsity of the representation, and if the statement induces the transferor to make a transfer of property to some other person and, as a proximate result, the transferor or the transferor's legal representatives or heirs are injured, then property has been obtained through fraud (Prosser, 1971, secs. 101–04).

A person who is mentally slow or unusually dependent on others for advice and guidance is especially susceptible to the fraudulent representations of a deceitful person. Consequently, the acts, conduct, and statements of the transferor would be relevant to show the nature of the misrepresentations made and the state of mind or mental opinion formed by the transferor in reliance on the misrepresentations (Wigmore, [1913] 1940, vol. 2, secs. 340–344).

It is much more difficult to prove a case of fraud than to prove a case of undue influence or lack of capacity. In order to establish that a defendant obtained a will, deed, trust instrument, or contract by fraudulent representations to the maker of the instrument, the plaintiff has to show that the defendant made a materially false representation to the person who executed the will, deed, trust, or contract with the intent to deceive that person. Additionally, the courts require the plaintiff to prove that the defendant made the statements with intent to convey an untrue idea to the person executing the instrument, which induced the person executing the instrument to act. This is called *knowing deception* or *scienter* in law and is very difficult to prove in court (Prosser, 1971, sec. 107). Consequently, a case of fraudulent inducement to execute a will, deed, trust, or contract is secondary in most instances to a case alleging the instrument was procured through undue influence.

Role of Human Services Worker in Postdeath Transfers

If lawyers and judges cling to what appear to be outmoded formulations of tests for mental capacity, they do so out of lack of knowledge of the state of medical or psychological knowledge, not out of bad faith or chicanery. Consequently, knowledgeable human services professionals may provide significant linkage between medical and psychological findings with respect to individuals and the legal consequences of those findings.

Detecting Early Signs of Impaired Mental Functioning

Particularly in older persons, the human services professional may be the one who will detect and recognize such early signs of mental deterioration as disorientation, confusion, random activity, and other indicators of inward mental disturbance.

The most commonly observed changes in elderly persons are the mental changes associated with cerebral atherosclerosis or cerebral arteriosclerosis—changes manifested in psychotic or disturbed behavior resulting from an insufficient supply of blood to the brain (Gray, 1972). Confusion, disorientation (as to place, time, or memory) (Aker, Walsh, and Beam, 1977, p. 116), irritability, lability of emotional state, and other signs of moderate to severe psychological changes should alert the human services worker to the possibility that the client is experiencing an emotional disorder. Similarly, some persons who are not elderly may show lability of mood to a marked degree or speak of seeing or hearing strange things (especially persons with a history of chronic drug or alcohol abuse over an extended period).

In all such instances, the human services worker should be able to detect early signs of mental disturbance in clients and take appropriate diagnostic steps or send for additional help—especially when these individuals begin to verbalize wishes to give all their property to strangers or to make wills disinheriting spouses or relatives. A thorough medical and psychiatric examination for such an individual may spare a family much grief in dealing with the emotional response to a disinheriting act by someone who was plainly disturbed mentally.

Bizarre or "Crank" Behavior. Many people illogically assume that an unusual behavior pattern is evidence of mental disturbance. Helping professionals must be aware, however, that there is a difference between an intellectually indefensible or unpopular opinion and a delusion. If an individual believes that world peace can be achieved through vegetarianism, but is otherwise well oriented in time, space, and memory and is able to do simple computations, read and write tolerably well, and otherwise behave normally, one should not facilely label the opinion delusional. It may be incorrect, in one's judgment, but it is not so far from the proper functioning of the human ego, or reality principle, as to be unacceptable. After all, thousands of people mistakenly believe that their current sexual partner is the most wonderful, thrilling, exciting, and lovable person in the world, and no one proposes locking them up for holding such socially acceptable opinions, even when the opinions seem absurd.

The kind of diminished mental competency that makes a transfer of property socially unacceptable and, therefore, moves the machinery of the law to set the transfer aside is the kind of low-level competency that prevents the law from enforcing the agreements of small children. In psychological terms, if a person has a level of mental functioning similar to that of a seven-year-old, then that person lacks mental competency to make a contract, prepare a deed or will, or transfer property of any kind. This means that certain types of mental illness, including psychoses, may not be the equivalent of the diminished mental competency that the law finds onerous. A manic-depressive psychotic may know the nature and extent of his property and the persons who would take his property at death as his heirs and may be able to integrate those considerations into a rational plan for distribution of his assets at death. Therefore, a psychosis of this type may not disable a person from making a will or a contract. A person who is convinced that the FBI and the CIA are out to get him and takes precautions—such as disguising himself or doubling back—to throw off his pursuers may be paranoid or a paranoid schizophrenic, but he may still be able to make a will involving persons outside his delusional state.

The human services worker should be aware that when a client verbalizes eccentric beliefs or dresses eccentrically or gives signs of some functional mental disorder and indicates that he or she wants to deed over a house or make a contract for managing his or her bank accounts, that client is sending a danger signal and may require psychiatric intervention.

Frequent Changes of Postdeath Distribution Plans. A final danger signal the human services worker should be able to recognize is the client's frequent changes of postdeath distribution plans. Such instability may be a sign of undue influence being exerted on the testator or of inner disturbance of some type, which may be traced to one of many factors. It is common for persons who are elderly and have no immediate family to revise their wills rather often, changing shares distributed to collateral relatives more or less at whim. It would be uncommon for a person who has a spouse and children to alternatively disinherit one member of his or her nuclear family within a relative short time frame or to discuss disinheritance with others as a means of manipulating them.

Advising Attorneys and Judges on Postdeath Transfer Cases

Human services workers may be required to advise an attorney or a judge on matters related to mental competency. Welfare guardianships, Veterans Administration guardianships, and the insanity process against recipients of public assistance are everyday examples of the collaboration of more progressive judges and lawyers with human services professionals in dealing with cases involving diminished mental capacity. Also, as counseling the elderly and the handicapped becomes more common, human services professionals are likely to be called into consultation in will or deed contests involving their now-deceased clients.

With the greater recognition given to the behavioral sciences and its practitioners as "experts" in legal parlance, more professionals in human services (especially those who have been trained as clinical psychologists) can be expected to be called as consultants to will contests by lawyers. Unfortunately, because most cases of diminished mental capacity deal with the mental capacity of a dead person, an imperfectly collected clinical history is all that is available and the chances of being able to have a well-developed psychological testing program for the alleged incompetent is nonexistent or practically nil. The challenge, then, is to reconstruct, from the available observations of lay persons and professionals, a meaningful "psychological autopsy" of the dead transferor. In this respect, the psychologist or social worker can aid attorneys in evaluating preliminary data gained through discovery processes and investigation.

Since most attorneys will have a limited vocabulary and background in psychiatric medicine or psychological theories of recall, perception, or judgment, part of the professional's task will be to educate the lawyer on professional investigative techniques and vocabulary. If a trial is anticipated, and the lawyer is required to produce evidence showing capacity (or want of capacity) or undue influence (or its lack), the professional in human services can present to the attorney various strategies for developing the data into the necessary factual proof in law, which permits an expert to testify from a hypothetical question written with the data in mind.

The human services professional can suggest what signs or symptoms the lawyer should ask about when he conducts preliminary interviews of witnesses who knew the deceased transferor well. He or she can suggest to the lawyer what questions should be asked of the transferor's treating physician about mental capacity and functional or organic disorders affecting mental competency. In short, a symbiotic relationship can exist between the human services professional and the attorney in competency cases.

Assisting Attorneys in Preventive Law Practice

The human services professional is also useful to attorneys in the preparation of preventive law measures to forestall unnecessary litigation over wills, deeds, or trusts. If a lawyer sees an individual who wants to disinherit a relative in favor of more distant relatives, or in favor of a nonfamily member, the lawyer knows that a will contest or deed contest is likely. If a person is alleged to be incompetent and an insanity process is started against him or her, such individual is entitled to counsel; and the lawyer assigned to represent the incompetent will need to have suitable psychological tests administered to the client, in order to show—if possible—that the client was mentally competent on a given date to make a will, deed, or trust. All this can be provided by human services workers who are trained to administer psychological tests and to interpret the results of the testing.

Consultative Practice. Lawyers may face professional malpractice liability suits for making wills or deeds for mentally incompetent persons (Reed, 1981). Consequently, lawyers will be more willing to reach out to others to obtain self-protective justification for making wills or deeds for persons whose competence may be questionable. Here the human services professional can devise a proper testing sequence, conduct or recommend a psychiatrist to conduct an evaluative examination, and otherwise prepare for medical and psychological justification for making the transfer of property. All this would be available if any later contest is initiated to break through the instrument.

Creating the Record. There are a number of ways in which a record showing mental capacity may be made in advance of litigation. A psychiatric evaluation of a potential transferor would be useful, particularly if the psychiatrist reduces his or her findings to a written evaluative summary. Psychological testing to determine the presence or absence of a learning disorder, depression, anxiety, and the like, would also be useful. A clinical psychosocial interview would be another way to detail the mental competency of a person before that person changes his or her will or makes out a deed to all his or her property. Also, the human services professional should be able to suggest to the lawyer what kinds of lay observations would be useful to collect and memorialize in present form for later use in a contest.

Since lawyers are required to execute wills or deeds before official witnesses in order to ensure compliance with legal formalities, the human services professional may suggest ways to conduct a formal signing of a will, in order to preserve for the record the competency of the maker. Lawyers have recommended various systems of recording execution ceremonies, such as videotape recordings and the like. The human services worker can assist in this process by indicating what data should be disclosed to the formal attesting witnesses and memorialized at the execution ceremony in a permanent fashion.

Dealing with Disappointed Family Members

Finally, the anger, grief, rejection, and guilt felt by members of an individual's family as a result of disinheritance should be kept in mind when one is planning preventive law measures. Lawyers often fail to take into account the psychological devastation suffered by a son or daughter who is disinherited by a parent. The human services worker should remind the lawyer that the nonclients in the situation are human and that positive steps must be taken to ensure that these wounded people do not undertake a will contest in order to reverse a parent's rejection of them as loved persons (Shaffer, 1970a, pp. 149–206)).

Lawyers generally assume that the motivation for will contests is purely utilitarian: a person who expected a legacy from a relative got no money and now pursues the estate, having nothing to lose and everything to gain if the will is broken down as the process of an unsound mind. Unfortunately, human motivation is too complex to be easily rationalized into utilitarian and economic categories alone. The motivation to attack a will may be deflected if a climate is created in which the disappointed relatives of a testator who made a disinheriting will can be allowed to vent their feelings in an appropriate conference setting.

Jeffrey C. Savitsky
Deborah Ann Karras

8

Rights of Institutionalized Patients

꧁꧁꧁꧁꧁꧁꧁꧁꧁꧁꧁꧁꧁꧁꧁꧁꧁꧁꧁

Concern for the welfare of the mentally ill has not been a routine characteristic of our past (Barton and Sanborn, 1978; Dingman, 1976; Halpern, 1976). On the contrary, the mentally ill were historically either ignored or badly treated by a superstitious and cruel society. If fortunate, the mentally ill person found shelter within the family. Without the protection of a sympathetic family, however, these hapless people often suffered abuse and neglect (Grob, 1973). The mental hospital was created as a refuge for such unfortunates. It represented a humanitarian effort to provide safety and shelter to a vulnerable segment of society. This purpose has not changed, and it continues today. Indeed, our efforts to provide care for the mentally ill seem to have increased. These efforts are reflected in research aimed at providing more effective methods of treatment and in the work of mental hospital staff members, who provide care under sometimes trying circumstances. Yet, despite the positive motivations that underlie the operation of the mental hospital, there is now also a growing mistrust of these institutions—a fear that this humanitarian experiment has gone awry and that the institutions created to help the vulnerable may ultimately harm them.

The concern about practices in these institutions can be observed among professional and lay groups alike; among legal and nonlegal observers. It is dramatically expressed in popular literature and films, which characterize both general and psychiatric hospitals as destructive agents of aggressive and power-oriented professionals (*The Snake Pit, Suddenly Last Summer, One Flew over the Cuckoo's Nest, The Hospital*). One of the more influential examples of this type of highly critical portrayal of the hospital environment, *One Flew over the Cuckoo's Nest*, a novel by Ken Kesey, and subsequently a film, portrayed life in a psychiatric hospital as anything but rehabilitative. Rather, the hospital was presented as a punitive and hostile environment that forced conformity to a sterile puritanical norm. Professionals working in that environment were described as either malicious or ineffectual. In place of preparation for return to the outside world, Kesey's novel suggested that patients were taught shame, robbed of their dignity, and threatened with punitive treatment that offered only physical and mental harm.

The impact of literature such as Kesey's novel cannot be accurately estimated. It is intriguing to note, however, that this book was highly critical of a variety of treatment forms, including electroshock therapy. The recently decreased use of this form of treatment (Chase, 1979) may have resulted, at least in part, from fears generated by accounts such as those offered in this book.

Concern that treatment in a mental hospital may be harmful and dehumanizing has not been limited to popular literature but has also found expression through recent litigation and legislation. Until recently, legal action challenging the admission or treatment of patients in the mental health system rarely occurred. In fact, the U.S. Supreme Court was able to express its surprise—given the large numbers of people affected by mental health services—about the lack of litigation in this area (*Jackson* v. *Indiana*, 406 U.S. 715 (1972)). This situation has changed radically, and there are now many legal challenges to mental health practice. Ennis (1978), a leading mental health attorney, has remarked that only a few years ago he could name most of the important mental health court cases from memory. There is now, in contrast, a vast body of mental health cases covering nearly every facet of patient care. Judges now assume a policy-making stance when reviewing mental health practices, while lawyers are encouraged to protect their clients against the mental hospital (Elkins, 1979; Mickenberg, 1979; "The Role of Counsel . . . ," 1975). Special journals now report mental health litigation (*Law and Human Behavior, Mental Disability Law Reporter, Law and Psychology Review, Journal of Psychiatry and Law*), whereas few such journals existed in the recent past.

The result of the legal scrutiny of the treatment given mental health inpatients is the topic of this chapter, but the real issue is the impact of this type of regulation on mental health services. Will patients benefit from greater attention to inpatient services, or will legal scrutiny simply succeed in causing inpatient care to become overregulated and static? Have we come to the point that nonexperts control mental health treatment, or has legal scrutiny managed to increase the quality of care and concern shown for the inpatient? If the former, we may have succeeded in discouraging mental health professionals from making innovative advances and thereby ultimately served to stymie progress. If the latter, however, recent legal challenges may have succeeded in providing the mental health inpatient with a significant measure of protection and hope.

Reasons for Increased Legal Scrutiny

The mental health professional who works in a mental hospital must sometimes feel, particularly when touched by the effects of legal scrutiny into the care of the inpatient, that this world is often irrational and unfair. The professional will certainly experience much frustration when he or she offers a patient treatment designed for the patient's benefit, only to have the patient refuse the treatment. But even worse professional frustration would result if a legal advocate supported the patient's seemingly misguided refusal. Yet this sequence is occurring with ever greater regularity. Patients view the hospital and its treatment with increasing skepticism, while others, from outside the hospital, are supporting their skepticism.

In some cases a patient's resistance may be a product of the very disorder that caused his hospitalization. However, psychiatric problems do not account for all of patient noncompliance. Rather, patient noncompliance appears to be a widespread phenomenon, not limited to the psychiatric client (Pomerleau and Brady, 1979; Prokop and Bradley, 1981). This subtle form of resistance characterizes many patients, some of whom suffer physical illnesses without mental health complications. Furthermore, attributing noncompliance to the patient's disorder does not explain why advocates from outside the hospital often support patient complaints.

There are undoubtedly many general reasons for the increase in skepticism toward mental hospital care, some of which have little to do with the mental hospital itself. For instance, our society has become increasingly litigious, so that the law courts play an ever more prominent role in routine daily interactions. It is reasonable, then, to expect that the mental hospital would not escape the challenges being leveled at all institutions. However, certain more specific concerns seem to underlie efforts to review mental health practices: concerns about unwanted physical and emotional side effects that can result from treatment, and concerns about intrusions on guaranteed legal rights caused by treatment.

Unwanted Side Effects. The unwanted side effects of mental hospital treatment include a variety of physical and psychological injuries, which occur with unfortunate regularity whenever a patient is committed to a state hospital. Nearly every facet of hospital treatment offers some degree of danger; there is no such thing as a completely risk-free treatment. Rather, the risk of psychological and physical harm accompanies the initial decision to place a patient in a hospital, and it continues through all phases of treatment and release.

The patient who is placed in a psychiatric hospital will routinely suffer massive feelings of loss and separation (Goffman, 1961; Rosenhan, 1973). Most hospitals are, unfortunately, both physically and psychologically removed from the community that contains the patient's family and friends (Korchin, 1976; Geiwitz, 1980). Some patients will, in addition, experience disruption in jobs and education. Of course, many patients become eligible for placement in the hospital precisely because of prior failure in adjustment, but the longer a patient remains in the hospital, and removed from the community, the greater will be the difficulties associated with ultimately reconstituting his or her social and economic network.

The very fact of hospitalization can have a profound impact on the patient's future, since a patient assumes a status that carries much negative stigma (Gallagher, 1980; Geitman, 1981). Surveys have shown that the status of being a mental patient causes others to develop a variety of negative beliefs about the patient's capacity for self-control, independence, and trustworthiness (Johannsen, 1969; Nunnally, 1961). The negative stigma associated with being a former mental patient may even limit future acceptability to employers (Farina and Felner, 1973; Miller and Dawson, 1969).

Life in a mental hospital, although meant to be a restorative experience, also presents a variety of potential physical and psychological dangers to the patient. Ward life sometimes carries with it demands for conformity, passivity, and cooperation. The rules of the institution, to the extent that they conflict with individual preference, will exert powerful control over an individual patient's lifestyle (Test and Stein, 1978). Even superlative care in the hospital can cause a patient harm, since swift attention to the patient's routine needs may soon encourage increased dependence and self-neglect. Because they are not subject to the demands inherent in independent living, patients may become institutionalized and lose many everyday coping skills (Goffman, 1961; Gruenberg, 1967; Hansell and Benson, 1971).

Ward life carries medical risks as well, particularly when the quality of the hospital environment is physically inadequate. Some psychiatric hospitals are unsanitary and have too few medical professionals (*Pennhurst State School* v. *Halderman*, 451 U.S. 1 (1981); *Wyatt* v. *Stickney*, 325 F. Supp. 781 (M.D. Ala. 1971)). Physical harm can also occur when hospital conditions encourage anonymity and overcrowding. Studies have shown, for instance, a variety of negative effects associated with long-term crowding (Paulus, McCain, and Cox, 1978; Sundstrom, 1978). Furthermore, when patients are anonymous and less than fully equal to their caretakers, they become potential targets for abuse and neglect. Research suggests that abuse results when caretakers come to have absolute power over their charges (Haney and Zimbardo, 1973).

Medication plays a central role in the treatment of the inpatient. The phenothiazines were initially heralded as a great breakthrough in the treatment of psychotic disorders, and these drugs continue to be a routine part of treatment in the psychiatric hospital. While initially it appeared that the side effects of psychotropic medications were easily controlled and minimal, it is now recognized that unwanted side effects can be profound and permanent.

For instance, the phenothiazine drugs may cause parkinsonian symptoms, including masklike face, retarded volitional movements, tremors, restlessness, and muscle spasms. In 10 to 40 percent of patients, these drugs also may produce tardive dyskinesia—a sometimes permanent condition characterized by involuntary movements of the mouth, limbs, and trunk (American Psychiatric Association, 1979; Freedman, Kaplan, and Sadock, 1976; Jarvik, 1965; Plotkin and Gill, 1979).

Even release from the hospital can have negative effects on patients. Patients who have become accustomed to a hospital environment need special training to prepare them for the outside world. Yet, in an effort to save money, some state hospitals release massive numbers of former patients into the community without any real effort to help these people establish a workable adjustment to the demands of their new environments (Dingman, 1976; Rachlin, 1976).

Intrusion on Legal Rights. A second major category of injury that can occur with psychiatric hospitalization is a loss of civil rights. Once in the hospital, the patient may lose the opportunity to exercise freedoms that are available to the nonpatient. Traditionally, mental patients were considered incompetent and therefore unable to exercise their rights in a self-protective manner. Consequently, it was assumed, the state was justified in denying the patient's civil rights, since this denial was in the patient's best interest. However, recognizing that many patients are quite capable of exercising many of their rights in a most competent fashion, many states have now lifted these imposed disabilities (Brooks, 1974). Whereas patients were once denied a variety of routine rights, they now have typically regained the ability to vote, divorce, draft a will, or sign a contract. The belief that all mental patients require paternalistic control has been replaced in many states by the recognition that patients should not be denied their rights in such a wholesale fashion. Rather, there must be a determination on an individual basis that a patient is unable to exercise these rights in a competent fashion. Several courts have held that patients should be denied their rights only when there has been a judicial determination that they are incompetent (*Rau* v. *Tannenbaum*, 444 N.Y.S.2d 635 (App. Div. 1981); *Winters* v. *Miller*, 446 F.2d 65 (2d Cir. 1971)).

But there remain significant hindrances, aside from statutory restrictions, to a patient's full exercise of civil liberties. These are the obstacles caused by separation from the outside world and internment in an institutional setting. Patients admitted to the hospital are, in varying degrees, cut off from their families, friends, and advisers. They will therefore find the exercise of civil liberties difficult, since they are removed from the people who might have encouraged and supported their efforts. It takes a great deal of coping ability to assert oneself despite feelings of isolation. Required conformity to hospital procedures also creates obstacles to the exercise of civil rights. These procedures are designed for efficiency, but they also, perhaps inadvertently, prevent the exercise of rights in an unfettered manner. For instance, either to protect people outside the hospital from patient-initiated nuisance calls or to avoid disruption of ward procedures, the hospital may limit the patient's use of the telephone. As a result, patients are even further isolated, and their ability to communicate freely with others outside the hospital—a right protected by the First Amendment—is limited.

The very fact of being housed in an institution causes a loss of fundamental and constitutionally protected rights. For instance, patients possess, as do all United States citizens, a right to privacy and to freedom of travel. These are fundamental liberties guaranteed by the Constitution. Privacy is the right to "do nothing," the right to be left alone by the government when one is not engaged in criminal or tortious activity. The constitutionally protected right to travel means that people can move about, go from state to state, without significant hindrance. Clearly, most mental hospital practices intrude heavily on both of these rights. Indeed, the U.S. Supreme Court has noted that civil commitment represents a "massive curtailment of liberty" (*Humphrey* v. *Cato*, 405 U.S. 504 (1972)).

In sum, there are a variety of reasons for the scrutiny of mental hospital practices. The mental hospital contains potential for abuse and neglect of inpatients. In addition, almost inescapable negative side effects result from hospitalization even when the patient receives the highest quality of care. These side effects may profoundly effect a patient's physical, emotional, and legal wellbeing. In essence, scrutiny of the mental hospital has begun because of the recognition that civil commitment is an extremely intrusive and potentially harmful experience.

There is much irony in the fact that mental hospitals are now the target of concern. As noted above, these institutions were originally created by the charitable motives of a well-intentioned society. Yet the scrutiny and potential restriction of hospital practices are products of these same motivations. Hospitals were constructed on the basis of society's wish to protect its weakest and most vulnerable members; yet we now find that the weak must also be protected against those very same institutions that were built to protect them. We now recognize that we must set limits on our own good intentions, that we must preserve a realistic balance between competing theories of what is best for society and for patients. In reality, there will never be a final or absolute solution. Rather, there will almost certainly continue to be a shifting between legal, psychological, and medical interests. But the challenge of resolving these interests is the task now faced by courts and legislatures. Their efforts at this task will be detailed throughout the rest of this chapter.

Sources of Legal Protection

Legal statements by courts and legislatures—statements reflecting alternative legal theories—have formed the conceptual basis for courtroom and administrative challenges to current conditions and practices in mental hospitals. The type of legal basis actually used in a specific challenge has implications for the types of changes, if any, that arise from this action.

Constitutional Theories

Constitutional theories suggested for use in mental hospital actions include claims that hospital practices have violated the Fourteenth Amendment's equal protection clause or the Eighth Amendment's prohibition against cruel and unusual punishment. However, the Constitution does not require that all people be treated in an identical fashion, only that differential treatment be supported by some reasonable state purpose. This reasoning makes equal protection challenges unlikely to be successful. Similarly, the Supreme Court has held that the prohibition against cruel and unusual punishment applies only to the treatment of those being punished because of criminal violations (*Ingraham* v. *Wright*, 430 U.S. 651 (1977)). Thus, this theory does not protect the rights of the civilly committed, since they are not being punished and are not guilty of criminal activity.

More successful challenges of mental hospital practices have been based on constitutional theories of due process: that all residents are guaranteed due process under the Fourteenth Amendment. Due process means "fairness" in state action. Thus, whenever the state acts in such a manner as to infringe on individual liberties, it must do so in an equitable manner. Fairness has two elements: procedural and substantive. Procedural due process requires that the methods used to arrive at a specific decision must include assurances that individual interests are being considered along with state interests. Substantive due process requires that the outcome of a state policy, the state's actions, must reflect a reasonable balance between individual rights and state interests; state actions cannot be unfairly one-sided.

Procedural Due Process. Procedural due process is a fluid concept. There is no single correct or absolutely required method of decision making. Rather, the courts have long recognized that the nature of due process protections will vary with the nature of the decision to be made (*Mathews* v. *Eldridge*, 424 U.S. 319 (1976); *Morrisey* v. *Brewer*, 408 U.S. 471 (1972)). Some governmental decisions will require elaborate protections, including a hearing and representation, while other decisions will require only that some official make an independent and considered judgment.

The most extensive form of procedural due process is typically provided by the criminal courts. In the criminal trial, the potential harm to the defendant, a loss of freedom, dictates that the procedures used to arrive at a final decision must contain elaborate protections against the possibility of a false positive. Thus, criminal defendants are guaranteed the assistance of legal counsel, whether or not they can pay for such help; an impartial fact finder to arrive at the final conclusions; and the right to present evidence or to cross-examine witnesses so as to ensure that all evidence is reliable. These extensive protections are provided because a wrong decision would cause a defendant to suffer irreparable harm.

Few decisions require the extensive protections provided to the criminal defendant because few decisions hold an equal potential for harm. Some decisions—decisions that do not jeopardize a legally protected right or that have only a trivial impact on individual rights—may merit no due process at all. However, a governmental action that has more than a trivial impact begins to raise the need for due process protections, although the amount of such protection will vary with the type of loss suffered by the individual.

The extent of required due process also is determined by the cost of alternative decision-making procedures and the administrative burden that these procedures would place on a governmental agency. The courts will not usually order an agency to use decision-making procedures that would paralyze the agency and prevent it from carrying out its duties. In general, the courts have given government agencies, such as hospitals, much discretion and freedom to develop their own forms of decision making, as long as the mechanism is equitable and allows an opportunity for later challenge and review by a regular court. However, when decisions made by hospital personnel weigh on the patient's rights, the courts require the hospital to provide due process protections, and these protections must represent a sincere effort to protect the patient's—and not only the hospital's—interests.

Courts and legislatures have responded to the recognition that mental health inpatients merit procedural due process protections with two separate maneuvers: (1) legal efforts, particularly by the courts, to carve out or define situations that clearly raise the need for procedural due process; (2) new methods of hospital decision making, including the creation of alternate forums and the provision of advocates to uphold the interests of the patient. Both of these maneuvers will be discussed later in this chapter.

Substantive Due Process. When evaluating the practices of mental hospitals, the courts have applied several principles for balancing state and individual interests and arriving at the conclusion that a particular practice is either fair or unfair. These principles, or yardsticks, include (1) an evaluation of the legitimacy of the state's purpose; (2) an insistence that the state act in the least intrusive manner; (3) an effort to ensure that there is a logical relation between state goals and actions; and (4) an insistence that there be a fair trade between individual losses and gains, a *quid pro quo*.

Under a substantive due process analysis, the state can infringe on the rights of the individual only if there is a sufficiently compelling or weighty reason for doing so. The courts will attempt to ensure that the state's goal is not completely trivial; it must be of sufficient importance so that it, on balance, justifies a deprivation of individual liberties. Furthermore, the curtailment of individual liberty must be done in a manner that is as minimally intrusive as possible. The state cannot sweep too broadly when it deprives individuals of their rights. Rather, the state can take away only the degree of liberty necessary to accomplish its goals. Substantive due process also requires that the purpose of the state's actions bear a logical relationship to the activities of the state, so that the purpose of the state is reflected in the actions used to carry out that purpose. The state cannot, for instance, claim that it is removing individual liberties for a specific goal and then fail to pursue that goal. Finally, the *quid pro quo* balancing principle requires that individuals who suffer a loss of individual liberties be compensated for their loss. The *quid pro quo* theory is, in essence, an economic analysis of individual liberties.

Two main rationales have been used to support the state's mental health activities. The government has justified these activities on the notion that it acts out of its duty to provide protection and care for those unable to be self-sufficient. This is the theory of *parens patriae*, an ancient duty on the state, which allows government agencies to act for the welfare and care of the weak or vulnerable whether or not these people actually request this type of help. A second justification is that the government must act to protect society against those who present a threat to the peace and harmony of society. This state duty, the police power, allows the state to intervene in the lives of residents who appear to present a high risk of danger to others. Unfortunately, and probably without sufficient justification, the mentally ill have been viewed as more dangerous than other groups. As a result, the government has traditionally been able to involuntarily commit and treat those who are shown to be mentally ill.

If the two most typical government justifications for involuntary treatment, *parens patriae* and the police power, are compared against the balancing analysis, several conclusions become possible. The notions of *parens patriae* and police power are clearly weighty or substantial state goals. Thus, the state's efforts to treat the mentally ill are supported by legitimate goals. However, even if the goal is legitimate, the methods used to achieve these goals must still represent the least intrusive form of state intervention possible. Thus, under a substantive due process analysis, some courts have concluded that the state must seek out methods of care that minimize, as much as is possible given the need for treatment, the restrictiveness of the treatment environment (*Lake* v. *Cameron*, 364 F.2d 657 (D.C. Cir. 1966); *Lessard* v. *Schmidt*, 349 F. Supp. 1078 (E.D. Wis. 1972)). Similarly, if the state claims that it is pursuing rehabilitation for the patient, due process demands that the stated goals of involuntary care must bear a logical relationship to the actual care provided to the patient (*Jackson* v. *Indiana*, 406 U.S. 715 (1972)). In the words of one court, "To deprive any citizen of his or her liberty upon the altruistic theory that the confinement is for humane therapeutic reasons and then fail to provide adequate treatment violates the very fundamental of due process" (*Wyatt* v. *Stickney*, 325 F. Supp. 781, 785 (M.D. Ala. 1971)). Finally, the *quid pro quo* argument suggests that the losses inherent in mental hospital treatment raise a duty on the state to provide some form of benefit to the patient. One influential court opinion has noted, for instance, that the procedures used to confine someone involuntarily in a mental hospital lack the extensive protections afforded by the criminal courts (*Donaldson* v. *O'Connor*, 493 F.2d 507 (5th Cir. 1974)). The *quid pro quo* argument was used to suggest that the state must provide a benefit that compensates the patient for this loss. This same court concluded that the compensation most typically recognized is adequate treatment.

A number of courts have concluded that there is a constitutionally mandated right to treatment for the involuntary patient. This conclusion was first set forth in *Wyatt* v. *Stickney*. Under this opinion patients were seen as having "a constitutional right to receive such individual treatment as will give each of them a realistic opportunity to be cured or to improve his or her mental condition" (at 784). In essence, the *Wyatt* decision first set out a broad definition of the constitutional right to treatment. Using this definition, the *Wyatt* court went on to outline a number of specific and rather sweeping changes in the conditions of several Alabama hospitals— changes designed to effect the cure or improvement of the patient's condition.

Other federal courts have also defined a constitutionally based right to treatment and, like the *Wyatt* court, have required hospitals to provide patients with environmental conditions and treatment that would enable them to improve their mental condition. For instance, in one federal district court opinion, a minor patient was granted a right to treatment in a program that offered "a reasonable chance to acquire and maintain those life skills that enable him to cope" (*Gary W.* v. *Louisiana,* 437 F. Supp. 1209, 1212 (ED. La. 1976)). Similarly, a federal appeals court defined the right to treatment as treatment that "will give . . . a reasonable opportunity to be cured or to improve [one's] mental condition" (*Wyatt* v. *Aderholt,* 503 F.2d 1305, 1312 (5th Cir. 1974)).

The original *Wyatt* holding was upheld in *Donaldson* v. *O'Connor.* This case arose on a complaint by a patient who had been involuntarily held in a mental hospital for nearly fifteen years. During that time, according to the patient, he had been given little treatment. Furthermore, the patient alleged, friends outside the hospital had made repeated offers to provide him with alternative forms of care and help; but despite these repeated offers, and despite his long history of violence-free behavior, hospital officials had continued his commitment. In its review of this case, the federal appeals court upheld the liability of hospital officials for their violation of the patient's rights. However, review of the *O'Connor* case by the U.S. Supreme Court (*O'Connor* v. *Donaldson,* 422 U.S. 563 (1975)) yielded a confused result. Although the Court upheld the liability of the hospital officials, it did so on grounds other than the right to treatment and, in fact, seemed to sidestep the right-to-treatment issue: "[There is] no reason now to decide whether mentally ill persons dangerous to themselves or others have a right to treatment upon compulsary confinement" (at 573).

In a dissenting opinion, Justice Burger specifically denied the existence of a right to treatment based on constitutional principles.

Burger expressed his belief that neither the *parens patriae* nor the *quid pro quo* rationales could support such a right. In Burger's view, the *parens patriae* rationale provides a justification for confinement but not necessarily a justification for a right to treatment. Similarly, a right to treatment based on a *quid pro quo* rationale suggests a variety of unacceptable conclusions. For instance, should the state be able to confine people merely because it can provide excellent treatment? Or, is it necessary that all judicial procedures, including civil commitment, be made to provide the same degree of procedural protections found in the criminal court to avoid the conclusion that these are a deprivation of procedural rights?

Although Justice Burger's position was clear, the Supreme Court's majority decision in *O'Connor* neither clearly denied nor clearly supported the right to treatment. As a result, lower court rulings based on a substantive due process analysis were left intact, but no apparent support for this form of reasoning was given. Not surprisingly, then, there was considerable variance in subsequent commentary and court rulings. Some commentators and courts felt that the Supreme Court had upheld a constitutional right to treatment (Bernard, 1977); others claimed that the ruling had denied the existence of a right to treatment (*Morales* v. *Turman*, 562 F.2d 993 (5th Cir. 1977)). Still others concluded that the Court's failure to overturn a right to treatment was an implicit support for this right (*Eckerhardt* v. *Hensley*, 475 F. Supp. 908 (W.D. Mo. 1979); *Welsch* v. *Likens*, 550 F.2d 1122 (8th Cir. 1977)).

A more recent Supreme Court decision again addressed the question of a constitutionally based right to treatment. In *Youngberg* v. *Romeo*, 102 S. Ct. 2452 (1982), a severely retarded and involuntarily committed patient was injured as a result of his own and others' violence. The patient's representatives alleged that the patient had been repeatedly subjected to prolonged periods of restraint and that the hospital had failed to provide him with appropriate "treatment or programs." The Court had little difficulty in concluding that involuntarily committed patients do have a constitutional right to be held in safe conditions and to be free from "undue restraint." However, the Court's conclusions about the extent of a right to treatment were more complex. In the words of the Court, the patient's claim to a "constitutional right to a minimally adequate habilitation" was more "troubling." The Supreme Court concluded that the *Youngberg* case did not present the question of a general right to treatment but, instead, the more narrow question of a right to "minimally adequate or reasonable training to ensure safety and freedom from undue restraint." That is, the right to treatment exists, and future cases may find it to be quite broad; however, the decision in *Youngberg* appears to have certified its existence only to a specific and limited level—the amount of treatment necessary to minimize the need for restraints and to limit danger to the patient. Under this decision, presumably, a patient would be entitled to treatment if without such treatment he was likely to be violent to himself or to others or if the absence of such treatment meant that the patient required constant restraints.

Clearly, many potential criticisms can be directed at the Supreme Court ruling in *Youngberg*. For instance, if treatment is to be restricted to those patients who are likely to be violent, then it may be withheld from the more numerous patients who are passive and withdrawn. Furthermore, as a concurring opinion by several of the justices points out, this definition might allow treatment to be withheld even from those patients who, while neither violent nor in need of restraints, might decay within the unstimulating institutional environment. Perhaps the greatest significance, the Court's opinion continues to preserve the confusion that has plagued the right-to-treatment area. That is, we still do not know whether the broader right to treatment exists. We still do not know whether there is indeed a right to a level of care that would provide patients with a reasonable opportunity to improve their mental condition. It appears the Supreme Court has again avoided a significant issue; and, as a result, lower federal and state courts will continue to wrestle with the threshold issue.

Statutory Enactments

State and federal legislators have also been active in providing legal umbrellas for the inpatient. Indeed, a seminal mental health case, *Rouse* v. *Cameron*, 373 F.2d 451 (D.C. Cir. 1966), which represented an initial judicial recognition of the right to treatment, was based on a Washington, D.C. statute.

Two federal acts seem to reflect the intention of federal legislators to provide mental health patients with a variety of specific
protections. Both of these acts, the Development Disabilities Assistance and Bill of Rights Act (DD Act), Pub. L. No. 94–103, 89 Stat.
486 (1975), and the Mental Health Systems Act (MHS Act), Pub. L.
No. 96–398, 94 Stat. 1598 (1980), include provisions that provide
inpatients with a variety of rights, including a right to receive adequate care. The DD Act states: "Persons with developmental disabilities have a right to appropriate treatment, services, and habilitation
for such disabilities." This treatment is to be provided in "the setting which is least restrictive of the person's liberty." Federal support is to be withdrawn if a facility fails to provide "appropriate"
medical and dental care or if the hospital uses either "excessive"
medication or physical restraints "unless absolutely necessary." The
MHS Act similarly states that persons admitted to mental health
programs "should" be accorded the "right to appropriate treatment" under conditions that restrict "liberty only to the extent necessary, consistent with such person's treatment needs."

Both the DD Act and the MHS Act, therefore, set out broad
guidelines that seem to outline a right to treatment. This conclusion
is heightened by the fact that both statutes make available federal
money for advocacy programs designed to remedy complaints raised
by patients. However, recent court cases and political events have
severely weakened the impact of the DD Act and have thereby probably weakened the argument that there exists a right to treatment
based on federal statutory authority. On the one hand, budgetary
cutbacks by the federal government will make meaningless statutory
threats to deprive noncompliant hospitals of federal funds. In addition, the U.S. Supreme Court has severely limited the importance of
the DD Act. In *Pennhurst State School* v. *Halderman*, 451 U.S. 1
(1981), the Court concluded that Section 6010 of the DD Act, the
section that appears to outline a right to treatment, does not create
substantive rights.

The *Pennhurst* case arose on allegations that conditions in a
state facility for the mentally retarded were "unsanitary, inhumane,
and dangerous." The Court majority opinion found the lower trial
court correct in its conclusion that conditions at Pennhurst School
were not only dangerous but also inadequate for treatment pur-

poses. But, in contrast to the lower court, the Supreme Court majority did not find that the DD Act created either rights for patients or obligations on the states to provide treatment. Instead, the Supreme Court found that the purpose of the DD Act was merely to "assist" states to improve their services. The Act, according to the Court, indicated only a congressional preference for certain kinds of treatment rather than a mandatory duty on the states. The Supreme Court also held in *Pennhurst* that federal funds are not necessarily contingent on compliance with Section 6010 of the DD Act. Furthermore, the Court noted that the language of Section 6010 kept the state's obligation largely indeterminate, since "it is difficult to know what is meant by providing 'appropriate treatment' in the 'least restrictive' settings" (at 24–25).

The courts have apparently not yet had occasion to construe the meaning of the MHS Act, but this statute can also be viewed as a statement of salutary policy rather than of mandatory duty. Similar to the DD Act, the wording of the MHS Act is quite vague and open-ended. Much discretion is left to treatment personnel since the Act does not order that certain therapeutic activities must be carried out, only that they "should" be implemented. The MHS Act was drafted, according to its legislative history, to supplement overvague constitutional and state statutory schemes. But, unfortunately, neither the MHS Act nor the DD Act seems to serve this purpose, since neither one sets out firmly defined minimal levels of treatment or environmental conditions. Instead, both appear to preserve the judgment-making autonomy of treatment staff and hospital administrators.

A number of states have also provided statutes that attempt to define the rights of hospitalized mental patients. An inspection of these statutes yields the conclusion that the states differ widely in the range of protections they provide the inpatient. For instance, in their survey of the extent to which the states provide statutory protections for each of the rights outlined in the MHS Act, Lyon, Levine, and Zusman (1982) concluded that Alabama statutes provide the fewest protections, failing to mention twenty-three out of the twenty-four categories contained in the federal law, whereas the California statutes provide the greatest number of protections (twenty out of twenty-four).

Applications of Legal Theories

Treatment personnel and hospital administrators can feel justifiably confused in their efforts to define acceptable treatment for the inpatient. Statutes and constitutional theories have set out broad policies; but these sources do not provide detailed guidance for hospitals, which must actually deal with individual cases. The Constitution does not provide the hospital administrator with concrete guidelines for determining which patient must be released or restricted. No single legal pronouncement outlines practices guaranteed to pass constitutional muster. Furthermore, much of the law in the mental health area has been developed in a reactive, rather than a proactive, manner. Consequently, judicial decisions often are announced only after there has been a "violation." The hospital worker seemingly treats patients at his or her peril, waiting apprehensively to learn whether a reviewing court will agree or disagree with previous decisions.

Some of the apprehension associated with the treatment of the inpatient is, frankly, warranted, since it is probably impossible to predict with certainty the specific practices that are needed to satisfy a reviewing court. However, the following sections will attempt to present the specific areas of hospital practice that have received court review. These prior decisions may give the mental health practitioner some guidance for setting treatment practices, and they will provide a "feel" for the types of hospital conditions and activities that should conform with the dictates of legal theory and generally applied judicial sensitivities. This type of review will also alert the practitioner to treatment areas that have already raised legal issues.

For several reasons, however, court decisions, administrative rulings, and statutory interpretations are all limited in their impact. Such rulings cannot be accepted as controlling in each subsequent mental health case. For instance, only U.S. Supreme Court rulings are binding on all states; the decisions of lower courts are binding on treatment practices only within each court's jurisdiction. Even Supreme Court decisions, however, may not determine practices in a particular jurisdiction, since these decisions merely set a minimum level of protection; a state may exceed that level by providing a greater amount of protection than the Supreme Court requires. Therefore, a state statute or local court decision may grant additional protections for the patient if, in the estimation of the local authorities, some local condition warrants these greater protections.

In addition to limitations on the basis of jurisdictional reach, court outcomes are further limited in their precedential value to the facts in a specific case. Thus, two individual cases may have many commonalities, but the decision in one may not determine the outcome of the other because of distinctions in the particular facts of the cases. Two cases may have many similarities, but rarely are they identical, and the most minor of differences can have radical effects on the outcome of a case. The best predictor of future cases is past cases, but cases are often controlled by the quality of the involved facts rather than by the nature of the underlying principles. Each legal controversy, in the end analysis, raises unique issues, and the final outcome of a specific case can never be fully predicted before its actual resolution.

Applying Procedural Due Process

The courts and state legislatures have found due process protections to be necessary in a variety of treatment-related situations. In general, however, these decision-making situations can be classified as either treatment decisions or as decisions that will change the patient's status (commitment, transfer, and release).

Commitment. The involuntary commitment process has received an extensive amount of judicial and legislative concern and review. Indeed, the degree of concern for the rights of potential patients has seemingly prompted hesitancy in the use of involuntary commitment and a greater effort to use voluntary forms of treatment. In New York, for instance, the number of involuntary commitments dropped from 12,000 in 1965 to 331 in 1967 after legal scrutiny of the commitment process was tightened. However, the number of persons actually entering New York mental hospitals did not decrease during this time period (Zitrin, Herman, and Kumasaka, 1970). Rather, only the status of these patients had changed. This suggests that the perceived need for hospital care had not abated, but that only the legal method for gaining this care had been altered.

Voluntary and involuntary forms of commitment seem, at first glance, to raise vastly differing types of legal concerns. Involuntary commitment is, of course, a coercive procedure, whereas voluntary commitment appears relatively benign. That is, since the voluntary patient apparently agrees to enter the hospital, there is presumably little need for due process protection against abuse of that patient's rights. The patient is, in essence, getting what he or she wants, and there should be little reason for complaint. Unfortunately, however, the notion that the voluntary patient enters the hospital after making a free and informed choice appears to be quite questionable. Instead, the actual process of voluntary commitment seems to contain great potential for coercion and misunderstanding.

Observations made in emergency rooms indicate that hospital personnel may pressure potential patients into accepting treatment (Gilboy and Schmidt, 1971)—either by threatening the patient with involuntary commitment or by reassuring the patient that voluntary commitment allows him or her to leave the hospital whenever he or she wishes. In fact, voluntary patients are sometimes required to remain in the hospital even after they indicate a desire to leave. That is, if hospital personnel seek to change the patient's status from voluntary to involuntary, the patient is typically required to remain in the hospital pending the outcome of a judicial hearing to determine the need for involuntary commitment. This waiting period of time, even if the patient is later found not to need further hospitalization, may span several days.

The threat to commit a patient involuntarily if he or she does not accept voluntary treatment may also be quite hollow; yet few patients probably know this. In fact, a patient might sometimes prefer the involuntary status because involuntary patients can enjoy protections that the voluntary patient does not receive. For instance, the involuntary patient often can refuse specific forms of treatment, whereas the voluntary patient is forced to choose between treatment or leaving the hospital. Similarly, and perhaps more important, involuntary patients may receive periodic review of their status by a court, whereas voluntary patients do not receive such review. In essence, a patient can be better protected under an involuntary status and, therefore, may wish to insist on involuntary commitment rather than accept a voluntary status.

Patients who enter a mental hospital under a voluntary commitment often do not fully grasp the meaning of their consent. Thus, forty patients who had signed voluntary commitment forms were asked ten days later to describe the contents of the forms they had signed (Palmer and Wohl, 1972). Only one of the patients was able to describe the document with any degree of understanding. The remaining patients either denied having signed or indicated ignorance of the contents. Therefore, thirty-nine out of forty voluntary patients had not truly given consent to their commitment, since they were not fully informed about the consequences of their agreement.

These observations suggest that voluntarily committed patients enter the hospital with legal risks that are equally as significant as the concerns of the involuntary patient. Yet, despite these concerns, patients who face voluntary commitment have not been afforded the extensive protections given in the involuntary commitment situation. While the involuntarily committed patient has typically received a variety of due process protections to avoid the possibility of needless commitment, the voluntary patient has only his or her own resources for support.

The due process protections provided for those who face involuntary commitment do vary but often include the right to timely notice, the right to a hearing before an impartial fact finder, the right to assess the reliability of evidence through cross-examination or exclusion, and the right to counsel. Most jurisdictions provide nearly as many protections for the involuntary commitment hearing as for the criminal trial, but critical differences do remain. For instance, many jurisdictions do not currently provide for the right to request a jury as the fact finder. Similarly, although the respondent in a civil commitment hearing may have a right to counsel, this may be a less than effective right if an indigent patient must provide counsel at his or her own expense. In a recent case, for example, the judge asked a prisoner facing involuntary commitment whether he wished to contest his commitment and, in particular, whether he wanted to be represented by counsel. The prisoner responded affirmatively to both questions, whereupon the judge produced a telephone directory, presumably so that the prisoner might look up the name of an attorney. Faced with this task, the prisoner quickly backed down and accepted the commitment. Not only was the prisoner penniless after many years of incarceration, and therefore unlikely to be successful at obtaining private counsel, but he was also illiterate and therefore unable to read the directory.

Mental health professionals who testify at civil commitment hearings can expect their conclusions to receive a greater degree of scrutiny by the judge and by opposing attorneys than they receive in the hospital. Instead of the hospital's atmosphere of negotiation and consensus, courtroom decisions are made in an atmosphere of opposing arguments, a win-or-lose perspective, with little room for compromise. The result for the mental health professional is often discomfort and frustration. Due process protections for the patient seem to make civil commitment hearings overformalized procedures that maximize legal interests but minimize treatment needs. In addition, these hearings seem to question the intentions, sincerity, and skill of the mental health professional.

Despite the obvious drawbacks associated with the formalized commitment hearing, there are few available alternatives. Rather than minimizing the need for these hearings, the courts have continued to demand that civil commitment decisions be made with due process protections, which require carefulness and proof beyond predictions espoused by a mental health professional. For instance, the U.S. Supreme Court has raised the level of proof required for a civil commitment. The Court held, in *Addington* v. *Texas*, 441 U.S. 418 (1979), that a "preponderance" standard of proof, the minimal level of proof that had previously formed a sufficient basis for commitment in a number of states, was insufficient. Instead, the Court ruled that a "clear and convincing" level of proof is required. These varying levels of proof cannot be defined precisely. However, a preponderance standard can be operationalized as 50 percent sure, while a clear and convincing level of proof requires 75 percent assurance. Criminal trials require a "beyond a reasonable doubt" standard or 90 percent sure, for a finding of guilt. Thus, while the level of proof required for a civil commitment has been raised, it is still less than the level required for criminal confinement. This Supreme Court decision means, in effect, that civil commitment cannot take place unless an impartial fact finder is nearly fully convinced of the need for this type of treatment. Given the substantive standards that underlie commitment in most states (mentally ill plus dangerous to self or others), the holding of the Court means that the mental health professional must present substantial evidence of the likelihood of future destructive behavior. Mere clinical intuition should no longer satisfy the scrutiny of the concerned judge. Indeed, the U.S. Supreme Court had held in another case, *O'Connor* v. *Donaldson*, 422 U.S. 563 (1975), that persons able to survive outside the hospital are not, without evidence of a real need for hospitalization, eligible for involuntary commitment.

One recent Supreme Court decision suggests a softening in judicial attitudes toward the autonomy of mental health professionals in the area of civil commitment. In this case, *Parham* v. *J. R.*, 442 U.S. 584 (1979), the Court seems to have supported the ability of mental health professionals to commit children without extensive due process safeguards. This case was brought on behalf of children who had been committed to mental health hospitals over their protests. In a number of states, children can be committed merely on request by their parents if the intake official at the hospital agrees on the need for commitment. This type of procedure affords the child only minimal due process protections. As long as the parents and the mental health professional are in agreement, the commitment will occur. By supporting this type of procedure, the Supreme Court has seemingly given the mental health professional great latitude and ultimate decision-making power in the commitment of children. However, it seems more likely that the Court was merely upholding parental autonomy. The Supreme Court has historically and recently shown considerable solicitude for the right of parents to raise their children as they see fit. For instance, the Court has upheld a Utah statute that requires physicians to make an effort to inform parents of their daughter's wish to obtain an abortion (*H. L.* v. *Matheson,* 101 S. Ct. 1164 (1981)). *Parham,* rather than indicating the Court's efforts to increase the autonomy of mental health professionals, seems to be an effort to preserve the prerogative of parents. Civil commitment, for independent adults at least, continues to require considerable due process protection.

The issue of the mental health professional's ability to make an independent decision to commit a patient for treatment was squarely faced by the U.S. Supreme Court in *Vitek* v. *Jones,* 445 U.S.

480 (1980). In this case a convicted felon challenged a Nebraska statute that allowed prisoners to be transferred from the state prison to a mental hospital merely on the order of a designated physician or psychologist. This statute allowed, in essence, the civil commitment of prisoners if a designated physician or psychologist diagnosed a mental disease that could not be treated in the prison. The Court, however, found this statute to be a deprivation of due process. Placement in a civil hospital, even of a convicted felon undergoing the considerable deprivation of liberty inherent in prison life, still merits due process protections beyond that which is provided by a treatment-oriented professional.

Treatment Decisions. The decisions that are most within the discretion of mental health professionals, and least open to judicial scrutiny, are those concerning treatment of the patient. These decisions take place in the hospital environment and therefore are relatively hidden from non-hospital personnel. Furthermore, these decisions depend on expertise; as a result, the nonexpert should be hesitant about second-guessing the professional, who presumably knows his or her business. Judges have also been hesitant to review treatment decisions, since this type of review would require them to scrutinize a trained expert. Indeed, the U.S. Supreme Court has acknowledged the importance of allowing professionals to exercise their expertise without fear of suit or legal action because of their decision (*Youngberg* v. *Romeo*, 102 S. Ct. 2452 (1982)). While judges continue to be hesitant to review the substantive aspects of treatment decisions, they have become more willing to review the decision-making procedures of the hospital. As Judge Bazelon, an influential jurist, has noted: "It makes little sense to guard jealously against the possibility of unwarranted deprivations prior to hospitalization only to abandon the watch once the patient disappears behind hospital doors" (*Covington* v. *Harris*, 419 F.2d 617, 623–624 (D.C. Cir. 1969)).

Various courts and legislatures have now held that procedural protections should be applied to treatment decisions that might deprive a patient of privileges or rights. The more profound or permanent the denial of rights becomes, the more necessity for procedural protections. Thus, the decision to medicate or carry out invasive medical procedures, such as electroshock or surgery, seems to require rather elaborate procedural protections, since these forms of medical treatment can intrude heavily on personal rights (whereas the decision to carry out less invasive procedures, such as psychotherapy, seems to require little real scrutiny). Certain procedures (most notably, hazardous or experimental forms of treatment that are not widely accepted by the mental health professions and pose special risks to the patient) are so profound that some courts and state legislatures have ruled that their use automatically requires impartial review ("Mental Health: A Model Statute . . . ," 1977; *Scott* v. *Plante,* 532 F.2d 939 (3d Cir. 1976)). Other treatment procedures have been found to require review only when the patient, or the patient's representative, refuses to accept the treatment.

If a patient refuses consent or is unable to give informed consent to a hazardous procedure, then review by a court or an ethics committee clearly seems warranted. More difficult problems arise, however, when the treatment to be applied is relatively routine, has typically achieved positive results, is accepted by most patients, but is refused by a particular patient for little apparent reason. Can the hospital override, for instance, a patient's efforts to avoid electroshock therapy even though this form of treatment has been widely applied and has been found to benefit many patients? What if this form of treatment appears to treatment personnel to be in the patient's best interest and only is being administered after much consideration and thought? In one recent court case, *Gundy* v. *Pauley,* (No. 80-CA-1737-MR (Ky. Ct. App. Aug. 21, 1981); cited in 5 Ment. Dis. L. Rep. 321 (1981)), the court decided that electroshock therapy could be forced on an involuntary patient only if there was a judicial finding that the patient was incompetent or if there was an emergency that posed a danger to the patient or to others. In essence, this court held that involuntary patients can be forced to accept electroshock therapy only when ordered to do so by a court or when extraordinary circumstances exist.

Patients can, of course, refuse all forms of treatment. And when a patient refuses some forms of treatment, such as psychotherapy, there is typically little real controversy. After all, a therapist would have little success in trying to force unwilling patients to reveal intimate information about themselves. However, controversy does arise when the patient refuses a form of treatment that can be applied to an unwilling participant. Some such treatments (for example, electroshock, surgery, and psychotropic medication) can still achieve an apparently beneficial result. These types of refusals precipitate a delicate balancing of competing interests by an impartial reviewer.

When courts review a patient's results of treatment, the judge will balance the patient's refusal against a variety of factors (*Price* v. *Sheppard*, 239 N.W.2d 905 (Minn. 1976)). One factor is the efficacy of the treatment but this is not the only issue that will be considered (although it might seem to the treatment personnel to be the most important). Rather, a court will evaluate the risk inherent in the treatment, the extent of the intrusion on the patient's liberty, and the competence of the patient to make independent decisions.

The administration of psychotropic drugs appears to be the most thoroughly litigated type of treatment refusal. The use of routine psychotropic drugs does not require judicial review unless the patient refuses to accept medication and the hospital wishes to pursue administration of the drugs over the patient's protest. When judicial review of this issue has occurred, the courts have considered all the factors listed above: risks, liberty interests, degree of emergency, and the patient's competence. In one of the earliest court cases on the right to refuse medication, *Winters* v. *Miller*, 446 F.2d 65 (2d Cir. 1971), a patient sued the hospital for refusing to recognize her right to refuse medication. In this instance, however, the patient's objection to medication was based on her religious convictions. This patient had been a practicing Christian Scientist for more than ten years prior to her hospitalization, and she claimed that the use of drugs would infringe on her constitutionally protected religious freedom. Despite her efforts to avoid medication, however, hospital authorities forcibly administered medication after her involuntary commitment. As justification for its actions, the hospital contended that it stood in a *parens patriae* relation to the patient because she was incompetent. However, the court disagreed. Despite her commitment, the patient had not been adjudicated incompetent. Indeed, the court noted that this type of finding, which would have presumably allowed forced medication, could easily have been made in two days' time. The patient had been admitted on a Thursday, and court hearings were held in the hospital each Tuesday. But, since the patient had not been found incompetent, her refusal to accept medication should have been honored.

The *Winters* case is somewhat atypical, in that it balances the value of medication against the patient's long-held religious beliefs. Because the freedom to exercise religious beliefs is a fundamental right, protected by the Constitution, the courts can be expected to be solicitous and protective of patients who demand protections based on their religion. The issue would, however, be more difficult if the patient's religious belief appeared delusional, as occurred in *Mayock* v. *Martin*, 157 Conn. 56, 245 A.2d 574 (1968). This case was not precipitated by the patient's efforts to refuse medication but instead by his efforts to gain release from the hospital. In this instance the patient's religious belief dictated that he sever his own body parts if he received divine orders to do so. The hospital characterized these beliefs as dangerous to the patient's welfare and refused his release. The court also saw the patient's beliefs as evidence of mental illness and continued the commitment. Thus, this case suggests that religious beliefs are not automatically accepted justification for treatment refusals.

In several recent cases, the right to refuse medication has been based not on religious freedoms but on the patient's right to privacy or his right to avoid intrusion by others into his bodily integrity. Using the rationale that involuntary patients have a right to refuse medication under certain circumstances, several federal courts have recently handed down decisions that could profoundly affect the practice of hospital psychiatrists (*Davis* v. *Hubbard*, 506 F. Supp. 915 (N.D. Ohio 1980); *Rennie* v. *Klein*, 653 F2d 836 (3d Cir. 1980); *Rogers* v. *Okin*, 478 F. Supp. 1342 (D. Mass 1979); 634 F.2d 650 (1st Cir. 1980)). Unfortunately, however, these decisions do not provide a uniform definition of the conditions that would allow hospitals to overcome the patient's protest and force medication.

In *Rogers* v. *Okin*, several patients brought litigation to uphold their right to resist the forced administration of psychotropic drugs. The district court upheld their refusals, noting that involuntary patients have privacy rights protected by the Constitution and that these patients had not been found incompetent. That patients' refusals to accept medication could be overcome by the hospital, according to this court, only when a judicial hearing had found the patients incompetent or when an emergency existed. The court narrowly defined an emergency as a condition that, without medication, would result in a "substantial likelihood of physical harm to the patient, other patients, or to the staff of the institution" (478 F. Supp. at 1365). This limited definition would prevent physicians from overriding a patient's wishes in a casual fashion by simply declaring that all mental illness is an emergency.

The appeals court upheld the right of patients to refuse medication but severely limited the application of this right. Seeking to return more decision-making power to the professional staff, the court limited the need for due process hearings and broadened the definition of an emergency. It held that medication can be forcibly administered when the danger of violence outweighs the danger of the drug to the individual patient or when the patient is found incompetent, but the procedures needed to make this finding need not be reviewed by a court. Perhaps most important, the court defined an emergency as existing when drugs are "necessary to prevent further deterioration in the patient's mental health." In essence, the appeals court removed much of the autonomy given to patients by the district court. Indeed, the appeals court removed all such rights from voluntary patients when it ruled that they must either accept the prescribed medication or leave the hospital.

Rogers and other cases involving a patient's right to refuse medication have raised many unanswered questions. For instance, what constitutes an adequate emergency? If an emergency situation is defined too broadly, a professional will be able to regard any inconvenience or negative emotion as an emergency; as a result, the patient is not protected at all. Yet, if an emergency is defined too narrowly, preventive intervention might be forestalled, and thereby the level of violence within the mental hospital might be increased. Similarly, what constitutes an adequate due process hearing for determining the competency of the refusing patient? If an adequate due process hearing requires a review by a court, then this process may become excessively slow and burdensome; but a due process hearing that simply requires consideration by an involved mental health professional may provide few real protections for the patient.

Aside from problems in definition, the status of the right to refuse medication varies widely by jurisdiction. Some states do not recognize it at all, and only sixteen states clearly accept it; other states accept it in a weakened form (Lyon, Levine, and Zusman,

1982). An Indiana statute (16-14-1.6–7), for instance, allows patients who wish to refuse treatment to petition a court with their refusal; in the absence of such a petition, the treatment facility may force the treatment. In essence, the Indiana statute places the burden on the patient, and treatment may be forcibly administered even though the state has not proved the patient to be incompetent.

In one federal district court case (*A. E. and R. R.* v. *Mitchell*, No. C-78-466 (D. Utah June 16, 1980); cited in 5 Ment. Dis. L. Rep. 154 (1981)), the court seemingly failed to follow the growing number of decisions that have upheld the right to refuse medication. This court held that involuntary patients have no right to refuse medication. However, the commitment statute in Utah, the site of this case, is quite stringent and allows commitment only after a finding of proof beyond a reasonable doubt that the patient is unable rationally to evaluate his or her need for treatment. The court contended that additional hearings on the patient's competency would be redundant, since, via the fact of commitment, the patient was already deemed incompetent to refuse treatment of any sort. Thus, the court's refusal to uphold the right to refuse treatment, or to require additional procedural protections, must be recognized as resulting from the existence of alternative safeguards rather than as a rejection of the concept.

The *Rogers* case (*Mills* v. *Rogers*, 50 U.S.L.W. 4676 (1982)) was recently argued before the U.S. Supreme Court. The Court could have taken this opportunity to clarify the rights of patients in this area; but, unfortunately, it did not. Instead, the Court decided that the facts in *Rogers* did not clearly present the issues involved in the right to refuse medication, since recent statutory changes in Massachusetts, the site of the *Rogers* case, had obviated some of the issues being argued. It appears, therefore, that the extent of a patient's right to refuse treatment, especially medication, will continue to require definition in each separate jurisdiction.

Transfers and the Least Restrictive Environment. In *Vitek* v. *Jones*, 445 U.S. 480 (1980), the U.S. Supreme Court required extensive due process protections for prisoners who were to be transferred from prison to a mental hospital. These protections included a hearing before an independent decision maker, written notice of the hearing, an opportunity to present and to cross-examine witnesses, counsel (although the counselor need not be an attorney or someone with legal training), a written statement of the reasons and facts supporting the final decision, and notice of these rights. In other words, prisoners facing commitment to a mental hospital must be provided with the same extensive procedural protections that a non-prisoner facing commitment must receive.

The *Vitek* decision, in the strictest sense, deals with the rights of prisoners; prisoners cannot be removed from the prison environment and hospitalized without a thorough consideration of the transfer. However, the *Vitek* decision also has implications for the transfer of patients in mental hospitals. In *Vitek* the Supreme Court reiterated its belief that placement in a mental hospital is a profound move and requires thoughtful consideration. It is surprising that the Court considered movement from a prison to a hospital as a potential loss of liberty, which requires protection for a prisoner—especially since the Court also has held that prisoners do not merit due process protections when transferred between different prisons (*Meachuna* v. *Fano*, 247 U.S. 215 (1976); *Montanye* v. *Haymes*, 427 U.S. 236 (1976)). But, in the *Vitek* case, the Court did label treatment in a hospital as a loss of individual rights, even for incarcerated prisoners; treatment in a mental hospital is not within the range of conditions that prisoners normally receive. If transfers to mental hospitals threaten the liberty of prisoners, then transfers within the mental hospital must also be considered a potential loss of freedom, which requires procedural protections.

This type of reasoning, that already institutionalized patients must receive due process protections before a transfer, was the basis of a recent district court opinion. In *Johnson* v. *Brelje*, 521 F. Supp. 723 (N.D. Ill. 1981), the court concluded that patients who are to be transferred to a more restrictive mental health facility must be given due process protections. These patients had been found incompetent to stand trial and were to be transferred to a state mental health facility purely on the basis of administrative decision-making procedures that were not designed to consider the individual needs of each patient. Prior to transfer, the patient was merely told, orally, about the impending move and given no opportunity to resist or protest the move. The court found these minimal procedures inadequate. It held that civilly committed patients have a right to be treated in the least restrictive environment suitable to their treatment needs and that due process protections must be provided before they can be transferred to a more restrictive setting. These protections include written notice to the patient of a hearing, an opportunity for the patient to appear at this hearing, an opportunity to present witnesses and evidence and to confront and cross-examine witnesses, a neutral and detached hearing body, and written reasons for the final decision.

Nearly identical results were handed down by a federal court that reviewed the transfer procedures in an Ohio mental hospital (*Davis* v. *Balson*, 461 F. Supp. 842 (N.D. Ohio 1978)). Again it was held that placement in a more restrictive setting requires written notice, the right to present evidence at a hearing, the opportunity to call witnesses, a written statement of findings, an impartial fact finder, and assistance from another resident or staff member. An interesting aspect of this case, aside from the fact of its close agreement with other federal court holdings, was that this court not only reviewed transfer decisions but also assessed hospital decision-making procedures that resulted in a loss of privileges. These decisions, since they weigh less heavily on fundamental liberties, require fewer due process protections. Thus, this court decided that the denial of privileges (grounds passes, commissary use, visits) requires notice of the impending loss, a hearing before someone other than the complainant who seeks to remove the privilege, and a written statement of the reasons for the removal.

The clear principle that arises from the transfer cases is that due process protections are required when the patient is to be placed in a more restrictive environment. But how can a hospital be sure that a transfer represents a move to a more or less restrictive environment? Furthermore, if all deprivations require due process to the extent of the deprivation, must the hospital create a balance between the extent of due process and the nature of specific environmental changes?

The exact extent of necessary due process protections will undoubtedly provide hospital administrators with occasional confusion. However, recent research indicates that mental health professionals agree closely on the relative restrictiveness inherent in varying treatment modalities (Ransohoff and others, 1982). This finding suggests that hospitals can create a rough correspondence between protections and degree of deprivation. In any event, since the extent of due process protections is not fixed, procedures that can be justified as fair will probably find support in most courts. The transfer cases presented above represent situations where the involved hospitals provided little or no protection for patient interests.

The degree of due process protection needed in transfer cases, just as in cases involving the right to refuse medication, will depend on specific circumstances. Thus, for instance, emergency situations lessen the due process requirement. The emergency exception is likely to arise when the hospital needs to employ the most severe form of transfer: isolation or restraint of the patient. These situations are undoubtedly more restrictive than the patient's former environment; yet the use of this type of control does not lend itself to procedural niceties. Faced with a violent patient, hospital staff have little time to arrange hearings or appoint representatives. However, despite these problems, a federal court has held that the decision to seclude or restrain a patient must be made in "a context designed to protect the patient from an arbitrary deprivation of personal liberty" (*Eckerhardt* v. *Hensley,* 475 F. Supp. 908, 926 (W.D Mo. 1979)). In essence, this court allowed aides to carry out restraints, but it also held that the need for restraints must be reviewed by a doctor within twenty minutes after initiation. Furthermore, the hospital must provide written reports describing each instance of restraint as well as attempted alternatives. These reports, the court ordered, are to be clear enough to be considered by a treatment team and by a separate review committee.

The procedures that must accompany decisions will also vary as a result of the purpose of these decisions. Specifically, there is less due process requirement when the decision is designed to implement treatment than when it is a punitive consequence used to prevent violations of institutional rules. This type of distinction, which has been followed by at least one court (*Eckerhart* v. *Hensley*) but rejected by another (*Gary W.* v. *Louisiana,* 437 F. Supp. 1209 (E.D. La. 1976)), might have an impact on the use of behavior modification techniques. Suppose, for instance, a patient in a behavior modification program violates a ward rule and suffers a loss of privileges. If the underlying reason for this loss is punishment, then there is a greater due process requirement than if it is therapeutic. However, this distinction may be a difficult one to support and might be open to considerable abuse.

Although the due process procedures outlined above seem elaborate, they can generally be implemented in the hospital with no outside hospital personnel. They allow easy implementation because the courts have not insisted that the due process hearings follow legal rules of evidence or that the hearing officer or patient representative be trained in the law. In other words, hearings may remain informal, and the requisite advocate for the patient and the impartial hearing officer can be hospital personnel from a different hospital unit who are, therefore, uninvolved with this particular decision. The courts, including the Supreme Court (*Vitek* v. *Jones*, 445 U.S. 480 (1980)), have repeatedly drawn a distinction between due process procedures that are adequate to protect the patient's interests and due process protections that meet the standards set in law courts. Hospital procedures need only meet the former standards and need not be so elaborate that they turn hospital decision making forums into criminal courts.

Release from the Hospital. A patient's release from a civil commitment has traditionally been a discretionary decision on the part of the hospital administrator or treatment personnel. Thus, persons were involuntarily committed until the hospital decided that they no longer required treatment. This type of discretionary power gives the patient little protection against overlong detention based on the arbitrary whims of hospital officials.

Several forms of due process protections have developed to ensure that patients are released from the hospital as quickly as possible. Thirty-seven states now provide for mandatory periodic review ("Procedural Safeguards . . .," 1979). Under this system state hospitals are directed by statute to review the status of each patient, after a specified time, to determine the need for further confinement. An Arizona statute, for instance, directs that there be "careful" and periodic reexaminations of each person by "appropriate professional persons, including a physician." These reexaminations are to be held each ninety days (Ariz. Rev. Stat. Ann. sec. 36-511).

A recent federal appeals court decision has added a constitutional dimension to the need for periodic review. In *Doe* v. *Gallinot,*

657 F.2d 1017 (9th Cir. 1981), the court held that the California commitment statute was constitutionally inadequate, since it allowed a fourteen-day period of hospitalization without an automatic review. The California statute had taken the burden of seeking review off the state and had placed it on the patient, who was required to seek release by initiating a habeas corpus action. This procedure placed a heavy burden on the isolated patient and allowed a commitment to continue for up to fourteen days without a real showing of need. Therefore, the court ordered that emergency detention could continue only for the time needed to arrange a review hearing. However, the court also found that the hearing could be conducted by someone in the institution, a "neutral decision maker," and did not require review by a law court.

Another form of periodic review is the requirement that commitment continue only for specified periods of time, after which the hospital must either release the patient or seek a renewed court order of commitment. Indiana, for instance, provides for differing periods of involuntary commitment. These periods of time are set during the original commitment procedure. While the hospital may release the patient prior to the expiration of the commitment period, it may not keep him or her any longer without a renewed commitment order. In essence, if the patient's involuntary hospitalization is to continue, the hospital must present the same stringent level of evidence, at specified times, that was presented at the original commitment hearing.

Applying Substantive Due Process

Substantive due process standards can serve to regulate the essential workings of the hospital. These standards might be used to determine the kind of environment, treatment, and care that patients must receive. But, despite the importance of substantive due process standards, they are all but impossible to define with precise certainty because hospitals and patients present an infinite variety of conditions. No court or legislature can hope to anticipate the needs of all patients in all hospitals. Even if it could, legislation binding all hospitals to a single standard would prevent progress and solidify errors. Each hospital must have enough freedom to develop treatment programs that are responsive to the needs of its patients, to innovations in practice, and to the realities of the surrounding community.

The courts realize that hospitals need freedom; but some judges have also concluded, after reviewing conditions in certain hospitals, that a floor of protection is needed—that is, a minimal level of care that will protect patients from harm and provide them with humane care. In setting substantive standards for mental hospitals, the courts seem to have adhered to a simple review formula: If the condition is grossly inadequate, then change it; otherwise, leave it alone. This formula has clearly had extensive guidance from the testimony of mental health experts. It has also been guided by constitutional principles, fiscal considerations, and traditional deference to the expertise of administrators. But, in the end analysis, substantive orders by judges reflect their own sense of humanity and moral concern.

Given the uniqueness of each court's substantive orders, it becomes an immense, confusing, and probably less than critical task to catalogue all the orders given by judges to hospitals. The next order received by a hospital will, undoubtedly, differ in specific detail from the last. A review of past cases, however, does suggest that certain vital aspects of hospital life have received the bulk of judicial concern and regulation.

Humane Environment. The general principle arising from court decisions and legislative enactments is that patients must receive treatment in a humane environment, one that does not expose them to excessive physical danger but is, instead, comfortable and protective. Unfortunately, as a number of recent court challenges indicate, the conditions in some mental hospitals continue to be inadequate and dangerous (*Pennhurst State School* v. *Halderman,* 451 U.S. 1 (1981)). This recognition formed the stimulus for the sweeping changes in Alabama hospitals ordered by the court in *Wyatt* v. *Stickney,* 325 F. Supp. 781 (M.D. Ala. 1971), an early right-to-treatment case. Other court orders have followed the original *Wyatt* model and directed changes designed to improve the physical environment of the hospital by normalizing it, adding activities, providing for privacy, ensuring that patients are safe against attack, providing for basic physical necessities, and making changes to increase patient comfort. Listed below are explanations and examples in each of these categories.

Some courts have attempted to normalize the hospital environment or to make life in the hospital similar to life outside the hospital. In their view, patients should be restricted from an aspect of a normal environment only if there is a significant reason for this restriction. For instance, in *Eckerhardt* v. *Hensley*, 475 F. Supp. 908 (W.D. Mo. 1979), the court noted that patient rooms contained only a bed and no other furniture—an inadequate match with the environment found under more normal circumstances. The court observed, therefore, that unless there was a specific medical justification for the lack of furniture (for example, that the patient is violent), the patient rooms should be supplied with furniture, including a desk and chair. In *Flakes* v. *Percy*, 511 F. Supp. 1325 (W.D. Wis. 1981), suit was brought because patients were kept locked in their rooms for long periods of time without bathroom facilities and were forced to use rubber chamber pots that were not kept adequately cleaned. The court held that the hospital could not confine patients to their rooms in excess of one hour unless the room contained a flush toilet and a washbowl. The absence of this type of facility was described as "so dehumanizing as to undercut minimally adequate treatment" (at 1339).

Many hospital programs fail to provide sufficient periods of activity for patients, whose enforced idleness increases their sense of frustration and futility. In reviewing the amount of outdoor activity offered in one hospital, the court in *Johnson* v. *Brelje*, 521 F. Supp. 723 (N.D. Ill. 1981), discovered that patients had been allowed outside on hospital grounds for only twenty-five hours over the course of a year. The court ordered that the time be increased.

The hospital facilities should also offer privacy to the patients. Thus, toilet facilities that allow no privacy are inadequate (*Eckerhardt* v. *Hensley*). Similarly, dormitory rooms are inadequate if they do not offer protection from attack. Even the absence of air conditioning has been ruled an inadequacy. While, of course, many people outside the hospital do not have air conditioning, this type of comfort was found to be a necessity in a hospital ward where the temperature sometimes soared over 100 (*Eckerhardt* v. *Hensley*).

The courts have not, however, granted every environmental change sought by complaining patients. On the contrary, the courts will not order substantive changes in the hospital environment if there is sufficient justification for the current state practice. In *Johnson v. Brelje*, for instance, patients were locked into separate rooms for two hours each day so that the staff could have this time for lunch. The reviewing court upheld this practice as necessary because of existing staff shortages and an overriding need for security among these patients.

Communication with Outside World. Patients have a right, guaranteed under the Constitution, to free speech and expression. This means, in essence, that patients cannot be deprived of the ability to communicate with the outside world. Thus, any policy that infringes on a patient's ability to make telephone calls, write letters, and receive visits faces stiff scrutiny by a reviewing court. Policies that restrict communication must be supported by state needs of considerable importance.

In addition to constitutional support for the right to communicate outside the hospital, nearly every state now has statutes that guarantee this right for the inpatient (Lyon, Levine, and Zusman, 1982). Typically, these state statutes provide for reasonable communication opportunities and for visitation during specified hours. Furthermore, many states provide specific statutory protection for the patient's ability to communicate with an attorney.

Litigation arising from complaints that hospital policy has infringed on free communication with the outside world appears to be rather infrequent—perhaps because the clear constitutional and statutory prohibitions in this area have provided hospital policy makers with concrete guidance. In the few cases where communication policies have been tested, however, the courts have required hospitals to provide patients with a reasonable opportunity to communicate with the outside world; the hospital may not censor this communication without a sufficiently compelling justification. Indeed, one federal appeals court opinion (*Morales* v. *Turman*, 562 F.2d 993 (5th Cir. 1977)), provides some insight into the stress placed by the courts on free communication. In this case the district court (*Morales* v. *Turman*, 383 F. Supp. 53 (E.D. Tex. 1974)) had ordered sweeping changes in the practices of the hospital. The appeals court felt, in contrast, that these changes were too great and that this type of intervention belonged exclusively to the legislature. As a result, it rescinded most of the orders made by the district court; but, despite this trend, it upheld the district court's finding that the hospital's policy on communication with the outside world was too restrictive. Courts apparently regard the right to communicate as even more essential than the right to treatment or care. The U.S. Supreme Court, in a different context (school discipline), held that the ability to communicate with the outside world cures a variety of other due process faults (*Ingraham* v. *Wright,* 430 U.S. 651 (1977)).

The telephone and visitation policies in one hospital were found to be so inadequate that the reviewing court labeled them punishment (*Eckerhardt* v. *Hensley*). These policies allowed for daily visits, which lasted for one hour and forty minutes, but hospital personnel could restrict visits without giving any justification for the restriction. Telephone calls to the patient from an attorney were allowed, but all other incoming calls were forbidden. Outgoing calls were allowed, but only if they were approved as an emergency or as beneficial to the patient. Patients were permitted to call their attorneys, but only prior to a legal event. These standards clearly set up many hindrances to free communication and were also quite arbitrary, since they allowed the staff to impede communication without any prior or objective rationale.

In its review of hospital telephone policies in *Johnson* v. *Brelje,* the court noted that many of the patients in this hospital were awaiting trial and needed an opportunity to prepare their legal defense. The court ordered that these patients must be provided with a law library or with free access to an attorney, and that a more liberal telephone policy would help provide the latter.

Ancedotal observations suggest that some hospitals censor or control mail that is sent or received by patients. This type of censorship is not disallowed, but it must be supported by substantial reasons, such as hospital security. The elaborate mail policy of one hospital was upheld in part but also struck down in those areas of censorship that allowed arbitrary infringement on patient rights to privacy and communication (*Johnson* v. *Brelje*). This policy allowed staff to open and inspect incoming mail even if the patient was not present, although the staff were not supposed to read the letters. Outgoing letters addressed to unusual people, such as famous dignitaries, were intercepted and not mailed. Letters sent to other patients in the same hospital were read and censored if deemed abusive or inappropriate. Finally, letters sent to private individuals who had complained to the hospital about previous letters were also intercepted and not mailed. The reviewing court upheld the practice of opening and inspecting incoming mail, but only in the patient's presence. The court disallowed the interception of outgoing letters to dignitaries or to people who had complained about previous letters, arguing that this function, the protection of the public from mail, does not belong to a hospital but rests with other government agencies. Because it is the hospital's function to protect patients against events that might harm them, the court allowed the hospital to intercept abusive and threatening mail from one patient to another. But even this last form of censorship was tightly controlled in that the hospital was allowed only to make spot checks rather than checking all such mail, and its standards for disallowing such mail was found to be impermissibly vague.

Patient Labor. Hospitals have relied historically on patient help to run the institution. To some extent, this practice seems appropriate. Patients probably should be made responsible for chores that affect their immediate well-being and health. The practice can, however, be carried to such extremes that the institution's viability comes to rest on patient labor. As a result, key patient-employees may be kept in the hospital when they should have been released, and individual therapeutic goals may be sacrificed for institutional efficiency.

Balanced against the fear that patient labor is mere involuntary servitude is the recognition that work is therapeutic. Work tasks, if chosen properly and with individualized concern, can contribute to the patient's feelings of mastery and independence. In essence, having a job is part of a normalized environment. In *Davis* v. *Balson*, 461 F. Supp. 842 (N.D. Ohio 1978), the Joint Commission on Hospital Accreditation is cited as having found this reasoning so persuasive that it directed hospitals to provide work for psychiatric inpatients.

The principle developed by courts and state legislatures is that patients cannot be required to perform uncompensated work which is designed merely to meet hospital goals rather than provide individualized therapy. In *Wyatt* v. *Stickney*, 325 F. Supp. 781 (M.D. Ala. 1971), the court set major guidelines for patient labor. Patients may be required to work to the extent that the tasks are therapeutic and do not serve the operation and maintenance of the hospital. Patients may volunteer for work that benefits the hospital as long as this work remains consistent with their therapeutic program and as long as they are compensated in accordance with minimum wage laws.

The subsequent federal district court ruling on patient labor in *Davis* v. *Balson* apparently followed the ruling in *Wyatt* but added several further guidelines. This court again held that patients may be required to work, but only if the tasks are for self-care or for individual rehabilitative purposes. To fit these criteria, the work tasks should be approved by a qualified mental health professional and be part of the patient's treatment plan. Work which had no purpose, in this case buffing already buffed floors or shining the shoes of staff members, was disallowed. All work that benefited the institution, even if voluntarily assumed by the patient, was ordered compensated at the level prevailing in the community (if an employee would have otherwise been paid for doing this work).

While the standards listed above may protect patients from forced uncompensated or nontherapeutic labor, these standards may also have unanticipated negative effects. Specifically, if patient labor is no longer cheap or if patient labor cannot be shown to be more efficient than nonpatient labor, then budget limitations may force the cessation of all compensated patient work programs. Worse yet, if hospital administrators become fearful that even nonessential therapeutic work programs must be compensated, then all work programs for patients, therapeutic or not, may soon grind to a halt. The case of *Schindenwolf* v. *Klein,* No. L-41293-75 P.W. (N.J. Super. Ct. Dec. 22, 1980), resulted in a consent order that would avoid these consequences. In this case both litigants endorsed an agreement whereby the hospital agreed to provide a minimum level of therapeutic work as part of the institutional program. Thus, this consent order outlined the state's agreement to provide employment or vocational rehabilitation programs to at least 25 percent of institutional residents. If this holding is carried further to other states, it would make work a routine part of all hospital treatment programs.

Staff Requirements. The *Wyatt* case was originally brought by hospital staff members rather than by the patients—although obviously the patients' concerns soon became paramount. The original complaint was precipitated by the state's effort to save costs by reducing staff numbers. This left the hospital understaffed, with the result that little treatment could take place. The *Wyatt* court sought to correct this situation by outlining acceptable staff-to-patient ratios. But how can a judge, who is not trained as a mental health expert or who has little familiarity with the daily work of the hospital, possibly set the specific composition of the hospital staff? One possible method of resolving this dilemma was used by a subsequent federal district court (*Eckerhardt* v. *Hensley,* 475 F. Supp. 908 (W.D. Mo. 1979)), which relied on expert opinion to set acceptable staff-to-patient ratios.

Another staff issue that has been litigated is the training and composition of the professional staff. The *Wyatt* court addressed the needs for an adequate professional staff in several ways. First, it ordered the hospital to hire more professionals. Second, it outlined the necessary training of the professional treatment staff. Finally, it ordered that activities and therapeutic programs be supervised by qualified mental health professionals (psychiatrists, psychologists, social workers, and graduate nurses).

Restraints and Isolation. As discussed above, the decision to restrain or isolate a patient raises procedural due process requirements. However, the use of this form of control also creates a need to define the protections and rights that the patient must be offered. In general, the substantive standards set forth by courts and state legislatures uphold the validity of using restraints when necessary but also recognize the psychological and physical risks created by these procedures. Of particular importance is the notion that the use of restraints is not justified by staff convenience, the absence of other forms of treatment, or violations by the patient of institutional rules. Patients cannot be punished through the use of restraints, although this form of control can be used to treat behavioral difficulties or to protect the patient or others from harm. In all instances the hospital must consider whether a less restrictive, but equally effective, form of treatment can be used. Finally, the hospital must provide clear safeguards for the welfare of the patient.

The central requirement for the legitimate use of restraints is that there be ongoing supervision by the professional staff, so that restraints will not be applied in an arbitrary manner by nonprofessionals. One plan upheld by a reviewing court (*Eckerhardt* v. *Hensley*) specified that restraints could be applied only on the written order of a physician; the orders were to be renewed every twenty-four hours; and the condition of the patient was to be checked by a physician within the first twenty minutes of restraint, so as to determine the need to continue the restraint. Nonprofessional staff were allowed to carry out the actual restraint process, check the patient's condition after each successive fifteen-minute period, and record the patient's condition.

Similar regulations were promulgated by a court that reviewed the use of isolation in the treatment of minor patients (*Gary W.* v. *Louisiana*, 437 F. Supp. 1209 (E.D. La. 1976)). The court held that isolation is a legitimate practice if it is the least restrictive alternative available, utilized under the close supervision of the professional staff on the basis of a written order, carried out in an unlocked room with staff members nearby and with access to a bathroom, and no longer than twelve hours in duration.

Directions for the Future

Legal review of the treatment of the inpatient will continue to affect hospital practices. Specifically, we can expect changes in advocacy forms used to advance patients' interests and in the very conceptualization that underlies our view of mental health treatment.

Forms of Advocacy for the Inpatient

The previous sections suggest that the inpatient has now gained a variety of rights. But patient rights are illusory unless there is an effective method of enforcing them—a method of providing review and encouragement for the patient and the institution. In response to this need, a number of advocacy techniques have emerged. These techniques or procedural mechanisms ensure that a large and impersonal institution becomes responsive to the rights of the individual patient. Some of these advocacy forms are listed here.

Patient Participation in Treatment. Perhaps the simplest safeguard for patient rights is to allow patients an active and effective participation in determining their hospital treatment. This type of safeguard is efficient and straightforward; preserves the confidential and personal nature of the therapist-patient relationship, since third parties, who might have interests of their own, cannot intrude on the patient's wishes; and recognizes that patients can make many competent and well-informed decisions. Morrison (1976) reports that inpatients can in fact make a positive contribution to the evaluation of hospital services.

While depending on patients to be their own advocates has a variety of positive features, there are also drawbacks. For instance, many patient decisions will reflect fear and mistrust rather than informed choice. Allowing patients to serve as advocates may also cause treatment to become a patchwork of indecision and impulsive guesswork, which, in the end, might make hospital functioning less efficient and less effective. Legitimate treatment may soon be overwhelmed with spurious complaints, since many patient-initiated complaints are without real substance (Brakel, 1978). On the other hand, concerns over the volume or impact of patient-initiated complaints may be exaggerated. For instance, not a single patient complained about treatment during the year following the passage of an Arizona statute that gave patients the right to refuse certain forms of treatment (White, 1976). Similarly, a court granted a temporary restraining order giving one thousand inpatients the opportunity to refuse medication; yet only twelve patients actually exercised this choice, and their refusals generally lasted for only a few days (*Rogers v. Okin*, 478 F. Supp. 1342 (D. Mass. 1979)).

Perhaps the most serious drawback to allowing patients to serve as their own advocates, without additional help, is that they may experience pressure to conform to the wishes of the hospital staff. Without outside help, they might not be able to withstand the superior bargaining position of hospital authorities. Even outpatients find it difficult to effectively voice complaints about the behavior of a professional (Sinnett and Thetford, 1975). The additional isolation suffered by inpatients would render their advocacy task all the more difficult. In one study 51 percent of the inpatients said that they wanted legal help to support their efforts to be released from the mental hospital (Epstein and Lowinger, 1975). Similarly, in a group of forty-three inpatients, eighteen said that their treatment raised legal concerns. These patterns suggest that large numbers of patients regard legal advocacy as a necessary adjunct to routine inpatient treatment.

Personal Representatives. The personal representative is an attorney or a mental health professional or a paraprofessional who serves the individual patient's needs in commitment and release hearings or in litigation and negotiations about problems that arise during the course of treatment. To perform these services effectively, the personal representative or advocate must be independent from allegiance to hospital goals (Wolfensberger, 1977). Some hospitals that claim to provide patients with personal advocates actually use these "advocates" to serve hospital interests, such as fee collection (Annas and Healey, 1974). It is not an easy task to represent a patient against the same institution that is also the advocate's employer. Several accounts from mental health professionals contain vivid descriptions of the many pressures on the therapist who assumes the "watchdog" role in an effort to pursue the civil rights of the patient (Simon, 1978; Suchotliff, Steinfeld, and Tolchin, 1970). To avoid such problems, some advocacy services are designed to be statewide and therefore able to remain independent from the influence of a particular hospital (Wilson, Beyer, and Yudowitz, 1977).

Nonattorneys can be effective personal representatives since most controversies, legal or not, are settled by negotiation rather than through actual litigation. However, advocates report that some questions will require the finality of a judge's decision for effective resolution (Broderick, 1973) and that therefore attorney advocates should be available.

Personal representatives ideally should be readily accessible to patients and familiar with their environment. One survey found that 20 percent of advocacy programs are, in fact, housed in hospitals (American Bar Association Commission on the Mentally Disabled, 1977). In one project, for instance, law students maintained offices in the hospital and were therefore able to respond with immediacy to patient needs (Lowry and Kennedy, 1968). Advocates within the hospital also serve to overcome difficulties that the patient might find in communicating with the outside world.

The impact of the personal advocate on treatment and hospital practices has not yet received extensive research attention, but it does appear that advocates are not disruptive and that they can have positive effects. When inpatients have attorneys, they are released more quickly from the hospital (Lewin, 1968). Similarly, when legal counsel is present at a commitment hearing, the hearing lasts longer (Wenger and Fletcher, 1969) and, therefore, probably is more thorough. Several reports suggest that advocates can serve a positive role in the hospital. Broderick (1973) has found that the professional staff members of the mental hospital typically cooperate with the advocate. In another survey 75 percent of professional staff members and 58 percent of nonprofessionals said that nonlawyer personal advocates either "definitely" or "probably" improved the quality of care for inpatients (Freddolino, 1981).

Advocates do face severe difficulties in defining the proper goals for their efforts, and the goals that they ultimately decide on may conflict with what the patient wants. For instance, the patient may want to be released from the hospital or to avoid a particular form of treatment. Although the advocate could simply pursue the patient's stated goals, the advocate may believe that these goals are ill advised and could ultimately harm the patient. But the advocate's own goal—for instance, to secure the form of treatment that the patient is resisting—reflects a value judgment and, as such, a personal bias that the patient may not share. Furthermore, few advocates are able to evaluate the many medical, legal, and psychological issues that may be raised by the patient's complaint. Therefore, an advocate's decision about the merit of a patient's complaint may be clouded by the advocate's own limited expertise.

Mental health attorneys continue to debate about the proper role for the advocate. Some feel that attorneys must, on occasion, ignore the wishes of the patient-client and pursue goals that appear correct in their own judgment (Brakel, 1981a, 1981b); others believe that attorneys should cling to a traditional client advocacy stance, supporting their client's expressed wishes at all costs (Schwartz and Fleischner, 1981). One court (*Lessard* v. *Schmidt*, 349 F. Supp. 1078 (E.D. Wis. 1972)) held that a guardian *ad litem*, who pursued a best-interest goal rather than a patient advocacy goal, was an insufficient protection for the patient and that the patient, therefore, needed an advocate instead.

Still another role definition problem faced by the advocate is the extent to which goals should be compromised by political realities or be aggressively pursued in individual cases. Brakel (1981a, 1981b) reviewed the effectiveness of six in-hospital advocacy programs and concluded that traditional aggressive legal advocacy is counterproductive for the mental health attorney. Instead, Brakel recommends that these attorneys become fact finders, mediators, counselors, and ombudsmen, since the overzealous advocate may alienate hospital personnel and forestall future communication. In contrast, Schwartz and Fleischner (1981) content that the mental health attorney can aggressively represent patient interests yet remain an accepted (if sometimes unpopular) member of the institution staff.

System-Wide Advocates. Personal advocates are beneficial because they are available to individual patients. While there is clearly a need for this type of availability, it also limits the impact that the advocate will have on system-wide needs. Patient interests will also be served by advocacy that has an impact on the total institution (Moore, 1976). A number of states as well as the federal government have supported this goal by creating statewide advocacy programs or by granting authority for government agencies to pursue advocacy on behalf of inpatients. For instance, the Civil Rights of Institutionalized Persons Act, Pub. L. No. 96-247, 94 Stat. 349 (1980), gives the federal Justice Department authority to intervene in suits by patients against mental hospitals. The goal of the Justice Department is to engage in a program of selective litigation against those institutions where the most egregious constitutional deprivations affect the largest number of people.

Because system-wide change is time-consuming and extremely costly, it can be undertaken only with extensive support from the government. Mental health organizations have not taken an active initiating role in suits against mental hospitals, although they have made appearances (Simon, 1975). Although these organizations typically support the interests of patients, suits that pursue patient rights may have the effect of limiting the freedom of the professional. Thus, the interests of patients and professionals are sometimes not synonymous.

Efforts by system-wide advocates have resulted in impressive courtroom victories. These advocacy services have been involved in most of the well-known right-to-treatment cases. Yet, after the courtroom arguments have ended, the difficult task of enforcement remains. System-wide advocacy sets the stage for many subsequent individual changes, but large-scale victories reveal even more clearly the need for advocacy on the individual level. The state hospital system is far too complex to undergo complete revision on the basis of a single judicial opinion ("Implementation Problems . . .," 1977).

Human Rights Committees. The human rights committee is another method of providing protection and advocacy for the inpatient. The most extensively studied ("Implementation Problems . . .," 1977; Mahon and others, 1975; "The *Wyatt* Case . . .," 1975) example of this type of advocacy was created in *Wyatt* v. *Stickney,* 325 F. Supp. 781 (M.D. Ala. 1971). This committee, composed of part-time volunteers from a variety of vocational backgrounds, was designed to monitor the efforts made by the hospital to comply with the court's order. The *Wyatt* committee, therefore, owed little allegiance to the hospital administration, so that the committee members were free from any conflict in loyalties. Other human rights committees have been composed of hospital employees. This type of composition exposes the committee to the problem of dual loyalties, but it also offers the advantages of availability, expertise in mental health matters, and efficiency. A committee composed of hospital employees has a greater awareness of the needs of the hospital as well. However, an investigation into the effectiveness of periodic reviews, which were conducted by hospital employees themselves, indicated that these review procedures became mechanical and so provincial that they failed to include information from nonhospital sources ("Project Investigates . . . ," 1976).

The human rights committee created by the *Wyatt* case faced many difficulties. The committee was hindered by its lack of enforcement ability. Its efforts to communicate with the court were often frustrated (for example, the sheer volume of memos resulted in some going unanswered). Finally, because of its part-time status, the committee apparently appeared to hospital personnel as an intruder; as a result, hospital employees were often uncooperative.

Notwithstanding these negative results, the human rights committee does seem to offer advantages. It is a nonadversarial method for allowing community input into the practices of the hospital. This may well serve to promote normalization of the hospital environment. Further, this type of committee offers a method for gathering patient complaints and evaluating them from a variety of different viewpoints.

Masters. Courts have, on occasion, made an extreme intervention into hospital administration and appointed a master (*Davis* v. *Watkins*, 384 F. Supp. 1196, 1212 (N.D. Ohio 1974); *Pennsylvania Association for Retarded Children* v. *Pennsylvania*, 343 F. Supp. 279 (E.D. Pa. 1972)). A master is an individual or committee that is given absolute power to change hospital practices; it is, in essence, a new administration that replaces the old one. This is a drastic step for a court to take, and it seems to be a last and generally unsatisfactory alternative. A new administration might be more willing to bring about changes, but it also loses the expertise, experience, and loyalty that the old administration would have accumulated. There is no guarantee that a new administration will avoid the pressures that afflicted its predecessors.

Changing Definition of Mental Health Treatment

In spite of the changes that legal scrutiny has brought to mental hospital practices, neither legal advocates nor mental health experts have abandoned a basic goal. Both groups continue to seek ways of helping patients reach a maximum level of functioning in the briefest possible time. In essence, both legal and mental health advocates continue to hold the best interests of patients as their ultimate value. A review of the literature in this area quickly convinces one that both groups also value the need to preserve mental health treatment and legal freedom. Both legal and mental health workers seem to recognize that mental health and civil liberty are dependent on each other. Freedom is a prerequisite to, as well as a product of, mental health. Mental illness forms an obstacle to the full exercise of civil liberties; treatment helps people change to the point that their exercise of freedom is based on legitimate feelings rather than on fears or distorted beliefs.

Despite unanimity in the underlying beliefs about the value of both freedom and mental health, major differences in viewpoints between legal and mental health workers remain and are probably unavoidable. No matter how dedicated each type of helper is to preserving the patient's interests in both civil liberties and mental health treatment, there will continue to be clashes in viewpoint. Those who provide treatment to the patient are concerned that an emphasis on legal protections will compromise the efficiency of treatment—that an overconcern with legal due process will delay and frustrate the delivery of effective treatment services. In many cases this concern is, unfortunately, well founded. Some patients, because of fear or distorted belief, will refuse treatment that would have been beneficial to them. Sometimes these refusals will have disastrous effects; some patients truly will "die with their rights on" (Treffert, 1973). These individual casualties, as senseless and as frustrating as they may appear to be, must be balanced against the ultimate effect of providing patients with a renewed sense of independence and self-determination. Individual casualties are the by-products, the unwanted side effects, of providing patients with the freedom to make mistakes; but autonomy and self-respect are the direct benefits associated with these mistakes.

There is also concern that legal advocates in general and the courts in particular have now come to play an inappropriate role in the treatment of the patient. If we allow these legal advocates to make final decisions about treatment, we will have created a new group of mental health experts—a group composed of those whose training does not prepare them for making treatment decisions. Furthermore, there are substantial drawbacks to using a legal forum for making mental health decisions. In particular, courts adhere to elaborate procedural and evidentiary rules. These legal rules, necessary in some contexts, result in delay, expense, complexity, and an overemphasis on adversarial representation. But mental health issues—which are often subtle, continuing, and highly personal—cannot be completely or effectively resolved by a judicial order. Using the courts as the arbiters of mental health issues will artificially limit the input of the mental health professional while inflating the input of the attorney.

The courts, then, are not appropriate mental health decision makers. However, the mental health professional is similarly not an appropriate arbiter of civil liberties. Throughout this chapter we have noted that mental health treatment can intrude on freedom. Therefore, a decision to give final decision-making power, without review, to mental health workers or any other group of professionals should be made only after careful consideration by all members of society. Thus far, mental health workers have not received a mandate to exercise this type of independent decision-making power.

The goal of reform should be to create a forum that can integrate mental health and legal expertise. This forum should be flexible enough to allow for input from a variety of sources; but it also should be authoritative enough that its decisions will receive the compliance of patients and of both legal and mental health groups. Advocacy for the mental patient is no longer the exclusive domain of either lawyers or mental health professionals—it has become a "community affair."

In many instances both legal and mental health advocates will experience much frustration in creating the necessary balance between legal and mental health issues. In particular, mental health professionals who work in mental hospitals will feel that their ability to make autonomous decisions is being eroded by other interests. These professionals undoubtedly do have a "right to treat," but they will have to recognize that this right is less substantial than the patient's rights. The recognition of patients' rights has created a new model of treatment—a due process model. Due process protections for patients bring with them profound changes in the way that patients and treatment must be viewed. Specifically, patients are given a full share of decision-making power. No longer are the decisions made by mental health professionals qualitatively different from those of the patient. Furthermore, treatment itself is no longer considered qualitatively different from human services provided by other social institutions, such as business and government. As a result, treatment decisions will receive the same type of scrutiny afforded to these other service areas. Mental health treatment and the efforts of practitioners will be evaluated, just as industry and government are, against a perspective that is much wider than mere "therapeutic progress."

Despite the difficulties that a due process model will cause for the mental health professional, there is consulation in the realization that this major conceptual shift reflects, in large part, the expanded understanding of emotional-behavioral disorders which the mental health professions have themselves gained. The legal professions may have ushered in changes, but mental health professionals were the catalysts. These professionals are partially to blame for their loss of autonomous decision making in that the mental health professions have encouraged a nonmedical definition of the problems faced by the mental inpatient. As long as the patient suffered an arcane, potentially dangerous medical disorder, then unfettered therapeutic services were required. But once it became apparent that many patient problems were the results of adverse social conditions, then it became necessary to provide patients with the conditions that encourage equality and independence. In the final analysis, the due process model is an alternative to the medical model.

Roberta S. Stick 9

Rights of Handicapped Children to an Education

Unique to the American experience and contributing to the American democratic form of government is the concept of free public education. Acknowledging the important role an educated citizenry plays in the effective functioning of a democracy, the various states have enacted laws mandating that children of certain prescribed ages must be provided with a free public education and must attend school in order to gain the benefits of such education. The states, in turn, have obligated themselves to provide this education. Under this system children of the rich and the poor, of the immigrant and of the native born, have learned and developed.

Within such a structure, it is hard to envision or justify separation or exclusion of classes of children from receiving such education. But such exclusion has, in fact, taken place. Handicapped students—children who, because of physical, emotional, or intellectual anomalies, differed from their peers—were systematically excluded. These differences were used as justification for excluding these children from public education with their peers—or even from public education altogether.

In many ways the exclusion of handicapped children was similar to that of black children, who did not receive a public education with their white peers. Because of this similarity, any analysis of litigation involving the rights of handicapped children to receive a publicly funded education must acknowledge its dependency on case law dealing with school desegregation.

During the 1970s proponents of the right of the handicapped child to a publicly funded education made significant progress toward achievement of their goals in two landmark cases. These cases, in turn, led to passage of state and federal legislation codifying and implementing the law that had evolved from the decisions. Subsequent litigation in this area has focused on interpreting the language of this legislation and on enforcing rights guaranteed by these laws. Such litigation will undoubtedly continue through the 1980s.

The battle for improved education will be waged not only with those local entities that administer educational programs for the handicapped but also with those legislators who passed the various laws. Proponents of defense-oriented budgets, the "new" federalism, and reduction in funding for social programs may succeed in curtailing and even cutting back on the advances that have been made in this area. Proponents of educatonal rights for handicapped children must now channel their efforts and resources not only to ensure that these rights are afforded to the children but also to keep in effect existing legislation and to preserve funding levels for such legislation.

This chapter will first analyze the historical milieu out of which the landmark litigation in this area arose. This analysis will be followed by a discussion of the two landmark cases that established a right to public education for handicapped children. Only by understanding the legal rationale behind affording handicapped children their educational rights can educators and other service providers who work with these children on a daily basis comprehend fully why they must afford these children and their parents certain protections. Litigation dealing with the testing procedures used to identify handicapped children also will be discussed. (For an application of the laws and principles discussed here to higher education, see Kaplin, 1978, pp. 191–193, 410–414; Kaplin, 1980, pp. 86–98, 146–149.)

From these seminal cases came Public Law 94-142, a federal codification of the right of handicapped children to appropriate public education and the procedural guidelines to ensure that such right is provided. The procedural protections set forth in Public

Law 94-142 and the regulations promulgated to implement it will be discussed, along with the evaluation procedures to be used to identify a handicapped child and the placement to be provided to a child once he or she is identified as having a handicapping condition.

The chapter will conclude with an analysis of litigation following Public Law 94-142—litigation that has focused mainly on interpreting what is an appropriate education for a handicapped child and on ensuring that educators and administrators provide such an education.

Historical Background

It has been said that we must study history in order to avoid the mistakes of history. A brief examination of early court decisions in which exclusion of handicapped children from public education was upheld will serve to place the current state of the law in its proper perspective.

Watson v. *City of Cambridge,* 157 Mass. 561, 32 N.E. 864 (1893), and *Beattie* v. *Board of Education of City of Antigo,* 169 Wis. 231, 172 N.W. 158 (1919), are two decisions representative of early judicial philosophy toward exceptional children.

In *Watson* the court held that the local school district could expel a student who displayed continued disorderly conduct either voluntarily or by reason of imbecility. The determination of what constituted disorderly conduct was to be made by school personnel. The Massachusetts court in that case said of the child in question: "He is so weak in mind as not to derive any marked benefit from instruction, and, further . . . he is troublesome to other children. . . . He is also found unable to take ordinary, decent, physical care of himself" (157 Mass. at 561).

The child involved in the *Beattie* decision was academically and physically capable of functioning within the school; however, he had cerebral palsy and as a result was slow in his speech and could not control his facial contortions or his drooling. In holding that this child could be excluded from school because he had a "depressing" and "nauseating" effect on the teachers and the other children, the court stated: "The right of a child of school age to attend the public schools of this state cannot be insisted upon when

the presence therein is harmful to the *best interests of the school.*
This, like other individul rights, must be subordinated to the
general welfare" (169 Wis. at 233).

This was the backdrop against which the struggle for public
education of the handicapped child would be played. However, understanding the social milieu in which *Watson* and *Beattie* took
place may in some way serve to put these decisions in perspective.
The economy was essentially agrarian; and the family was a stable,
multigenerational unit, with all members helping and caring for
each other. Given these factors, the devastating impact of excluding
handicapped children from school and education was somewhat
mitigated. Although they would be deprived of the opportunity to
develop their own potential, they could be assured that there would
be someone to care for them and provide for their needs. However, as
society became more mobile and interpersonal dependencies and
relationships more fractured, this weak justification for exclusion
from educational opportunity lost whatever validity it might have
had in earlier times.

As alluded to previously, the legal route taken by advocates of
the right of the handicapped child to a public education begins at
and in many ways parallels the road taken by those who opposed
school segregation. In 1954 the constitutionality of racially segregated schools was challenged in *Brown* v. *Board of Education,* 347
U.S. 483 (1954). The United States Supreme Court, in holding that
separate but equal educational facilities are inherently unequal, acknowledged the important role that education plays in preparing
the individual for full participation in the democratic process. Education, as viewed by the Court, has both academic and social aspects:
"Today education is perhaps the most important function of state
and local governments. Compulsory school attendance laws and the
great expenditures for education both demonstrate our recognition
of the importance of education to our democratic society. It is required in the performance of our most basic public responsibilities,
even service in the armed forces. It is the very foundation of good
citizenship. Today, it is a principal instrument in awakening the
child to cultural values, in preparing him for later professional
training, and *in helping him adjust normally to his environment.* In
these days, it is doubtful that any child may reasonably be expected

to succeed in life if he is denied the opportunity of an education"
(347 U.S. at 493, emphasis added).

In the Court's view, the purpose of education is to prepare the
student for life; such preparation involves both the teaching and
development of certain cognitive skills *and* an emphasis on living
skills; black children cannot effectively take their place in the majority white society unless they are educated during their formative
years with white children; integration cannot be forestalled; and it
must begin at an early age in order for it to be meaningful.

In post-*Brown* litigation, efforts were made to show that
black children would benefit from a segregated education. But
the courts remained true to their belief that segregation, no matter
what the justification, is unconstitutional. In *Stell* v. *Savannah-
Chatham County Board of Education*, 318 F. 2d 425 (5th Cir. 1963),
certiorari denied, *Gibson* v. *Harris*, 376 U.S. 908 (1964), psychological and educational evidence was offered to show that segregation
had a more beneficial effect on black children than integration did.
The court, however, said that *Brown* had established as a matter of
law that segregation is inherently unequal and that segregated programs cannot be justified even if they provide a more adequate education and a better psychological experience for students.

Just as black children must be educated with their white peers
in order to prepare them for assuming their role in society, so, too,
must handicapped children be educated with nonhandicapped
children to assume their role in the majority nonhandicapped society. And, just as black children or handicapped children cannot
effectively function in majority society unless they have experience
with and exposure to those who constitute the majority, so, too, the
majority cannot react appropriately and positively unless they have
a bank of experience on which to draw in interacting with blacks or
with handicapped children.

The educational term for integration is *mainstreaming*—or
education in a least restrictive environment. This means that a
handicapped child will be integrated with nonhandicapped children
for some portion of a school day and during that time will receive
appropriate support personnel to assist him or her. Generally speaking, children are mainstreamed during activity periods, such as recess and lunch, and for nonacademic classes, such as physical

education, music, and art. These educational and integrational experiences are extremely important to handicapped children because they can learn only in a structured educational environment, whereas nonhandicapped children do acquire skills on their own through the process of living. Moreover, exposure to normal peers affords handicapped children the opportunity to observe and model the behaviors of normal children.

Just as blacks were slow to assert their rights to equal treatment under the law, so, too, were proponents of the handicapped child's right to an education slow to assert their position. By the 1970s, however, there occurred a shift in responsibility for the handicapped child from the professional educator—whom the parents had feared and revered—to the increasingly more militant and assertive parents to the attorney acting on behalf of the parents and the child. As part of the movement characterized by increased assertion of individual rights, there emerged a new group of attorneys, involved and committed, eager to take up the fight for individual liberty. As all these undercurrents and cross-currents operated, the time became propitious to seek judicial acknowledgment of the exceptional child's right to an education.

Litigational Achievements

Landmark Cases: PARC *and* Mills. The year 1972 marked the beginning of the era of landmark litigation in the area of special education. Two decisions, *Pennsylvania Association for Retarded Citizens* v. *Pennsylvania*, 343 F. Supp. 279 (E.D. Pa. 1972) (hereinafter referred to as "PARC"), and *Mills* v. *Board of Education*, 348 F. Supp. 866 (D.D.C. 1972), signified this new trend in the law.

In *PARC* the plaintiffs alleged that the state's compulsory education statute violated the equal protection and due process safeguards embodied in the Fourteenth Amendment of the Constitution. One of the state statutes that was challenged provided that the state would furnish a proper education for all its exceptional children unless they were certified to be uneducable or untrainable. Also challenged were provisions permitting exclusion of children who had not attained a mental age of five and those who, in the opinion of a psychologist, could not profit from school attendance.

Under such existing laws, it is easy to see how handicapped children could have been excluded. The state merely had to find a professional who would certify that a child was uneducable, untrainable, or unable to benefit from school attendance. And many professionals were willing to provide such certification, since they shared the commonly held belief that the handicapped could not be educated.

The equal protection argument advanced by the plaintiffs in *PARC* centered on the fact that Pennsylvania was already providing a public education to most of the children in the state. The Fourteenth Amendment constitutional guarantee of equal protection requires that people in similar situations should be treated similarly. Since the Commonwealth of Pennsylvania was providing an education for some children, it should provide an education for all children.

The constitutional guarantee of equal protection is not necessarily an absolute guarantee. There has evolved the concept that like people can be treated in an unlike manner if the state has a rational basis for this disparity in treatment. This "rational basis" test is not uniformly applied to assess the constitutionality of all situations created by the state that result in unequal treatment of otherwise similarly situated individuals. When the discrimination affects individuals because of traits over which they have no control—traits such as age, sex, or color—the test to be applied to determine violations of the equal protection clause is not whether the state has a rational basis for making such discrimination but whether the state has a compelling interest in imposing such discrimination. This test is referred to as the "strict scrutiny" test, and the state has the burden of showing the compelling state interest.

In *PARC* the important point made by the plaintiffs in advancing their equal protection argument was that handicapped children *could* be educated—even though the expectation level for them was different from that of normal children. *PARC* was a landmark case because it introduced a massive amount of incontrovertible expert testimony showing that handicapped children could learn and benefit from a publicly funded education. Moreover, for such children a formalized education was even more critical to their learning progress than it was to the progress of a normal child.

As to the second issue raised in *PARC*—namely, the due process argument—the focus was on asserting the right of parents and children to speak out on the appropriateness of educational placement. The Fourteenth Amendment, in addition to affording individuals equal protection guarantees, also assures that they will be provided with due process. Before individuals are deprived of life, liberty, or property interests, such as a right to an education, certain procedural safeguards must be afforded to them. The type of procedure afforded depends on the type of deprivation involved. But, as a general guide, inherent in the concept of due process is the notion of telling individuals what is occurring and affording them the opportunity to respond.

According to the plaintiffs in *PARC*, labeling a child as "handicapped" has the effect of stigmatizing that child and depriving him of rights enjoyed by his nonhandicapped peers. If a child is to be stigmatized by this labeling, then, at the very least, fairness and justice dictate that the labeling must be valid.

Two reasons were given for conceptualizing "handicapped" as a stigmatizing label. First, the general community was thought to deprecate handicapped individuals, compounding the tragedy of not being truly mentally disabled with having to endure scorn. Second, the educational programs offered for handicapped children at the time of *PARC* were segregated from the regular classroom curriculum and did not easily permit crossover. In such a situation, if a child had been incorrectly labeled, there would be little opportunity to rectify the error.

The *PARC* decision that exclusion of handicapped children from a public education was unconstitutional resulted from a consent decree entered into between the parties. That is, the parties agreed to a resolution of the controversy, rather than having the judge make the decision. Although the court indicated that the plaintiffs did have a constitutional claim, its decision does not have precedential value because the matter was resolved between the parties.

Mills v. *Board of Education*, in contrast to *PARC*, established by court decision what had been agreed to between the parties in *PARC*—namely, that to exclude the exceptional child from a publicly funded education, while affording such a benefit to all other children, was a denial of due process. In *Mills,* also, the plaintiffs were not only handicapped children but all children excluded from school because of mental, behavioral, emotional, or physical handicaps. Finally, *Mills* was significant because, by way of a defense, the defendant school district asserted that it did not have the funds to provide special education programming for all children who needed it. The school district stated that it could not adequately handle the proposed influx of students without a tremendous expenditure of funds and that because of these funding problems the system would be unable to furnish services to *both* normal and exceptional children. The court found this argument less than persuasive:

> The defendants are required . . . to provide a publicly-supported education for these "exceptional" children. Their failure to fulfill this clear duty to include and retain these children in the public school system, or otherwise provide them with publicly-supported education, . . . cannot be excused by the claim that there are insufficient funds. In *Goldberg* v. *Kelley* . . . the Supreme Court . . . held that *Constitutional rights must be afforded citizens despite the greater expense involved.* . . . Similarly, the District of Columbia's interest in educating the excluded children clearly must outweigh its interest in preserving its financial resources. If sufficient funds are not available to finance all of the services and programs that are needed and desirable in the system then the *available funds must be expended equitably in such a manner that no child is entirely excluded from a publicly-supported education consistent with his needs and abilities to benefit therefrom.* The inadequacies of the District of Columbia Public School System, whether occasioned by insufficient funding or administrative inefficiency, certainly cannot be permitted to bear more heavily on the "exceptional" or handicapped child than on the normal child [348 F. Supp. at 876; emphasis added].

Because funds were available to educate normal children, these funds had to be expended equitably, so as not to exclude any child from an education.

As indicated earlier, *PARC* and *Mills* were the landmark cases in the area of education for the handicapped child. There followed a plethora of litigation in many other states, raising the same issues and relying on the same constitutional arguments. At the same time that litigation was moving forward to establish handicapped children's rights to education, other litigation was challenging the testing procedures used to identify handicapped children and seeking to ensure that the labeling process was accurate.

Challenges to Testing Procedures. The *PARC* court evidenced its concern with the procedures by which children were placed in a special education class or designated as in need of specialized assistance, with no notice or opportunity for a hearing at which to challenge the placement: "Experts agree that it is primarily the *school* which imposes the mentally retarded label and concomitant stigmatization upon children, either initially or later on through a change in educational assignment. This follows from the fact that the school constitutes the first social institution with which the child . . . comes into contact. . . . The stigma of bearing the label 'retarded' is bad enough, but to bear the label when the placement is questionable or outright erroneous is an intolerable situation" (343 F. Supp. at 295).

The commonly accepted tool for conducting evaluations of handicapped children had been the IQ test. However, as an outgrowth of the movement that asserted the rights of handicapped children and other minority groups, actions were brought by children of ethnic, cultural, or socioeconomic minorities alleging that the evaluation procedures used to label them as handicapped had, in fact, improperly identified them. As the weaknesses of the various tests were exposed through this litigation, the challenge was given to the psychologists to develop assessment tools that were not ethnically, culturally, or socioeconomically biased.

Hobson v. *Hansen*, 269 F. Supp. 401 (D.D.C. 1967), was the first case to consider the validity of standardized tests, although it ostensibly dealt with the legal implications of ability grouping. Judge Skelly Wright struck down the "tracking system" that had been used in the public schools of the District of Columbia. In so doing, he criticized the tracking system itself for locking children into the track in which they had been placed. His focus was on the manner in which children had been sorted—through teacher's observations and standardized testing. In the court's view, the use of teachers' evaluations was predicated on the erroneous assumption "that school personnel can with reasonable accuracy ascertain the maximum potential of each student and fix the content and pace of his education accordingly. If this premise proves false, the theory of the track system collapses" (269 F. Supp. at 474).

As for the use of standardized aptitude tests to categorize students, expert testimony showed that such tests created a substantial risk of the student's being wrongly labeled. For this reason the court concluded that such tests were "completely inappropriate for use with a large segment of the student body. Because these tests are standardized primarily on and are relevant to a white middle class group of students, they produce inaccurate and misleading test scores when given to lower class and Negro students. As a result, rather than being classified according to their ability to learn, these students are in reality being classified according to their socioeconomic or racial status, or—more precisely—according to environmental and psychological facts which have nothing to do with innate ability" (269 F. Supp. at 514).

Tracking, as practiced in the District of Columbia, was abolished because of the type of evaluative scheme used to channel students into the system. However, a later appellate court decision limited the applicability of the *Hobson* court order to the existing tracking system and did permit "full scope . . . ability grouping."

Whereas *Hobson* stressed the socioeconomic and racial bias of IQ tests, *Diana* v. *State Board of Education*, Civ. No. C–70 (N.D. Cal. Jan. 7, 1970 and June 18, 1973), focused on test bias against ethnic minorities. The plaintiffs in *Diana* were nine Mexican American children who came from homes where Spanish was the chief language spoken. They alleged that they had been improperly placed in classes for the educable mentally retarded and that the IQ tests that had been used for their placement had an inherent cultural bias because they focused on English verbal skills and had been standardized on a population composed entirely of white, native-born Americans. Statistical evidence was introduced to show the disparate effect of the tests on Mexican Americans. For example, although children from this ethnic background made up only 13 percent of the school population in Monterey County, California, they comprised almost 30 percent of the children enrolled in the program for educable mentally retarded children. Moreover, studies done by the California State Department of Education showed that in 1966–67, of the 85,000 children in classes for the educable mentally retarded in California, 26 percent were Spanish-surnamed children, while these same children accounted for only 13 percent of the total school population.

The case was resolved in a stipulated settlement between the parties. The defendant school board agreed that in the future it would test all children in their primary language, it would retest those currently enrolled in classes for the educable mentally retarded, it would submit annual reports explaining the percentage disparity between Mexican Americans in the total school population and in classes for the educable mentally retarded, and it would undertake immediate efforts to develop and standardize an appropriate IQ test for children from a Spanish-speaking family background. Interestingly, when the nine plaintiff children were retested in Spanish, seven of the nine scored higher than the IQ level used to determine mental retardation.

Racial bias of tests was challenged by black Californians in *Larry P. v. Riles*, 343 F. Supp. 1306 (N.D. Cal. 1972). The plaintiffs showed that the IQ tests being used as evaluative tools had the effect of classifying a disproportionate number of black children as retarded. The plaintiffs thereby established a system of de facto racial discrimination, and the burden of proof shifted to the defendants to show that this unequal treatment—that is, the disparate results of testing—was rationally related to the purpose of evaluating the student's ability to learn.

The school district tried to justify the test it was using by alleging that it did not rely solely on the test in classifying children. However, the court held that it was sufficient that "substantial emphasis" was placed on the test results. The court also rejected the defendant's second contention—namely, that the parental consent required before a child could be placed in a special education class barred the parent from complaining. In adopting this position, the court acknowledged that such consent tends to be pro forma because of parental awe of the educational process: "Parents are likely to be overawed by scientific-sounding pronouncements about I.Q.: and if their decisions whether to provide their consent are so colored by I.Q. results, then the I.Q. tests again appear as prime determinants of EMR [educable mentally retarded] placement. Furthermore, if the I.Q. tests are found in fact to be biased against the culture and experience of black children, any consent which is obtained from the parents of such children absent communication of full information to that effect is not effective communication" (343 F. Supp. at 1313). The defendants, as their final defense, suggested that "since black people tend to be poor, and poor pregnant women tend to suffer from inadequate nutrition, it is possible that the brain development of many black children had been retarded by their mother's poor diet during pregnancy" (at 1310). In response to this, the court refused to assume "otherwise than that the ability to learn is randomly spread about the population" (at 1311).

The result of this litigation was that the San Francisco school district was enjoined "from placing black students in classes for the educable mentally retarded on the bases of criteria which rely primarily on the results of I.Q. tests as they are currently administered, if the consequence of use of such criteria is racial imbalance in the composition of such classes" (at 1315).

The foregoing case discussions deal with only a sampling of the litigation challenging the correctness of testing procedures. The volume of cases parallels that found in the area of right-to-education cases. Several lessons are to be gleaned through examination of the litigation in these two areas.

First, the number of cases brought before the courts is indicative of the tedious process that must be followed in order to achieve full and meaningful educational rights for the handicapped. Parents and advocacy groups must be constantly vigilant. They must police the educational system to be sure that handicapped children are being provided with an appropriate education. It is unfortunate that they are thrust into the role of enforcers, since they must also work with those whom they police—namely, the school personnel. To handle this difficult situation, tolerance and understanding are required of both sides.

The professionals working with handicapped children should endeavor to learn as much as possible about the children with whom they are working: their families, their environment, their native language. In this way they will be able to select the most effective assessment instruments for use with these children. Moreover, gathering this information will facilitate future communication with the parents; the key to better relationships between the school and the family is this better communication.

A second lesson to be derived from a study of litigational achievements is to discover that the courts have essentially functioned in a punitive rather than a remedial capacity. Resort to the court *is* a last resort. Parents take this ultimate step in frustration, when they feel that they can no longer accomplish their goals through reasoned discussion with school personnel. This insight is important to the professionals working with the parents. They should conduct a dialogue with the parents and maintain communication even when both sides seem to be far apart in their goals. As long as the parties can interact, progress is being made. When communication breaks down, the parties cannot fashion a suitable remedy, and often the court cannot either. In such a situation, all that may remain is for one side or the other to be punished.

One final point to be gleaned from these cases is that implementation of these decisions requires a vast expenditure of finances and human energy, and some people feel that providing educational services for the exceptional child is a wasteful expenditure of public funds. This point will be discussed later in this chapter.

Statutory Implementation

The "law" is not only embodied in decisional or judicial law such as that previously discussed. There is also statutory law enacted by local, state, or national government entities. The interplay between these two types of law varies. Judicial decisions may interpret statutes, and sometimes, as in the area of educational law for the handicapped, statutes serve to codify decisional law. Public Law 94-142 (Education for All Handicapped Children Act, 20 U.S.C. sec. 1401 *et seq.*), enacted by Congress in 1974, incorporated many of the themes set out in *PARC* and *Mills*. Public Law 94-142, in turn, led to legislation enacted by each state, except New Mexico, which complemented and implemented the provisions of Public Law 94-

142. States that refused to enact such legislation would not have received federal reimbursement for monies expended to provide special education services.

Public Law 94-142 seeks to ensure that all handicapped children have available to them a free appropriate education designed to meet their individual needs. The law tries to achieve this goal by two means. First, it provides a mechanism whereby large amounts of federal aid are disbursed to the individual states to reimburse them for a large percentage of the costs of providing special education services. Second, as a condition for receipt of this federal assistance, the law requires protections for handicapped children and their families: procedural due process protection in evaluation and decision making for placements, rights to hearings and appeals, requirements of confidentiality of and access to school records, and requirements concerning educational programming.

At the time of passage of Public Law 94-142, regulations were being promulgated under Section 504 of the Rehabilitation Act of 1973, 29 U.S.C. sec. 794. Generally speaking, the Rehabilitation Act of 1973 may be considered a civil rights statute prohibiting discrimination against the handicapped by any program receiving any type of federal assistance. Certain provisions of these regulations dealing specifically with the activities of educational institutions also protect the interest of children requiring special education by expanding federal requirements on aid recipients. Ironically, the state of New Mexico, which rejected receipt of federal funding in order not to be forced to comply with the procedural due process required by Public Law 94-142, was forced to provide a free appropriate public education to its handicapped children because of the regulations promulgated to enforce Section 504—this without receiving the reimbursement afforded to states in compliance with Public Law 94-142.

Public Law 94-142 was designed to ensure correct evaluation and to implement an appropriate educational program for a child designated as handicapped. The following procedural safeguards (the due process referred to in *PARC*) are afforded to parents and children:

(a) Any state educational agency, any local educational agency, and any intermediate educational unit which receives assistance under this part [20 U.S.C. sec. 1411 *et. seq.*] shall establish and maintain procedures in accordance with subsection (b) through subsection (e) of this section to assure that handicapped children and their parents or guardians are guaranteed procedural safeguards with respect to the provision of free appropriate public education by such agencies and units.

(b) (1) The procedures required by this section shall include, but shall not be limited to—

    (A) an opportunity for the parents or guardian of a handicapped child to examine all relevant records with respect to the identification, evaluation, and educational placement of the child, and the provision of a free appropriate public education to such child, and to obtain an independent educational evaluation of the child;

    (B) procedures to protect the rights of the child whenever the parents or guardian of the child is a ward of the State, including the assignment of an individual (who shall not be an employee of the State educational agency, local educational agency, or intermediate educational unit involved in the education or care of the child) to act as a surrogate for the parents or guardian;

    (C) written prior notice to the parents or guardian of the child whenever such agency or unit—(i) proposes to initiate or change, or (ii) refuses to initiate or change the identification, evaluation, or educational placement of the child or the provision of a free appropriate public education to the child;

    (D) procedures designed to assure that the notice required by clause (C) fully inform the parents or guardian, the parents' or guardian's native language, unless it clearly is not feasible to do so, of all procedures available pursuant to this section; and

    (E) an opportunity to present complaints with respect to any matter relating to the identification, evaluation, or educational placement of the child or the provision of a free appropriate public education to such child.

(2) Whenever a complaint has been received under paragraph (1) of this subsection, the parents or guardian shall have an opportunity for an impartial due process hearing which shall be conducted by the State educational agency or by the local educational agency or intermediate educational unit, as determined by State law or by the State educational agency. No hearing conducted pursuant to the requirements of this paragraph shall be conducted by an employee of such agency or unit involved in the education or care of the child.

(c) If the hearing required in paragraph (2) of subsection (b) of this section is conducted by a local educational agency or an intermediate educational unit, any party aggrieved by the findings and decision rendered in such a hearing may appeal to the State educational agency which shall conduct an impartial review of such hearing. The officer conducting such review shall make an independent decision upon completion of such review.

(d) Any party to any hearing conducted pursuant to the subsections (b) and (c) shall be accorded (1) the right to be accompanied and advised by counsel and by individuals with special knowledge or training with respect to the problems of handicapped children, (2) the right to present evidence and confront, cross-examine, and compel the attendance of witnesses, (3) the right to a written or electronic verbatim record of such hearing, and (4) the right to written findings of fact and decisions (which findings and decisions shall also be transmitted to the advisory panel established pursuant to section 613(a)(12))[20 U.S.C. sec. 1414(a)(12)].

(e) (1) A decision made in a hearing conducted pursuant to paragraph (2) of subsection (b) shall be final, except that any party involved in such hearing may appeal such decision under the provisions of subsection (c) and paragraph (2) of this subsection. A decision made under subsection (c) shall be final, except that any party may bring an action under paragraph (2) of this subsection.

(2) Any party aggrieved by the findings and decision made under subsection (b) who does not have the right to an appeal under subsection (c), and any party aggrieved by the findings and decision under subsection (c) shall have the right to bring a civil action with respect to the complaint presented pursuant to this section, which action may be brought in any State court of competent jurisdiction or in a district court of the United States without regard to the amount in controversy. In any action brought under this paragraph the court shall receive the records of the administrative proceedings, shall hear additional evidence at the request of a party, and, basing its decision on the preponderance of the evidence, shall grant such relief as the court determines is appropriate.

(3) During the pendancy of any proceedings conducted pursuant to this section, unless the State or local educational agency and the parents or guardian otherwise agree, the child shall remain in the then current educational placement of such child, or, if applying for initial admission to a public school, shall, with the consent of the parents or guardian, be placed in the public school program until all such proceedings have been completed.

(4) The district courts of the United States shall have jurisdiction of actions brought under this subsection without regard to the amount in controversy [20 U.S.C. sec. 1415].

Other sections of the Act set forth the mechanics of state reimbursement.

The regulations, codified at 45 C.F.R. Part 121a, amplify the procedural safeguards found in Public Law 94-142. Once again, the emphasis is on correct evaluation, an individual education program (IEP) for each child in need of special services, and monitoring to ensure progress.

Throughout the regulations, there is continual reference to providing a "free appropriate education to each handicapped child." Unfortunately, no definition of a "free appropriate education" is contained in the regulations. Educators charged with providing this appropriate education must rely on their own discipline for direction on what constitutes an appropriate education for each individual child. As will be dealt with more fully later in this chapter, considerable litigation has evolved in different states in an effort to grapple with what constitutes this nebulous concept and to formulate guidelines for it.

The regulations require that this free appropriate education must take place in the least restrictive environment. What this means is that public agencies must ensure "(1) that to the maximum extent appropriate, handicapped children, including children in public or private institutions or other care facilities, are educated with children who are not handicapped and (2) that special classes, separate schooling, or other removal of handicapped children from the regular educational environment occurs only when the nature or severity of the handicap is such that education in regular classes with the use of supplementary aids and services cannot be achieved satisfactorily" (45 C.F.R. Part 121a). In order to ensure "education in the least restrictive environment," educators must provide a continuum of alternative placements to meet the needs of handicapped students for special education and related services. This continuum includes instruction in regular schools, special classes, special schools, home instruction, and instruction in hospitals or institutions. Where a student fits on this continuum is determined by the severity of his or her handicapping condition.

The "related services" to be provided to handicapped students are defined as "transportation and such developmental, corrective, and other supportive services as are required to assist a handicapped child to benefit from special education." Specific services mentioned in the regulations are "speech pathology and audiology, psychological services, physical and occupational therapy, recreation, early identification and assessment of disabilities in children, counseling services, and medical services for diagnostic or evaluation purposes," as well as "school health services, social work services in schools, and parent counseling and training." The courts, as will be discussed more fully later in this chapter, have focused on what services are required to help the handicapped child *benefit* from special education. As a result, the definition of "related services" has been expanded to include administration of medication, intermittent catheterization, eyeglasses, orthopedic equipment, and hearing aids needed for students to benefit from education.

One important aspect of the regulations implementing Public Law 94-142 is the involvement of parents in devising the educational programming for their children. Whereas, before *PARC* and *Mills,* parents of handicapped children generally played a minimal role in their children's education, informed and participating parents now work with the educators to carry out the educational programming at home and thereby complement the school program. Moreover, these parents can also monitor compliance by the school district with the law's requirements when such monitoring becomes appropriate.

There are various ways in which parents are involved in decisions about their handicapped child's education: They must give written consent prior to an evaluation that will determine whether their child needs special education; they are to participate in the actual writing of the child's IEP; they are to be provided with a list of places where they can receive free or low-cost legal services if they qualify for such services; they are to give written consent prior to the initial placement of their child in special education; and they must be provided with access to information about their child if they request it. All these requirements permit parents to have knowledge of and to participate in their child's educational program. In this way, they can assist in monitoring the quality of their child's program.

Procedures are set forth to guarantee, as much as possible, an accurate assessment of each student who may be in need of special educational services. This is an acknowledgment of the finding in *PARC* that identifying a child as handicapped is stigmatizing and that, before such stigmatization is imposed, there should be guarantees that the labeling is accurate. To ensure this accuracy, provision is made that children whose native language is not English should be tested in their native language. Moreover, the tests must have been validated for the specific purpose for which they are used, and they must be administered by trained personnel in conformity with instructions provided by their producer. These requirements undoubtedly have their genesis in the previously discussed litigation involving testing procedures.

Elaborate due process procedural safeguards for parents and children are set forth in the regulations. These include the right to have an independent educational evaluation if the parents do not agree with the school's assessment and the right to receive prior notice before any changes are made in a child's program. Educators must inform parents of their child's planned placement and must give the parents an opportunity to give their opinions about the propriety of the placement.

Certain requirements concerning testing are set out in the regulations: Students must be reevaluated every three years; a multidisciplinary approach must be used in evaluations of handicapped children, and multifaceted evaluations must be conducted; there must be standards for establishing the validity and reliability of the tests used to evaluate students; those who administer the tests must have specific qualifications; parents have the right to obtain independent educational evaluations at public expense; and someone who evaluated the student or understands the evaluation must participate in that student's IEP meeting. This clearly spelled-out procedure is an acknowledgment of the importance to all concerned—parents, children, and educational providers—of correctly identifying children and providing them with an educational program appropriate to their needs.

Regrettably, the survival of these procedural safeguards is threatened. In financially troubled times, advocates of reduced spending in the area of social services may seek to dilute the effectiveness of the regulations. Compliance with the law can be costly, but what fiscal conservatives may overlook is the total picture. Education of the handicapped child may be initially expensive. But if the child, through the educational process, can learn enough life skills to enable him or her to live independently in the community as an adult rather than in an institution, then the cost to society of that child's education will be more than recouped, since it is more expensive to maintain an individual in an institution than in a residence in the community. Moreover, if the child is capable of learning vocational skills, then he or she will become a contributor to society rather than a taker from society.

Litigation Following Public Law 94-142

The focal point of litigation initiated after enactment of Public Law 94-142 has centered on defining what is an appropriate education. Regrettably, the decisions only serve to inject more uncertainty into the area.

In *Campbell* v. *Talladega County Board of Education and Board of Education of the State of Alabama,* 518 F. Supp. 47 (N.D. Ala. 1981), the court held that the determination of "appropriateness" is a proper judicial function. Basing its conclusions on the legislative history of the Education of All Handicapped Children Act, the court said that an IEP must at least embody practical objectives. That is, the educational program must enable a handicapped child to be as independent as possible, to become a productive member of society, and to achieve approximately the same academic success as his or her nonhandicapped peers. In the court's view, the defendant had failed to "design an education to further [the plaintiff's] progress in attaining such self-sufficiency as he may be capable of" (at 54). Specifically, the program did not impart to the plaintiff, an eighteen-year-old severely retarded student, any functional or communicative skills that might increase his independence. Therefore, it failed to meet "even a minimally stringent standard of appropriateness" (at 54). The court also noted that the plaintiff had had virtually no contact with nonhandicapped students outside of his lunch period—even though there was considerable evidence that increased interaction with nonhandicapped students was essential to provide him with role models and to increase his ability to act independently.

The court ordered the school district to change the child's IEP so that it would cover the entire school year, including the summer session; provide for significantly increased contact with nonhandicapped students (either by moving his special education class into the main high school building or by educating nonhandicapped students as well as handicapped students in the special education center); focus on acquisition of functional skills; and include instruction in social and community adjustment and in appropriate nonverbal communication skills. In addition, the school district was required to make provisions for measuring the plaintiff's progress in all areas. The defendants in *Campbell* also were ordered to provide suitable in-service training to the child's teacher and special education coordinator. Finally, the defendants were ordered to provide the plaintiff with a free appropriate education for two years past his twenty-first birthday (when the state's obligation ordinarily would end) and to pay reasonable attorney's fees for the plaintiff.

For professionals working with handicapped children, there are definitive lessons to be learned from *Campbell*. Education is not just an academic experience. It is training for living. For students who cannot benefit from an academic program, the focus should be on life skills, on training the child to be a productive member of society. School districts that fail to provide appropriate programs for each student will be penalized to the extent that they may have to compensate for years of improper education by providing educational services for a student beyond the age of twenty-one.

The *Campbell* decision focused on a functional and practical definition of an appropriate education. At the other end of the spectrum, *Rowley* v. *Board of Education of the Hendrick Hudson Central School District*, 483 F. Supp. 528 (S.D.N.Y. 1979), affirmed, 632 F. 2d 945 (2d Cir. 1980), involved an action brought by an eight-year-old deaf child against the school district because of its failure to provide her with the services of a sign language interpreter in the classroom. The trial court concluded that the definition of an appropriate education was not clear. It could mean "an education substantial enough to facilitate a child's progress from one grade to another and to enable him to earn a high school diploma"; or it could mean an education "which enables the handicapped child to achieve his or her full potential" (483 F. Supp. at 534). The court adopted a definition falling somewhere between these two poles: an education that gives "each handicapped child . . . an opportunity provided to other children" (at 534). "Appropriate" education was considered to require something more than "adequate" education. However, since even the best public schools lack the resources to enable *every* child to achieve his or her full potential, schools were not required to afford students the chance to do so. Although the court found that the plaintiff's academic performance was better than that of the average child, the court held that she was not receiving an appropriate education (that is, something more than an "adequate" education). The court ordered that the child be allowed to have a sign language interpreter. The case was subsequently appealed to a federal appeals court, and the holding was affirmed.

The case was then appealed to the United States Supreme Court. In its first decision involving the Education for All Handicapped Children Act, *Hendrick Hudson School District v. Rowley,* 50 U.S.L.W. 4925 (June 28, 1982), the Court reversed the lower court order requiring that the Hendrick Hudson School District provide Amy Rowley with a sign language interpreter. In a 6-to-3 decision, the Court said that Congress did not intend to give handicapped children a right to the best possible education—that is, education that would "maximize their potential." It also rejected the standard used by the lower courts—namely, that handicapped children are entitled to an educational opportunity "commensurate with the education available to nonhandicapped children" (483 F. Supp. at 534). This standard, said Justice Rehnquist, writing for the majority, requires comparisons between the needs and potential of handicapped children and nonhandicapped children, and such comparisons are impossible to make. The Court held instead that *a state is required to provide "meaningful" access to an education for each handicapped child:* "The 'basic floor of opportunity' provided by the Act consists of access to specialized instruction and related services which are individually designed to provide educational benefit to the handicapped child" (50 U.S.L.W. at 4932). Moreover, stated the justices, sufficient supportive and related services must be provided to permit the child to benefit educationally from special instruction.

When the Court applied this standard to Amy Rowley, it found that she did not need interpreter services because she was making exemplary progress in the regular educational system with the help of the extensive special services her school was providing—namely, a special tutor for the deaf one hour each day, a speech therapist three hours a week, and a sound amplifier for Amy to use in class. The Court was careful to point out, however, that merely passing from grade to grade did not mean that a child's education is appropriate under Public Law 94-142. The services that constitute an appropriate education must be based on each child's individual needs. Therefore, although Amy was found not to need a sign language interpreter, a child who must have the help of an interpreter to benefit from his or her education would have a right to receive that service.

The Court held that judicial review under the Act is *not* limited to review of a state's compliance with procedural requirements. The role of the federal court is twofold: (1) to determine whether the state has complied with the procedures of the Act (including development of an IEP) and (2) to determine whether the substance of the IEP is reasonably calculated to enable the child to receive educational benefits.

Justice Rehnquist's opinion suggested that courts should hesitate to substitute their own notions of sound educational practices for the programs developed by educational agencies in cooperation with each child's parents. Nonetheless, the federal courts do retain the power to review the substance of the state's proposed educational program and to order additional services if that program is not individually designed to give each child meaningful access to education.

The *Rowley* decision leaves intact all the major components of Public Law 94-142. Effective implementation of the Court's definition of appropriate education—an education individually designed to provide educational benefit to a child—will make active parental involvement and advocacy in the development of each child's education plan even more important than it has been in the past. Because the Court decided that the facts of this particular case did not warrant the school district's provision of a particular service does not mean that school districts can rely on *Rowley* to justify cutbacks in services for handicapped children. Such cutbacks are not justified by a fair reading of the opinion.

The Court's opinion makes clear that the Education for All Handicapped Children Act imposes extensive legal requirements on state education agencies and school systems. Specifically, the opinion states and affirms that:

• Handicapped children must be educated by the public schools without charge.
• Handicapped children must be provided meaningful services.

- Those services must be designed, through the individual education plan (IEP) to benefit the specific child.
- Related services and supportive services needed to enable a child
  to benefit from his education must be provided.
- Parents must be actively involved in the planning for their
  child's education.
- Due process procedures and federal court review are available to
  parents who wish to challenge either the procedure used in developing their child's program or the capacity of the program to
  provide a meaningful education for their child.

While the parents in *Rowley* had sought a quality education
for their child, one that would maximize her potential, the parents
in *Springdale School District* v. *Sherry Grace and Arkansas Department of Education,* 494 F. Supp. 266 (W.D. Ark. 1980), 656 F.2d 300
(8th Cir. 1981), were motivated by other goals. They sought placement for their profoundly deaf daughter in their home school district, while the school district wished to have her placed at the
Arkansas School for the Deaf. In that case, the school district sued
the parents of Sherry Grace, seeking review of a determination of the
Arkansas State Department of Education that Sherry's education
should take place in the local school district rather than at the Arkansas School for the Deaf. The school district lost in the district
court and appealed to the U.S. Court of Appeals for the Eighth
Circuit. The appellate court affirmed the lower court's decision. The
Arkansas School for the Deaf, which Sherry had attended before the
parents moved to Springdale, was located far from their new home.
Moreover, this residential placement is on the extreme end of the
placement continuum and constitutes education in the *most* restrictive environment. However, for a profoundly deaf child such as
Sherry, education with deaf peers would provide more intensive
educational opportunities. A similar argument had been advanced
and rejected in *Stell* v. *Savannah-Chatham,* 318 F.2d 425 (5th Cir.
1963), a school segregation case discussed earlier.

The *Grace* court relied on the definition of appropriate education contained in the *Rowley* trial court opinion to aid it in determining whether Sherry Grace was receiving an appropriate
education: "An 'appropriate education' could mean an 'adequate'

education—that is, an education substantial enough to facilitate a child's progress from one grade to another and to enable him or her to earn a high school diploma. An 'appropriate education' could also mean one which enables the handicapped child to achieve his or her full potential. Between those two extremes, however, is a standard which . . . is more in keeping with the regulations, with the Equal Protection decisions which motivated the passage of the Act, and with common sense. This standard would require that each handicapped child be given an opportunity to achieve his full potential commensurate with the opportunity provided to other children" (494 F. Supp. at 272). Using this standard, the *Grace* court was able to conclude that Sherry could receive an appropriate education in the Springdale schools. The education would be comparable to that received by other students in that she would not receive the *best* education; however, "Springdale School does not turn every one of its students into academicians or professionals or even successful secondary school students" (at 272).

The segregation that would be imposed on Sherry were she to be placed at the Arkansas School for the Deaf was most persuasive on the court. The court noted that in Springdale Sherry could be with nonhandicapped children for physical education, health, social studies, music, or art. No such contacts during the regular school day would be available at the Arkansas School for the Deaf. Although the Arkansas School for the Deaf had better facilities for teaching the deaf, teachers skilled in total communication, role models, peers with whom she could communicate, and the opportunity for full participation in after-school activities, placement at that institution would not meet the mainstreaming requirements of Public Law 94-142.

Since the *Grace* decision predated the final *Rowley* decision, the Supreme Court ordered the court of appeals to reconsider its earlier decision in *Springdale School District* v. *Grace* concerning an "appropriate" education under Public Law 94-142.

The court of appeals reaffirmed its pre-*Rowley* ruling that a profoundly and prelingually deaf child could receive an "appropriate" education in the local public school even though the "best" place for the child would be at the Arkansas School for the Deaf. In reconsidering its earlier ruling, the court of appeals answered the two questions which the *Rowley* Court required lower courts reviewing actions under Public Law 94-142 to address: (1) whether the state has complied with the Act's procedures (including fully and properly developing an IEP); (2) whether the IEP is reasonably calculated to enable the child to receive educational benefits.

The appellate court found that the state had complied with the procedures of the Act. The Springdale School District had prepared an IEP for Sherry Grace, providing that she be taught by a certified teacher of the deaf at the Arkansas School of the Deaf. The child's parents challenged the proposed placement, and a hearing officer reversed the school district's determination.

In finding that the IEP developed through the administrative process was reasonably calculated to enable Sherry to benefit from the public school program, the court of appeals relied on the Supreme Court's emphasis in *Rowley* on the goals of mainstreaming, and its finding that the public school could provide an appropriate education through personalized instruction by a certified teacher of the deaf and through other supportive services.

In another post-*Rowley* case, *Doe* v. *Anrig*, 507 F. Supp. 802 (D. Mass. 1980), the Court of Appeals for the First Circuit upheld as consistent with the principles of *Rowley* a trial court's finding that a residential placement was appropriate for a teenaged boy with Down's Syndrome who had been institutionalized from birth, even though this judgment set aside a state-level administrative decision.

Contrary to assertions by the appellants, the court of appeals found nothing in the record to suggest that the lower court had failed to accord "due weight" to state proceedings. Mindful of the Supreme Court's admonition to lower courts in *Rowley* not to substitute their own notions of educational policy for those of the school authorities, the appellate court stated that the trial court's finding was not a choice of educational policy but a resolution of an individualized factual issue: whether John's handicap would affect his ability to benefit from the proposed school setting. Such an issue, the appeals court ruled, is clearly within the scope of judicial review contemplated under Public Law 94-142.

While *Rowley* and *Grace* affirm the concept that a handicapped child has a right to a free appropriate education, *Levine* v. *Institutions and Agencies Department of New Jersey* and *Guempel*

v. *New Jersey*, 418 A.2d 229 (1980), are in sharp contrast. The issue presented in these cases was whether the New Jersey Constitution's free education clause—the essential purpose of which was to maximize public education so that citizens may "function politically, economically, and socially in a democratic society"—includes within its guarantee profoundly retarded institutionalized children and the total-habilitation programs entailed in their residential care. Focusing on a definition of education similar to that articulated by the *Brown* court, the New Jersey court concluded that the free education clause did not cover this type of residential care: "It is neither realistic nor meaningful to equate the type of care and habilitation which such children require for their health and survival with 'education' in the sense that that term is used in the Constitution" (418 A.2d at 237). Perhaps the provisions of the New Jersey state constitution led to this particular decision. As opposed to most other state constitutions, it provides for a thorough and efficient education for the children of New Jersey. Perhaps this emphasis on a quality education led to the *Levine* and *Guempel* decision.

The dissent in *Levine* is worth quoting because it remained constant to the concept of handicapped children's rights: "I cannot accept a definition of education which does not provide to each child the training and assistance necessary to function as best [he] can in whatever will be [his] environment—even if that environment will be separated from the world of politics and economic competition. The ability of even profoundly impaired children to benefit from education is universally acknowledged" (418 A.2d at 250–251).

While *Levine* and *Guempel* (for the present time) may have little impact beyond the state of New Jersey, they might indicate the wave of the future in right-to-education cases if the provisions of Public Law 94-142 and its accompanying regulations were to be substantially weakened or even repealed at some future time. This decision does harken back to the previously espoused position that retarded children cannot be "educated." Moreover, it seems result oriented; that is, if handicapped individuals cannot become politically, socially, and economically involved in society, the treatment provided should not be categorized as education.

The law mandates that education must be provided even for profoundly retarded children. Out of this requirement has come litigation seeking year-round educational programs. The rationale for such request lies in the fact that during the summer months retarded children regress in their educational progress. When school resumes, it takes several weeks or even months before they again return to their prior level of functioning.

In *Armstrong* v. *Kline*, 476 F. Supp. 583 (E.D. Pa. 1979), remanded, 629 F.2d 269 (1979), the court was confronted with an administrative policy of the state of Pennsylvania, which limited to 180 days the instruction that handicapped children could receive. The district court held that the inflexibility of the defendant's policy of refusing to provide more than 180 days of education was incompatible with the Education for All Handicapped Children Act's emphasis on the individual. Where an inflexible rule, such as the 180-day rule, had not been submitted to the federal government for its approval, that rule must fall. Other subsequent cases have basically followed the reasoning in the *Armstrong* decision and have mandated a year-round program when it is appropriate. The courts do acknowledge that year-round programming would be beneficial to all children, handicapped or nonhandicapped; therefore, twelve-month programming is provided only in exceptional situations. It should also be noted that successful requests for twelve-month programming occur when school districts have policies absolutely mandating shorter periods of education.

An area of increasing concern in Public Law 94-142 cases deals with "related services." In *Gary B.* v. *Cronin*, No. 79-C-5383 (N.D. Ill. 1980), emotionally disturbed children alleged that they had been denied a free appropriate public education because the defendants had failed to provide them with counseling and therapeutic services. The court held that "while psychotherapy may be related to mental health, it also may be required before a child can derive any benefit from education" (at 4–5). Therefore, these services should be considered part of the child's *educational* needs and provided at no cost to parents.

In *Tatro* v. *State of Texas*, 625 F.2d 557 (5th Cir. 1980), the plaintiffs alleged that catheterization services were among the "related services" required by Public Law 94-142 and Section 504 of the Rehabilitation Act. The case involved five-year-old Amber Tatro, who had been born with spinal bifida. Her birth defect caused a bladder condition requiring catheterization every three or four hours. This treatment was provided through a procedure known as clean intermittent catheterization (CIC), a procedure that need not be performed in a sterile environment and that a person could learn to perform in less than an hour. The parents requested that the school district provide the catheterization for Amber at no cost and that the procedure be part of her IEP. The district declined. A hearing officer found that the procedure was a "related service . . . required to assist a handicapped child to benefit from special education." This finding was affirmed by the state commissioner of education but overruled by the state department of education. The parents then filed suit in federal court. That court found that CIC was a related "school health service" and not a medical service.

Confusion still exists as to what constitutes a related service. The list of related services in Public Law 94-142 is not exhaustive, and it does include categories that arguably encompass formerly noneducational services. The statutory definition is qualified by the phrase "as may be required to assist a handicapped child to benefit from special education." Courts have struggled to understand and use this limitation. If a child can still benefit from his program without the service, then it may not be "required." But courts do not have the expertise to decide what is basically an educational issue. Given the ambiguity surrounding the expression "related services," it is easy to comprehend why there is so much litigation in this area.

Another area in which there has been appreciable litigation involves disciplinary proceedings and the handicapped student. In one such case, *Blue* v. *New Haven Board of Education*, Civ. No. N-81-41 (D. Conn. 1981), the action was brought by a sixteen-year-old emotionally disturbed student challenging the disciplinary procedures employed by the school district against him. The court found that because responsibility for changing the placement of handicapped students rests with a group of trained professionals knowledgeable about evaluation data and placement options, the plaintiff was entitled to have his educational placement changed by the pupil placement team, and not through the school's normal disciplinary procedures. The defendant's action in placing the student on home-bound instruction pending an expulsion hearing and seeking to place him in an alternative educational setting following his expulsion deprived him of his right to an education in the least restrictive environment. Expulsion would have the effect of excluding the plaintiff from a placement that was appropriate for him and restricting the availability of alternative placement in violation of Public Law 94-142.

In *S-1* v. *Turlington,* 635 F.2d 342 (5th Cir. 1981), nine mentally retarded children were expelled for alleged misconduct for the remainder of the 1977-78 school year and for the entire 1978-79 school year. The court found that under Section 504 no handicapped student may be expelled for misconduct that results from or is related to his or her handicap. An expulsion of a handicapped child resulting in a termination of educational services constitutes a change in educational placement and requires the application of the procedural protections of Public Law 94-142. Expulsion was found to be a proper disciplinary tool under Public Law 94-142 and Section 504 when proper procedures were utilized and under proper circumstances. The court went on to hold that the burden was on the school district to determine whether the student's misconduct was a manifestation of his handicap.

Conclusion

Human services professionals have long-term involvement with handicapped children and their parents. In order to serve their client population effectively, human services professionals must be familiar with the scope of the rights of handicapped children. They can best advocate for these children if they understand those essential services to which these children are entitled. They can best counsel with parents and children if they can accurately assess whether mandated opportunities are being afforded to the children.

The goal of professionals who work with handicapped children—the physicians, physical therapists, educators, and human services providers—is to maximize the potential of these children. One essential way to maximize potential is through education. Education is often symbolically presented as a key—to unlock the future—and a light—to show the way. It is this and more for the handicapped child who does not learn through normal channels. For this reason all who work with handicapped children must be totally familiar with their right to an education, so that they can ensure that these children are afforded this right.

Robert Henley Woody   # 10

Professional Responsibilities and Liabilities

The relationship established between the client or patient and the human services professional is vested with many features that set it apart from all other human relationships. Foremost, the entire relationship is devoted, at least ostensibly, to promoting the welfare of the client. Because of this unilateral service objective, public policy has cast a protective net around what transpires in the relationship. Notwithstanding this protection, public policy also prescribes that the net must be rent on occasion—and these occasions may be beyond the personal preference of either the client or the professional. Having this self-determination removed often leads to dissatisfaction with how the professional relationship is handled, and the client and the society are given means by which to seek legal remedies.

This chapter will explore four critical dimensions of the human services professional relationship: informed consent, privileged communication, the duty to warn, and professional malpractice. Analysis and understanding of these dimensions will improve the client's welfare and help the human services professional avoid unnecessary legal actions. (For additional discussion of these dimensions, see Schutz, 1982; Van Hoose and Kottler, 1977, chap. 5.)

Informed Consent

Consent to receiving or being administered human services, particularly when they are in the realm of diagnostics and therapeutics, creates a composite of legal issues. The composite contains such diverse considerations as constitutional rights and contract law. Since many of these factors must be interpreted by judicial decisions tailored to a set of circumstances, as opposed to having some definite legislative document that provides an incontrovertible service framework, human services professionals are commonly left to let good intentions provide their only safeguard against legal liability.

Involuntarily committed mental patients, because of their "patient" status, have long been subjected to excursions by professionals into their constitutional rights (Robitscher, 1966). Historically, the legal posture has been that, once committed, a mental patient is incapable of individual decision making; consequently, the choice of administering a treatment was left to the professional, not the patient. Now, however, the courts have directed that patients must give "informed consent" before they enter treatment.

Informed consent "is one in which the patient has received sufficient information from his physician concerning the health care proposed, its incumbent risks, and the acceptable alternatives to that care so that the patient can participate and make an intelligent, rational decision about himself" (Hemelt and Mackert, 1978, p. 94). For the human services professional, "the ideology of *informed* consent is of paramount importance . . . because of the profession's commitment to individual autonomy and to facilitating reasoned decision making. An understanding of the need to deal with the whole person is becoming a concern for all professions involved with matters of informed consent. . . . The right to know when you are sick what is happening to you, how it is happening, by whom, and under what conditions of risk, is a basic human need" (Parry, 1981, p. 537). In other words, a patient's personal integrity is enhanced when he is given responsibility for consenting to treatment. The act of giving consent, in turn, becomes one of the essential conditions for psychotherapeutic advancement; that is, the patient internalizes responsibility for his being, even when he is overtly under the care and control of a professional.

The importance of informed consent underlies the American Hospital Association's (1973) *Patient's Bill of Rights.* Similarly, a U.S. Department of Health, Education and Welfare (1971) position statement stresses that human subjects who are to be used in research projects must be competent to consent, must give voluntary consent, and must receive adequate information about what will transpire.

In spite of these authoritative pronouncements, not all professionals endorse informed consent. Amazingly, many professionals, perhaps because of the notion that "doctor knows best," still refuse to give patients all the information they need if they are to be involved in the choice of treatment (Kelly, 1976; Parry, 1981); and in mental hospitals many treating physicians are even reluctant to allow attorneys access to mental patients (Brakel, 1981b). Such professionals, for whatever motive, have kept hospital patients from having communications that might influence their understanding of the treatment and might thus alter their consent. In one case a psychiatrist offered to eliminate the charges for treatment if the patient would agree not to talk with an attorney about the quality of treatment and whether or not his rights had been upheld. In other instances hospital personnel have been rude to attorneys and constructed logistical barriers to their visiting with clients.

As is often the outcome when professionals fail to live up to the expectations directed at them by society, legislatures have moved more and more toward prescribing the required approach to informed consent. As an example and as mentioned in Chapter One, portions of the *Florida Statutes* are devoted to patient's rights: "All persons entering a facility shall be asked to give express and informed consent for treatment after disclosure to the patient if he is competent, or his guardian if he is a minor or is incompetent, of the purpose of the treatment to be provided, the common side effects thereof, alternative treatment modalities, the approximate length of care, and that any consent given by a patient may be revoked orally or in writing prior to or during the treatment period by the patient or his guardian" (Fla. Stat. sec. 394.459(3)). Statutes may specify that the professional can require treatment, but only on an emergency basis and for the safety and health of the patient or others. Even here, there has been public uneasiness about allowing professional discretion, and in some jurisdictions emergency treatments that cannot or will not be consented to by a mental patient must be reviewed by an objective third party, such as a professional (or mental health team) other than the treating source.

The professional should be the last person to object to a requirement of informed consent. If anything, the professional should reach to the maximum allowed by public policy to ensure that the service recipient does, in fact, understand and consent to the treatment. To do otherwise is to court a disciplinary action for unethical conduct and/or a legal suit for malpractice (in one of several possible forms, to be discussed later).

The rights of patients—both "involuntary" patients and voluntary patients whose needs are not being met—have been explored in depth in Chapter Eight. In this chapter comment on the topic is necessary only as a reminder of its importance to the professional relationship, such as in professional responsibility and liability.

The right to treatment finds solid justification in social and legal theory: "The rationale for the right to treatment is clear. If society confines a man for the benevolent purpose of helping him— "for his own good," in the standard phrase—then its right to so withhold his freedom depends entirely upon whether help is in fact provided. It may be that the person is not treatable or that the treatment effort is too costly in light of the chances of success. If this is the view of the professional, it should be spread clearly upon the record so that we do not delude ourselves by calling these unfortunates 'patients'" (Bazelon, 1970, p. 102). The legal underpinnings for the right to treatment are in constitutional law. Schwitzgebel and Schwitzgebel (1980, p. 51) identify "three constitutional grounds: cruel and unusual punishment, equal protection, and due process." From this unequaled authority, the United States Constitution, judicial opinions proscribe and prescribe the conditions for patients.

Maintaining the conditions for treatment at an acceptable qualitative level can be a problem. In a landmark Alabama case, *Wyatt* v. *Stickney*, 325 F. Supp. 781 (M.D. Ala. 1971), (enforced in 334 F. Supp. 1341 (M.D. Ala. 1971), 344 F. Supp. 373 (M.D. Ala. 1972), affirmed under the name *Wyatt* v. *Aderholt*, 503 F.2d 1305 (5th Cir. 1974)), the court connected the right to treatment with the quality of treatment. (See the extended discussion of *Wyatt* in Chapter Eight.) It therefore issued a judicial order mandating such details as space, the number of professionals for a given patient population, and the training required for the professionals. Thus, resources become an issue.

The scientific stature of the treatment also becomes an issue: "Treatment is not likely to be adequate, appropriate, or suitable if it is not also 'effective' in achieving a primary goal of the commitment process: namely, the restoration of the patient to normal mental functioning and . . . to satisfactory living in the community" (Schwitzgebel and Schwitzgebel, 1980, p. 52). Given the widely heralded battles over the efficacy of therapeutic interventions (Woody, 1971), it seems dubious that any human services professional can proceed with treatment and be totally certain that its quality is, unquestionably, compatible with the legal expectations for adequacy.

In addition to a right to treatment, the courts have spoken decisively in favor of a constitutional right to refuse treatment. For practice purposes the guideline should be: "Treatment should probably not be forced upon a committed but legally competent mental patient who refuses treatment unless there has been a prior judicial review" (Schwitzgebel and Schwitzgebel, 1980, p. 53). In any case, the prudent approach is to honor the doctrine of the least restrictive alternative, meaning that whatever treatment approach is offered or imposed should carry the minimal possible infringement or adverse consequences. There must be a careful weighing of the positive and negatives, and the selection of treatment should be to maximize benefits at the minimum of risks.

Because of the patient's right to refuse treatment, the professional is, in effect, "stripped of authority to force individuals to submit to psychological interventions [and therefore] must deal with individuals committed to institutions in the same manner as [he] does with any other individual. . . . As with all other patients seen by the mental health professional, the committed patient must be given all information at the professional's disposal that the patient requires to make a reasonable, intelligent decision regarding choice of treatment. This includes not only information about the patient's condition, but also about alternative courses of treatment and the potential advantages and disadvantages and dangers of each.

The patient's informed consent to a specific treatment plan must be obtained, and the treatment must be terminated at the patient's demand" (White and White, 1981, p. 959). For the traditionalist (read "old-fashioned") professional, this requirement may seem an affront to expertise. It is actually, however, a redefinition of professionalism. The human services practitioner must accept the fact that the ultimate responsibility for treatment rests with the recipient and that human dignity requires freedom of choice and a professional who can meet unique health needs. Florida statutory language spells out this definition: "Each patient in a facility shall receive treatment suited to his needs, which shall be administered skillfully, safely, and humanely with full respect for his dignity and personal integrity" (Fla. Stat. sec. 394.459(4) (a)).

Again, recognition of informed consent—with its powerful nexus to the legally endorsed right to treatment and right to refuse treatment—is a cornerstone for professional responsibility. Failure to fulfill this standard is to jeopardize one's professional liability.

Whether in an institution or in the private practitioner's office, the final goal is to equip the patient or client to exercise informed consent in a manner consonant with public policy, ethics, and the law. Margolin (1982, p. 794) provides a reasonable set of guidelines for attaining informed consent: "(a) an explanation of the procedures and their purpose, (b) the role of the person who is providing therapy and his or her professional qualifications, (c) discomforts or risks reasonably to be expected, (d) benefits reasonably to be expected, (e) alternatives to treatment that might be of similar benefit, (f) a statement that any question about the procedures will be answered at any time, and (g) a statement that the person can withdraw his or her consent and discontinue participation in therapy or testing at any time." Unless these guidelines are adequately followed, the human services professional runs the risk of an eventual ethical or legal action based on lack of informed consent.

In most instances the professional need only discuss the foregoing issues (inherent to the guidelines) with the client (and record what was discussed in the case notes). This should be done, of course, at any early point in the treatment and should be modified immediately whenever new considerations arise. In some instances it may be necessary to write out the issues and have the client give written approval. These "contracts," however, may be vulnerable in the event of a legal action. That is, if there is any evidence that the powerful influence wielded by the professional was inappropriately used to misinform a client or to coercively extract acceptance from the client, such evidence will certainly be used against the professional. For example, if the therapist fully informed a client of a therapeutic intervention—and if that intervention was "unconscionable" in the eyes of the court, as deduced from public policy—the client's written informed consent might be set aside as a way of shaping the professional's conduct and safeguarding the public against similar unconscionable activities by professionals. Similarly, as Margolin (1982) points out, informed consent obtained from a participant in marital and family therapy who is there merely to appease another family member might also be regarded as coercion and consequently set aside.

The professional must exercise reasonable effort to be sure that all persons receiving treatment of any form do, in fact, accept the treatment without any condition that would denigrate the kind of informed consent required by public policy, ethics, and the law. To proceed into treatment without informed consent is foolish and irresponsible.

Privileged Communication

In human services a client's communication is protected by two types of law: confidentiality and privileged communication (DeKraai and Sales, 1982). The former, with roots in professional codes of ethics, becomes of legal concern through legislative recognition and court decisions. Disclosure of confidential information could be the basis for professional discipline (through an ethics complaint) or legal action (through civil or criminal liability).

Confidentiality does not prevent the professional from testifying in a court of law; such a prohibition would require statutory authority for establishing privileged communication. Even then there would be exceptions. Fisher (1964) recognizes three exceptions to the therapist's honoring privileged communication: when the court appoints a psychologist to perform an examination; when professonal opinion about mental or emotional problems may be necessary to assure proper legal handling or justice; and when the client bases a legal claim or defense on his or her mental condition (note that these exceptions are often incorporated into statutes).

Wigmore ([1913] 1940, vol. 8, p. 531) delineates the criteria that would justify confidentiality: "(1) the communications must originate in a confidence that they will not be disclosed; (2) this element of confidentiality must be essential to the full and satisfactory maintenance of the relation between the parties; (3) the relation must be one which in the opinion of the community must be sedulously fostered; and (4) the injury that would inure to the relation by disclosure of the communications must be greater than the benefit thereby gained for the correct disposal of the litigation." Unless these four criteria are fulfilled, confidentiality cannot be justly expected, and failure to establish confidentiality negates the possibility of privileged communication.

Privilege refers to "a freedom from compulsion to give evidence or to discover-up material, or a right to prevent or bar information from other sources, during or with a view of litigation, but on grounds extrinsic to the goals of litigation" (Rothstein, 1970, p. 303). In other words, persons may have a right to keep certain information from legal proceedings and to restrict the access of others to information about themselves, but in certain situations public policy may require that the privilege be set aside.

Although confidentiality is endorsed by the constitutional right to privacy, such confidentiality has to be reasonably expected. That is, if one were to stand before a general audience of thirty people—for instance, at a political rally or a public lecture—and say, "Now don't tell anyone, keep this confidential," and then proceed to tell a personal bit of information, he or she could not *reasonably* expect that confidentiality to be maintained. If, on the other hand, the thirty people in the audience shared a common employment commitment—for instance, if they were all law enforcement personnel or members of a hospital staff—statements about the confidential information would be reasonable.

The right to privacy also requires conditions that would justify it. For example, the right of privacy has often been extended to legal cases that allege a governmental violation of privacy in marriage. If the conditions surrounding the intrusion are truly in the realm of the marital privacy, constitutional support is found. Consider the case of *Lovisi* v. *Slayton*, 539 F.2d 349 (4th Cir. 1976). Aldo and Margaret Lovisi, husband and wife, were convicted of sodomy with each other, and they challenged the constitutionality of the state statute. They based their challenge on a right to privacy. It seems that they had placed advertisements in a "swinger's" magazine for sex partners and allowed a man who responded to the advertisement to take Polaroid pictures of them performing fellatio (while two daughters witnessed the act). The constitutional defense came from *Roe* v. *Wade*, 410 U.S. 113 (1973), where the Supreme Court stated that the personal intimacies of marriage, the home, procreation, motherhood, childbearing, and the family are "fundamental" and encompassed within the protected rights of privacy. In *Lovisi*, however, a federal appeals court held that "once they accept onlookers, whether they are close friends, chance acquaintances, observed 'peeping Toms', or paying customers, they may not exclude the state as a constitutionally forbidden intruder" (at 351). There was no reasonable expectation of marital privacy with the third person present. This same principle applies to psychotherapy. While there may be a reasonable expectation of privacy between a client and the therapist, group therapy or marriage therapy, with other persons being involved, could potentially create conditions that negate a reasonable expectation of privacy and/or confidentiality.

The most common idea for the context of human services is that a client has a right to confidentiality. That may be true, but the "right" comes from legislative enactments, not from constitutional bases (Slovenko, 1973; Lempert and Saltzburg, 1977). Even then, confidentiality, with its expectancy for privacy, does not always reach to the level of privileged communication. Privileged communication is a statutory declaration of a right to keep certain information, as long as it conforms to the reasonable basis of privacy and confidentiality, from legal proceedings. Often there is gross misunderstanding about the existence of privileged communication, and seldom is there a realistic knowledge of how even information that is privileged by statute can still be brought into legal proceedings via the rules of evidence and procedure.

Trainees in the human services are frequently misled into believing that, because they assure their clients that their sessions are confidential, they will be immune from revealing the communications. That is not true. To be immune, even to the slightest extent, one must have an established membership (such as by being licensed) in a professional discipline that is specified by state statute as having privileged communication. As mentioned in Chapter One, for example, the *Florida Statutes* give privileged communication to the lawyer-client, psychotherapist-patient, clergyman-parishioner, and accountant-client relationship. Contrary to popular misconception, the physician-patient relationship (in Florida) does not receive privileged communication unless the physician is treating an emotional or mental problem and thereby qualifies under the psychotherapist subsection.

At this juncture, it is important to underscore that the professional does not have privileged communication; the recipient of services has the privilege, and it can be either waived or invoked. According to Rothstein (1970, pp. 318-319), there may be "two types of 'holders' of a privilege that is intended to encourage accurate communication of potentially self-damaging information. The primary holder is the one whose immediate interests are harmed if disclosure occurs. He is the communicator. It is he whom the laws seek to encourage. His assertion or express waiver of the privilege should thus always prevail over anyone else's wishes, including those of a secondary holder. A secondary holder is one who is allowed to assert the privilege in certain instances where the primary holder is unable to assert the privilege for himself." Stated differently, the human services professional is not at liberty to invoke privileged communication—that must be done by the client. However, if the client is suing the professional, the privileged communication surrounding the relationship disappears, and the professional is free to communicate anything to a source relevant to the legal action. Moreover, the professional is free to set aside the privileged communication if there is a substantial threat to the safety and welfare of the client and/or others. That is, the professional has a "duty to warn" (as discussed later in this chapter).

The public policy that justifies privileged communication comes from the belief that "some values are . . . important enough to justify restrictions on the search for truth" (Lempert and Saltzburg, 1977, p. 606). This public policy has, however, come under repeated attacks, and the modern trend seems to be clearly toward setting aside these once sacrosanct personal privileges.

Aside from the duty to warn for the welfare of the society and the person, public policy has endorsed third-party payments for health services. In such instances there can be no reasonable expectancy of privacy. When a client submits the bill for human services to his insurance company for reimbursement, there is an implicit (and often explicit) waiver of confidentiality and privileged communication. That is, information required by the insurance company to jusify reimbursement—for instance, a psychiatric diagnosis—will not be treated with the sanctity of the protective nature of the professional relationship. Furthermore, some employers, by virtue of paying all or part of the health insurance costs, acquire a right to information that would otherwise be privileged.

Of most concern for human services professionals is privileged communication for psychotherapeutic interventions. For a variety of reasons, the psychotherapist-patient section was not included in the *Federal Rules of Evidence* but was offered as an option for adoption at the state level. State versions typically limit the professionals covered by this section. For example, the *Florida Statutes* (sec. 90.503) define a psychotherapist as a licensed physician or psychologist (although the licensure or certification need not be from Florida but may be "under the laws of any state or nation").

Even if covered by a privileged communication statute, the human services professional may still have to release information that would otherwise be privileged. Rule 35 of the *Federal Rules of Civil Procedure* allows a court to order a physical or mental examination when those conditions are at issue, and all information must be made available to both sides of the legal dispute. Similar rules at the state level allow for court-ordered examinations.

What if the professional does not want to release all the information? He or she can ask the court to allow submission of an abridged version of the results—because, for instance, the client might not be able to handle the confrontation with a specific diagnostic label. In all but the most rare instances, however, the court will not accept such a request (unless the requested abridgment allows for an equal degree of justice to be accomplished).

There are practical means for handling this situation. Donnelly (1978, pp. 203–204) states: "Data should be recorded always with the possibility in mind that the record may be open to inspection by other persons, including those in a court of law, so that statements potentially damaging to the patient in any of a range of circumstances will be avoided. . . . Thus, from the viewpoints of both patient care and training, there is no need to record the innermost secrets of the patient nor to detail fantasies, erotic or otherwise, about which so much concern is expressed. The English language is particularly suited to the selection of words which, while vague and nonspecific to the nonprofessional, alert a psychiatrist to areas he may wish to explore with the patient." This is the view of one psychiatrist. It may not be shared by other professionals and would likely be disputed by legalists.

While Donnelly's view is certainly understandable from the vantage point of preserving the professional tenets of treatment (for example, the patient's assurance that the doctor will put the patient's welfare ahead of all else), the public policy for maximizing information for justice and fair play could be potentially circumvented by incomplete records of evidence. A more contemporary public policy stance would be to record all pertinent information, recognizing that justice supersedes personal privacy. Any ploys to conceal information—for example, by "keeping a special set of more detailed notes at home under my bed" are socially unethical and demonstrate a lack of respect for the rules of evidence.

The legal system has established means for opening the previously privileged communications to the eyes and ears of those seeking justice. This means that the professional must yield any information appropriately sought by the court. To offer information, the initial move could be by the client through a waiver. Any holder of privileged communication can knowingly waive the right—through a signed release form (which is common practice in mental health facilities) or through the introduction of a mental status issue into judicial proceedings (referred to in legal circles as "opening the door"). Once the door has been figuratively opened on an issue, the party-opponent has a right to plunge through and gain access to any and all information, privileged or otherwise, that relates materially to that issue.

A second move may be made through subpoena. This amounts to a court order that information be provided to the party-opponent. When subpoenaed, the professional must yield the information regardless of the client's preference. In other words, the client may object to the professional's providing information, but the subpoena controls the decision. Subpoenas may be used for two reasons. First, the professional may actually prefer to testify only if subpoenaed, because this creates a legal mandate to breach the privileged communication and will make the professional immune to any objections or claims or legal actions leveled by the client. Second, some attorneys for the party-opponent will strive to intimidate the professional; they believe that being served a subpoena by the sheriff will "shake up" the professional and adversely affect his or her testimony. Professionals should keep in mind, therefore, that a subpoena is simply a court order for the production of information. It contains no allegations and need not be endowed with any positive or negative connotation.

The professional cannot refuse to cooperate with a subpoena on the ground that the psychotherapeutic process will be contradicted by the therapist's speaking out. Public policy has clearly relegated these arguments to a position secondary to the goal of maximizing fair play in the judicial process by bringing in all relevant information (note the later discussion of the *Tarasoff* case). The professional may, however, question whether providing the information will do more harm than good. Responding respectfully to a subpoena, the professional can set forth a reasoned request to withhold certain information to avoid hurting someone—the client or someone else—and asserting that justice will not be substantially furthered if the full account (as opposed, perhaps, to a summary) is entered into the record. If the court deems that the subpoena must be met (by issuing an order to produce), the professional should forthwith produce any and all information specified. To do otherwise would potentially mean being held in contempt of court. Similarly, to "conveniently forget" information during the process of giving testimony could potentially be perjury.

The release of human services records to certain individuals may be legitimately questioned. Legally, a subpoena can require any and all records—such as original test protocols—relevant to the matter. However, the court might allow a clinical psychologist to withhold certain protocols—such as the Rorschach, Thematic Apperception Test, or Wechsler Adult Intelligence Scale protocols—from a witness for the party-opponent who did not meet licensing standards in the state for using those instruments and who was seeking them to provide impeachment or contradictory testimony. In a child custody case, for example, the attorney for the mother wanted the father's psychologist to photocopy test protocols and turn them over to a marriage and family counselor (one without a doctorate of any kind and without any licensure or certification). The psychologist's objection to turning these tests over to anyone other than a licensed psychologist proved to be persuasive, and the request was denied.

The courts have held that professionals have a "limited property right" in their records, such as test protocols. This means that if a client wants all records destroyed—for instance, to avoid discovery by a party-opponent in an approaching legal action—the professional does not have to comply with the demand. In fact, the professional would be foolish to do so. He or she could be charged with purposefully destroying evidence, with all the possible sanctions that could accordingly be imposed, and could also incur personal liability if, for example, the records were later needed as a defense in a malpractice action brought by the client. As an example, one client had been told the results of her psychological tests by her therapist and, despite efforts by the therapist to resolve her paranoid reactions, demanded that the therapist turn over the entire file to her to be destroyed. Both the therapist and the client sought legal counsel, and both received the same legal advice—namely, that the therapist has a right to the test protocols and is justified in retaining them for professional and personal protection (but would, of course, keep them confidential).

Retention of records can be jeopardized by the so-called "best evidence" rule. The *Florida Statutes*, for example, state: "Except as otherwise provided by statute, an original writing, recording, or photograph is required in order to prove the contents of the

writing, recording, or photograph" (sec. 90.952). With a few exceptions, however, duplicates are "admissible to the same extent as an
original" (sec. 90.953). The "best evidence" rule translates into
warning the professional that records brought to the court may be
"taken away" to become part of the court record. Therefore, before
appearing for a deposition, court appearance, or otherwise, the prudent professional should prepare one or more sets of duplicates of
any and all materials, thereby allowing him or her to retain the
original records without having to copy them later from the court
record. The admissibility of duplicates usually requires only that the
professional certify, either by written affidavit or verbally during testimony, that the duplicates are, in fact, true copies of the originals.

The professional is entitled to charge a reasonable fee for any
activity associated with the legal proceedings. Thus, the costs for
photocopying records, preparing a report, participating in a deposition, or giving courtroom testimony should be billed at an established rate. Some attorneys for the party-opponent might try to
minimize expense to their clients by claiming that the only fee legally required is the one paid to lay persons subpoenaed to testify.
Although a few jurisdictions do impose the lay person fee on a
professional giving testimony (or whatever), in most jurisdictions
the court will order payment of the established professional fee for
case-related services (or for a uniform per deum professional fee).

In addition to information subpoenaed for legal proceedings,
there may be statutory requirements for the human services professional to breach confidentiality. Many statutes specify that professionals must notify health or law enforcement authorities of clients
who have contagious diseases, are drug dependent, or are involved
in child abuse. The statutes typically include an express immunity
from legal action for any professional who, in good faith, attempts
to comply with this statutorily required breach of confidentiality
(and the statutes may include a penalty for those who do not comply
with the reporting requirement).

Information given because of a statutory requirement or a
court order removes the professional from any kind of liability for
alleged breach of confidentiality. Otherwise, the professional might
be subject to various types of legal actions—namely, suits charging
defamation, invasion of privacy, or breach of contract.

388   The Law and the Practice of Human Services

Defamatory language (as alleged in slander or libel suits) is
language that blemishes the client's honesty, integrity, virtue, sanity, or any other personal characteristic that could potentially create
damage. The defamatory statement must go to a third person
(known as "publication") and must be made either intentionally or
negligently. It is no defense to claim "I had no idea that I was
defaming." It may, however, be a defense if the comments were true,
known to a number of others, and not made with malice.

Many legal distinctions are made to establish whether a defamation charge is actionable. Among these distinctions are the type
of person involved (such as a public figure versus a private individual) and the context in which the comments were made (for instance, a professional making seemingly negative comments about a
client during a staff meeting would probably be privileged to do so,
but to utter the same comments at a party could be a basis for a legal
action).

A defamation suit typically must establish that the person
has, in fact, suffered damages, and these often have to be computed
as an out-of-pocket loss. But damage to reputation and standing in
the community, mental anguish and suffering, and so on, may also
be viewed by the court as damages and transposed into a dollar
figure. If the plaintiff can prove that the defendant made the defamatory statements with knowledge of their falsity or with reckless disregard for the truth, the court is likely to presume damages (which,
in some states, may be "punitive"—to teach the professional a
lesson).

In addition to the legal sanctions for a breach of confidentiality that results in defamation, the codes of ethics for the human
service disciplines are replete with restrictions on such statements.
This is one area where the prudent professional must err on the side
of conservativism: Do not talk about clients except with helpful
intent and in contexts associated with professional services.

A tort action alleging invasion of privacy might be brought
against a person who uses a picture or the name of a client (or any
other person) for commercial advantage (such as publishing the
picture or name in a book without express permission), intrudes
into the client's affairs or seclusion, publishes facts that place the
client in a false light, and makes public disclosures of private facts
about a client.

An alleged breach of confidentiality can also be the basis for a suit in contract because the professional human services relationship creates an implied, if not express, contractual relationship that encompasses confidentiality. If the professional has failed to fulfill all terms of a contract, a court might levy damages to "make the claimant whole."

While damages are commonly thought of in terms of money, the penalty will typically go far beyond dollars. For example, one's license to practice could be revoked, especially if the breach of confidentiality were willful or malicious in purpose. Professional associations could impose sanctions, such as a censure made before the total membership or the removal of certification and/or membership therein. Perhaps the most damaging consequence of such a charge—whether proved or not—is that the professional suffers a loss of credibility in the community. To illustrate the wide-ranging effects, one professional was alleged to have breached confidentiality by making comments about a client's criminal conduct. Although the professional's comments were true and were restricted to criminal conduct that was on the public record, the client thought they were slanderous and filed a legal action. After discovery procedures, it became evident that the professional had not, in fact, breached confidentiality or made slanderous comments, and the plaintiff agreed to drop his suit. In the meantime, however, the professional had spent about two thousand dollars in legal fees counteracting the suit, and the professional grapevine carried the story to colleagues in a manner that probably tarnished her professional image. As a result, her professional credibility began to be questioned, even though she was not guilty of any legal wrong. Clearly, professionalism carries a unique duty to safeguard information. Legal actions against a professional can be costly in terms of monetary damages as well as diminution of reputation.

Duty to Warn

There was a time when whatever was said during psychotherapy was awarded sacrosanct protection from being revealed to anyone else. Theories of psychotherapy were developed around the tenet that an iron-clad guarantee of confidentiality is essential to therapeutic progress. As public policy evolved toward a different stance on confidentiality—namely, that justice is best served when all relevant information is brought in—the very essence of psychotheraphy came under attack. The courts have made it clear that the welfare and safety of the client and of others come before confidentiality for the therapy relationship. In order to clarify the evolution of this legal position, three cases should be reviewed.

In *Merchants National Bank and Trust Co. of Fargo* v. *United States*, 272 F. Supp. 409 (D.N.D. 1967), a mental patient, hospitalized for a considerable length of time in a Veterans Administration hospital, was released on a work placement. Precautions were not taken to prevent his leaving his placement, and so he returned to his home town and killed his wife—something that many persons had warned the treatment team would happen if the patient were not supervised and restricted. The court held that the hospital staff were "tortiously negligent" and that their failure to diagnose the dangerousness posed by this patient constituted "gross negligence."

In the hallmark case in this area, *Tarasoff* v. *Regents of the University of California*, 17 Cal. 3d 425, 551 P.2d 334, 131 Cal. Rptr. 14 (1976), a university-based psychologist was told by a client that he intended to harm a girlfriend. Although some effort was made to hospitalize him, the client remained free, the victim was not warned, and the client subsequently killed her. The girl's parents brought suit against the university, charging negligence by hospital personnel. The California Supreme Court held: "Once a therapist does in fact determine, or under applicable professional standards reasonably should have determined, that a patient poses a serious danger of violence to others, he bears a duty to exercise reasonable care to protect the foreseeable victim of that danger. While the discharge of this duty of due care will necessarily vary with the facts of each case, in each instance the adequacy of the therapist's conduct must be measured against the traditional negligence standard of this rendition of reasonable care under the circumstances." (17 Cal. 3d 358, at 440). At the same time, the court recognized "the difficulty that a therapist encounters in attempting to forecast whether a patient presents a serious danger of violence. Obviously we do not require that the therapist, in making that determination, render a perfect performance; the therapist need only exercise that reasonable degree of skill, knowledge, and care ordinarily possessed and exercised by members of that professional specialty under similar circumstances" (at 438). The court noted that the psychotherapeutic dialogue should be confidential and that the therapist should "not disclose a confidence unless such disclosure is necessary to avert danger to others, and even then . . . he [should] do so discreetly, and in a fashion that would preserve the privacy of the patient to the fullest extent compatible with the prevention of the threatened danger. . . . In this risk-infested society we can hardly tolerate the further exposure to danger that would result from a concealed knowledge of the therapist that his patient was lethal" (at 441–442).

As a follow-up to *Tarasoff, McIntosh* v. *Milano*, 403 A.2d 500 (N.J. Super. Ct. 1979), involved a psychiatrist's failure to prevent a fifteen-year-old patient from killing his girlfried, even though he knew of the threats and the youth's potential to carry them out. The psychiatrist also failed to warn the victim. As in *Tarasoff,* the court held that the welfare of the victim and the community must come before confidentiality and that, even though complete accuracy in prediction is impossible, therapists must make an effort to predict. A review of the post-*Tarasoff* cases indicates that the matter is not settled and that states are making individualized interpretations. Some states, following *Tarasoff,* require that the professional warn the victim; others require that the warning go to the police or another responsible third-party source. Similarly, Knapp and VandeCreek (1982, p. 516) have noted that one court "refused to extend the duty to protect suicidal persons," and that courts "have differed as to the liability when patients have harmed persons who were not specifically threatened." They conclude, however, "that most but not all courts have found *Tarasoff* applicable to their jurisdiction."

In one post-*Tarasoff* case (*Lipari* v. *Sears, Roebuck,* 497 F. Supp. 185 (D. Neb. 1980)), a mental patient who had been under long-term treatment in a Veterans Administration hospital had bought a gun (from Sears, Roebuck, which then filed a third-party complaint against the hospital for being negligent in dealing with a dangerous person) and shot and killed one person and wounded numerous others. Since the hospital personnel were aware that he had purchased a shotgun, it was alleged that the treatment team had acted unreasonably in failing to involuntarily hospitalize the patient and/or remove the shotgun from his possession. The court refused specifically to rule that a reasonable therapist would never be required to take precautions other than warnings or that there is never a duty to attempt to detain a patient. Instead, basing its opinion on its interpretation of Nebraska law, the court held that the relationship between a psychotherapist and his patient gives rise to an affirmative duty for the benefit of third persons; this duty requires the therapist to initiate whatever precautions are necessary to protect potential victims of his patient. As might be expected, the duty arises only when the therapist knows or should know that his patient's dangerous propensities present an unreasonable risk of harm to others.

While these are the landmark cases, there have been numerous other comparable cases—many of which do not appear in print because of out-of-court settlements. To be sure, this body of law is still evolving and should not be considered fixed. At this time, however, the court's message seems clear: The safety and welfare of others must be protected, even if it is at the expense of the confidentiality of psychotherapy. This protection involves a duty to warn and a duty to predict dangerousness to others or to the client, and failure to fulfill this duty can result in professional liability (*Frank* v. *State of Utah*, 613 P.2d 517 (Utah) (1980)).

Without doubt, the prediction of dangerousness is unsure. However, as summarized by Walters (1980), substantial research has been conducted in this area. Furthermore, public policy maintains that the benefits of being deemed a professional entail a concomitant duty to predict. Failure to accomplish this charge is to leave one's professional functioning vulnerable to legal attack.

Professional Malpractice

One of the heaviest words in professional practice today is "malpractice." It is public policy, however, to hold professionals, regardless of discipline, accountable for the quality of their services. Some human services professionals are aghast that the legal system is intervening on their turf. Their position is that professionals should be responsible for their own regulation, with no outside governors. Many people believe, however, that professional self-regulation has "frequently failed to achieve the basic purpose that it was designed to serve. The professions either could not or would not effectively eliminate from their midst those who abused their patients or clients" (Bierig, 1983, p. 617). According to Bierig, the self-regulators have also used this trust for their own interest, as opposed to the public interest. Despite these criticisms, he endorses self-regulation and recommends that antitrust laws "should take greater account of public-spirited motivation and should permit professionals to confront inferior, unnecessary, or injurious practices without substantial fear of imposition of antitrust liability or even of the debilitating costs of plenary antitrust proceedings" (p. 619). For such a recommendation to be effective, professionals would have to be unrelenting in their allegiance to the public interest.

Malpractice constitutes a breach of professional responsibility. The foundation for a legal action is a violation of an established standard of care for the particular professional service, with the outcome being damage to a client.

There is a *duty of care* facing every person at every moment of life. For example, in professional or in private life, one may not create an unreasonable risk of injury to another person. The fundamental question, again in professional or private life, is: What would a reasonable person do in this situation? The "reasonable person" is a mythical being with the same physical characteristics as the defendant (thus, being blind or deaf might enter into establishing the duty of care required) and the amount of knowledge possessed by an average person in the community. Individual mental handicaps are not considered in the standard of care.

As for professional standards of conduct, the practitioner need not be superior but must possess and exercise the knowledge and skill of a member of the profession in good standing: "Professional men in general, and those who undertake any work calling for special skill, are required not only to exercise reasonable care in what they do, but also to possess a standard minimum of special knowledge and ability" (Prosser, 1971, p. 161). Much of the standard of conduct for professional practice comes from legal analyses of the medical profession, but "many of the legal principles governing such actions may apply with equal force to malpractice claims asserted against other health care providers" (King, 1977, p. 7).

The standard that applies to human services professionals in general is contained in Prosser's (1971, p. 162–163) authoritative treatise on torts:

> [The medical professional] does not warrant or insure the outcome of his treatment, and he will not be liable for an honest mistake of judgment, where the proper course is open to reasonable doubt. But by undertaking to render medical services, even though gratuitously, he will ordinarily be understood to hold himself out as having standard professional skill and knowledge. The formula under which this usually is put to the jury is that he must have the skill and learning commonly possessed by members of the profession in good standing; and he will be liable if harm results because he does not have them. Sometimes this is called the skill of the "average" member of the profession; but this is clearly misleading, since only those in good professional standing are to be considered; and of these it is not the middle but the minimum common skill which is to be looked to.

Some practitioners believe that if they practice in a discrete theoretical framework, such as Gestalt therapy, the tenets of that theory, and that theory alone, should determine what is acceptable—and not, for example, the tenets of psychoanalysis or behaviorism. Prosser (1971, p. 163) states: "A 'school' must be a recognized one with definite principles, and it must be the line of thought of at least a respectable minority of the profession. In addition, there are minimum requirements of skill and knowledge as to both diagnosis and treatment, particularly in the light of modern licensing statutes, which anyone who holds himself out as competent to treat human ailments is required to have, regardless of his personal views." This means that a discrete theoretical approach will be considered but that the standards of the discipline in general also will be presented for consideration before the court. Glenn (1974) analyzes nontraditional forms of psychotherapy and concludes that the closest theoretical school would likely be the defining source for the standard of care. Stated differently, it seems doubtful that a human services practitioner, especially one who is licensed as a general practitioner in a particular discipline, could find legal refuge in the confines of a theoretical school, since other theoretical views would enter into the legal analysis of whether the standard of care had been achieved.

Increased legal risk may be associated with new approaches to psychotherapy. Serban (1981, p. 77) believes that new psychotherapeutic approaches are having an impact on the patient-therapist relationship: "In the new modalities of therapy, which basically are a mixture of sensitivity training and behavior-modification techniques, with a touch of popular existentialism, the relationship between the doctor and patient is highly flexible, to the point of improvisation. If in classical therapy the emphasis was on interpretation, in the modern one it has shifted to closeness, empathy, warmth, love, expression of mutual feelings, and bodily contact. With the loose conceptualization of authentic human interaction, the boundary between the professional involvement and a personal one becomes increasingly blurred." In addition to new theories, new contexts for applying human services may elevate legal risk. For example, Knapp and VandeCreek (1981) believe that the holistic framework, with its emphasis on medically oriented procedures, can increase the possibility of malpractice actions against psychologists.

Traditionally, the standard of care for human services practices was based on what other practitioners in the same geographical community would do under the circumstances. This is still the predominant frame of reference; but nationwide certification programs—for example, those of the Academy of Certified Social Workers and the boards that certify "diplomates" in various areas of psychology—are in effect, and there seems to be a trend toward a national standard. This trend has particular relevance to specialization (Shrallow, 1977). In some states local geographically defined criteria are used for the standard of care expected of general practitioners, but for specialists the standard of care is derived from national criteria. Thus, any human services professional who professes to be a "specialist" in a particular area will likely have national standards imposed on his or her practice—even if the professional is not a member of the national association that promulgated standards but has a specialized practice in the area covered by that association's position statements.

Specifications concerning standards of care seem to be increasingly present in state statutes, as opposed to coming from court decisions. In the *Arkansas Statutes Annotated*, actions for medical injuries are defined as "any action against a medical provider, whether based in tort, contract, or otherwise, to recover damages on account of medical injury" (sec. 34-2613 (A)) and "medical care providers" as, among other professionals, psychologists (sec. 34-2613 (B)). How the medical injury (which would include psychological injury) must be proved (sec. 34-2614) and what damages may be recovered (sec. 34-2619) are detailed in the statutes. Finally, the issue of how the standard of care will be determined is stated: "In determining whether the person against whom a malpractice claim has been made has met the applicable standard of care, the hearing panel shall not be bound or limited by the standard of care accepted or established with respect to any particular geographical area or locality, but shall consider only whether the person against whom the claim is made has acted with due care, having in mind the standards and recommended practices and procedures of his profession, and the training, experience, and professed degree of skill by the average practitioner of such profession, and all other relevant circumstances" (sec. 34-2608). This Arkansas example, which is similar to specifications in the statutes of other states, makes it clear that a psychologist (and probably other mental health professionals by implication) faced with a malpractice action would have little room to maneuver a unique standard of care.

The fact that no other comparable practitioner employs a certain safeguard will not constitute an absolute defense. For example, if dangerousness could be predicted by a psychological test (such as elevations on the Psychopathic Deviate and Hysteria scales on the Minnesota Multiphasic Personality Inventory), it would be no sure-fire defense to assert that "no other psychologist in town uses that test." Courts have held that the potential benefit should be weighed against the costs and that an entire profession could be held liable for failing to embrace a reasonable method for enhancing safety and welfare (Prosser, 1971).

Informed consent is the best defense against a charge of malpractice. If the client has been adequately informed of the procedures and has knowingly and intelligently consented to them, the professional is protected if the procedures are properly administered. Documented consent that is truly informed can be a bit difficult, and the prudent practitioner would be well advised to take steps early in the treatment program—for instance, by preparing a written acknowledgment of the procedures, signed by the client or patient—to ensure that there will be no later question about the consent.

Perhaps it could go without saying, but public policy will not accept any attempt by a professional to avoid total liability for his or her practices—for example, by requiring a client to sign an agreement that absolves the professional of all liability before the services are rendered.

The greater public awareness of liability for human services professionals has not yet—at least in the case of psychologists—resulted in "proportionately significant increases in malpractice action" (Wright, 1981a, p. 1485). Nonetheless, this is an era where every practitioner should consider carefully the acquisition of professional liability/malpractice insurance. Even with malpractice insurance, the human services professional may be poorly protected. There are two reasons.

First, some insurance policies cover only the damage portion of a lawsuit. That is, the policy may or may not cover the legal fees. Most lawsuits against psychologists fall in the nuisance category (Wright, 1981b), yet they still must be defended against by acquiring legal representation. If the malpractice insurance policy does not cover legal fees, the professional will have to pay them. The insurance committee for one national human services association estimated that it could average as much as $100,000 in legal fees to defend against even a nuisance suit in (expensive) New York City. It seems doubtful that the average suit would bring on that high of an expense, but even a few thousand dollars can drain much-needed resources away from a practitioner, including those who are perfectly innocent. One can, under some circumstances, petition the court to tax the legal fees to the party-opponent, especially in suits that are clearly nuisance or harassment in nature, but if there is an iota of legal justification for the suit, the court is prone to designate that each party will pay his or her own legal fees.

Second, as Wright (1981b, p. 1535) cautions: "By training, experience, and life-style, psychologists are ill equipped to defend themselves against formal allegation of malpractice, and many well-intentioned actions may actually increase the psychologist's vulnerability in the courtroom." Wright is referring to the human services professional's tendency to be open and to be inclined to confront the accuser in an attempt to "therapeutically resolve" the conflict. This stance is well and good for the therapy relationship, wherein there is only the client and the therapist. But in the legal relationship, the client and the therapist are joined by an attorney for the party-opponent, whose *raison d' être* is maximum advocacy of the client's legal claim against the therapist. The outcome may well be that the therapist provides the opposition with emotions or statements that will lead to a judgment against the therapist. Any time a legal action is brought against a human services professional, all inclinations to take on the legal challenge without an attorney should be avoided. The adage "Anyone who tries to serve as his own lawyer has a fool for a client" has been repeated over and over in the courtroom. The professonal should run, not walk, to a qualified attorney. It seems ironic that a human services professional, who does not hesitate to charge clients a substantial fee, becomes reluctant to pay legal fees.

In accepting employment with any type of hospital, agency, or university, the human services professional should, from the onset, have an express written agreement about the employer's responsibility for providing legal representation and malpractice insurance. Professionals too often assume that their employer will accept these responsibilities—only to find, after a legal action has commenced, that the employer expects the individual to pay for any expenses incurred.

Being employed by an institution, even one supported by public tax dollars, does not ensure that a lawsuit cannot be sustained against the individual. More will be said later about the demise of governmental or sovereign immunity.

A frequent misconception is that malpractice occurs only when there is malicious abuse of a client. Such is not the case. To be sure, in some malpractice actions a therapist has purposefully inflicted danger, harm, or abuse on the client. In other instances, however, a client has misconstrued something that was said or done or, worse yet, has let delusions create a nonexistent happening between the therapist and client. One middle-aged female client, in the first treatment session, asked the psychologist whether he would be having sexual relations with her. When told that such relations were definitely outside the therapeutic relationship and would not occur under any circumstances, she replied, "Well, my last four therapists," and she proceeded to name them, "had sexual relations with me, and so I guess I'll just have to find a therapist other than you." The psychologist discretely investigated the matter with her preceding therapist, who convincingly indicated that he had never had any sexual contact with her and had reason to believe that delusions were the basis for her allegations about the other three therapists.

Whatever leads up to a malpractice action, there are numerous forms that the suit can adopt. King (1977) cites intentional misconduct, breaches of contracts guaranteeing a specific therapeutic result, defamation, invasions of privacy, unauthorized postmortem procedures, and failures to prevent injuries to certain nonpatients. Trent (1978) specifies improper hospital commitment, death, pressing for fee collection, testifying against the patient's wishes without a subpoena, sexual behavior with patients, drug reactions, unauthorized release of confidential information, suicide, improper administrative handling, inappropriate use of electroconvulsive therapy, improper treatment, and injury to a nonpatient during professional services as the potential bases for malpractice actions against psychiatrists (and presumably the forms would, for the most part, be applicable to other mental health professionals as well). Wilkinson (1982), analyzing malpractice cases in psychiatry, offers the categories of liability for patient-inflicted injuries and suicide, harm by the patient to third persons, errors in judgment, faulty treatment methods, drug-related liability, and sexual misconduct. Finally, Hogan (1979) studied 300 cases involving psychotherapists and found that "more than twenty-five types of action were brought, including involuntary servitude, false arrest, trespass, malicious infliction of emotional distress, abuse of process, loss of liberty, misrepresentation, libel, assault and battery, malicious prosecution, and false imprisonment. Outnumbering all actions put together, however, is the negligence or malpractice suit, which occurs in more than two thirds of the cases" (p. 7).

To the chagrin perhaps of the human services professional, public policy seems to be creating a greater vulnerability to being sued, regardless of the employment setting. This trend is particularly evident in the demise of immunity.

At one time the doctrine of sovereign immunity precluded a legal action from being taken against the state and, in the process, its employees. Today discretionary functions (which are policy making in nature) are generally protected from legal actions, but the governmental cloak of protection has been removed from ministerial duties (which are technical or service in nature). In *Frank* v. *State of Utah*, 613 P.2d 517 (Utah, 1980), the Supreme Court of Utah held that the acts of a psychologist employed by a state mental health facility were not legally discretionary and that (since they were ministerial) the psychologist could be sued for allegedly being negligent in the handling of the case of a university student who had committed suicide. In *Koepf* v. *County of York*, 251 N.W.2d 866 (Neb. 1977), the Nebraska Supreme Court allowed immunity to a county judge, the public prosecutor, and the sheriff for their roles in a case where an illegitimate child, removed from the custody of the natural mother, was allegedly allowed to die wrongfully while in the care of a foster home; but the social worker who arranged the placement, and whose actions were ministerial (clinical), was denied immunity and was subject to legal suit on a negligence theory.

The prudent human services professional should (1) have a clear delineation of the standard of care that would be applied to his or her services; (2) adopt assessment procedures to ensure that the services were reasonably tailored to the needs of the client and were consonant with standard of care; (3) maintain a system by which clients are informed about and consent to the professional interventions; and (4) consistently exercise safeguards against any knowing or inadvertent deviations from or any real or imagined breaches of the established standard of care.

Conclusion

These four dimensions of the human services relationship—informed consent, privileged communication, duty to warn, and professional malpractice—constitute the core of legal concerns *vis à vis* practice. Both the client and the professional can benefit when the existence of these dimensions is openly acknowledged very early in the therapeutic relationship. Some professionals are hesitant to talk to their clients about the inherent duty to breach confidentiality in order to ensure the safety and welfare of all persons—but such a possible breach must be confronted.

As has been repeatedly stated, professionalism is the child of society. It cannot exist without the endorsement of society. Public policy prescribes what will earn endorsement. Like it or not, the human services professional of today must function under a public policy that imposes many possible legal sanctions, as herein discussed. It is unprofessional to attempt to deny, consciously or unconsciously, that these public policy legal sanctions are justified.

References

"Affidavits." In *American Jurisprudence*. Vol. 3. (2nd ed.) Rochester, N.Y.: Lawyers Co-operative Publishing, 1962.

Aker, J. B., Walsh, A. C., and Beam, J. R. *Mental Capacity: Medical and Legal Aspects of Aging*. Colorado Springs: Shepard's, 1977.

American Bar Association. *Code of Professional Responsibility*. Chicago: American Bar Association, 1971.

American Bar Association Commission on the Mentally Disabled, National Commission on Patients' Rights. *Legal Advocacy Programs for the Mentally Disabled: A Preliminary Survey and Directory*. Chicago: American Bar Association, 1977.

American Hospital Association. *A Patient's Bill of Rights*. Chicago: American Hospital Association, 1973.

American Law Institute (Ed.). *Restatement of the Law of Trusts*. (2nd ed). St. Paul, Minn.: West, 1959.

American Law Institute (Ed.). *Restatement of the Law of Contracts*. (2nd ed.). St. Paul, Minn.: West, 1981.

American Psychiatric Association. *Tardive Dyskinesia*. Washington, D.C.: American Psychiatric Association, 1979.

American Psychiatric Association. *Diagnostic and Statistical Manual of Mental Disorders*. (3rd ed.) Washington, D.C.: American Psychiatric Association, 1980.

Annas, G. J., and Healey, J. M. "The Patient Rights Advocate: Redefining the Doctor-Patient Relationship in the Hospital Context." *Vanderbilt Law Review*, 1974, *27*, 243–269.

Arthur, L. G. "Status Offenders Need a Court of Last Resort." *Boston University Law Review*, 1978, *57* (4), 631–644.

Baker, R., and Meyer, F., Jr. *The Criminal Justice Game: Politics and Players*. North Scituate, Mass.: Duxbury Press, 1980.

Barton, W. E., and Sanborn, C. J. (Eds.). *Law and the Mental Health Professions*. New York: International Universities Press, 1978.

Bazelon, D. L. "Implementing the Right to Treatment." In G. H. Morris (Ed.), *The Mentally Ill and the Right to Treatment*. Springfield, Ill.: Thomas, 1970.

Bedwell, M. A. "The Rights of Fathers of Non-Marital Children to Custody, Visitation, and to Consent to Adoption." *U.C. Davis Law Review*, 1979, *12*, 412–451.

Belli, M. "Loss of Consortium: Academic Addendum or Substantial Right?" *Trial*, 1980, *16*, 73–75.

Belli, M. *Modern Trials*. (2nd ed.) St. Paul, Minn.: West, 1982.

Bernard, J. L. "The Significance for Psychology of *O'Connor* v. *Donaldson*." *American Psychologist*, 1977, *32*, 1026–1035.

Bersoff, D. N. "Representation for Children in Custody Decisions: All That Glitters Is Not *Gault*." *Journal of Family Law*, 1976, *15*, 27–49.

Besharov, D. J. "Terminating Parental Rights: The Indigent Parent's Right to Counsel After *Lassiter* v. *North Carolina*." *Family Law Quarterly*, 1981, *15*, 205–221.

Besharov, D. J. "Representing Abused and Neglected Children: When Protecting Children Means Seeking the Dismissal of Court Proceedings." *Journal of Family Law*, 1982, *20*, 217–239.

Bierig, J. R. "Whatever Happened to Professional Self-Regulation?" *American Bar Association Journal*, 1983, *69*, 616–619.

Blinder, M. "The Abuse of Psychiatric Disability Determinations." *Medical Trial Technique Annual*, 1979, pp. 84–91.

Bodenheimer, B. M. "Interstate Custody: Initial Jurisdiction and Continuing Jurisdiction Under the UCCJA." *Family Law Quarterly*, 1981, *14*, 203–227.

Bowlby, J. *Attachment and Loss*. Vol. 2: *Separation*. New York: Basic Books, 1973.

Brakel, S. J. "Legal Problems of People in Mental and Penal Institutions: An Exploratory Study." *American Bar Foundation Research Journal*, 1978, pp. 565–645.

Brakel, S. J. "Legal Advocacy for Persons Confined in Mental Hospitals." *Mental Disability Law Reporter*, 1981a, *5*, 274–277.

Brakel, S. J. "Legal Aid in Mental Hospitals." *American Bar Foundation Research Journal*, 1981b, pp. 21–93.

Broderick, A. "One-Legged Ombudsman in a Mental Hospital." *Catholic University Law Review*, 1973, *22*, 517–562.

Brooks, A. *Law, Psychiatry, and the Mental Health System*. Boston: Little, Brown, 1974.

Brophy, K. M. "A Surrogate Mother Contract to Bear a Child." *Journal of Family Law*, 1982, *20*, 263–291.

Brosky, J. G., and Alford, J. G. "Sharpening Solomon's Sword: Current Considerations in Child Custody Cases." *Dickinson Law Review*, 1977, *81*, 683–731.

Browning, C. M., and Weiner, M. L. "The Right to Family Integrity: A Substantive Due Process Approach to State Removal and Termination Proceedings." *Georgetown Law Journal*, 1979, *68*, 213–248.

Bruch, C. S. "Property Rights of De Facto Spouses Including Thoughts on the Value of Homemakers' Services." *Family Law Quarterly*, 1976, *10*, 101–136.

Callner, B. W. "Boundary of the Divorce Lawyer's Role." *Family Law Quarterly*, 1977, *10*, 389–398.

Cantor, P. D. (Ed.). *Traumatic Medicine and Surgery for the Attorney*. Vol. 6. Woburn, Mass.: Butterworth, 1962.

Chamber of Commerce of the United States. *An Analysis of Workers' Compensation Laws*. Washington, D.C.: Chamber of Commerce of the United States, 1981.

Charney, M. A. "Review of *Divorce Mediation* by H. H. Irving." *Journal of Family Law*, 1982, *20*, 147–149.

Chase, I. H. "An Affair to Remember." In R. C. Allen (Ed.), *Mental Health in America: The Years of Crisis*. Marquis Academic Media, 1979.

Chemerinsky, E. "Defining the 'Best Interests': Constitutional Protections in Involuntary Adoptions." *Journal of Family Law*, 1979, *18*, 79–113.

Children's Rights Report. Vol. 1. New York: American Civil Liberties Union, 1977.

Clark, H. H., Jr. *The Law of Domestic Relations.* St. Paul, Minn.: West, 1968.

Clarke, S. H. "Status Offenders Are Different: A Comparison of Status Offender Careers by Type of First Known Offense." In R. Allison (Ed.), *Status Offenders and the Juvenile Justice System.* Hackensack, N.J.: National Council on Crime and Delinquency, 1978.

Cleary, E. W. (Ed.). *McCormick's Handbook of the Law of Evidence.* (2nd ed.) St. Paul, Minn.: West, 1972.

Connell, M. J. "Property Division and Alimony Awards: A Survey of Statutory Limitations on Judicial Discretion." *Fordham Law Review,* 1981, *50,* 415–449.

Coogler, O. J. *Structured Mediation in Divorce Settlement.* Lexington, Mass.: Heath, 1978.

"Couples Place Want Ads for Babies in Newspapers." *Atlanta Constitution,* Oct. 19, 1981, p. 7A.

Cross, M. B. "The Expert as Educator: A Proposed Approach to the Use of Battered Woman Syndrome Expert Testimony." *Vanderbilt Law Review,* 1982, *35,* 741–768.

Crutchfield, C. F. "Nonmarital Relationships and Their Impact on the Institution of Marriage and the Traditional Family Structure." *Journal of Family Law,* 1981, *19,* 247–261.

Davis, K. C. *Discretionary Justice: A Preliminary Inquiry.* Baton Rouge: Louisiana University Press, 1969.

DeKraai, M. B., and Sales, B. D. "Privileged Communications of Psychologists." *Professional Psychology,* 1982, *13,* 372–388.

Derdeyn, A. "Child Custody Consultation." *American Journal of Orthopsychiatry,* 1975, *45,* 791–801.

"Developments in the Law: The Constitution and the Family." *Harvard Law Review,* 1980, *93,* 1156–1383.

Dickens, B. M. "Legal Responses to Child Abuse." *Family Law Quarterly,* 1978, *12,* 1–36.

Dingman, P. R. "The Alternative Care Is Not There." In P. I. Ahmed and S. C. Plog (Eds.), *State Mental Hospitals.* New York: Plenum, 1976.

Donnelly, J. "Confidentiality: The Myth and the Reality." In W. E.

Barton and C. J. Sanborn (Eds.), *Law and the Mental Health Professions.* New York: International Universities Press, 1978.

Douthwaite, G. *Unmarried Couples and the Law.* Indianapolis: Allen Smith, 1979.

Elkins, J. R. "Legal Representation of the Mentally Ill." *West Virginia Law Review,* 1979, *83,* 157–250.

Emery, R. E. "Interparental Conflict and the Children of Discord and Divorce." *Psychological Bulletin,* 1982, *92,* 310–330.

Ennis, B. J. "Judicial Involvement in the Public Practice of Psychiatry." In W. E. Barton and C. J. Sanborn (Eds.), *Law and the Mental Health Professions.* New York: International Universities Press, 1978.

Epstein, L., and Lowinger, P. "Do Mental Patients Want Legal Counsel: A Survey." *American Journal of Orthopsychiatry,* 1975, *45,* 88–92.

Farina, A., and Felner, R. D. "Employer Interviewer Reactions to Former Mental Patients." *Journal of Abnormal Psychology,* 1973, *82* (2), 268–272.

Fisher, R. M. "The Psychotherapeutic Professions and the Law of Privileged Communications." *Wayne Law Review,* 1964, *10,* 609–654.

Fleming, J. B. *Stopping Wife Abuse: A Guide to the Emotional, Psychological, and Legal Implications for the Abused Woman and Those Helping Her.* New York: Doubleday, Anchor Books, 1979.

Folberg, H. J., and Graham, M. "Joint Custody of Children Following Divorce." *U.C. Davis Law Review,* 1979, *12,* 523–581.

"Fornication, Cohabitation, and the Constitution." *Michigan Law Review,* 1978, 77, 252–306.

Foster, H. H., Jr., and Freed, D. J. "Joint Custody: Legislative Reform." *Trial,* 1980, *16,* 22–27, 62.

Frankel, C. (Ed.). *Lawyer's Medical Cyclopedia.* Vol. 3. Indianapolis: Allen Smith, 1970.

Franklin, R. L., and Hibbs, B. "Child Custody in Transition." *Journal of Marital and Family Therapy,* 1980, *6,* 285–292.

Freddolino, P. P. "Recipient Rights Evaluation Project." Unpublished report, School of Social Work, Michigan State University, 1981.

Freed, D. J., and Foster, H. H., Jr. "Divorce in the Fifty States: An Overview." *Family Law Quarterly*, 1981, *14*, 229–284.

Freedman, A. M., Kaplan, H. E., and Sadock, B. J. *Modern Synopsis of Psychiatry*. (2nd ed.) Baltimore: Williams & Wilkins, 1976.

Gallagher, B. J. *The Sociology of Mental Illness*. Englewood Cliffs, N.J.: Prentice-Hall, 1980.

Geitman, H. *Psychology*. New York: Norton, 1981.

Geiwitz, J. *Psychology: Looking at Ourselves*. (2nd ed.) Boston: Little, Brown, 1980.

Gilboy, J. A., and Schmidt, J. R. " 'Voluntary' Hospitalization of the Mentally Ill." *Northwestern University Law Review*, 1971, *66*, 429–453.

Girardeau, J. E. "Determining the Custody of Minor Children." In *Program Materials for Seminars on Family Law Practice*. Athens: Institute of Continuing Legal Education in Georgia, 1982.

Glendon, M. A. "Modern Marriage Law and Its Underlying Assumptions: The New Marriage and the New Property." *Family Law Quarterly*, 1980, *13*, 441–460.

Glenn, R. D. "Standard of Care in Administering Non-Traditional Psychotherapy." *U.C. Davis Law Review*, 1974, *7*, 56–83.

Goffman, E. *Asylums*. New York: Doubleday, Anchor Books, 1961.

Goldstein, J., Freud, A., and Solnit, A. J. *Beyond the Best Interests of the Child*. New York: Free Press, 1973.

Goldstein, J., Freud, A., and Solnit, A. J. *Before the Best Interests of the Child*. New York: Free Press, 1979.

Gozansky, N. "Court-Ordered Investigations in Child Custody Cases." *Willamette Law Journal*, 1976, *12*, 511–526.

Gray, R. N. (Ed.). *Attorneys' Textbook of Medicine*. Vol. 3B. New York: Bender, 1972.

Green, C. "Homicide Rated as Top Child Killer." *Atlanta Constitution*, June 12, 1982, p. 6B.

Grilliot, N. J. *Introduction to Law and the Legal System*. Boston: Houghton Mifflin, 1975.

Grob, G. N. *Mental Institutions in America*. New York, Free Press, 1973.

Gruenberg, E. "The Social Breakdown Syndrome: Some Origins." *American Journal of Psychiatry*, 1967, *123*, 1481–1489.

Guernsey, T. F. "The Psychotherapist-Patient Privilege in Child

Placement: A Relevancy Analysis." *Villanova Law Review,* 1981, *26,* 955–966.

Gulley, K. G. "The Washington Child Abuse Amendments." *Gonzaga Law Review,* 1977, *12,* 468–491.

Halpern, C. R. "The Right to Habilitation: Litigation as a Strategy for Social Change." In S. Golann and W. J. Fremouw (Eds.), *The Right to Treatment for Mental Patients.* New York: Irvington, 1976.

Hancock, E. "The Power of the Attorney in Divorce." *Journal of Family Law,* 1981, *19,* 235–245.

Handel, W. W., and Sherwyn, B. A. "Surrogate Parenting." *Trial,* 1982, *18,* 57–60, 77.

Haney, C., and Zimbardo, P. B. "Interpersonal Dynamics in a Simulated Prison." *International Journal of Criminology and Penology,* 1973, *1,* 69–97.

Hansell, N., and Benson, M. L. "Interpreting Long-Term Patienthood: A Cohort Study." *Archives of General Psychiatry,* 1971, *24,* 238–243.

Harp, B. S., Jr. "Post Judgment Proceedings." In *Program Materials for Seminars on Family Law Practice.* Athens: Institute of Continuing Legal Education in Georgia, 1982.

Haynes, J. "Divorce Mediation: A New Role." *Journal of Social Work,* 1978, *23,* 5–9.

Hemelt, M. D., and Mackert, M. E. *Dynamics of Law in Nursing and Health Care.* Reston, Va.: Reston Publishing, 1978.

Hennessey, E. F. "Explosion in Family Law Litigation: Challenges and Opportunities for the Bar." *Family Law Quarterly,* 1980, *14,* 187–201.

Henning, J. S. "Child Advocacy in Adoption and Divorce Cases: Where Is the Wisdom of Solomon When We Really Need It?" *Journal of Clinical Child Psychology,* 1976, *6,* 50–53.

Hetherington, E. M. "Divorce: A Child's Perspective." *American Psychologist,* 1979, *34,* 851–858.

Hetherington, E. M., Cox, M., and Cox, R. "Divorced Fathers." *Family Coordinator,* 1976, *25,* 417–428.

Hirschberg, B. A. "Who Speaks for the Child and What Are His Rights? A Proposed Standard for Evaluation." *Law and Human Behavior,* 1980, *4,* 217–236.

Hogan, D. B. *The Regulation of Psychotherapists.* Vol. 3: *A Review of Malpractice Suits in the United States.* Cambridge, Mass.: Ballinger, 1979.

House, M. P., Jr. "Pretrial Discovery and the Use of Experts." In *Program Materials for Seminars on Family Law Practice.* Athens: Institute of Continuing Legal Education in Georgia, 1982.

"Implementation Problems in Institutional Reform Litigation." *Harvard Law Review,* 1977, *90,* 428–463.

Irving, H. H. *Divorce Mediation: A Rational Alternative to the Adversary System.* New York: Universe Books, 1981.

Jarvik, M. E. "Drugs in the Treatment of Psychiatric Disorders." In L. S. Goodman and A. Gillman (Eds.), *The Pharmacological Basis of Therapeutics.* (3rd ed.) Toronto: Macmillan, 1965.

Johannsen, W. J. "Attitudes Toward Mental Patients: A Review of Empirical Research." *Mental Hygiene,* 1969, *53,* 218–228.

Kalmanoff, A. *Criminal Justice: Enforcement and Administration.* Boston: Little, Brown, 1975.

Kamisar, Y., LaFave, W., and Israel, J. *Basic Criminal Procedure.* (5th ed.) St. Paul, Minn.: West, 1980.

Kaplin, W. A. *The Law of Higher Education: Legal Implications of Administrative Decision Making.* San Francisco: Jossey-Bass, 1978.

Kaplin, W. A. *The Law of Higher Education 1980.* San Francisco: Jossey-Bass, 1980.

Katz, S. N. *Child Snatching: The Legal Response to the Abduction of Children.* Chicago: American Bar Association Press, 1981a.

Katz, S. N. "Legal Remedies for Child Snatching." *Family Law Quarterly,* 1981b, *15,* 103–147.

Kazen, B. A. *When Father Wants Custody: A Lawyer's View.* Austin: State Bar of Texas, 1977.

Kelly, J. B., and Wallerstein, J. S. "Part-Time Parent, Part-Time Child: Visiting After Divorce." *Journal of Clinical Child Psychology,* 1977, *6,* 51–54.

Kelly, L. Y. "The Patient's Right to Know." *Nursing Outlook,* 1976, *24,* 26–32.

Kern, M. N. "Unwed Fathers: An Analytical Survey of Their Parental Rights and Obligations." *Washington University Law Quarterly,* 1979, *1979,* 1029–1062.

Ketchum, O. W. "Why Jurisdiction over Status Offenders Should Be Eliminated from Juvenile Courts." *Boston University Law Review*, 1977, *57* (4), 645–662.

King, J. H., Jr. *The Law of Medical Malpractice*. St. Paul, Minn.: West, 1977.

Kionka, E. J. *Torts: Injuries to Person and Property*. St. Paul, Minn.: West, 1977.

Kittrie, N. N. "Can the Right to Treatment Remedy the Ills of the Juvenile Process?" *Georgetown Law Journal*, 1969, *57*, 848–885.

Klaff, R. L. "The Tender Years Doctrine: A Defense." *California Law Review*, 1982, *70*, 335–372.

Knapp, S., and VandeCreek, L. "Behavioral Medicine: Its Malpractice Risks for Psychologists." *Professional Psychology*, 1981, *12*, 677–683.

Knapp, S., and VandeCreek, L. "*Tarasoff:* Five Years Later." *Professional Psychology*, 1982, *13*, 511–516.

Korchin, S. J. *Modern Clinical Psychology*. New York: Basic Books, 1976.

Krause, H. D. *Family Law in a Nutshell*. St. Paul, Minn.: West, 1977.

Krause, H. D. "Child Support Enforcement: Legislative Tasks for the Early 1980s." *Family Law Quarterly*, 1982, *15*, 349–370.

Krech, D., Crutchfield, R., and Livson, N. *Elements of Psychology*. (2nd ed.) New York: Knopf, 1969.

Kressel, K., and others. "Professional Intervention in Divorce: The Views of Lawyers, Psychotherapists, and Clergy." *Journal of Divorce*, 1978, *2*, (2), 119–155.

Kurdek, L. A. "An Integrative Perspective on Children's Divorce Adjustment." *American Psychologist*, 1981, *36*, 856–866.

LaFave, W. R., and Scott, A. W. *Handbook on Criminal Law*. St. Paul, Minn.: West, 1972.

Lassen, G. "The Psychologist as an Expert Witness in Assessing Mental Disease or Defect." *Journal of the American Bar Association*, 1964, *50*, 239.

Lavori, N. *Living Together, Married or Single: Your Legal Rights*. New York: Harper & Row, 1976.

Lempert, R. O., and Saltzburg, S. A. *A Modern Approach to Evidence*. St. Paul, Minn.: West, 1977.

Levine, J. P., Musheno, M. C., and Palumbo, D. J. *Criminal Justice:*

A Public Policy Approach. New York: Harcourt Brace Jovanovich, 1980.

Levitt, E. E. "The Psychologist: A Neglected Legal Resource." *Indiana Law Journal,* 1970, *45,* 83.

Lewin, T. H. "Disposition of the Irresponsible: Protection Following Commitment." *Michigan Law Review,* 1968, *66,* 721–736.

Litwack, T. R., Gerber, G. L., and Fenster, C. A. "The Proper Role of Psychology in Child Custody Disputes." *Journal of Family Law,* 1980, *18,* 269–300.

Lowry, D. R., and Kennedy, R. M. "Clinical Law in the Area of Mental Health." *Wisconsin Law Review,* 1968, *66,* 721–736.

Lyon, M. A., Levine, M. L., and Zusman, J. "Patients' Bill of Rights: A Survey of State Statutes." *Mental Disability Law Reporter,* 1982, *6,* 178–201.

Mahon, S., and others. "A Mechanism for Enforcing the Right to Treatment: A Human Rights Committee." *Law and Psychology Review,* 1975, *1,* 131–149.

Margolin, E. "Hypnosis-Enhanced Testimony: Valid Evidence or Prosecutor's Tool?" *Trial,* 1981, *17,* (10), 42–46, 83–84.

Margolin, G. "Ethical and Legal Considerations in Marital and Family Therapy." *American Psychologist,* 1982, *37,* 788–801.

Martin, D., and Lyon, P. *Lesbian—Women.* San Francisco: New Glide, 1972.

Meade, D. "Consortium Rights of the Unmarried: Time for a Reappraisal." *Family Law Quarterly,* 1981, *15,* 223–251.

"Mental Health: A Model Statute to Regulate the Administration of Therapy Within Mental Health Facilities." *Minnesota Law Review,* 1977, *61,* 841–886.

"Mental Illness and the Law of Contracts." *Michigan Law Review,* 1957, *57,* 1020–1114.

Mickenberg, N. H. "The Silent Clients: Legal and Ethical Considerations in Representing Severely and Profoundly Retarded Individuals." *Stanford Law Review,* 1979, *31,* 625–636.

Miller, D. J. "Joint Custody." *Family Law Quarterly,* 1979, *13,* 345–412.

Miller, D., and Dawson, W. H. "Effects of Stigma on Reemployment of Ex-Mental Patients." *Mental Hygiene,* 1969, *49,* 281–287.

Miner, M. G., and Miner, J. B. *Employee Selection Within the Law.* Washington, D.C.: Bureau of National Affairs, 1979.

Mnookin, R. "Foster Care in Whose Best Interest?" *Harvard Educational Review,* 1973, *43,* 599–638.

Moore, M. L. "Systems Change Advocacy." *Amicus,* 1976, *1,* 13–16.

Moore, W. C. "Affidavits." In *Nebraska Practice.* Vol. 1. St. Paul, Minn.: West, 1964.

Morrison, J. K. "An Argument for Mental Patient Advisory Boards." *Professional Psychology,* 1976, *7,* 127–131.

Muench, J. H., and Levy, M. R. "Psychological Parentage: A Natural Right." *Family Law Quarterly,* 1979, *13,* 129–181.

Mussehl, R. C. "From Advocate to Counselor: The Emerging Role of the Family Law Practitioner." *Gonzaga Law Review,* 1977, *12,* 442–454.

National Conference of Commissioners on Uniform State Laws. "Uniform Marriage and Divorce Act." *Family Law Quarterly,* 1971, *5,* 205–251.

Neubauer, D. W. *America's Court and the Criminal Justice System.* Belmont, Calif.: Wadsworth, 1979.

Nunnally, J. C. *Popular Conceptions of Mental Health.* New York: Holt, Rinehart and Winston, 1961.

Okpaku, S. R. "Psychology: Impediment or Aid in Child Custody Cases." *Rutgers Law Review,* 1976, *29,* 1117–1153.

Orlando, F. A. "Conciliation Programs: Their Effect on Marriage and Family Life." *Florida Bar Journal,* 1978, *52,* 218–221.

Orthner, D. K., and Lewis, K. "Evidence of Single-Father Competence in Child-Rearing." *Family Law Quarterly,* 1979, *13,* 27–47.

Page, W. *The Law of Wills.* Vol. 1. Cincinnati: W. H. Anderson, 1960.

Palmer, A. B., and Wohl, I. "Voluntary Admission Forms: Does the Patient Know What He Is Signing?" *Hospital and Community Psychiatry,* 1972, *23,* 250–252.

Parry, J. K. "Informed Consent: For Whose Benefit?" *Social Casework,* 1981, *62,* 537–542.

Patton, R. G. "Deeds." In A. J. Casner (Ed.), *American Law of Property.* Boston: Little, Brown, 1952.

Paulus, P. B., McCain, G., and Cox, V. "Death Rates, Psychiatric Commitments, Blood Pressure, and Perceived Crowding as a

Function of Institutional Crowding." *Environmental Psychology and Nonverbal Behavior*, 1978, *8*, 107–116.

Pittoni, M. *Brief Writing and Argumentation*. (3rd ed.) Mineola, N.Y.: Foundation Press, 1967.

Plotkin, R., and Gill, K. R. "Invisible Manacles: Drugging Mentally Retarded People." *Stanford Law Review*, 1979, *31*, 637–678.

Podolski, A. L. "Abolishing Baby Buying: Limiting Independent Adoption Placement." *Family Law Quarterly*, 1975, *9*, 547–554.

Pomerleau, O. F., and Brady, J. P. "Introduction: The Scope and Promise of Behavioral Medicine." In O. F. Pomerleau and J. P. Brady (Eds.), *Behavioral Medicine: Theory and Practice*. Baltimore: Williams & Wilkins, 1979.

President's Commission on Law Enforcement and Administration of Justice. *Task Force Report*. Washington, D.C.: U.S. Government Printing Office, 1967.

"Procedural Safeguards for Periodic Review: A New Commitment to Mental Patients' Rights." *Yale Law Journal*, 1979, *88*, 850–867.

"Project Investigates Periodic Review in Massachusetts." *Amicus*, 1976, *1*, 2–3.

Prokop, C. K., and Bradley, L. A. *Medical Psychology*. New York: Academic Press, 1981.

Prosser, W. L. *Handbook of the Law of Torts*. (4th ed.) St. Paul, Minn.: West, 1971.

Rachlin, S. "The Case Against the Closing of State Hospitals." In P. I. Ahmed and S. C. Plog (Eds.), *State Mental Hospitals*. New York: Plenum, 1976.

Ransohoff, P., and others. "Measuring Restrictiveness of Psychiatric Care." *Hospital and Community Psychiatry*, 1982, *33*, 361–366.

Reed, T. J. "The Stolen Birthright: An Examination of the Psychology of Testation and an Analysis of the Law of Testimentary Capacity." *Western New England Law Review*, 1979, *1*, 431–522.

Reed, T. J. "Breaking Wills in Indiana." *Indiana Law Review*, 1981, *14*, 865–925.

Regan, J. J. "Protective Services for the Elderly: Commitment, Guardianship, and the Alternatives." *William and Mary Law Review*, 1972, *13*, 569–622.

Reiss, A. J., Jr. *The Police and the Public.* New Haven, Conn.: Yale University Press, 1971.

Robitscher, J. B. *Pursuit of Agreement: Psychiatry and the Law.* Philadelphia: Lippincott, 1966.

"The Role of Counsel in the Civil Commitment Process: A Theoretical Framework." *Yale Law Journal,* 1975, *85,* 1540–1563.

Roman, M., and Haddad, W. *The Disposable Parent: The Case for Joint Custody.* New York: Holt, Rinehart and Winston, 1978.

Rombauer, M. D. *Legal Problem Solving: Analysis, Research, and Writing.* St. Paul, Minn.: West, 1978.

Rosen, R. "Children of Divorce: What They Feel About Access and Other Aspects of the Divorce Experience." *Journal of Clinical Child Psychology,* 1977, *6,* 24–27.

Rosenhan, D. L. "On Being Sane in Insane Places." *Science,* 1973, *179,* 250–258.

Rothman, D. "Decarcerating Prisoners and Patients." *Civil Liberties Review,* 1973, *8,* 12–23.

Rothstein, P. F. *Evidence.* St. Paul, Minn.: West, 1970.

Rubin, T. *Juvenile Justice Police: Practice and Law.* Santa Monica, Calif.: Goodyear, 1979.

Saposnek, D. T. *Mediating Child Custody Disputes: A Systematic Guide for Family Therapists, Court Counselors, Attorneys, and Judges.* San Francisco: Jossey-Bass, 1983.

Sarri, R. C. *Under Lock and Key: Juveniles in Jails and Detention.* Ann Arbor: National Assessment of Juvenile Corrections, University of Michigan, 1974.

Scaletta, D. I. "Divorce Courts and Conciliation Services: An Interface of Law and the Social Sciences." *Manitoba Law Journal,* 1981, *11,* 321–328.

Schechter, L. F. "The Violent Family and the Ambivalent State: Developing a Coherent Policy for State Aid to Victims of Family Violence." *Journal of Family Law,* 1981, *20,* 1–42.

Schur, E. M. *Radical Nonintervention.* Englewood Cliffs, N.J.: Prentice-Hall, 1973.

Schutz, B. J. *Legal Liability in Psychotherapy: A Practitioner's Guide to Risk Management.* San Francisco: Jossey-Bass, 1982.

Schwartz, S. J., and Fleischner, R. D. "Legal Advocacy for Persons Confined in Mental Hospitals." *Mental Disability Law Reporter,* 1981, *5,* 274, 277–280.

Schwitzgebel, R. L., and Schwitzgebel, R. K. *Law and Psychological Practice.* New York: Wiley, 1980.

Sepler, H. J. "Measuring the Effects of No-Fault Divorce Laws Across Fifty States: Quantifying a Zeitgeist." *Family Law Quarterly,* 1981, *15,* 65–102.

Serban, G. "Sexual Activity in Therapy: Legal and Ethical Issues." *American Journal of Psychotherapy,* 1981, *35,* 76–85.

Shaffer, T. L. *Death, Property, and Lawyers.* Port Washington, N.Y.: Dunellen, Kennikat Press, 1970a.

Shaffer, T. L. "Undue Influence, Confidential Relationship, and the Psychology of Transference." *Notre Dame Lawyer,* 1970b, *45,* 197–237.

Shaffer, T. L. *The Planning and Drafting of Wills and Trusts.* Mineola, N.Y.: Foundation Press, 1972.

Sharp, S. B. "Divorce and the Third Party: Spousal Support, Private Agreements, and the State." *North Carolina Law Review,* 1981, *59,* 819–866.

Shell, R. "Scientific Jury Selection." *Barrister,* 1980, 7, 47–52.

Shlensky, R. "Psychiatric Expert Testimony and Consultation." *Medical Trial Technique Annual,* 1978, pp. 38–44.

Shrallow, D. F. "The Standard of Care for the Medical Specialist in Ohio: *Bruni* v. *Tatsumi.*" *Ohio State Law Journal,* 1977, *38,* 203–218.

Shultz, M. M. "Contractual Ordering of Marriage: A New Model for State Policy." *California Law Review,* 1982, *70,* 204–334.

Siegel, D. M., and Hurley, S. "The Role of the Child's Preference in Custody Proceedings." *Family Law Quarterly,* 1977, *11,* 1–58.

Sigler, J. A. *Understanding Criminal Law.* Boston: Little, Brown, 1981.

Simon, O. C. "Psychology and the 'Treatment Rights Movement.'" *Professional Psychology,* 1975, *6,* 243–251.

Simon, O. C. "The Psychologist as a Whistle Blower: A Case Study." *Professional Psychology,* 1978, *9,* 322–340.

Simon, R. J., and Altstein, H. *Transracial Adoption.* New York: Wiley, 1977.

Sinnett, E. R., and Thetford, P. E. "Protecting Clients and Assessing Malpractice." *Professional Psychology,* 1975, *6,* 117–126.

Slovenko, R. *Psychiatry and Law.* Boston: Little, Brown, 1973.

Smith, C., and others. *A Preliminary National Assessment of the Status Offender and the Juvenile Justice System.* Washington, D.C.: National Institute for Juvenile Justice and Delinquency Prevention, 1980.

Smith, R. G., and Hager, L. M. "The Senile Testator: Medicolegal Aspects of Competency." *Cleveland-Marshall Law Review,* 1964, *13,* 397–435.

State Bar of Georgia, Legal Status of Women Committee of the Younger Lawyers Section. *Handbook for Battered Women.* Atlanta: State Bar of Georgia, 1981.

Steinberg, J. L. "The Therapeutic Potential of the Divorce Process." *American Bar Association Journal,* 1976, *62,* 617–620.

Steinberg, J. L. "Toward an Interdisciplinary Commitment: A Divorce Lawyer Proposes Attorney-Therapist Marriages or, at the Least, an Affair." *Journal of Marital and Family Therapy,* 1980, *6,* 259–268.

Strickman, L. P. "Marriage, Divorce, and the Constitution." *Family Law Quarterly,* 1982, *15,* 259–348.

Suchotliff, L., Steinfeld, G., and Tolchin, G. "The Struggle for Patients' Rights in a State Hospital." *Mental Hygiene,* 1970, *54,* 230–240.

Sundstrom, E. "Crowding as a Sequential Process: Review of Research on the Effects of Population Density on Humans." In Y. M. Epstein and A. Bawn (Eds.), *Human Response to Crowding.* Hillsdale, N.J.: Erlbaum, 1978.

Sussman, A. "Child Abuse Reporting: A Review of the Literature." In A. Sussman and S. J. Cohen (Eds.), *Reporting Child Abuse and Neglect: Guidelines for Legislation.* Cambridge, Mass.: Ballinger, 1975.

Test, M. A., and Stein, L. I. "The Clinical Rationale for Community Treatment: A Review of the Literature." In L. I. Stein and M. A. Test (Eds.), *Alternatives to Mental Hospital Treatment.* New York: Plenum, 1978.

Thar, A. E. "The Admissibility of Expert Testimony on Battered Wife Syndrome: An Evidentiary Analysis." *Northwestern University Law Review,* 1982, *77,* 348–373.

Thomas, C. W. "Are Status Offenders Really So Different?" *Crime and Delinquency,* 1978, *24* (4), 438–455.

Treffert, D. A. "Dying with Their Rights On." *American Journal of Psychiatry,* 1973, *130,* 1041.

Trent, C. L. "Psychiatric Malpractice Insurance and Its Problems: An Overview." In W. E. Barton and C. J. Sanborn (Eds.), *Law and the Mental Health Professions.* New York: International Universities Press, 1978.

Trombetta, D. "Joint Custody: Recent Research and Overloaded Courtrooms Inspire New Solutions to Custody Disputes." *Journal of Family Law,* 1981, *19,* 213–234.

Uniform Laws Annotated. Vol. 9: *Matrimonial, Family, and Health Laws.* St. Paul, Minn.: West, 1979.

U.S. Bureau of the Census. *Statistical Abstract of the United States.* Washington, D.C.: U.S. Government Printing Office, 1981.

U.S. Department of Health, Education and Welfare. *Institutional Guide to Department of Health, Education and Welfare Policy on Protection of Human Subjects.* Washington, D.C.: U.S. Government Printing Office, 1971.

Van Hoose, W. H., and Kottler, V. A. *Ethical and Legal Issues in Counseling and Psychotherapy.* San Francisco: Jossey-Bass, 1977.

Walker, L. *The Battered Woman.* New York: Harper & Row, 1979.

Wallerstein, J. S., and Kelly, J. B. *Surviving the Breakup: How Children and Parents Cope with Divorce.* New York: Basic Books, 1980.

Walters, H. A. "Dangerousness." In R. H. Woody (Ed.), *Encyclopedia of Clinical Assessment.* Vol. 2. San Francisco: Jossey-Bass, 1980.

Watson, A. *Psychiatry for Lawyers.* (2nd ed.) New York: International Universities Press, 1978.

Weis, J. G. *Jurisdiction and the Elusive Status Offender: A Comparison of Involvement in Delinquent Behavior and Status Offenses.* Washington, D.C.: National Institute for Juvenile Justice and Delinquency Prevention, 1980.

Weiss, R. S. "Issues in the Adjudication of Custody When Parents Separate." In G. Levinger and O. C. Moles (Eds.), *Divorce and Separation.* New York: Basic Books, 1979.

Weitzman, L. J. "Legal Regulation of Marriage: Tradition and Change." *California Law Review,* 1974, *62,* 1169–1277.

Weitzman, L. J. *The Marriage Contract: Spouses, Lovers, and the Law.* New York: Free Press, 1981.

Weitzman, L. J., and Dixon, R. B. "Child Custody Awards: Legal Standards and Empirical Patterns for Child Custody, Support, and Visitation After Divorce." *U.C. Davis Law Review*, 1979, *12*, 473-521.

Weitzman, L. J., and Dixon, R. B. "The Alimony Myth: Does No-Fault Divorce Make a Difference?" *Family Law Quarterly*, 1980, *14*, 141-185.

Wenger, D., and Fletcher, R. "The Effect of Legal Counsel on Admissions to a State Hospital: A Confrontation of Professions." *Journal of Health and Social Behavior*, 1969, *10*, 66-72.

Weyrauch, W. O. "Metamorphoses of Marriage." *Family Law Quarterly*, 1980, *13*, 415-440.

White, G. "New Laws Help in Collecting That Check." *Atlanta Constitution*, April 9, 1982, p. 1B.

White, M. D., and White, C. A., "Involuntarily Committed Patients' Constitutional Right to Refuse Treatment: A Challenge to Psychology." *American Psychologist*, 1981, *36*, 953-962.

White, M. E. "Protection Following Commitment: Enforcing the Rights of Persons Confined in Arizona Mental Health Facilities." *Arizona Law Review*, 1976, *17*, 1070-1134.

Wice, P. B. *Freedom for Sale.* Lexington, Mass.: Heath, 1974.

Wigmore, J. H. *Evidence.* (3rd ed.) (10 vols.) Boston: Little, Brown, 1940. (Originally published 1913; Vol. 3 rev. 1970, vol. 4 rev. 1972, by J. H. Chadbourn.)

Wilkinson, A. P. "Psychiatric Malpractice: Identifying Areas of Liability." *Trial*, 1982, *18*, 73-77, 89-90.

Wilson, J. P., Beyer, H. A., and Yudowitz, B. "Advocacy for the Mentally Disabled." In L. E. Kopolow and H. Bloom (Eds.), *Mental Health Advocacy: An Emerging Force in Consumer Rights.* Washington, D.C.: U.S. Government Printing Office, 1977.

Winks, P. L. "Divorce Mediation: A Nonadversary Procedure for the No-Fault Divorce." *Journal of Family Law*, 1981, *19*, 615-653.

Wolfensberger, W. "A Model for a Balanced Multi Component Advocacy/Protective Services Schema." In L. E. Kopolow and H. Bloom (Eds.), *Mental Health Advocacy: An Emerging Force in Consumer Rights.* Washington, D.C.: U.S. Government Printing Office, 1977.

Wooden, K. *Weeping in the Playground of Others.* New York: McGraw-Hill, 1976.

Woody, R. H. *Psychobehavioral Counseling and Therapy: Integrating Behavioral and Insight Techniques.* New York: Appleton-Century-Crofts, 1971.

Woody, R. H. "Psychologists in Child Custody." In B. D. Sales (Ed.), *Psychology in the Legal Process.* New York: Spectrum, 1977.

Woody, R. H. "The Pain/Intelligence Nexus in Personal Injury Litigation." *Medical Trial Technique Quarterly,* 1979, *25,* 249–257.

Wright, R. H. "Psychologists and Professional Liability (Malpractice) Insurance: A Retrospective Review." *American Psychologist,* 1981a, *36,* 1485–1493.

Wright, R. H. "What to Do Until the Malpractice Lawyer Comes: A Survivor's Manual." *American Psychologist,* 1981b, 36, 1535–1541.

"The *Wyatt* Case: Implementation of a Judicial Decree Ordering Institutional Change." *Yale Law Journal,* 1975, *84,* 1338–1379.

Zitrin, A., Herman, M., and Kumasaka, Y. "New York's Mental Hygiene Law: A Preliminary Evaluation." *Mental Hygiene,* 1970, *54,* 28–36.

Legal Abbreviations in This Volume

※※※※※※※※※※※※※※※※※※※※※※※

A., A.2d *Atlantic Reporter.* Regional reporter for state court cases in Connecticut, Delaware, Maine, Maryland, New Hampshire, New Jersey, Pennsylvania, Rhode Island, Vermont, and Municipal Appeals cases in District of Columbia. Sample citations: 304 A.2d 819 (Md. 1973) or 34 N.J. 494, 170 A.2d 39 (1961); 430 A.2d 1321 (D.C. 1981).

A.D., A.D.2d *Appellate Division Reports.* Reporter for cases in New York Supreme Court, Appellate Division.

Ala. *Alabama Reports.* Official state reporter for cases in Alabama Supreme Court. Sample citation: 1 Ala. 20.

A.L.R., A.L.R.2d, A.L.R.3d *American Law Reports.* Contains annotations on selected cases in specific legal areas; discusses historical background, current law, and probable future developments.

Ann. Annotated. As in Wash. Rev. Code Ann. (*Revised Code of Washington Annotated*).

Ariz. *Arizona Reports.* Official state reporter for cases in Arizona Supreme Court. Sample citation: 1 Ariz. 20.

Ariz. App. *Arizona Appeals Reports.* Reports of cases in Arizona Court of Appeals.

Ark. *Arkansas Reports.* Official state reporter for cases in Arkansas Supreme Court. Sample citation: 1 Ark. 20.

Cal., Cal. 2d, Cal. 3d *California Reports.* Official state reporter for cases in California Supreme Court. Sample citation: 1 Cal. 3d 20.

Cal. App., Cal. App. 2d, Cal. App. 3d *California Appellate Reports.* Reporter for cases in California Courts of Appeal.

Cal. Rptr. *West's California Reporter.* Unofficial reporter for cases in California Supreme Court, California Courts of Appeal, and Appellate Departments of the Superior Court in California.

C.F.R. *Code of Federal Regulations.* Contains regulations and rules of all federal administrative agencies (except Treasury). Sample citation: 34 C.F.R. Part 104; 34 C.F.R. sec. 104.27(a)(1).

Ch. Chancellor's Court. English court of nineteenth century. Now called Chancery Division.

Civ. Civil. As in Tex. Rev. Civ. Stat. Ann. (*Texas Revised Civil Statutes Annotated*).

C.J.S. *Corpus Juris Secundum.* Series of publications containing discussions of legal issues.

Colo. *Colorado Reports.* Official state reporter for cases in Colorado Supreme Court. Sample citation: 1 Colo. 20.

Conn. *Connecticut Reports.* Official state reporter for cases in Connecticut Supreme Court of Errors. Sample citation: 1 Conn. 20.

D. District. Used in U.S. District Court citations: 368 F. Supp. 38 (D. Mass 1977). See also E.D., M.D., N.D., S.D., W.D.

D.C.Cir. District of Columbia Circuit. Used in citations to U.S. Court of Appeals for the District of Columbia Circuit: 528 F.2d 658 (D.C. Cir. 1976).

D.D.C. District Court, District of Columbia. Used in citations to U.S. District Court: 358 F. Supp. 38 (D.D.C. 1977).

Del. *Delaware Reports.* Official state reporter for cases in Delaware Supreme Court. Sample citation: 1 Del. 20.

E.D. Eastern District. Used in U.S. District Court citations: 368 F. Supp. 38 (E.D. Pa. 1977).

Empl. Prac. Dec. *Employment Practices Decisions.* Looseleaf service publishing cases in area of employment relations.

Eng. Rep. *English Reports.* Reporter for cases tried in English courts before 1865.

Ex. Exchequer. Reporter for cases in English Court of Exchequer between 1865 and 1880.

F., F.2d *Federal Reporter.* Official reporter for cases heard by U.S. Courts of Appeals. Sample citations: 513 F.2d 347 (6th Cir. 1975), 622 F.2d 397 (2d Cir. 1975).

F.R.D. *Federal Rules Decisions.* Reporter sometimes cited for U.S. District Court decisions. Most frequently such cases are cited to F. Supp.

F. Supp. *Federal Supplement.* Official reporter for cases heard by U.S. District Courts. Sample citations: 381 F. Supp. 718 (D. Del. 1974), 382 F. Supp. 1328 (W.D. Pa. 1974).

Fed. R. Evid. *Federal Rules of Evidence.*

Fed. Reg. *Federal Register.* Publishes federal administrative rules and regulations when they are enacted, prior to their codification in C.F.R.

Fla. *Florida Reports.* Official state reporter for cases in Florida Supreme Court. Sample citation: 1 Fla. 20.

Ga. *Georgia Reports.* Official state reporter for cases in Georgia Supreme Court. Sample citation: 1 Ga. 20.

Hawaii *Hawaii Reports.* Official state reporter for cases in Hawaii Supreme Court. Sample citation: 1 Hawaii 20.

H.R. House of Representatives.

Idaho *Idaho Reports.* Official state reporter for cases in Idaho Supreme Court. Sample citation: 1 Idaho 20.

Ill., Ill. 2d *Illinois Reports.* Official state reporter for cases in Illinois Supreme Court. Sample citation: 1 Ill. 2d 20.

Ill. App., Ill. App. 2d, Ill. App. 3d *Illinois Appellate Court Reports.* Reporter for cases in Appellate Court of Illinois.

Ind. *Indiana Reports.* Official state reporter for cases in Indiana Supreme Court. Sample citation: 1 Ind. 20.

Ind. App. *Indiana Court of Appeals Reports.* Reporter for cases in Indiana Court of Appeals.

Iowa *Iowa Reports.* Official state reporter for cases in Iowa Supreme Court. Sample citation: 1 Iowa 20.

Kan. *Kansas Reports.* Official state reporter for cases in Kansas Supreme Court. Sample citation: 1 Kan. 20.

K.B. Court of King's Bench. English court. Also called Court of Queen's Bench if a queen is monarch at the time.

Ky. *Kentucky Reports.* Official state reporter for cases in Kentucky Supreme Court. Sample citation: 1 Ky. 20.

L. Ed., L. Ed. 2d *U.S. Supreme Court Reports, Lawyers' Edition.* Unofficial reporter for U.S. Supreme Court cases. Sample Citation: 71 L. Ed. 2d 533 (1982).

L.R.R.M. *Labor Relations Reference Manual.* Looseleaf service.

La. *Louisiana Reports.* Official state reporter for cases in Louisiana Supreme Court. Sample citation: 1 La. 20.

Mass. *Massachusetts Reports.* Official state reporter for cases in Massachusetts Supreme Judicial Court. Sample citation: 1 Mass. 20.

Md. *Maryland Reports.* Official state reporter for cases in Maryland Court of Appeals. Sample citation: 1 Md. 20.

M.D. Middle District. Used in U.S. District Court citations: 368 F. Supp. 38 (M.D. Ala. 1977).

Me. *Maine Reports.* Official state reporter for cases in Maine Supreme Judicial Court. Sample citation: 1 Me. 20.

Mich. *Michigan Reports.* Official state reporter for cases in Michigan Supreme Court. Sample citation: 1 Mich. 20.

Minn. *Minnesota Reports.* Official state reporter for cases in Minnesota Supreme Court. Sample citation: 1 Minn. 20.

Misc., Misc. 2d *New York Miscellaneous Reports.* Reporter for cases in New York lower courts, such as the Court of Claims and the New York Criminal Court.

Miss. *Mississippi Reports.* Official state reporter for cases in Mississippi Supreme Court. Sample citation: 1 Miss. 20.

Mo. *Missouri Reports.* Official state reporter for cases in Missouri Supreme Court. Sample citation: 1 Mo. 20.

Mont. *Montana Reports.* Official state reporter for cases in Montana Supreme Court. Sample citation: 1 Mont. 20.

N.C. *North Carolina Reports.* Official state reporter for cases in North Carolina Supreme Court. Sample citation: 1 N.C. 20.

N.D. (1) *North Dakota Reports.* Official state reporter for cases in North Dakota Supreme Court. Sample citation: 1 N.D. 20. (2) Northern District. Used in U.S. District Court citations: 368 F. Supp. 38 (N.D. Ill. 1977).

N.E., N.E.2d *Northeastern Reporter.* Regional reporter for state court cases in Illinois, Indiana, Massachusetts, New York, and Ohio. Sample citations: 249 N.E.2d 366 (N.Y. 1969) or 79 Mass. 1171, 389 N.E.2d 83 (1979).

Neb. *Nebraska Reports.* Official state reporter for cases in Nebraska Supreme Court. Sample citation: 1 Neb. 20.

Nev. *Nevada Reports.* Official state reporter for cases in Nevada Supreme Court. Sample citation: 1 Nev. 20.

N.H. *New Hampshire Reports.* Official state reporter for cases in New Hampshire Supreme Court. Sample citation: 1 N.H. 20.

N.J. *New Jersey Reports.* Official state reporter for cases in New Jersey Supreme Court (1948 to date). Sample citation: 1 N.J. 20.

N.J. Eq. *New Jersey Equity Reports.* Reporter for New Jersey Supreme Court cases (1790–1948).

N.J.L. *New Jersey Law Reports.* Reporter for New Jersey Supreme Court cases (1830–1948).

N.M. *New Mexico Reports.* Official state reporter for cases in New Mexico Supreme Court. Sample citation: 1 N.M. 20.

N.W., N.W.2d *Northwestern Reporter.* Regional reporter for state court cases in Iowa, Michigan, Minnesota, Nebraska, North Dakota, South Dakota, and Wisconsin. Sample citations: 204 N.W.2d 568 (Neb. 1973) or 291 Minn. 310, 191 N.W.2d 185 (1971).

N.Y., N.Y.2d *New York Reports.* Official state reporter for cases in New York Court of Appeals. Sample citation: 1 N.Y.2d 20.

N.Y.S., N.Y.S.2d *West's New York Supplement.* Unofficial reporter for cases in New York Court of Appeals.

Ohio St., Ohio St. 2d *Ohio State Reports.* Official state reporter for cases in Ohio Supreme Court. Sample citation: 1 Ohio St. 2d 20.

Okla. *Oklahoma Reports.* Official state reporter for cases in Oklahoma Supreme Court. Sample citation: 1 Okla. 20.

Or. *Oregon Reports.* Official state reporter for cases in Oregon Supreme Court. Sample citation: 1 Or. 20.

P., P.2d *Pacific Reporter.* Regional reporter for state court cases in Alaska, Arizona, California, Colorado, Hawaii, Idaho, Kansas,

Montana, Nevada, New Mexico, Oklahoma, Oregon, Utah, Washington, and Wyoming. Sample citations: 18 Cal. 3d 660, 134 Cal. Rptr. 815, 557 P.2d 106 (1976) or 444 P.2d 25 (Or. 1968).

Pa. *Pennsylvania State Reports.* Official state reporter for cases in Pennsylvania Supreme Court. Sample citation: 1 Pa. 20.

P.C. Judicial Committee of the Privy Council. English court.

P.R.R. *Puerto Rico Reports.* Official reporter for cases in all Puerto Rico courts. Sample citation: 1 P.R.R. 20.

Prerog. Prerogative Court. Early English court.

Pub. L. Public Law. Cited as Pub. L. No. 96-398, 94 Stat. 1598 (1980).

Rev. Revised. As in Tex. Rev. Civ. Stat. Ann. (*Texas Revised Civil Statutes Annotated*).

R.I. *Rhode Island Reports.* Official state reporter for cases in Rhode Island Supreme Court. Sample citation: 1 R.I. 20.

Rich. *Richardson's Cases.* Reporter for certain South Carolina cases before 1868.

S. Senate.

S.C. *South Carolina Reports.* Official state reporter for cases in South Carolina Supreme Court. Sample citation: 1 S.C. 20.

S. Ct. *Supreme Court Reporter.* Unofficial reporter for U.S. Supreme Court cases. Sample citation: 101 S. Ct. 2587 (1981).

S.D. (1) *South Dakota Reports.* Official state reporter for cases in South Dakota Supreme Court. Sample citation: 1 S.D. 20. (2) Southern District. Used in U.S. District Court citations: 368 F. Supp. 38 (S.D.N.Y. 1977).

S.E., S.E.2d *Southeastern Reporter.* Regional reporter for state court cases in Georgia, North Carolina, South Carolina, Virginia, and West Virginia. Sample citations: 239 Ga. 541, 238 S.E.2d 81 (1977) or 162 S.E.2d 468 (Ga. 1968).

So., So. 2d *Southern Reporter.* Regional reporter for state court cases in Alabama, Florida, Louisiana, and Mississippi. Sample citations: 373 So. 2d 200 (la. 1979) or 291 Ala. 701, 287 So. 2d 824 (1973).

Stat. (1) Statutes. As in Ark. Stat. Ann. (*Arkansas Statutes Annotated*). (2) *Statutes at Large.* Publication containing federal session laws, cited as Pub. L. No. 96-398, 94 Stat. 1598 (1980); also includes congressional resolutions, presidential proclamations, international agreements.

S.W., S.W.2d *Southwestern Reporter.* Regional reporter for state court cases in Arkansas, Kentucky, Missouri, Tennessee, and Texas. Sample citations: 341 S.W.2d 591 (Ky. 1981) or 252 Ky. 4, 66 S.W.2d 48 (1933).

Tenn. *Tennessee Reports.* Official state reporter for cases in Tennessee Supreme Court. Sample citation: 1 Tenn. 20.

Tex. *Texas Reports.* Official state reporter for cases in Texas Supreme Court. Sample citation: 1 Tex. 20.

U.S. *United States Supreme Court Reports.* Official reporter for United States Supreme Court cases. Sample citation: 344 U.S. 203 (1963).

U.S.L.W. *United States Law Week.* Looseleaf service reporting recently decided U.S. Supreme Court cases. Sample citation: 50 U.S.L.W. 4333 (1982).

U.S.C. *United States Code.* Publication containing collection of federal statutes. Sample citations: 38 U.S.C. sec. 2012, 20 U.S.C. sec. 1087a *et seq.*

U.S.C.A. *United States Code Annotated.* Annotated edition of *United States Code.*

Utah *Utah Reports.* Official state reporter for cases in Utah Supreme Court. Sample citation: 1 Utah 20.

Va. *Virginia Reports.* Official state reporter for cases in Virginia Supreme Court. Sample citation: 1 Va. 20.

Vt. *Vermont Reports.* Official state reporter for cases in Vermont Supreme Court. Sample citation: 1 Vt. 20.

Wash., Wash. 2d *Washington Reports.* Official state reporter for cases in Washington Supreme Court. Sample citation: 1 Wash. 2d 20.

W.D. Western District. Used in U.S. District Court citations: 386 F. Supp. 38 (W.D. Pa. 1977).

Wend. *Wendell's Reports.* Reporter for certain cases heard in early nineteenth-century New York courts.

Wis. *Wisconsin Reports.* Official state reporter for cases in Wisconsin Supreme Court. Sample citation: 1 Wis. 20.

W. Va. *West Virginia Reports.* Official state reporter for cases in West Virginia Supreme Court of Appeals. Sample citation: 1 W. Va. 20.

Wyo. *Wyoming Reports.* Official state reporter for cases in Wyoming Supreme Court. Sample citation: 1 Wyo. 20.

Case Index

General Index

O

Odegard, G., 270
Odegard, G. D., 270-271
Odell, A., 242
Office of Child Support Enforcement, 152-153
Ohio: capacity to contract case in, 245; contracts as voidable in, 233; in Northeastern region, 425; patient rights cases in, 315, 319, 327, 336; procedural fairness case in, 52; professional negligence case in, 177; reporter for, 425; self-incrimination case in, 68; temporary detention case in, 61
Oklahoma: contracts as voidable in, 233; in Pacific region, 426; reporter for, 425; testamentary capacity case in, 249
Okpaku, S. R., 144, 413
Olsen, M., 238-239
Omnibus Crime Control and Safe Streets Act of 1968, Title III of, 64
Opinion, briefing an, 25-26
Opinion testimony: on capacity to transfer property, 244, 258-259, 278; and rules of evidence, 11
Oregon: assumption of risk case in, 172-173; contracts as void in, 233; neglected and dependent juveniles case in, 106; in Pacific region, 426; reporter for, 425; testamentary capacity case in, 257; undue influence case in, 275-276
Organic impairment: and capacity to contract, 239-241; and capacity to transfer property, 231; and testamentary capacity, 248-249
Orlando, F. A., 133, 413
Orth, G., 280-281
Orth, M. A., 280-281

P

Pacific region cases: assumption of risk, 172-173; capacity to contract, 232, 233-234, 235-236, 238-239, 240-241, 244, 245; citation

system in, 32; confidentiality, 178; consequential damages, 197; duty to warn, 390-391, 392; intentional torts, 156, 157; preventive detention, 78; professional negligence,174; 175; reporter for, 425-426; surrogate parenthood, 125; testamentary capacity, 248, 249, 257; undue influence, 274-276, 278; workers' compensation, 186; wrongful death, 34-35
Page, W., 248, 413
Palagi, R. J., 155-198
Palmer, A. B., 309, 413
Palumbo, D. J., 40, 411-412
Parens patriae theory: and institutionalized patients, 299-300, 302, 314; and juvenile law, 84, 89, 96, 105, 107, 112
Parent-child relations: and abortion, 121-122; and adoption, 123-125; analysis of, 121-129; initiating, 121-126; and juvenile law, 96-98; legitimacy of, 122-123; and parental rights and responsibilities, 126-129; and paternity, 123; and surrogate parenthood, 125-126; termination 109-111
Park, M. B., 270
Parry, J. K., 374, 375, 413
Party-opponent, concept of, 11
Paternity, family law on, 123
Patients, institutionalized: advocacy for, 330-336; analysis of rights of, 289-339; applications of legal theories to, 306-320; background on, 289-291; changing definition of treatment for, 336-339; commitment of, 307-312; communication with outside world by, 325-327; constitutional protections for, 5, 296-303; future directions for rights of, 330-339; humane environment for, 323-325; increased legal scrutiny of rights of, 291-296; intrusion on legal rights of, 294-296; labor by, 327-328; legal protection for, sources of, 296-305; and medication, 293-294, 314-317; partici-

S

Sadock, B. J., 294, 408
Sales, B. D., 379, 406
Saltzburg, S. A., 381, 382–383, 411
Sanborn, C. J., 289, 404
Saposnek, D. T., 134, 145, 415
Sarri, R. C., 415
Savitsky, J. C., 289–339
Scaletta, D. I., 133, 415
Schechter, L. F., 120, 127, 415
Schmidt, J. R., 308, 408
Schur, E. M., 95, 415
Schutz, B. J., 373, 415
Schwartz, S. J., 333, 334, 415
Schwitzgebel, R. K., 10, 376, 377, 416
Schwitzgebel, R. L., 10, 376, 377, 416
Scienter, concept of, 231, 281
Scott, A. W., 46, 411
Search and seizure: and arrest warrants, 60; and consent searches, 65–66; and juveniles, 66–67; protection against unreasonable, 58–67; reasonableness determination for, 61; and third-party consents, 66–67; and vehicles, 64–65; of words, 62–63
Search warrant: and informants, 59–60; probable cause for, 58–60
Seek, D. S., 265–266
Seek, J. E., 265–266
Self-incrimination: and juveniles, 73–74; and police practices limitations, 71; protections against, 67–74; and right to counsel, 70–72; and voluntariness, 69
Senile party: and capacity to contract, 235–237; and testamentary capacity, 249–252
Separation, legal, in family law, 130–131
Sepler, H. J., 133, 416
Serban, G., 395, 416
Shaffer, T. L., 230, 277, 279, 287, 416
Sharp, S. B., 130, 416
Shell, R., 80, 416
Shepard volumes, 32
Sherwyn, B. A., 125, 126, 409
Shlensky, R., 194, 416
Shotwell, M. B., 237

Shrallow, D. F., 395, 416
Shultz, M. M., 114, 416
Siegel, D. M., 143, 416
Simon, O. C., 332, 334, 416
Simon, R. J., 124, 416
Sinnett, E. R., 331, 416
Sixth Amendment, and right to counsel, 54, 66, 74, 81
Slovenko, R., 9–10, 141, 194, 381, 416
Smith, C., 97n, 99, 417
Social Security, 117
Solnit, A. J., 126, 129, 145, 408
South Carolina: contracts as voidable in, 233; foster care board in, 112; reporters for, 426; in Southeastern region, 426; undue influence case in, 263
South Dakota: divorce in, 132; in Northwest region, 30, 425; reporter for, 426; warrantless search case in, 64–65
Southeastern region cases: capacity to contract, 239; child custody, 146; cohabitation, 118–119; contributory negligence, 171; reporter for, 426; separation agreement, 130; testamentary capacity, 253; undue influence, 273–274, 278
Southern region cases: child custody, 149–150; confidentiality, 178; reporter for, 426; undue influence, 264, 277
Southwestern region cases: breach of duty, 168; capacity to contract, 232–233, 241, 244; contributory negligence, 171; intentional torts, 156; negligence, 163–164, 166; reporter for, 427; testamentary capacity, 248, 249, 251, 255, 256, 257, 259; undue influence, 265–266
Sparine, 90
Spouse: abuse by, 119–121; and privileged communication, 16–17; undue influence by, 265–266. *See also* Marriage
Springer, J. R., 155–198